Alternative Perspectives on Lawyers and Legal Ethics

The study of legal ethics and the legal profession has emerged as a distinct and important field of scholarship over the last 30 years. However, as in other disciplines, academic recognition can in turn entrench static and powerful meta-theories and narratives about professional ethos and practice. This collection seeks to disrupt this homogenizing impulse and to present alternative voices by bringing together a range of international scholars writing about legal ethics and the legal profession.

The book features significant and timely contributions which take contemporary and non-mainstream perspectives on the current and future shape of the legal profession. The essays not only describe the rapidly changing profession but canvas different approaches to scholarship on the legal profession. The collection seeks to explore a diverse and contextualized profession from a number of angles. Authors examine how the public sees lawyers and how lawyers see their own profession; how we practise law and how this practice shapes lawyers; how such cultural and professional practice intersects with institutional structures of the law to create certain legal outcomes; and how we regulate the legal profession to modify or institute ethical practice.

The volume provides insights into legal culture and ethics from the perspective of authors from Australia, Canada, England, the United States, New Zealand and Kenya – a diversity of national perspectives that give valuable insights into developments in the profession at the local and global level. It also illustrates diversity within the profession by tracing differing professional career trajectories based on raced or gendered barriers, alternative ethical strategies and the impact of organizational cultures in which lawyers practise.

Francesca Bartlett is College of Law Lecturer in Legal Ethnics at the TC Beirne School of Law, University of Queensland, Australia.

Reid Mortensen is Professor of Law at the University of Southern Queensland, Australia.

Kieran Tranter is a Senior Lecturer and Managing Editor of the Griffith Law Review at Griffith University, Australia.

Routledge Research in Legal Ethics

Available titles in this series include:

Reaffirming Legal Ethics: Taking Stock and New Ideas
Kieran Tranter, Francesca Bartlett, Lillian Corbin, Reid Mortensen and Michael Robertson

Forthcoming titles in this series include:

The Ethics Project in Legal Education
Michael Robertson, Lillian Corbin, Kieran Tranter and Francesca Bartlett

Alternative Perspectives on Lawyers and Legal Ethics

Reimagining the Profession

Edited by Francesca Bartlett, Reid Mortensen and Kieran Tranter

Routledge
Taylor & Francis Group

LONDON AND NEW YORK

First published 2011
by Routledge
2 Park Square, Milton Park, Abingdon, Oxon OX14 4RN

Simultaneously published in the USA and Canada
by Routledge
270 Madison Avenue, New York, NY 10016

Routledge is an imprint of the Taylor & Francis Group, an informa business

Typeset in Baskerville by
RefineCatch Limited, Bungay, Suffolk
Printed and bound in Great Britain by
CPI Antony Rowe, Chippenham, Wiltshire

British Library Cataloguing in Publication Data
A catalogue record for this book is available
from the British Library

Library of Congress Cataloging in Publication Data
Alternative perspectives on lawyers and legal ethics : reimagining the
profession / edited by Francesca Bartlett, Reid Mortensen and Kieran
Tranter
     p. cm.
     Includes index.
1. Legal ethics.   I Bartlett, Francesca.   II. Mortensen, Reid.
III. Tranter, Kieran.
K123.A95 2010
340′.1—dc22

2010003242

ISBN13: 978-0-415-54652-2 (hbk)
ISBN13: 978-0-203-84688-9 (ebk)

ISBN10: 0-415-54652-4 (hbk)
ISBN10: 0-203-84688-5 (ebk)

Contents

Preface

This book, the second of three, arises out of papers delivered at the Third International Legal Ethics Conference held on the Gold Coast, Queensland, Australia in July 2008. The conference was hosted jointly by Griffith Law School at Griffith University and the TC Beirne School of Law at the University of Queensland. This conference, building on the successes of the first two in the series – in Exeter, the United Kingdom in 2004 and in Auckland, New Zealand in 2006 – was one of the largest specialist gatherings of legal ethicists in the new millennium.

For us, the privilege of working with the contributors in this book followed from the success of the conference itself. It is fitting that our expressions of thanks extend to colleagues from many countries who assisted in making the conference and this volume possible. We would first like to thank Kim Economides and Julian Webb for their foundational work in establishing the international legal ethics conference series, and for their encouragement in organizing the third conference. We would also acknowledge Tim Dare's role in organizing the second conference, which provided the platform for the third. We owe a particular debt to Brad Wendel, Christine Parker, Adrian Evans and Neil Watt for their help and enthusiasm over the two years of planning for the Gold Coast conference. Our thanks are also due to our respective Deans and others who contributed to the resources needed to run the conference: Charles Rickett and Ross Grantham from the TC Beirne School of Law and Paula Baron and Richard Johnstone from Griffith Law School; and to Teola Marsh from the University of Queensland and Linda Brauns from Griffith University. Substantial financial support for the conference was also given by the College of Law, for which we are especially grateful.

We extend our thanks to the contributors to this volume for their willingness to work with us and for their patience during the editing process. We would also like to thank Katie Carpenter and Khanam Virjee from Routledge for their support and encouragement. And a special mention must go to Griffith Law School student Stevie Martin, who not only worked tirelessly as the administrator for the conference, but also joyfully undertook the task of helping to edit the manuscripts in her final year at law school.

Finally, we wish to express our heartfelt thanks to colleagues, friends and most importantly to our families for their faith and support over these past few years.

Francesca Bartlett, Reid Mortensen and Kieran Tranter
November 2009

Contributors

Francesca Bartlett is a Lecturer at the TC Beirne School of Law, University of Queensland, Brisbane.

Paula Baron is Dean and Professor of Law, Griffith Law School, Griffith University, Brisbane.

Tina Dolgopol is Associate Professor of Law, Flinders University of South Australia, Adelaide.

Rachael Field is a Senior Lecturer at the School of Law, Queensland University of Technology, Brisbane.

Elizabeth Gachenga is affiliated to Strathmore University, Kenya.

Vivien Holmes is a Senior Lecturer in Law at the Australian National University College of Law, Canberra.

Judith Maute is William J. Alley Professor of Law, College of Law, University of Oklahoma.

Reid Mortensen is the Foundation Professor of Law, School of Law, University of Southern Queensland, Toowoomba.

Simon Rice OAM is an Associate Professor at the Australian National University College of Law, Canberra.

Michelle Sharpe is a Lecturer with Melbourne Law School, University of Melbourne and a member of the Victorian Bar.

Rachel Spencer is the Director, Professional Programs with the School of Law, University of South Australia, Adelaide.

Kieran Tranter is a Senior Lecturer at Griffith Law School, Griffith University, Gold Coast.

Duncan Webb is the Legal Complaints Review Officer for New Zealand and a Professor at the School of Law, University of Canterbury, Christchurch.

Lisa Webley is a Reader at the School of Law, University of Westminster, London.

Alice Woolley is an Associate Professor at the Faculty of Law, University of Calgary.

1 Introduction

*Francesca Bartlett, Reid Mortensen and
Kieran Tranter*

The contributions to this volume are both united by a common, underlying perspective on legal ethics and the legal profession and, somewhat paradoxically, different in the alternative approaches they have taken when adopting it. This perspective is that the established modus through which legal ethics and its professional context have been comprehended is limited and limiting. This reveals two strains that tie the contributors together. The first is the identification of a familiar pattern – of an orthodoxy and its critical reaction. The second concerns the location of this critique in method.

Legal ethics, as a discipline, is a twinned project.[1] One branch of it concerns the law of lawyering – that is, the positive law that formally governs legal practice. As a scholarly enterprise concerned with the law of lawyering, legal ethics has regularly been criticized as methodologically conservative.[2] The instruments through which the law of lawyering has traditionally been examined are predominantly taken from the positivist toolbox. The questions have been concerned, *inter alia*, with what law exists, its clarity and its jurisdictional diversity. The evaluative concerns tended to remain modest, and in general the focus has been on how reform to the law has impacted on existing legal practice. However, parallel to this doctrinal emphasis has been a normative task of constructing moral arguments about the role of the lawyer, particularly concerning the ethics and politics of role morality. For this branch of legal ethics, a different set of intellectual resources has been evident. For the normative task, positivist description has been displaced by moral philosophy. The scholarship that occupies this branch of legal ethics is characterized by an ethical lexicon, reasoned argument and 'proofs' via abstract hypotheticals.

We reaffirm, and have reaffirmed,[3] the importance and efficacy of these established methods of legal ethics. The law of lawyering needs to be known according to traditional measures. Old laws need to be assessed in new contexts, and new laws need to be assessed in old ones. Further, the clarity of moral dissection has been – and continues to be – important to shock a powerful, and often complacent, profession into self-reflection concerning its responsibility to individuals and the body politic. At least one of the contributors to this volume – Elizabeth Gachenga (Chapter 7) – implicitly presents a strong view of the importance of philosophy for resolving questions of legal ethics that other approaches have not resolved. However, as David Luban notes in his reflection on Max Weber's 'Science as vocation',[4] in the context of legal scholarship, 'legal scholars ... are comfortable' and a deep, dedicated commitment to knowledge 'does not come naturally to people who are comfortable'.[5] There is much of value in scholarship that draws upon the established methods of legal ethics; both the law and lawyering have been, and can be, changed through such scholarship. However, at one level it is a comfortable space. Its perimeters and methods are known and well practised. As Luban's remembering of Weber reminds us, the search for knowledge, for ideas, requires the seeker to go beyond the comfortable: 'a kind of astringent designed to extinguish the ego in the name of knowledge'.[6] For Weber, being a scholar was a vocation to a particularly modern form of asceticism.

The body of research that has grown around understanding the legal professional is not a comfortable space, at least for lawyers. For common lawyers, the archaic self-representation lay within myths of community, unwritten law and artificial reason.[7] Lawyering was a calling to a pre-modern asceticism that mingled symbol, place and law, and now only lies as a faint shadow in some of the architecture and language of legal institutions.[8] As Weber has so keenly observed, in modernity, law moved from the charismatic to the rational, from the informal to the formal.[9] With modernity's emptying of the symbolic realm, lawyers pieced together an impoverished self-representation; to be a lawyer was to be a technician for the law machine.[10] In many respects, the absence of a truly lived self-representation has opened the study of the legal profession up to another of Weber's legacies: the social sciences.[11] As a consequence, the practice of law has come to be understood not just as a technical process of rule application and role performance, but as a complex and contestable social, cultural and economic activity, concerned with power, status, gender, language and exchange.[12] Whereas legal ethics expresses a stable bifurcation – which on the methodological level breaks down to positivism concerning the law of lawyering and moral philosophy concerning the normative task – studies into the legal profession have become subject to the full gamut of contemporary social scientific research methods.

However, the impact on legal ethics of both such findings and the methods of this scholarship has been minimal.[13] Legal ethics remains a field mainly concerned with rule application and role performance, even in the face of ever-growing research that has endeavoured to make sense of lawyering as a social, political and economic activity. This leads to the rationale for this volume: to bring together alternative ways of thinking about legal ethics and the legal profession; about who comprises it, where it operates and how.

For this reason, it is tempting to locate this volume under the label 'interdisciplinarity' or 'interdisciplinary legal scholarship'. Indeed, in a recent article, Carrie Menkel-Meadow has traced the increasing embrace of 'context' by legal theory through the twentieth century, and explored the impact this has had on legal education.[14] Her stated purpose was to 'realize the potential of true interdisciplinary study'.[15] There is a similarity between Menkel-Meadow's appreciation of the insertion of context into the theory of law by the realists, law and economics, law and society, critical legal studies, feminist legal studies, virtue ethics, ethical relativism and law and cultural studies, and the scope of this volume. Each contribution in this volume can be seen as drawing foundational concepts and methods from a discipline beyond the legal ethics orthodoxy; there are chapters drawing on law and culture, feminism and empirical legal studies, as well as chapters that challenge the orthodox conception behind the role morality of a lawyer in private practice. We remain agnostic when it comes to the term 'interdisciplinary', with its overtures of 'post-modernity'[16] and 'crumbling of disciplinary fences'.[17] Instead, each of the chapters is located in a recognized discipline. The unity across the contributions is not a performative commitment to an abstract and possibly empty ideal of interdisciplinarity, but a more basic manifestation of the type of scholarship about which Luban was writing. The contributions are not comfortable. Each, in its own way, stretches understanding about legal ethics and the legal profession. Each challenges some of the orthodox conceptions that ground legal ethics scholarship. As such, they are not comfortable reading – for lawyers or legal ethicists. For example, Michelle Sharpe – who, in Chapter 12, discusses an empirical study that reports on the predominance of mental ill-health in the legal profession – directly challenges a foundational representation common to legal ethics and in the ego-ideal of most lawyers: that to be a lawyer is to be a rational decider confidently engaging with the world. Another example is Paula Baron (Chapter 4) who, writing with reference to psychoanalytical theory, questions the desire for the father in the idealization of *To Kill a Mocking Bird*'s Atticus Finch, and offers a subversive alternative in *Boston Legal*'s Denny Crane.

An alternative perspective, and alternative perspectives, on legal ethics and the legal profession mean not being comfortable. In going beyond the orthodox methods of legal ethics, the contributors to this volume are continuing in a spirit of intellectual endeavour championed by Weber. They seek and report ways to know beyond the pragmatics of mainstream scholarship. The primal registry is that of knowledge. But in seeking knowledge they do legal ethics – as a practical task of thinking about, regulating and challenging lawyering – a significant service. In making legal ethics uncomfortable, they challenge it to know and do better.

1.1 Challenging legal ethics

In Chapter 2, Judith Maute undertakes a detailed comparative examination of the changes to the regulation of the legal profession. She notes that the reforms in the eastern states of Australia that led to the establishment of government agencies charged with the regulation of lawyer conduct effectively displaced professional self-regulation and were mirrored by recent reforms in the United Kingdom. This chapter presents two challenges to legal ethics. The first is her contextual approach. She locates the change within social pressures, in Australia and the United Kingdom, to consider lawyering as a service to customers, and as such as something that should be subject to similar consumer protection regulations as other service industries. In this chapter, the law of lawyering is considered in its political and cultural context, and Maute particularly emphasizes how cultural factors in Australia and the UK influenced the reforms. Her second challenge is directly to the profession in the United States. The end point of the Australian and UK reforms has been the establishment of a co-regulatory regime between the newly established 'Commissioner' and the organized profession, but with the profession playing a minor supporting role. It also has led in Australia to a movement towards a unified national regime for regulation. This is a direct challenge to the 'balkanized' United States: a challenge to state Bars to reform discipline processes and become more responsive to 'consumer concerns' – or else to risk losing self-regulation.

In Chapter 3, Vivien Holmes and Simon Rice argue for an alternative source of values to inform legal ethics. Their challenge is directly to the traditional concepts of moral philosophy that have informed the normative task in legal ethics. Holmes and Rice are not comfortable with the way in which lawyering is conceived, nor with its political impact. Beginning with the pre-eminent global challenges of the present – the global financial crisis and global warming – they argue that lawyers acting as corporate advisers or facilitating trans(even pan)-jurisdictional transactions play an essential role in the activities responsible for these crises. However, they note that the ethical expectations of, and obligations on, these lawyers remain in the realm of role morality – a theory grounded on a traditional vision of the lawyer in private practice, working in a specific jurisdiction and representing human clients. This is not the reality for corporate legal advisers, nor trans-jurisdictional transaction lawyers. Drawing upon calls for contextual ethics that have been heard in legal ethics, Holmes and Rice suggest that lawyers whose work directly relates to global challenges cannot rely upon claims of neutral partisanship to absolve them of moral responsibility. Instead, the context of interconnectedness, and the possibility that corporate actions and trans-jurisdictional transactions can have impacts of global significance, mean a responsibility for consideration, for self-reflection and for self-conscious action.

In Chapter 4, as mentioned above, Paula Baron revisits the law and culture literature that laments an increasingly negative depiction of lawyers in popular imagery, marked especially by the contrast of Atticus Finch in *To Kill a Mockingbird* and Denny Crane in *Boston Legal*. For many, this shows how, in the popular imagination, the lawyer has fallen from grace. It has also led some to call for the profession to wage something of a public relations campaign to counter the negative stereotyping. Baron, however, suggests that there is greater significance in the similarities that Finch and Crane share, and that these are drawn out by psychoanalytical theory. These similarities are manifest in the symbolic role of father: the father who symbolically 'institutes law in the social sense [and] who institutes law in the individual through the exercise of the so-called "paternal function"'. In many respects, lawyers represent that 'paternal function' for their clients, bringing together both our 'love' of the protection that law and fathers represent and our 'fear' of their power. Finch and Crane exemplify both, but Crane also represents the loss of paternal authority and the loss also of the symbolic function it serves. So, while Finch symbolizes the disciplined restraint of that authority – and even that is challenged – Denny Crane 'is obscene enjoyment', the *joisseur* who represents the undermining of symbolic authority. This is disturbing reading for men and women – not only for what is says about lawyers but, we suggest, for its implications regarding law itself. It has important unresolved implications for women in the legal profession. Baron recalls the continuing symbolic and unconscious confusion of the paternal function and the law, and the resulting inability of popular culture to develop satisfying images of hard-working women lawyers.

In Chapter 5, Rachel Spencer examines legal ethics from the perspective of law and culture (as does Baron in part). Spencer's texts are *The Verdict* (1982) and *Regarding Henry* (1991). For Spencer, the challenge initially presented in both films is what William Simon has termed 'moral pluck'.[18] Both lawyer protagonists end the film as heroes. Frank Galvin (Paul Newman) wins his case, and Henry (Harrison Ford) leaves law practice a better man who has redeemed himself. However, as Spencer makes clear, both are heroes despite the laws of lawyering. Frank does not follow his client's wish to accept the settlement, and Henry discloses confidential documents. The films tell a problematic story concerning public representations of lawyers and ethical conduct: Frank and Henry resonate with audiences not because they are lawyers, but because they are anti-lawyers. The challenges that Spencer's chapter communicates go two ways. The first is the established challenge that law and culture reveals: that popular representations of lawyers exhibit a cultural mistrust and cynicism towards the legal profession.[19] The second challenge lies in Spencer's negation of the moral pluck hypothesis. She argues that both Frank and Henry could have achieved their outcomes without having to break the laws of lawyering – that for actual lawyers in daily practice, the films give the wrong message. It is not a choice between a stark dichotomy of lawyering or doing what is right. Spencer, at one level, affirms that the sophistication within contemporary legal ethics can allow a thoughtful and reflective practitioner to remain a lawyer and do what is right.

In Chapter 6, Lisa Webley challenges legal ethics with both empirical research methods and feminist legal theory. Webley's 'data' are the material produced by the various professional bodies in England and Wales concerning training, accreditation, best practice and professional code requirements in the family law field. She does not read these at face value. Instead, these texts are sources through which she reveals the deep conceptions of what it means to be a lawyer that is being encoded and transmitted. The practical tasks of professional legal training and compliance are not innocent, but construct categories that are gendered. Drawing upon feminist legal theory's identification of gender ideals within law and legal discourse – that there are identifiable masculine and feminine characteristics – Webley argues that the professional bodies construct various gendered images of lawyers who practise in family law. The non-specialist solicitor was identified as possessing the most masculine traits, while the United Kingdom College Family Mediator had the most feminine. This continuum of gender, traits and styles of lawyering represents a direct challenge to legal ethics. Webley reveals not that gender is an important factor in how a specific lawyer might practise law – a point discussed by Gachenga in Chapter 7 (see below) – but that representations of lawyering produced by the organized profession have a gendered commitment.

The implications of gender in the legal profession are also explored in Chapter 7 by Elizabeth Gachenga. Gachenga responds to tensions within an ethics of care and persistent questions about it. To what extent is an ethics of care distinctive of the moral reasoning of women? If it is distinctive of women, why do many women not exemplify an ethics of care, yet some men do? How is care reconciled with justice? The school of care for lawyers' ethics has been dominated by feminist perspectives, with Christian views having been the only alternative ground for an ethics of care presented. It is therefore promising that Gachenga attempts to resolve the inconclusive studies on the extent to which women lawyers bring an ethics of care to legal practice by reference to the thought of the philosopher-nun Edith Stein. Gachenga suggests that the unresolved problems of an ethics of care in the mould of Carol Gilligan's *Different Voice*[20] stem from its grounding in psychology, with the different conclusions that emerge from empirical studies being somewhat inevitable. Drawing from Stein, she then suggests that a more adequate means of dealing with these questions is found in philosophy. Stein's view of empathy as the means by which we move from ourselves and encounter others is that it is a primary way in which we possess others' experience and care for them. But it is nevertheless an act of logic. Stein also concludes that humans are a double species – woman and man – and that the complete human being is characterized by the two. Man and woman are therefore marked by ontological difference, although both have the same basic human traits. As a result, there are qualities that predominate in one sex rather than another (such as care in women), but there are also qualities that predominate in one individual rather than another. Gachenga claims that this addresses the place of gender in an ethics of care: women tend to search for a harmonious development of personal relations, but are still capable of more markedly masculine traits such as abstract analysis. This re-examination of the place of care, and of women, in the legal profession – so dependent on Stein, Aristotle and Aquinas – brings the very distinction of an ethics of care from an account of the virtues into question.[21]

In Chapter 8, Tina Dolgopol provides a rare consideration of a particular lawyering role (and its impact) in the context of international justice: the prosecutorial role in the International Criminal Court (ICC). She contends that, while the ICC has been given the mandate to pursue those crimes that 'violate the conscience of humanity as a whole', it is the specific functioning of the Office of the Prosecutor (OTP) by which this laudable goal is defined and pursued. This perspective illuminates the importance of the role and the necessity for it to be performed within a clearly defined, and publicly known, ethical framework. The OTP 'selects the situations to be investigated, the individuals to be prosecuted and determines the charges to be brought against those individuals'; providing it with a 'broad discretion' and shaping the content of international criminal justice. As such, Dolgopol asserts that, while a discretionary function is necessary, there must be public accountability for a process of ethical decision-making. She asserts that a 'morally reflective' practice that encompasses an obligation to understand the 'social context' in which decisions are made is particularly appropriate for the OTP. This thesis is dramatically illustrated by her critique of the OTP's current approach to, or lack of consideration of,[22] 'the gender dimensions of victims' concerns'.

In Chapter 9, Rachael Field's consideration of mediator practice in Australia provides another insight into an 'alternative' lawyer role: the mediator. While many mediators in Australia do not have legal training, this emerging vocation is playing an increasingly important role in the administration of justice in this jurisdiction. Field's chapter closely examines the 'complex, nuanced and contextualized nature of mediation practice'. By this characterization, her contention is that an alternative ethical framework for practice is necessary. Her critique is an important one for mediators and ethical precepts applied to the legal profession broadly, as it disputes the logic (and reality) of a legal actor who does not influence the autonomy of the client. Field explains that the generally accepted goal, and thus *good*, to be achieved in mediation is 'is to maximize participants' decision-making'. Thus the mantra in mediation is participant 'self-determination'. It is understood that there must be a concomitant impartiality in the role of the mediator; the mediation must only 'facilitate' the process, not affect the outcome or the will of the parties. However, Field contends that this ideal is 'practically unattainable, unreal and unworkable'. Thus the theory and the practice of the professional role appear to be in conflict. She suggests that the solution is in the practice of a 'contextual ethics' to replace the rule-like standards of mediator impartiality that currently predominate.

In Chapters 10 and 11, Alice Woolley and Duncan Webb provide complementary arguments for the abolition of the character test applied in the admission of lawyers in Canada, Australia and New Zealand. Their contention is that the legal, logical and empirical arguments for such considerations regarding the fitness of a person to perform the legal role are weak, if not hollow. Thus, on a number of bases, they challenge the notion that ethics dictates a certain type of person, or personal conduct, to be necessary in order for someone to be a *good* lawyer.

Webb examines disciplinary body cases in several jurisdictions where personal misconduct has been considered decisive as to whether a person is permitted to continue in legal practice. He shows that certain conclusions about a person's character and future propensities in the practice of law are drawn from types of personal (mis)conduct. Alternatively, he notes a concern that lawyer character is bigger than the person him or herself, and a resulting apprehension that individual personal misconduct will bring the profession as a whole into disrepute. However, Webb contends that 'there is little evidence either that such lawyers harm the reputation of the wider profession, or that the profession needs such reputational protection to discharge its duties'. He also questions whether egregious conduct ought necessarily to preclude the practice of law, especially when the failings of the lawyer bear no direct relationship to the effective discharge of their duties as a lawyer.

Webb's consideration of the history, legislative framework and current application of this regulatory doctrine in Australia, New Zealand and Canada provides the background for his and Woolley's contention about a lack of basis for the standard normative justifications offered by disciplinary authorities for the relevance of a character test. Woolley argues that the lack of a proper basis for this gatekeeping test seriously undermined the legitimacy of regulation of the legal profession. This thesis is based on what she argues is a lack of foundation for the character requirement. She provides further argument that any proper empirical basis for drawing conclusions as to future professional conduct is lacking.[23] She employs the psychological method to test how reliable these predictions can be, and finds them based on 'empirically doubtful assertions about the existence of ascertainable "moral character"'. Finally, she considers alternative bases for legitimacy of disciplinary bodies' reliance on 'moral character': economic and democratic theories of regulation. Yet again, she considers these unsatisfactory because it cannot be 'normatively justified as necessary to correct for the numerous imperfections in the market for legal services [and] ... fails to achieve the necessary standards of [democratic] legitimacy'.

In Chapter 12, Michelle Sharpe addresses the ever-mounting evidence of mental illness in the legal profession. Focusing on the problem in Victoria, but drawing on empirical evidence gathered elsewhere in Australia and the United States, she responds to consistent findings that lawyers have higher rates of depression than the general population, and that the legal profession is above the norm for professional groups. Lawyers also have high levels of 'self-medication' – trying to deal with depression or anxiety with alcohol or non-prescription drugs. As Sharpe recounts, the problem begins in law school. There are normal levels of psychiatric distress among students before they commence studies in law, but these rise rapidly and never return to normal levels. To some extent, the problem is attributed to characteristic values and personality traits that lawyers demonstrate: one study lists competitiveness and aggression, an orientation towards achievement and thinking (rather than feeling) types of personalities. It is therefore potentially a problem that both stems from values and (given other evidence) compounds lawyers' difficulties with the management of ethical problems and standards. Mental illness is a common feature of disciplinary cases. However, returning to the situation in Victoria, Sharpe refuses to leave the problem at the point of description. She suggests a comprehensive, integrated programme for dealing with mental illness in the profession. Education, counselling, health assessments and implications for the right to practise if a lawyer either avoids or ignores treatment are suggested, with the programme to be funded by levies on practising certificates. Undoubtedly this would be a controversial solution, but Sharpe maintains that it is a profession-wide problem, significantly attributable to the nature of law school and of legal practice, and that it demands a whole-of-profession response.

In summary, all of these chapters offer an alternative perspective on legal ethics and the legal profession. They present a heterogeneity of approaches to understanding both legal ethics and the legal profession. What is challenged is the comfortable orthodoxy that legal ethics concerns the positivism of the law of lawyering and moral philosophizing concerning the normative task. In the alternative view, legal ethics and legal practice can be conceived as complex and contested – concerned with the global, the image, gender, representations, context and well-being. As such, the lasting challenge to legal ethics from this volume is for it to engage more deeply with these alternative perspectives – and to shape and guide the legal professional towards a more global, responsive, inclusive and caring future.

Notes

1 K. Tranter, F. Bartlett, L. Corbin, R. Mortensen and M. Robertson, 'Introduction', in K. Tranter, F. Bartlett, L. Corbin, R. Mortensen and M. Robertson (eds), *Reaffirming Legal Ethics*, London: Routledge, 2010, pp. 1–19.
2 D. B. Wilkins, 'Legal realism for lawyers', *Harvard Law Review*, 1990, vol. 104, 469.
3 Tranter et al., 'Introduction'.
4 M. Weber, 'Science as vocation', trans. H. H. Gerth and C. Wright Mills, in H. H. Gerth and C. Wright Mills (eds), *From Max Weber: Essays in Sociology*, London: Routledge, 1948, p. 129.
5 D. Luban, 'Legal scholarship as vocation', *Journal of Legal Education*, 2001, vol. 51, 173.
6 ibid.
7 Gerald Postema, *Bentham and the Common Law Tradition*, Oxford: Clarendon Press, 1986, pp. 1–33.
8 Peter Goodrich, *Languages of Law: From Logics of Memory to Nomadic Masks*, London: Weidenfeld & Nicolson, 1990.
9 M. Weber, *Economy and Society: An Outline of Interpretive Sociology: Volume 2*, G. Roth and C. Wittich (eds), Berkeley, CA: University of California Press, 1968, p. 848.
10 J. Boyd White, 'Law as rhetoric, rhetoric as law: The arts of cultural and communal life', *University of Chicago Law Review*, 1985, vol. 52, 686.
11 W. T. Murphy, 'The oldest social science? The epistemic properties of the common law tradition', *Modern Law Review*, 1991, vol. 54, 182.
12 See, for example, J. E. Carlin, *Lawyers' Ethics: A Survey of the New York City Bar*, New York: Russell Sage Foundation, 1966; J. P. Heinz and E. O. Laumann, *Chicago Lawyers: The Social Structure of the Bar*, Evanston, IL: Northwestern University Press, 1994; J. Flood, 'Doing business: The management of uncertainty in lawyers' work', *Law and Society Review*, 1991, vol. 25, 41; R. Granfield, *Making Elite Lawyers: Visions of Law at Harvard and Beyond*, New York: Routledge, 1992; A. Sarat and W. L. Felstiner, *Divorce Lawyers and Their Clients: Power and Meaning in the Legal Process*, New York: Oxford University Press, 1995; L. Mather, C. A. McEwen and R. J. Maiman, *Divorce Lawyers at Work: Varieties of Professionalism in Practice*, New York: Oxford University Press, 2001.
13 M. Robertson and K. Tranter, 'Grounding legal ethics learning in social scientific studies of lawyers at work', *Legal Ethics*, 2006, vol. 9, 211.
14 C. Menkel-Meadow, 'Taking law and – really seriously: Before, during and after "the law"', *Vanderbilt Law Review*, 2007, vol. 60, 555.
15 C. Menkel-Meadow, 'Taking law and – really seriously', 594.
16 B. Statham, 'Postmodern jurisprudence: Contesting genres', *Law and Critique*, 2008, vol. 19, 141.
17 S. Feldman, *American Legal Thought from Premodern to Postmodern: An Intellectual Voyage*, New York: Oxford University Press, 2000, p. 9.
18 W. H. Simon, 'Moral pluck: Legal ethics in popular culture,' *Columbia Law Review*, 2001, vol. 101, 421.
19 L. Friedman, 'Law, lawyers and popular culture,' *Yale Law Journal*, 1989, vol. 89, 1598–1603.
20 C. Gilligan, *In a Different Voice: Psychological Theory and Women's Development*, Cambridge, MA: Harvard University Press, 1982.
21 R. Mortensen, 'The lawyer as parent: Sympathy, care and character in lawyers' ethics', *Legal Ethics*, 2009, vol. 12, 27–28.

22 Dolgopol refers to a policy paper released in 2007, in which 'the OTP expresses its view that it will operate from the premise that investigations and prosecutions are generally in the interests of justice and that only extraordinary circumstances would warrant a determination that it would *not* be in the interests of justice to proceed'.
23 This argument relies on an earlier chapter by the author: A. Woolley and J. Stacey, 'The psychology of good character: The past, present and future of good character regulation in Canada', in K. Tranter, F. Bartlett, L. Corbin, R. Mortensen and M. Robertson (eds), *Reaffirming Legal Ethics*, London: Routledge, 2010, p. 306.

2 Global continental shifts to a new governance paradigm in lawyer regulation and consumer protection: riding the wave

Judith L. Maute

2.1 Introduction

The legal profession in the United Kingdom is undergoing a period of regulatory and constitutional reforms. These reforms have culminated in the passage of the Legal Services Act 2007. This Act implemented a single regulatory oversight entity with authority over all categories of legal service providers. Three driving forces lay behind the eventual legislation: (1) competition policy to improve the availability and quality of legal services; (2) elimination of trade barriers that restricted innovative forms of practice, making way for 'alternative business structures'; and (3) consumer protection concerns with the existing discipline and complaint handling systems run by the respective professional associations.

This chapter compares the progressive reforms in the United Kingdom with the balkanized state-based lawyer regulation in the United States. The UK reforms should not be viewed in isolation, but as possible byproducts of earlier reforms in Australia. While reforms in Australia and the United Kingdom can be seen as a global trend in the regulation of lawyers, the reform efforts also reflect contextual differences among each nation's history, demographics and policies of market regulation. These differences affect whether the legal professions maintain primary control over regulatory enforcement.

Lawyers, like other service providers, operate in a competitive and increasingly global market.[1] Advancements in Internet and communications technology facilitate innovative delivery systems, including outsourcing, commoditization of legal products and affiliations with non-lawyers.[2]

In a global sense, these regulatory reforms reflect a sea change in the worldwide legal market. Some commentators use dramatic geological terms to describe the enormity of these changes – as 'seismic' or the regulatory counterpart of a 'tsunami'[3] – terms aptly used because the innovations occurred on different continents, triggering further reforms elsewhere. However, the regulatory reforms taking hold in other countries are unlikely to cut the destructive path of a tsunami.

Instead, they may take the form of a big wave, savoured by surfers, beachcombers and those who appreciate the cleansing effect brought in by a new current.

As we learn from the ongoing international economic crisis, no nation is an island unto itself: what happens in one nation impacts what happens in the others. Lawyer regulators and trade representatives have strong incentives to participate in ongoing regulatory discourse within the international trading community.[4] Lawyers in the United States must take heed, initiating local reforms that respond to the seismic shift that is under way. If they do not, they risk both external governmental regulation and impaired competitiveness in the globalized legal marketplace.[5]

This chapter contains four parts. The first part discusses the trailblazing efforts by Australian lawyer regulators in the states of New South Wales and Queensland. The Australian co-regulatory model engages cooperatively with the professional associations as well as the individual lawyers or firms with which it interacts. It places much regulatory authority with an independent Legal Services Commissioner, giving the public greater confidence in the regulator's integrity and independence. While the Commissioners lack binding authority to order that a lawyer make redress to a dissatisfied former client in the non-disciplinary complaint handling scheme, they have achieved remarkable success resolving complaints. Recent amendments allow incorporation by firms after the firm has undergone a self-audit process that focuses on management-based regulation, helping it incorporate best practices and thus minimizing the risk of common-place ethical violations. By stressing 'compliance through education', this approach engages in positive, preventative interaction with those regulated, in contrast to reactively addressing ethical problems only in the disciplinary context. These localized experiments hold great potential for developing ethical infrastructures appropriate to specific firms, rejecting a 'one size fits all' template. The Australian Model Law looks to build further, aiming for some national uniformity. These innovations have influenced regulatory reform efforts in the United Kingdom and elsewhere.

The second part surveys developments in the United Kingdom since 1990, in which the public interest, consumer protection and market competition play key roles in the massive regulatory reforms contained in the Legal Services Act 2007, now in the early stages of implementation. UK reformers apparently learned from their Australian regulatory counterparts and have gone even further. The 2007 law creates the Legal Services Board, an independent oversight entity with regulatory authority over all UK legal professionals, which will work in collaboration with approved regulators formed by existing professional bodies. Part of the board infrastructure, a new Office of Legal Complaints ombudsman scheme, will serve as a single point of entry for all consumer complaints seeking redress from legal professionals with the authority to issue legally binding directives.

The third part considers lawyer regulation in the United States by the state disciplinary entities, together with the limited available redress for dissatisfied clients through civil liability for legal malpractice or dispute-resolution programmes. It suggests that malpractice carriers may provide ongoing regulation of insured lawyers through education, rate-setting and both claim prevention and cure. The traditional US model draws a distinct line between complaints giving rise to discipline (there must be a violation of an applicable rule of professional conduct) and non-disciplinable client grievances about other matters. This dichotomy leaves a huge gap when it comes to dissatisfied consumers of legal services with no meaningful recourse in either forum. This part looks back at the reform processes in Australia and the United Kingdom and suggests ways in which the United States can learn from them as it develops its own strategy for reform.

The fourth part argues that these global changes represent changing views in professionalism, in which lawyers are service providers who must be open to innovations in delivery of legal services, both to ordinary consumers and to large corporate clients. The reforms in Australia and the United Kingdom provide useful templates that can be adapted to fit the legal framework in the United States, with cooperation between the federal and state regulatory structures. Both nations embrace a co-regulatory model that works in partnership with approved regulators, focusing on management-based regulation that aims for compliance through education. By taking a proactive approach to identify best practices, they seek to improve the quality of legal services and reduce the need for punishment through the disciplinary process. The regulatory innovations are endorsed by theoretical scholarship articulating a 'new governance' paradigm that uses collaborative organizational networks to set and enforce standards; no one set of actors is vested with 'command and control' authority.[6] If successful, these reforms will dramatically improve regulation. Only time will tell whether the law as written and practised will have such positive long-term effects. Finally, this chapter cautions the United States and other nations that want to be competitive in the globalized legal marketplace: their regulatory systems must function well, enforce professional conduct standards, provide meaningful redress to persons injured by inadequate professional services and remain open to market changes that enhance affordable access to legal services. If they have not yet undertaken such modernization, entrepreneurial nations are advised to join the continental shifts in regulation so their lawyers are not left adrift, excluded from the international currents of regulatory reform.

2.2 Australia's regulatory reforms: a continuing work in progress

From a comparative perspective, the Commonwealth of Australia has pioneered important regulatory reforms. Although it inherited much of its legal culture and structure from the United Kingdom, the federation's relative youth, demographics and global entrepreneurial aspirations have freed it to move beyond the hidebound constraints of England's regulatory structure. Unlike that of the United Kingdom, the Australian Parliament lacks plenary constitutional power to regulate the legal professions. Regulation is done through the individual states and territories, both through legislation and the Supreme Courts' inherent powers.[7] The six states and two self-governing territories maintain their own regulatory structures, resulting in a balkanized system akin to, but far smaller than, that of the United States. New South Wales, Queensland and Victoria have co-regulatory systems in which an independent Legal Services Commissioner (LSC) oversees enforcement activities, which may be delegated to the relevant professional bodies.

Among the Australian co-regulatory states, the independent LSCs in Queensland and New South Wales have achieved notable success at consumer protection, notwithstanding limited statutory powers to intervene and order redress. Discussion of the many subtle variations among the regulatory regimes would more confuse than clarify and hence is beyond the scope of this work. The present focus is on New South Wales, which started the progressive innovations and on Queensland, which joined in collaborative efforts to modernize lawyer regulation.

2.2.1 Trailblazing in New South Wales

In 1993, the NSW Law Reform Commission reported on complaint handling administered by the professional bodies, finding that the disciplinary approach to 'get rid of the bad apples' was 'too static and ... gives pitifully little value directly to the consumer'.[8] Legal commentators and consumers had become increasingly dissatisfied with what they saw as 'an undue emphasis on economic factors [which] ha[d] led, in recent times, to a lessening of sensitivity to, and the importance of, the old ethic and culture of professional service'.[9] They saw a profession that had worked to 'exclude the public from any real role in the regulation of the profession' in the Legal Profession Act 1987.[10]

As a result, the New South Wales Office of the Legal Services Commissioner (OLSC) was created in 1994 by amendments to the Legal Profession Act 1987. It is an independent statutory body reporting directly to state Parliament through the Attorney-General.[11] Comprehensive reviews of the revised complaint handling system occurred in 2001–02, when Parliament replaced the earlier statute with the Legal Profession Act 2004.[12] The newer law clarifies the statutory purposes and objectives – ensuring that laypersons have readily available information about the means of redress, and promoting transparency and openness about how the complaints scheme operates.[13] It also improves the complaint handling procedure, facilitating dispute resolution at various stages of the process. The OLSC may refer to voluntary mediation of both consumer disputes not involving misconduct and hybrid complaints alleging professional conduct issues.[14] The OLSC identifies as consumer disputes not involving misconduct complaints about communication, mistakes, delays and poor service.[15] The Commissioner is authorized to give notice of compulsory mediation of consumer disputes. The practitioner who fails to comply is susceptible to discipline.[16] Mediation outcomes can range from an apology or explanation from the practitioner, additional work performed without charge to correct a mistake or a fee adjustment.[17] An alternative mechanism provides for binding cost assessment of fee disputes not through the OLSC, but via an independent court-appointed system.[18]

The Commissioner's office provides a single point of entry for all complaints about lawyers. It makes a preliminary assessment whether to dismiss a complaint as non-meritorious, refer it to mediation as a consumer dispute, or exercise its co-regulatory authority to refer for investigation by the Law Society or Bar Association allegations of unsatisfactory professional conduct or a more serious category of professional misconduct. Alternatively, the OLSC may retain jurisdiction to investigate and prosecute complaints presenting issues of public interest or conflicts of interest with the professional associations. The single gateway streamlines the process, avoiding the confusion on where to start and problems with the 'regulatory maze' encountered in more complex schemes.

Because of its independence from the professional associations, the OLSC's dismissal rate (15 per cent of complaints) carries greater legitimacy in the public perception, as contrasted with the high dismissal rate (90 per cent) under the prior scheme administered by the professional bodies. This also alleviates pressure on the associations to justify their inaction as something other than that of a self-protectionist 'fox guarding the henhouse'. By referring many complaints back to the professional associations for investigation and prosecution, Commissioner Steve Mark believes this co-regulatory regime 'encourages the profession to continue on its path of self-regulation and improvement, albeit with direction from my Office'.[19]

It remains to be seen whether this structure could be replicated elsewhere. In the view of Christine Parker and Adrian Evans, the New South Wales model of co-regulation is 'workable' perhaps because 'the current Commissioner's personal skills and powers of persuasion are, in practice, sufficient to discretely manage what could be described as a continuing conflict of interest in the involvement of the profession in its own disciplinary processes' and 'may not be sustainable with different personalities in key positions'.[20]

Under the Legal Profession Reform Act 1993, the OLSC had no stand-alone authority to issue a binding compensation order.[21] That has changed so that, where requested by a complainant, the Commissioner or relevant Council may order compensation in dismissing a complaint when 'it is in the public interest' – language suggesting possible settlement and no good reason to pursue prosecution.[22] Similarly, compensation may be ordered when a complaint is brought to a summary conclusion where there is a reasonable likelihood the Tribunal would find the practitioner engaged in unsatisfactory professional conduct, but is otherwise generally competent and diligent.[23] Compensation orders by the Commissioner or Council are subject to review by the Tribunal.[24] Disciplinary matters are prosecuted before the Administrative Decisions Tribunal, which can issue binding compensation orders, up to $25,000, whether as part of a consent agreement or after hearing on the merits.[25] Despite the statutory authority to award compensation to the aggrieved person, this power is rarely used.[26] As in the United States, claims for compensation for negligence are to be pursued through private litigation. In New South Wales, smaller claims can be brought in a special tribunal.[27]

2.2.2 New South Wales' regulatory reforms spread to Queensland

The Legal Profession Act 2004 (Queensland) created an Office of Legal Services Commissioner (LSC), appointed by the Attorney-General, with exclusive authority to receive and administer complaints about lawyers. Although the LSC can refer matters for investigation and recommendation to the relevant professional bodies, prosecutorial authority remains with the LSC.[28] If, after preliminary review, the LSC characterizes the complaint as a 'consumer dispute', raising no issue of 'unsatisfactory professional conduct or unprofessional conduct', the statute only grants the discretion to suggest voluntary mediation or to refer to the relevant professional body for assistance in resolving the dispute.[29] As a practical matter, the Queensland LSC has limited authority to pursue dispute resolution unless a complaint can be termed subject to prosecution before a tribunal, as either unsatisfactory professional conduct or as professional misconduct.[30] Upon making this determination, the LSC has substantial latitude to facilitate a suitable resolution that is in the public interest, with redress for the complaint possibly including an apology, a fee refund or monetary compensation for harm caused by the professional failing.

Because the Act broadly defines 'unsatisfactory professional conduct' to include commonplace failures of competence and diligence, theoretically it gives the Commissioner leeway to obtain redress for complainants with small claims not worth the bother of civil litigation.[31] Disciplinary powers can be reserved for more serious and persistent incompetence, in which the public interest warrants intervention, as well as individual redress.[32] The Queensland LSC does not purport to be 'an alternative forum to the courts for hearing and deciding claims of negligence against lawyers'.[33] Thus the most common harms to clients from delays and incompetence go unremedied, risking criticism that the LSC may be an expensive bureaucracy that focuses too much on the 'small stuff', inadequately protecting the public interest.[34] When the Commissioner refers a matter for disciplinary action, the Tribunal or a committee of the professional body, upon finding of misconduct, can order compensation up to $7,500 for pecuniary loss.[35] Unfortunately, the Act confers no such authority on the Commissioner. If the Commissioner had the power to order redress for ordinary negligence, this would give lawyers a stronger incentive to improve the quality of routine legal services, with 'claims prevention' assistance from malpractice carriers requiring sound office procedures.

2.2.3 Progressive collaboration among regulatory stakeholders

Discipline and complaint handling schemes are reactive, narrowly focused on whether an individual practitioner has failed to comply with minimum standards of conduct.[36] In 2001, New South Wales pioneered a more revolutionary, proactive reform requiring that any firm seeking to incorporate must conduct a self-assessment on whether it has 'implemented and maintained' 'appropriate management systems' so that legal services are provided in accordance with professional obligations.[37] Using that statutory language as a base, the OLSC collaborated with stakeholders to identify 10 criteria relevant to whether that standard was met. The criteria included competence, communication, timeliness, conflicts, record-keeping, supervision and trust accounts.[38] Online self-assessment materials were developed for the incorporating firm to evaluate itself, reporting to the regulator whether it was fully, partially or non-compliant on each of the issues. When a firm self-assesses as fully compliant and the OLSC concurs, incorporation proceeds without further action. When the self-audit indicates partial or non-compliance, the OLSC enters into dialogue with the firm to help identify and implement mechanisms that will bring it into compliance.

'Management-based regulation' adopts the key strategy that 'education towards compliance' will deter future violations by helping firm management become aware of possible pitfalls and the type of systems that could avoid problems.[39] Recognizing that firms vary in size, locale and types of practice, there is no 'one size fits all' management system. The OLSC believes 'that if people build their own systems they usually own them more than if they are imposed. They are more appropriate to individual needs and requirements and more likely to be followed than just given lip service'.[40]

The vast majority (74 per cent) of incorporated firms have five or fewer lawyers. Experience has shown that smaller firms are more likely to be the subject of complaints and thus stand to benefit most from going through the process of self-assessment.[41] While relatively few larger firms have sought to incorporate and may already have in place formal risk-management mechanisms required by their malpractice carriers, they too could benefit from going through the self-assessment process. Every firm can benefit from a period of deliberation about creating an ethical infrastructure that actively promotes a culture supporting ethical values.[42] The self-assessment process allows firms autonomy in developing an ethical infrastructure suited to their particulars. Because the act allows both multidisciplinary practices and outside investment by non-lawyers, at least one legal practitioner director must be responsible for maintaining the appropriate management systems so that the non-lawyer providers or investors cannot override lawyers' ethical obligations. All lawyer partners share this responsibility and risk discipline for failing to do so.[43] Recent empirical research on the New South Wales management-based regulation found that incorporated legal practices (ILPs):

> do in fact manage themselves better and have better behavior than before they self-assessed, as indicated by lower complaints rates. On average the complaint rate for each ILP *after* self-assessment was one third the complaint rate *before* self-assessment ... This is a huge drop in complaints, which is statistically significant at the highest level.[44]

The proactive focus on deterrence through education has proved its effectiveness as a system of co-regulation. It starts with the proposition that lawyers and firms aspire to comply with their ethical obligations, but may not know of mechanisms that can avoid common pitfalls, resulting in complaints, consumer disputes or negligence claims. The external regulator is not a threatening force to be avoided, but rather functions as an expert consultant in sound law practice management. Although it has the power to conduct external audits, this rarely occurs – and only after less drastic efforts to bring about compliance fail.

The United States' constitutional concept of 'cooperative federalism' recognized the right of individual states to experiment with novel ideas not pre-empted by federal law. If successful, such local activity serves as an incubator for ideas that may work nationally and elsewhere. It appears that New South Wales and Queensland have served such roles for the federation of Australia.

In 2006, a cooperative effort undertaken by the respective Attorneys-General and the Australian Law Council (the umbrella organization for the respective professional bodies) produced the Legal Profession – Model Laws Project Model Provisions ('Model Laws'), a nationally uniform structure for lawyer regulation, leaving to local control a wide range of issues relating to the standards and procedure for discipline and complaints.[45] The Model Laws identified 'core provisions' requiring textual uniformity: the definitions of 'unsatisfactory professional conduct'; the more serious 'professional misconduct' requiring disciplinary proceedings; and hybrid matters capable of treatment under either category.[46] Those responsible for implementing the local Legal Profession Acts report continuing frustration with the myriad variations and subtle differences, which limit the Commissioner's authority to mediate consumer claims that fall short of professional misconduct but confer no binding authority to order redress.[47] The many inconsistencies between local regulations have impaired the ability of Australian lawyers to practise nationwide and compete internationally. The Prime Minister recently announced that legal profession reform is part of the government's national economic reform agenda. Reform is needed to simplify and harmonize lawyer regulation, to reduce compliance costs and provide a consistent, transparent approach for consumers. The Law Council of Australia welcomes the prospect of a single piece of federal legislation and regulatory structures.[48]

Because of the successful New South Wales approach, the 2006 Model Laws project adopted comparable language requiring 'appropriate management systems' and audits of ILPs. Every Australian state and territory is following suit, enacting almost identical statutory language. Queensland and Victoria have joined New South Wales in adopting the 'education towards compliance' strategy, and in developing a self-assessment audit form that can be completed online. Queensland is expanding the system to obtain information about a firm's non-legal directors, shareholders and their relationship to the practice, its non-legal services performed and its gross revenue.[49] Collaborative efforts are underway to draft audits on workplace culture and on billing practices – the latter being a prevalent cause of unethical behaviour, especially in medium and large firms.[50]

Self-assessment confers significant benefits to both firms and regulators, with little downside risk. The required process gives firms the opportunity to address potential problems before they become serious. Increased awareness about their own ethical infrastructure can only improve the quality of services to clients and lessen the likelihood of consumer disputes and conduct complaints. The additional information supplements existing complaint data, helping regulators set risk-management priorities and target resources where they are most needed. Regula-tors can also view the self-assessment data in evaluating complaints, to determine whether there might be a problem with the current management system.

Convinced that the benefits are well worth the effort, some regulators are considering whether to expand the requirement to all law firms, not just those seeking to incorporate.[51] Ironically, US scholarship on ethical infrastructure of law firms has persuaded Australia's regulators and scholars of the wisdom of management-based regulation.[52] Self-assessment reflects the normative position of Chambliss and Wilkins, that an ILP must 'designate at least one partner [to be] the firm's compliance specialist', who is 'personally liable for ensuring [his or her firm] maintain[s] the appropriate structural controls'.[53]

2.3 The United Kingdom's regulatory reforms: past, present and future

Over the last 30 years, the UK government has increased pressure on the legal professions to improve the quality of self-regulation and responsiveness to consumer complaints over inadequate legal services. The legal professions' self-regulatory models have 'been in more or less perpetual turmoil', with vast changes in their economic and political setting and closer involvement with government agencies 'that is proving fatal to key components of self-regulation as traditionally balanced'.[54]

Lord Mackay laid the groundwork for reform with the radical proposals in his 1989 Green Paper.[55] The resulting furor led to the somewhat modest reforms in the Courts and Legal Services Act 1990, which created a Legal Services Ombudsman (LSO) to oversee complaint handling by the professional bodies.[56] When problems continued, Parliament expanded the LSO's powers and author-ized the Lord Chancellor to appoint a Legal Services Complaints Commissioner (LSCC), yet another independent regulator to improve complaint handling.[57] Continued criticism focused on the Law Society, which had regulatory authority over the solicitor branch. In her 2002 Annual Report, LSO Zahida Manzoor found it had achieved little progress in improving complaint handling over 15 years. The quality of service 'failed to keep pace with consumer expectations or to reverse the decline in public confidence in lawyers'[58] – 'the professional bodies have been warned on countless occasions ... self regulation is a privilege, not a right – and ... can be taken away if it is no longer warranted'.[59]

The Blair administration turned up the heat that next summer, appointing Sir David Clementi to undertake a comprehensive review of the legal professions' regulatory structure.[60] Two strands of criticisms prompted the Clementi Review: (1) increased consumerism and widespread dissatisfaction with how lawyers and their professional bodies handled client complaints; and (2) competition law administered by the Office of Fair Trading, which investigated whether restrictive practices impeded professional competition.[61] Had lawyers – especially the solicitors – been able to clear up backlogs of complaints and been responsive to consumer watchdogs, 'they might have prevented or postponed what was to come'.[62] After extensive consultation among stakeholders, Clementi's final report produced a comprehensive set of proposed regulatory reforms.[63] The Blair government fast-tracked proposed legislation incorporating Clementi's proposals, which culminated in the Legal Services Act 2007.[64]

The Legal Services Act includes three categories of reforms that will completely overhaul lawyer regulation, complaint handling and permissible forms of practice. First and foremost, it establishes the Legal Services Board (LSB or Board) as an independent, non-governmental entity charged with oversight of all approved regulators of legal professionals, which must perform their duties to the Board's satisfaction. Approved regulators – for now, the existing professional bodies – must separate their regulatory functions from the politicized representative functions, to ensure regulatory independence. The Act envisions a co-regulatory model in which the board would only exercise its powers of intervention upon finding serious or persistent failures by the front-line approved regulators. Second, the Act creates an independent Office of Legal Complaints (OLC) as a single point of entry for all complaints seeking non-disciplinary redress for unsatisfactory services, and grants the Ombudsman authority to issue binding orders against practitioners. Third and potentially with greater future global impact, the Act authorizes alternative business structures – between legal service providers and non-lawyers, and with the possibility of outside investors. Each component of the Act requires ongoing consultation with multiple stakeholders, including the competition authority and consumer representatives. It appears that drafters of this multi-tiered, collaborative regulatory structure were in tune with other regulatory innovations, both actual and theoretical. The innovative work in Australia has likely gained the attention of those concerned with UK regulatory reforms.

The following discussion briefly summarizes the regulatory failings preceding the Clementi Review under the 1990 and 1999 Acts. It then focuses on the Legal Services Act 2007, with particular attention to the co-regulatory regime, complaint handling by the Legal Services Ombudsman and efforts at management-based regulation that are part of the new licensing system for Legal Disciplinary Practices (LDP). Finally, it identifies some of the many ongoing implementation activities. Because any reform project of this scope is a continuing work in progress, readers are advised to update information on developments occurring after 1 October 2009.

2.3.1 Regulatory failings preceding the Clementi Review

2.3.1.1 *1989–98: Lord Mackay's 1989 Green Paper and oversight entities authorized by courts and the Legal Services Act 1990*

Before considering recent developments, discussion of lawyers in the United Kingdom requires note of what gave rise to the traditional distinctions between barristers and solicitors. Those distinctions fostered a quasi-contractual division of territory, which gave each branch a monopoly over its respective field of trade.[65] Barristers, who had exclusive rights of audience to appear in court, were selected and instructed by the solicitors who maintained all client contact. Barristers had the technical legal knowledge, etiquette and advocacy skills required in court, but maintained a distance from the client. Solicitors involved in litigation would handle the paperwork, client interactions and financial matters. The solicitor branch also worked on a wide range of transactional matters and exercised its monopoly over conveyancing. These divisions evolved over time, and have, in recent decades, eroded incrementally under pressure from competition law and other efforts to ease artificial restrictions on delivery of legal services. Meanwhile, numerous other categories of legal professionals have proliferated.

Modern regulatory reforms go back to 1989. Prime Minister Margaret Thatcher's policies favoured open competition in the marketplace. Thatcher replaced then Lord Chancellor Hailsham, a staunch advocate for the bar, appointing Lord Chancellor Mackay of Clashfern, a Scotsman willing to make radical proposals that upset many in the stodgy English legal professions.

Mackay's 1989 Green Paper, 'The work and organization of the legal profession', aimed to create a system to provide the public with the most efficient, affordable and competent legal services, courtesy of market discipline.[66] Mackay proposed removing anti-competitive rules that restricted rights of advocacy, conveyancing and forms of practice between lawyers and non-lawyers. He sought to permit both barristers' direct access to clients and multidisciplinary practices, and to create extensive government control over professional regulation, including a Legal Services Ombudsman.[67] Not surprisingly, the Green Paper drew intense opposition, especially from the bar and judiciary. Michael Zander doubted that 'any single event in the long history of the English legal profession ever evoked so fierce and so broadly based a negative reaction'.[68] The Bar Council 'violently attacked' Mackay's proposals, and the then Lord Chief Justice, Lord Lane, called it 'one of the most sinister documents ever to emanate from government'.[69] In retrospect, Lord Mackay was ahead of his time; many of his proposals foreshadowed later reforms, including those in the Legal Services Act 2007 (LSA).

Overwhelming opposition to the Green Paper forced government retreat. Parliament enacted the Courts and Legal Services Act 1990 (CLSA), most of which made structural alterations to the complex English court system. Although some provisions opened the theoretical possibility for solicitors' rights of audience and repealed statutory bars to certain lawyer practices, the Act then authorized the relevant professional bodies to retain those trade restraints and most of their self-regulatory powers. Nevertheless, the CLSA represented a significant intrusion on the professional bodies' traditional prerogatives. The Act's stated objective sought to expand the range of eligible providers of advocacy, litigation, conveyancing and probate services, and to innovate the delivery of those services.[70]

Among the various oversight entities established in the CLSA, two are relevant here. The Lord Chancellor's Advisory Committee on Legal Education and Conduct (ACLEC) was to assist in developing and maintaining standards in the education, training and conduct of those offering legal services, both for initial training and continuing education, and to 'have regard' to the practices of other members of the European Union and 'the desirability of equality of opportunity'.[71] ACLEC also shared the broad oversight functions of the professional bodies: a body proposing changes to qualification standards and rules of conduct required ACLEC approval.[72] The CLSA structured a cumbersome and time-consuming procedure for amending such standards or rules, routing the proposal through ACLEC, the Lord Chancellor or designated judges and the Office of Fair Trading.[73]

The CLSA also created the Legal Services Ombudsman (LSO), a non-lawyer appointed by the Lord Chancellor to exercise oversight of complaint handling by the different professional bodies, to recommend improvements of their systems, with limited authority to investigate individual complaints and to suggest reconsideration of a complaint or redress for the complainant.[74]

In 1995, Rhoda James and Mary Seneviratne conducted a comprehensive study on the LSO's operations. While they found that the LSO was truly independent from both government and the professions, they found it ineffective at resolving grievances and recommended that Parliament expand its powers to act on its own initiative, conduct unannounced inspections and random file reviews, and issue binding orders as opposed to recommendations.[75]

The arduous route to get a matter considered by the LSO took several completed steps, available only to tenacious and knowledgeable complainants who did not drop out from frustration or fatigue. First, the complainant had to go through the lawyer or firm's internal complaint handling procedure. Although Law Society Practice Rule 15 required all solicitors to have an in-house procedure and to ensure clients knew how to access it, empirical research showed that many firms either had no procedure or failed to inform clients about it. Complainants who sought resolution through the in-house procedure were very dissatisfied.[76] Yet the Solicitors' Complaint Bureau (SCB) would not accept a complaint until exhaustion of the in-house procedure. Those who filed a written complaint with the SCB generally hoped it would contact the solicitor and help sort things out; fewer expected the solicitor be punished or made to pay compensation.[77] Survey respondents were also very dissatisfied with the SCB process and outcome, believing it was heavily influenced in favour of the solicitor and the legal profession and that it was rife with incompetence, delay and poor communication.[78] The SCB would only inform complainants of their right to seek assistance from the LSO if they lost an appeal of the SCB's determination. Because few dissatisfied complainants pursued an appeal, they never got notice that further recourse might be available through the LSO scheme.[79] Although 30 per cent of SCB complaints were not resolved to the consumer's satisfaction, only about 8 per cent contacted the LSO.[80]

2.3.1.2 *Access to Justice Act 1999*

Parliament revisited some of those issues in the Access to Justice Act 1999 (ATJA), which more generally addressed legal aid in civil and criminal matters and procedural court rules.[81] The CLSA intended the ACLEC to be a lead policy-making body with a lay majority and designated judges to play a subsidiary monitoring role. That committee, perhaps stymied by the statute's carefully balanced representation of various interest groups, was unsuccessful at achieving the stated objectives. The new Act abolished the ACLEC and created the Legal Services Consultative Panel, charged with duties similar to those of the ACLEC but providing for appointments based on individual expertise instead of interest group representation.[82] The Consultative Panel was smaller and more focused to provide specialist advice on proposed rule changes; the role of judicial members was demoted to a consultative role without their prior veto power.[83] The ATJA empowered the Lord Chancellor to set timetables on consultations about proposed rule changes and to make minor rule changes on his own, in order to expedite the amendment process.[84] Nevertheless, the consultation process required interaction between professional bodies and other interested persons who raised public and consumer interests. The Consultative Panel made recommendations to the Lord Chancellor, who had the final authority to approve any changes.

The ATJA expressly opened to solicitors the rights of audience and to conduct litigation in all courts, subject to their satisfying the qualification standards of the Law Society. This effectively broke the bar's gridlock resisting solicitors' efforts to obtain rights of audience in higher courts. The Act also eased the Bar Council's permissible restrictions on the rights of audience for employed advocates, such as barristers who worked for the Crown Prosecutor but who lacked the independence of sole practitioners practising in chambers.[85]

The solicitor branch gained advocacy rights, but also became subject to much closer oversight on complaint handling. Solicitors, who are the primary point of contact for clients, outnumber barristers by a ratio of nine to one, so it is not surprising that most complaints pertained to solicitors.[86] The cumulative number of complaints brought to the LSO reflected the same ratio.[87] Nevertheless, the LSO was far more satisfied with the Bar Council's handling of complaints compared with that of the Law Society, which had a long history of poorly handled complaints and few indications of improvement over time.[88]

The ATJA expanded the LSO's authority to issue binding orders against both individuals and professional bodies.[89] It also enhanced the Lord Chancellor's authority to assess professional bodies for expenses incurred by the LSO and to appoint an additional oversight authority, the Legal Services Complaints Commissioner (LSCC), vested with enforcement powers over professional bodies, and the ability to demand reports, conduct further investigation, audit, recommend specific improvements, set targets and require self-improvement plans. For failure to submit or implement an adequate plan for handling complaints effectively and efficiently, the LSCC may fine a professional body up to £1 million.[90] In 2004, the Lord Chancellor exercised that reserve authority to appoint LSO Zahida Manzoor to also act as LSCC.

Between 2003 and 2005, Manzoor's annual reports about the Law Society became increasingly strident, noting little improvement after 15 years of oversight and repeated warnings about unacceptable delays, poor administration, decision-making, service and basic errors. Solicitors comprised 95 per cent of the LSO caseload. In 2005, she assessed a £250,000 penalty against the Law Society for failing to achieve the targets she previously had set.[91] At the same time, she applauded the government's proposed radical reforms, which adopted many of the recommendations set forth in Clementi's final report, as a 'a once in a lifetime opportunity to put things right for consumers and professionals who have laboured for too long under an archaic system of regulation which has lacked transparency or consumer focus'.[92]

2.3.2 The Clementi Review and Report lead to enactment of the Legal Services Act 2007

In July 2003, Secretary of State Lord Falconer appointed Sir David Clementi to undertake an independent review of the legal profession's regulatory framework.[93] Clementi's appointment followed a Scoping Study conducted by the Department for Constitutional Affairs (DCA), which found the existing framework 'outdated, inflexible, over complex, and insufficiently accountable or transparent', concluding that 'the status quo [was] not an option'.[94] Clementi was charged to consider 'what regulatory framework would best promote competition, innovation and the public and consumer interest in an efficient, effective and independent legal sector'.[95]

The Clementi Review Consultation Paper, released on 8 March 2004, addressed three main issues: the architectural framework of a more rational regulatory system; a better system to regulate complaint handling and discipline issues; and the possibility of alternative business models for legal practices.[96] Clementi doubted that professional bodies, which serve as representative lobbying organizations, could also provide legitimate regulatory oversight.[97] Consumers were confused by the regulatory maze of the professional bodies' existing complaint systems.[98] Clementi presented for discussion three regulatory models, ranging from complete separation of trade and regulatory functions, with all regulation controlled by an independent government entity akin to the UK Financial Services Authority, to establishing a light-touch oversight agency to monitor self-regulatory conduct by the professional bodies.[99]

Clementi's final report endorsed the B+ model, in which a new Legal Services Board would have overarching regulatory and oversight authority. If professional bodies wanted to become approved regulators, they must create new entities vested only with regulatory powers, subject to oversight by the LSB. Their representational activities could continue unfettered by government control. The Office of Legal Complaints (OLC) would consider all consumer complaints against legal professionals[100] – although, under the authority and general supervision of the LSB, complaint handling would function independently.[101] The proposed OLC would play a strategic role in setting targets for practitioners' in-house complaint handling, monitoring indemnity insurance schemes and compensation funds controlled by the front-line bodies.[102] The final report cautiously opened the door to modern business structures for delivering legal services, including Legal Disciplinary Practices (LDPs), which would allow professional associations among all legal professionals comparable to US law firms, and Alternative Business Structures, which would allow partnerships between lawyers and non-lawyers with the possibility of outside investors.[103]

In May 2006, the government introduced its draft Legal Services Bill into Parliament.[104] The Bill mostly followed Clementi's final report, proposing the LSB oversee front-line regulators (now called 'approved regulators'), who must perform their duties in a manner compatible with stated regulatory objectives.[105] It endorsed Clementi's OLC proposal for an office with exclusive authority over complaints for redress up to £20,000.[106] The Bill prohibited approved regulators from providing redress as part of their regulatory arrangements,[107] and prevented them from contractually limiting or excluding a person's right to seek relief through the OLC ombudsman scheme.[108] It advanced more controversial proposals to permit alternative business structures and outside ownership of law firms. In anticipation of eventual passage, the Law Society and Bar Council segregated their regulatory and representative functions, delegating the regulatory functions to new, independent entities.[109]

No UK law reform occurs without extensive consultations open to all interested groups and individuals, from the initial proposals through to final enactment. The LSA 2007 was no exception. Objecting to the end of self-regulation and diminished core values of professional independence, UK professional bodies voiced concern that the reforms risked excluding them from practice in other European Union nations.[110] Overseas bars also raised independence concerns.[111] Fearing the UK reforms would adversely impact their competitive standing, the Scottish and Irish legal professions sought local legislation to address consumer complaints against lawyers.[112]

These lobbying efforts proved successful, persuading the government that continued global competitiveness of UK firms required respect for professional independence. Amendments built in a co-regulatory regime that granted approved regulators primary frontline authority, subject to the board's oversight and limited intervention powers. Other amendments granted authority to appoint the Board chair and its members to the Lord Chancellor, head of the judiciary, in consultation with the Lord Chief Justice.[113] Clementi had endorsed the B+ regulatory model, but these changes may have shifted the Board's oversight role closer to the B model, with light-touch authority to influence approved regulators. Only time will tell.

A brief description of the new regulatory oversight structure is in order, given its multi-tiered collaborative relationships and mechanisms for transparency and accountability. LSA 2007, s. 1(1) identifies regulatory objectives that the board, approved regulators and other stakeholders must promote, including public and consumer interests, competition, the constitutional rule of law and access to justice through a strong and diverse legal profession. The Board chair and a majority of its members must be laypersons, not authorized to engage in activities reserved to legal professionals.[114] Board composition (seven to 10 members) should reflect knowledge in diverse areas, including legal, consumer and commercial affairs, competence and complaint handling.[115] Regulatory activities 'should be transparent, accountable, proportionate, consistent and targeted' only where action is needed.[116] The Board's internal governance rules should aim to protect the regulatory independence of approved regulators, including adequate resources, open communications among regulatory actors, the Board and the Office of Legal Complaints.[117]

For the first time, legislation articulates specific activities reserved to licensed legal professionals and defines the unauthorized practice of law. The LSA identifies types of reserved legal activities and sets criminal sanctions for persons not authorized by relevant approved regulators.[118] Schedule 4 lists existing professional bodies that had served as regulators for subsets of legal professionals and authorizes their continued service as approved regulators. Approved regulators' 'regulatory arrangements' concerning rules of conduct, discipline, education, licensure, indemnification and compensation for redress or misconduct must further the regulatory objectives. Acts or omissions that adversely affect those objectives are subject to dialogue and sanctions between the Board and a regulator, starting with target-setting and ending with cancellation of status.[119] Under the statutory model, the Board's progressive intervention powers are limited and may be exercised only as warranted by proof of serious ongoing failures.

The UK model of regulatory discourse through consultations among stakeholders is incorporated throughout. For example, policy statements on the Board's planned oversight functions must allow time for comments and final publication, reflecting any interim changes.[120] Board oversight of approved regulators should attempt informal resolution before it invokes formal mechanisms, such as setting targets, giving directions or intervention.[121] Under Board auspices, an independent Consumer Panel of non-lawyers may conduct research and advise the LSB about regulatory activities.[122] The Office of Fair Trading (OFT) may issue a report opining that an approved regulator's regulatory arrangements impede competition; after receiving input from the relevant regulator and the Consumer Panel, the Board gives notice of its proposed action, which is subject to further review by the Lord Chancellor and the European Union Competition Commission.[123] Principles of accountability and transparency require annual reports both from the Office of Legal Complaints (OLC) to the Board and from the Board to the Lord Chancellor, who presents them to Parliament.[124]

The OLC is an independent body under Board oversight, which will administer an ombudsman scheme to investigate and determine all complaints seeking redress from legal service providers.[125] As a jurisdictional prerequisite, a complainant must first seek resolution using the practitioner's in-house complaints procedures.[126] When operational, it will provide a single point of entry for all complaints from persons who received legal services from those authorized to engage in reserved legal activities (regulated persons), whether or not the alleged conduct related to legal services. Vicarious responsibility extends to the acts or omissions of employees and partners acting within the customary scope of their duties.[127] The ombudsman scheme has a broad remit to determine complaints and, where appropriate, to issue direction that the respondent apologize, reimburse fees, pay up to £30,000 compensation, rectify the error at the practitioner's own expense or take other actions in the interest of the complainant.[128] Remedial authority is not limited 'to cases where the complainant may have a cause of action against the respondent for negligence', and 'may be available in cases of "simple" inadequate professional service'.[129]

The ombudsman can provide redress but not discipline, which remains under the jurisdiction of the relevant approved regulator.[130] The ombudsman may dismiss a complaint without consideration of the merits if the complaint is 'frivolous or vexatious', would be better dealt with under another ombudsman scheme, has already been addressed under another ombudsman scheme, arbitration or legal proceedings, or if there was undue delay in making the complaint or providing evidence.[131]

When the OLC receives a complaint within its jurisdiction, it first is assigned to a non-ombudsman caseworker for investigation and attempted mediation. The caseworker may not summarily dismiss or issue a determination. If the parties do not accept the caseworker's proposed resolution, the complaint then proceeds to consideration and disposition by the Chief Ombudsman or is delegated to an assistant ombudsman.[132] An ombudsman's determination of a complaint should have reference to what is 'fair and reasonable in all the circumstances of the case'. Upon making a determination, the ombudsman must prepare and provide a written statement of reasons to the complainant, respondent and relevant professional body. If the complainant accepts the determination or is deemed to have accepted because of failure to reject in a timely fashion, the ombudsman will issue a certificate of determination which has a binding and preclusive effect on both parties.[133] If a respondent does not comply with the Chief Ombudsman's binding directions, a court may order enforcement, notifying the OLC and approved regulator. The ombudsman may notify the Board, triggering possible intervention if an approved regulator 'persistently failed adequately to discharge its regulatory function'.[134] The Act creates a 'polluter pays' system, requiring the respondent to pay charges to the OLC unless the complaint is resolved in the respondent's favour and the ombudsman is satisfied that the respondent took all reasonable steps to resolve the issue through in-house procedures.[135]

The Act does not expressly state what may happen if the complainant rejects the determination. If this new ombudsman scheme receives positive performance reviews after a few years of operation, civil action by dissatisfied complainants will face an uphill battle to establish liability. Because the Act requires larger liability claims to be brought in court, a well-functioning ombudsman system will provide clients of UK lawyers a meaningful opportunity to seek redress. The Chief Ombudsman's authority to issue binding and enforceable determinations is the envy of commissioners who administer complaint handling systems elsewhere. As the UK system comes into existence, perhaps it will trigger additional law reforms in those countries.

2.3.3 Implementation to date: the UK way ahead
(as of 1 October 2009)

Lawyer regulation in the United Kingdom is in the middle of transition. Zahida Manzoor accepted terminal reappointment as LSO and LSCC, with limited transitional authority. The first LSB chair, nine board members and chief executive were appointed and began work in 2008. If their backgrounds and nine months of work in 2009 are predictive, the LSB has potential to be a very effective oversight regulator that communicates and collaborates well. Chair David Edmonds has an extensive background in senior management in both the public and private sectors, including regulatory work and oversight of the UK Legal Aid programme. The Board includes two lawyers with powerful backgrounds, as general counsel to Reuters and the Financial Services Agency Board. Lay members come with diverse expertise in executive, regulatory, administrative and consumer matters.

Since January 2009, the Board has issued its business plan, which sets forth a vision for a dynamic, modern and consumer-oriented organization that 'work[s] constructively with the (approved regulators) and all our other partners to . . . tackle the objectives systematically'.[136] After announcing it was 'open for business', the Board issued consultations on regulatory independence and developing a regulatory regime for alternative business structures. Since November 2008, the Board has appointed Elizabeth France as Chair of the OLC, six OLC board members and the Chief Ombudsman.[137] Each of the appointees has extensive expertise with Ombudsman, mediation or consumer protection matters.[138] As of 1 October 2009, the staff has grown to 35.[139] The Board published proposed rules on regulatory independence and is now evaluating the alternative business submissions and the construction of licensing rules.[140]

Until the OLC becomes fully functional in 2011, the relevant approved regulators bear continued responsibility for complaint handling, besides licensure and discipline.[141] The Law Society and Bar Council established separate regulatory entities, the Solicitors Regulation Authority (SRA) and Bar Standard Board (BSB) respectively. Positioned for future practice innovations, as of 31 March 2009, the SRA assumed responsibility for regulating Legal Disciplinary Practices and amended the Code of Conduct to introduce firm-based regulation similar to recent Australian innovations. Because membership in their representative components is now voluntary and other entities already cater to the interests of other legal professional subsets, there is some uncertainty about the future roles of the Law Society and Bar Council. The Law Society seeks to leave little to chance. It hired long-time Bar Council executive and founding LSB Director Mark Stobbs to head legal policy issues and commissioned additional independent regulatory reviews.[142] Stay tuned. The question remains: what impact will the LSA 2007 have on regulation of lawyers elsewhere? Is it the regulatory equivalent of a tidal wave with global implications? Or will the new regulatory structure become yet another cumbersome bureaucracy resulting in limited meaningful change?

2.4 Lawyer regulation in the United States

The United States has been a strong international leader in the law and ethics of lawyering. At present, however, it appears to lag behind as Australia and the United Kingdom take the lead on regulatory reforms. US lawyers claim robust privileges of self-regulation are needed to uphold the rule of law, unfettered by partisan impulses that could influence executive or legislative action.[143] Lawyers exercise substantial regulatory authority over licensure, professional conduct standards and disciplinary enforcement, subject to final approval and oversight by the highest state court exercising its inherent authority to regulate the practice of law.[144]

The American Bar Association's national leadership in crafting model lawyer codes has influenced state courts and bar associations, which exercise their prerogative to consider local modifications based on policy differences or sensibilities. Federal and state legislation has, to some extent, subjected lawyers to external regulation by governmental entities.[145] Consumer protection, in the form of redress to clients or third persons harmed by incompetent or dishonest lawyers, falls outside the usual scope of lawyer discipline. While some states provide for mediation of non-fee disputes or mandatory fee arbitration,[146] US lawyer disciplinary agencies typically do not obtain relief for injured clients as part of the discipline imposed. As a practical matter, most dissatisfied former clients can only wish for redress through civil litigation. Unless the lawyer carries malpractice insurance, liability is strong and damages large, recovery is unlikely.

The next section discusses lawyer regulatory systems in the United States, mostly controlled by local authorities with vast differences in their views on enforcement, dispute resolution and resource allocation. In recent decades, federal statutes imposed additional restrictions on lawyers in specialized practice areas. As contrasted to the balkanized state enforcement systems, the following section considers the expanding risks of civil liability with reference to limited available statistical evidence about malpractice claims, and the growing importance of malpractice carriers on the behaviour of those they cover. Given the prevalence of compulsory insurance and other types of consumer protection required in other developed countries, it criticizes states' failure to provide mechanisms for consumer protection, including minimum indemnity coverage by all lawyers who provide services to private clients.

2.4.1 Balkanized state-based regulation overlaid with pockets of federal law

Self-regulation of the American legal profession is something of a misnomer. More accurately, it is regulation and enforcement delegated to professional bodies and overseen by the judicial branch. In each state and the District of Columbia, the court of highest appellate jurisdiction has inherent authority to regulate the practice of law.[147] Because most regulatory authority resides in individual states, and because those states vary significantly in their standards, enforcement mechanisms and general approach to ethical issues, lawyer regulation in the United States is considered 'balkanized' or 'fractionalized'.

State supreme courts' regulatory authority includes power to adopt rules for Licensure, rules of professional conduct, and rules and procedures for disciplinary enforcement to fulfil the primary purpose of professional regulation: protection of the public. The organized bar may formulate proposed rules for adoption by the state court. State legislative efforts to regulate lawyers have met with mixed success.[148] Courts invoke inherent authority doctrine as a fundamental tenet of separation of powers when invalidating such legislation.[149] When courts uphold state statutes or regulations based on their Tenth Amendment police power that incidentally affect the practice of law, they reiterate that such laws neither supersede nor detract from the judiciary's inherent authority to regulate the practice of law.[150]

Location of the regulatory function varies among jurisdictions. Thirty-three US jurisdictions maintain unified (previously referred to as mandatory or integrated) bar associations, in which membership is required as a condition of licensure to practise law in the state.[151] Compulsory state bar membership has been accomplished through court rule, inherent power doctrine, legislation or some combination thereof.[152] In 21 states, the unified bars exercise both representative and regulatory functions within the same organization, reinforcing the perception that politics and collective self-interest taint regulatory decisions. Those states' supreme courts delegate to the state bar associations administrative authority to investigate and prosecute alleged misconduct and authorize hearing tribunals to recommend findings of fact, conclusions of law and disciplinary sanctions. Such delegation to the bar is non-binding and advisory, with the high court retaining final and exclusive authority. While judicial regulation aims to protect the disciplinary process from undue political influence by the legislative and executive branches of government, delegation of regulatory functions to the state bar association risks under-regulation due to actual or perceived conflicts of interest. The public often views as protectionist regulatory conduct that appears to benefit the profession's political, ideological or trade interests rather than being seen to advance legitimate public interest in the legal system.[153] Twelve of the 33 unified bar states maintain a separate lawyer admissions and discipline entity in order to isolate regulatory activities from those advancing the bar's business or professional interests.[154] This structural segregation of regulatory and trade functions alleviates public concerns about accountability.

In the 18 non-unified or voluntary bar states, lawyers are regulated by the highest state court, administered through a stand-alone agency of the court. Voluntary state bars are most firmly established in the North Atlantic and Midwestern states.[155] Voluntary bars function as trade associations representing the collective interests of their members; while they provide input on some regulatory questions, including changes to the rules governing ethical standards, their views lack official imprimatur and may or may not influence adoption by the state supreme court.

Over the last century, debates periodically have resurfaced about unification and whether compulsory state bars are sufficiently accountable to the public in their regulatory actions, and whether the bar's political speech violates the First Amendment rights of dissenting members.[156] To date, efforts to force states' conversion from a unified to a voluntary bar have failed, although some challenges persist.[157]

The purpose of discipline, it is commonly said, is to 'protect the public, the bar, and legal institutions against lawyers who have demonstrated an unwillingness to comply with minimal professional standards'.[158] While it is sound to involve lawyers in the disciplinary process as prosecutors, grand jurors, adjudicators, disciplinary board members and appellate judges, their dominant role in the process furthers the public perception that US lawyers are regulated exclusively by their professional colleagues.[159] Regulatory reforms throughout the United States now include lay representatives in the process. This is a step towards bringing the United States in line with the Australian and UK reforms, which both require significant participation by non-lawyers on all regulatory matters.

It is difficult to make generalized observations about lawyer discipline systems in the United States. The 1970 Clark Report declared that existing disciplinary systems were 'scandalous', with lawyers' prevailing attitudes ranging from 'apathy to outright hostility' and enforcement 'practically nonexistent in many jurisdictions'.[160] That scathing review prompted important but uneven reforms. Eric H. Steele's and Raymond T. Nimmer's 1976 empirical research concluded that most disciplinary entities focused on lawyer deviance in which the offending lawyer 'is defined as unfit, a malefactor', who warrants removal by suspension or disbarment in order to purify the profession, and disregarded more pervasive client complaints about fees, delays and quality of performance.[161] Scholars continued to question the effectiveness of professional self-regulation, with particular focus on the bar's inattention to competence and consumer protection.[162] Deborah Rhode noted the serious mismatch between client needs and the regulatory response by lawyer discipline agencies. Even where conduct violates black-letter provisions of an applicable rule and the unhappy client files a grievance, discipline seldom results and even more rarely provides any redress for the harmed client. The traditional disciplinary model declines to act upon the vast majority of client grievances about isolated instances of neglect, inadequate services and excessive fees.

In 1989, the ABA McKay Commission again studied US disciplinary systems, reaffirming that the judicial and not the legislative branch should have regulatory authority over the profession.[163] The commission report noted that most common law countries, including the United Kingdom and Australia, had mechanisms to address less serious client complaints, redress for consumers and other non-disciplinary mechanisms to bridge the gap between legitimate client expectations and existing regulations. It recommended that states consider expanding their regulatory structures to include multi-door pilot programmes, mediation, fee and malpractice arbitration and management assistance programmes.[164] The ABA House of Delegates adopted, with modifications, the report's 21 recommendations.[165]

States widely implemented some recommendations, providing peer assistance and education, and expediting procedures for minor misconduct, substance abuse counselling and interim suspensions where conduct poses a substantial threat of serious public harm.[166] Many adopted centralized intake systems to facilitate efficient screening and referral of grievances to the appropriate entity.[167] Some states resisted more visionary consumer protection recommendations to require fee arbitration or other dispute-resolution mechanisms.[168] Unified bar jurisdictions also resisted major structural recommendations that would ensure the independence and adequate funding of disciplinary entities housed within.[169]

Many states have increased funding and hired professional staff to administer discipline, as opposed to relying on local volunteer committees that produced inconsistent outcomes reflecting political and personal connections. A majority of states (12 unified Bar states and the 18 voluntary Bar states) have established separate regulatory entities to protect their independence from political and trade interests. It is likely that most states now employ advisory ethics counsel carefully isolated from the disciplinary staff. Diversion programmes and attention to backlogs are common. Although most states now allow public access to disciplinary proceedings after a finding of probable cause and filing of a formal complaint, there is still limited public transparency.[170]

No jurisdiction has formally implemented what Tom Morgan has suggested would have been most visionary: to create 'a professionally staffed system within which a client could file a charge and get a decision ordering payment of damages as well as see traditional discipline imposed'.[171] In the absence of that type of system, Morgan contends the legal profession lacks 'the leverage with which to force our brothers and sisters at the bar to take professional obligations seriously'.[172] It appears he was referring to a resolution by the ABA Standing Committee on Dispute Resolution, which found that lawyer discipline and client protection funds had limited ability to compensate clients or order restitution, denying a feasible remedy for most clients with legitimate claims for redress.

While the traditional discipline–malpractice dichotomy leaves a huge gap of viable complaints without recourse, some jurisdictions have quietly shifted to more of a consumer protection model not expressly addressed in the rules or court opinions. Chief counsel of an independent lawyer regulator observed a 'sea change' in which the state Supreme Court now routinely approves plea bargains for discipline that include fee restitution and other forms of client-focused relief.[173]

Although sound analysis of comparative budget data on enforcement budgets in unified bar states is challenging, it may raise additional concerns about regulatory independence from bar politics and trade concerns. Inherent tension exists where bar administrators and elected leaders must allocate limited resources to both regulatory and membership service programmes.

The annual ABA Survey on Lawyer Discipline Systems (SOLD) presents quantified data, but carefully avoids any qualitative analysis. My preliminary statistical analysis of the 2006 survey indicates that the per-lawyer annual disciplinary budgets of 13 US jurisdictions are under $100; 11 of these jurisdictions have unified bars. While the issue warrants further study, it also appears that seven of the 11 low-funded disciplinary programmes have significantly lower rates of filing charges against lawyers after probable cause determinations have been

made. Anecdotal information suggests a possible correlation between low disciplinary budgets for unified bars, lengthy delays and continued risk of harm to
unsuspecting current and future clients. Focus on formal charge rates may overlook potential disciplinary matters that are resolved informally. Comparison
among jurisdictions is difficult because of differences in local legal culture, procedure, rules, terminology and the possible perception that bar leaders owe
members protection from increased regulation. There also may be jurisdictional
differences in reporting rules, prosecutorial discretion or informal resolutions.
Nevertheless, this unscientific study of available data suggests a strong correlation
at both the high and low ends of budgets and per-lawyer charge rates.[174]

When major financial scandals surface, external federal regulators become
involved, whether through regulatory action to hold accountable professional
advisers who facilitated the fraud, or through new legislation or rule-making to
prevent recurrences. Federal intervention requires lawyers, along with other service providers, to impose gatekeeping duties 'to monitor their clients for the sake
of other interests'. Each of these federal initiatives has 'been limited in scope and
require[d] relatively rapid [defensive] responses from [the ABA, state and federal
Bars]'. Ted Scheyer's survey of these skirmishes in the last 30 years contends that
these federal regulators may no longer pay deference to the tandem professional
regulatory programmes designed by the legal profession. Instead, 'the ABA must
now be prepared to *shape, not merely oppose, external initiatives*'.[175]

2.4.2 Expanded risk of civil liability and regulatory role of malpractice carriers

Risk of civil liability to both clients and non-clients has exploded over the last
three decades, in terms of both the frequency and severity of claims.[176] Several
factors may account for this, including heightened consumerism, developments in
the underlying substantive law and the greater availability of lawyers to sue or
testify against a professional colleague. Despite expansion of the substantive law,
prospective claimants have little chance of recovery unless the offending lawyer is
insured or has substantial personal assets vulnerable to collection.

Risk of malpractice liability has become a serious concern for US lawyers only
recently. Reliable statistical data are scarce. In recent years, the frequency of
'claims made' has levelled, but the severity of claims and amounts of indemnity
payouts have increased significantly.[177] The aftermath of huge financial failures
has resulted in mega-claims, sometimes against large and prestigious firms.[178]
Because settlements often condition payouts and other remedial terms subject to
confidentiality provisions, the consuming public remains unaware that wronged
clients may have civil recourse against malfeasant lawyers.[179]

The datum identify known risky practice areas, including plaintiffs' personal
injury, insurance defence, real estate, family law, estate, trust and probate.[180] Only
15 per cent of all claims are brought against larger firms – those with 40 or more
lawyers – which may indicate that growth in firm size increases the likelihood of
insurance coverage and an ethical infrastructure to prevent or cure potential

claims.[181] Most claims allege substantive errors of law or administrative error.[182] Viable allegations of conflict of interest in garden-variety negligence cases present major hurdles for effective defence.[183]

Several factors may account for the expanded liability risks. The growing consumer movement corresponded with an increase in the number of lawyers and competition among them.[184] Public opinion polls in recent decades show sizeable drops in the profession's reputation for honesty, veracity and ethics.[185] When lawyers were fewer in number, fraternal collegiality viewed legal malpractice as an unpopular cause in which it was difficult to find a lawyer willing to bring a claim or to find an expert willing to testify that another lawyer had violated the accepted standard of care. Even today, when the prospective plaintiff can find a lawyer willing to take a case and break the 'conspiracy of silence', otherwise viable claims are dropped when it appears the malfeasant lawyer is uninsured and effectively judgment proof.[186] Smaller claims also fall through the cracks when a low likely recovery leaves little financial incentive to bring suit. Some observers assert that appellate judicial decisions by judges who rose through the ranks of local practitioners and selected with lawyers' political and financial support perpetuate protectionist doctrines, imposing difficult barriers to recovery.[187]

The underlying substantive law in the United States has changed notably in recent decades. Evolutionary development of the law governing lawyers, including successive drafts of the Model Rules of Professional Conduct, the Restatement (Third) of the Law Governing Lawyers and expanded case law allowing potential recovery improves the likelihood prospective claimants can find a lawyer willing to sue – if the damages are large and the prospective defendant maintains adequate malpractice insurance.[188] Influential scholarship supports expanded theories of liability.[189] Breach of fiduciary duty and breach of contract claims are on the rise.[190] Economic downturns prompt disappointed clients and non-clients to search for deep pockets to cover their losses from high-risk matters.[191]

Knowledgeable observers maintain that malpractice carriers provide the most effective means of regulating US lawyers today.[192] Carriers, who must indemnify for any claims within the scope of coverage, have first-hand ability to educate and affect the conduct of the lawyers they insure. They provide ongoing education on loss prevention through good management structure, starting with the initial application and premium and then repeated through annual renewals and rates based on a firm's claim history. They issue regular newsletters and consultations aimed to prevent claims, provide guidance and active assistance to cure a potential claim and further educate their insureds during the defence of claims brought.[193] Carriers have the greatest ability to interface with those they insure, to establish workable ethical infrastructures suitable for the firm's size and practice areas. Their enforcement mechanism is based on money and business models, not hortatory reference to high moral ethics.

There is little reliable data on the number of uninsured or under-insured practising lawyers whose conduct risks exposure to malpractice liability.[194] The 1992 McKay Report recommended that states consider whether to compel malpractice insurance.[195] Oregon remains the only US jurisdiction that compels malpractice coverage as a condition of licensure.[196] The Oregon experience has achieved notable success at providing affordable coverage to lawyers and appropriate claims handling and resolution, reserving defence costs for significant claims warranting such expenditures. Its captive carrier starts out charging each lawyer the same annual premium, with later adjustments based on actual claims experience.[197]

Present discussion of compulsory insurance has shifted to a debate on whether lawyers must reveal whether they maintain a minimum level of liability coverage and to whom that must be disclosed.[198] Twenty-five jurisdictions now require lawyers to disclose in some manner whether they maintain a minimum level of professional liability insurance, either on bar registration statements or directly to prospective clients. Five jurisdictions have rejected proposed compulsory disclosure rules.[199]

In the aftermath of the current economic crisis, legal professionals worldwide can expect unprecedented liability claims against lawyers and other advisers connected to the massive frauds perpetrated on investors and home buyers. While actual recovery remains doubtful, to avoid future recurrences, regulators in the United States and elsewhere must provide better oversight, with fair and impartial mechanisms through which claimants can seek redress without expensive litigation costs. Liability must become recoverable through malpractice insurance.

2.5 Riding the wave of regulatory reforms

2.5.1 The importance of context

The dynamic process though which smaller-scale experiments in New South Wales and Queensland have taken hold has enjoyed proven success, inspiring nationwide reforms in the federation of Australia and elsewhere. Besides the United Kingdom, recent legislation in New Zealand, Scotland and the Republic of Ireland has also authorized the creation of a complaint handling structure. While there are significant differences among the new organizations, the local reforms indicate that the status quo is not an option: principles of consumer protection and competition have taken hold, indelibly changing traditional concepts of professionalism. Rather than resist change, to remain competitive in the global marketplace, the US legal profession must realize that these regulatory reforms do not conflict with core professional values. The pending changes encourage market innovations that allow new forms of practice, enhanced access to lower cost, competent services and improved consumer protection.[200]

Demographics and historical context affect a jurisdiction's ability to experiment. Experimentation is more feasible in newer jurisdictions with smaller numbers of affected persons.[201] If they are successful, localized experiments can be replicated elsewhere, with modifications to reflect differences in law, culture and political realities. Federalism principles in the United States have long respected the role of local jurisdictions to serve as 'incubators' for law reform efforts on matters not pre-empted by federal regulation. For example, federal environmental law sets national standards, delegating to the states responsibility for more specific regulation and implementation.[202]

Compare the differing contexts of Australia, the United Kingdom and the United States. To some extent, each country has a public persona that also may be reflected in their legal professions. Australia's government is the youngest, with the country becoming a federation in 1901. Although its landmass is comparable in size to that of the United States, its population of 21 million includes about 6,600 barristers and solicitors concentrated in the more populous states of New South Wales, Victoria and Queensland.[203] The Australian federal government has authority over national issues but respects the autonomy of states and territories on local matters. With its vast expanses of territory, Australian popular culture portrays images of adventurous explorers willing to try new things.[204] Perceiving that Australia is 'over-lawyered', its top-tier firms reportedly have adopted entre-preneurial strategies to internationalize, forming strategic alliances or referral systems and considering outside investors. Changes in the federal and state regula-tory structures discussed in the first section of this chapter have facilitated these efforts.[205] Commissioner Steve Mark:

> truly believe[s] that the legal ethics sky has not fallen in Australia. 'The NSW experience has clearly shown that the practice of law can be regarded as both a profession and a business and in ILPs we witness the overt merger of the two roles. I am convinced that in NSW, chicken little has survived!'[206]

In contrast to that of Australia, the UK legal system developed over 1,000 years, with incremental changes resulting from historical accidents and entrenched social stratification based on class, heritage and wealth.[207] The United Kingdom's general population exceeds 60 million, with 140,000 legal professionals contained in a relatively small land mass. Parliament has long regulated some aspects of the legal professions, with input from the judicial branch. Parliamentary sovereignty confers unfettered legislative authority, not subject to an over-riding power of judicial review. This could change dramatically with the new UK Supreme Court and other actions within the European Union to promote competition.

Finally, consider the United States, which declared independence from Britain in 1776. The young nation expanded westward, fostered by rugged individualism and entrepreneurial spirit. The Constitution established a federal government of limited powers; it reserved to the states or citizens all powers not specifically delegated.[208] Because lawyer regulation is balkanized, significant local differences warrant criticism that some regulatory entities are ineffective, poorly funded, politicized or do not adequately protect legitimate consumer interests. Entry to the legal profession is open to all who qualify by education, bar examination and proof of character, regardless of class, family of origin or wealth. In practical terms, this means that over 1 million lawyers for its population of 300 million reflect great diversity in demographics, political and economic views. Licence to practise in a jurisdiction permits one to engage in the full range of tasks broadly defined as the practice of law, without the need for specialist training, but only in that jurisdiction or as authorized for temporary practice under local rules. Although there have been some federal intrusions on the regulatory autonomy of individual jurisdictions, the organized bars and state judiciary have resisted any comprehensive federal reforms. In the globalized legal marketplace, this also has hampered the ability of US trade negotiators to speak collectively on behalf of the nation's lawyers.[209]

This discussion warrants a brief comment on the reciprocal perceptions of US and UK lawyers, as it were, across the pond. While broad generalizations are fraught with danger, it can be said there is some mutual ambivalence. US lawyers observe with bemusement barristers' stodgy rules of etiquette and court attire of wigs and robes. They respect the barrister's professional independence, unsullied by client contact or fee collection, but do not understand the sole practitioner model of barristers' chambers and trade restrictions that prohibit familiar US forms of practice among different categories of legal professionals. US lawyers probably relate better to the diverse legal tasks performed by solicitors, acknowledging the business aspects of their practice, but do not understand the complex rules limiting solicitors' rights of audience in all levels of courts. On the other hand, many UK lawyers perceive that the United States has too many generalist lawyers who are overzealous or motivated by greed, with great variance in their litigation skills and courtroom etiquette. UK law reform discussions often include statements wishing to avoid changes that could deteriorate into unruly American-style litigation and unprofessional conduct. Where US lawyers resoundingly rejected the concept of multi-disciplinary practices, professional regulators and many practitioners in Australia and the United Kingdom warmly embrace the economic benefits of allowing such innovations.

2.5.2 What drives regulatory reforms?

The UK Legal Services Act 2007 must be viewed in the greater context of social reforms geared to modernize and democratize the nation, to erode unwarranted distinctions based on heritage and social class and to streamline an unwieldy government bureaucracy. Competition law, consumer protection and meritocracy are core principles underlying the greater reform agenda. Since Lord Mackay's 1989 Green Paper, earlier attempts to achieve sweeping reforms have failed in the legislative process, thwarted by powerful segments of an entrenched profession. Viewed in context, some of the LSA 2007 reforms are nothing short of breathtaking, creating a streamlined co-regulatory structure that aims to modernize the profession, enhance affordable access to legal services and expand the scope of available services. Because oversight regulation will now reside in a single nationwide entity working in cooperation with other stakeholders, the Act holds great potential to accomplish sweeping reforms that will give UK lawyers a strong competitive edge in the globalized legal market. Some forecast that competitive advantages from the LSA will further enhance London's role in international legal practice.

The United Kingdom's membership in the European Union (EU) has provided additional impetus for change. Although traditional lawyer regulation has been within the province of individual European states, the EU has played an important role 'in shaping the contours of contemporary European legal practice', with some recent proposals 'nothing short of breath-taking'.[210] The EU aims to create a single market, facilitating circulation of goods and services among member states and limiting artificial trade restrictions. Its Parliament is authorized to enact legislative directives requiring member states to achieve a particular result, giving members flexibility on the choice of form and methods by which the directive should be accomplished.[211] In areas outside its exclusive competence, the principle of subsidiarity limits its authority to take legal or regulatory action 'unless action at the EU level would be more effective than action at the national, regional or local level'.[212] EU lawyers now have much greater cross-border mobility than those in the United States. Directive 77/249 generally allows EU lawyers to provide temporary services in other member states. Directive 98/5 more broadly permits EU lawyers to become permanently established in another state after three years of practice and compliance with minimal registration requirements.[213] In 2002, the European Court of Justice held that activities of a European bar association constitute economic activity subject to EU anti-trust law.[214] While the potential reach of EU competition law to the service professions remains uncertain, it further supports the new UK regulatory reforms.

2.5.3 Portability to the United States?

US federalism principles consistently resist comprehensive national regulation on matters traditionally reserved to the states.[215] Although the organized bar has managed to forestall the loss of state-based regulation, nationalized federal oversight remains a possibility if its leaders do not respond to the 'paradigm-shifting developments' concerning the increasingly international nature of the legal profession.[216] Since 1987, the number of US lawyers working in international offices of US firms increased tenfold, to 15,000. Between 1993 and 2003, the dollar value of US exported legal services rose by 134 per cent, but the value of legal services imported to the United States rose by 174 per cent.[217]

Is portability to the United States of the international reforms feasible? Yes, especially considering the adverse effect of doing nothing. Besides disadvantaging US lawyers in the international marketplace, the balkanized status risks criticism as arcane, self-interested and disserving the public interest. Harvard Law School Professor Howell Jackson acknowledged envy of his:

> academic and regulatory counterparts working in other jurisdictions. While the United States prides itself in having a dynamic economy that fosters innovation, the country's capacity to reform the structure of its regulatory institutions pales in comparison to the ability of [EU member states and Australia] ... to modernize their regulatory bodies ... [The US] national taste for federalism ... and aversion to concentrated sources of governmental

power ... [explains overlapping and fragmented systems of state and federal oversight of the financial services sector] ... On top of these latent political preferences and historical accidents, the political impediments inherent in our divided and increasingly partisan political system ... a national predilection to review any idiosyncratic aspect of governmental structure as a manifestation of American exceptionalism, and one can develop a relatively rich though not always inspiring explanation of why the American system of financial regulation has strayed so far from the models of supervisory oversight upon which the rest of the world is converging.[218]

The Australian and UK reforms provide valuable templates adaptable to the US constitutional structure and commitment to state-based regulation. EU directives and principles of subsidiarity are analogous to US principles of federalism, encouraging local autonomy and experimentation to achieve particular nationalized results. Despite periodic threats to federalize lawyer regulation, most knowledgeable observers would concede a nationalized lawyer regulatory agency would be unwieldy and ineffective. In considering the way ahead, US regulators and state courts should look closely at the Australian and the UK reforms, and begin constructing independent state regulatory entities with collaborative, co-regulatory regime that aims at deterrence through education, management-based regulation and consumer protection backed by redress.

The United States has a strong federal interest in eliminating anti-competitive professional restrictions that interfere with access to competent legal services and in requiring that states provide reasonable consumer protection mechanisms. Congress should not try to nationalize lawyer regulation. Instead, this moment in history presents an excellent opportunity for Congress to enact legislation excouraging cooperative federalism, requiring that state regulatory entities satisfy specific minimum standards of independence, competence and access to justice. States should be encouraged to experiment with co-regulatory models designed to achieve those ends. As Congress addresses the financial difficulties made possible by regulatory lapses, it should enact a Legal Services Act requiring each local regulatory entity, at a minimum, to do the following:

1   Mandate separation of regulatory and trade functions of state-based lawyer entities. Unified bar states that maintain control over lawyer discipline should promptly implement McKay Recommendation 5, creating a separate, independent regulatory entity controlled and managed exclusively by the highest state court, with assurance of its economic and political independence.
2   Create national standards setting minimum levels of compulsory malpractice insurance for lawyers who deliver services to private clients.
3   Require local lawyer regulatory entities to establish workable, unbiased mechanisms to evaluate and issue binding orders for claims of redress against US lawyers with a stated minimum cap on recovery.
4   Encourage state regulatory entities to experiment with management-based regulation and compliance through education by using their version of ABA

Model Rule 5.1(a), to require that partners 'make reasonable efforts to ensure that the firm has in effect measures giving reasonable assurance' that the firm conforms with the rules. Internal audit procedures should be implemented, encouraging cooperative and collaborative relations between firms and state regulators.

5   Direct federal and state competition authorities to examine ethical restrictions that may present unreasonable restraints on trade and require that lawyer regulators provide justification on their necessity. Congress should consider narrowing permissible exemptions to anti-competitive regulations under the state action doctrine.

In view of the innovative reforms in Australia, the United Kingdom and elsewhere, leadership of the US legal profession must join the international movement to advance regulatory reforms that improve the quality of and access to legal services, relax unnecessary trade restrictions and provide meaningful consumer protection for clients falling within the huge gap left by the US discipline–civil liability dichotomy.[219] State-based lawyer regulators must move beyond a narrow focus on punishing miscreants, moving ahead to improve consumer protection with systems of redress. Those with authority over the leadership of US regulators may perceive broad-based reform as daunting and politically unfeasible. Australia's regulatory innovations have demonstrated the effect of deterrence through education, improving the quality of legal services. For years, the UK legal professions used political clout to forestall meaningful regulatory reforms. If the LSA 2007 fulfils its potential, it will be powerful proof that the status quo is not set in stone. In both Australia and the United Kingdom, reform continues to be a work in progress; more ambitious reforms are being realized only after it has become clear that incremental reforms have been ineffective. The legal profession can benefit greatly from the new governance paradigm, with multi-tiered co-regulation, collaboration and adaptability for future situations. That, indeed, can be the new wave of professionalism for lawyers.

Acknowledgements

The author gratefully acknowledges the earlier research assistance of Adam L. Mitchell and Valerie Grey (JD, University of Oklahoma 2006, 2009) on the evolution of UK regulatory reforms. Amy Lee Kamp (JD candidate, University of Oklahoma 2010) provided significant editorial assistance. The University of Oklahoma provided research support. Library Director Darin K. Fox and Law Reference Librarian Jennifer Gerrish provided invaluable help accessing international materials. Many professional and academic colleagues generously shared their ideas. While there are too many to name individually, special thanks go to Anthony Davis, Art Garwin, Drew Kershen, Ellyn Rosen and Laurel Terry. Kieran Tranter and the editors of this book provided invaluable comments on earlier drafts. Any mistakes or omissions are mine alone.

Notes

1 L. Terry, 'The future regulation of the legal profession: The impact of treating the legal profession as "service providers" ', *Journal of the Professional Lawyer*, 2008, vol. 18, 205–9 (arguing that there has been a paradigmatic shift in international trade discussions including lawyers as service providers subject to market regulation, and that this shift will have future impact on who has authority to regulate lawyers and how they will be regulated).

2 R. Susskind, *The End of Lawyers? Rethinking the Nature of Legal Services*, Oxford: Oxford University Press, 2008, pp. 1–6, 28–36, 253–79.

3 ibid., p. 189 ('seismic shift'); P. Paton, 'Between a rock and a hard place: the future of self-regulation – Canada between the United States and the English/Australian experience', *Journal of the Professional Lawyer*, 2008, vol. 18, 95 (stating English and Australian reforms cast as 'global tsunami against self-regulation'), quoting R. Devlin and Porter Heffernan, 'The end(s) of self regulation', *Alberta Law Review* vol. 45, 2008, 169: 182.

4 See J. Goldsmith, 'The core values of the legal profession for lawyers today and tomorrow', *Northwestern Journal of International Law and Business*, 2008, vol. 28 (discussing globalization of ideas and 'market rules all' as impetus to treat legal services as commodities, need to return to core values as embodied in Charter of Core Principles of the European Legal Profession); Organization for Economic Co-operation and Development, *OECD Policy Roundtables: Competitive Restrictions in Legal Professions*. Available from: <www.oecd.org/dataoecd/45/16/43046091.pdf> (accessed 20 November 2009); Council of Bars and Law Societies of Europe, *Code of Conduct for European Lawyers*, 2006. Available from: <www.ccbe.eu/fileadmin/user_upload/NTCdocument/2006_code_enpdf1_1228293527.pdf> (accessed 20 November 2009).

5 Susskind, *The End*, pp. 280–81.

6 C. Touhy, 'Agency, contract, and governance: shifting shapes of accountability in the health care arena', *Journal of Health Politics, Policy and Law*, vol. 28, 2003, 202–5; H. Jackson, 'Learning from Eddy: A meditation upon organizational reform of financial supervision in Europe', in M. Tison et al. (eds), *Perspectives in Company Law and Financial Regulation*, Cambridge: Cambridge University Press, 2009, pp. 523–39 (discussing the advantages of a consolidated regulatory body, such as the British Financial Services Authority and its regulatory counterparts in the European Union, Japan and Australia).

7 C. Parker and A. Evans, *Inside Lawyers' Ethics*, Melbourne: Cambridge University Press, 2007, pp. 46–47; Ross Ray, President, Law Council of Australia, *Speaking Points: ABA Centennial of the Canons of Professional Ethics* (8 August 2008) (on file with author).

8 S. Mark, 'The Office of the Legal Services Commissioner – Consumer protection', *Precedent*, 2009, vol. 90, 12–13.

9 The Honourable Justice Michael Kirby, 'Legal professional ethics in times of change', *Australian Bar Review*, 1996, vol. 14, 170–84.

10 J. Slee, 'Lawyers' contempt for public', *Sydney Morning Herald*, 11 December 1992, 12.

11 See Legal Profession Reform Act 1993 (NSW), Sch. 2; Website of the Office of the New South Wales, Legal Service Commissioner. Available from: <www.lawlink.nsw.gov.au/lawlink/olsc/ll_olsc.nsf/pages/OLSC_aboutus> (accessed 20 November 2009); C. Parker, 'Regulation of the ethics of Australian legal practice: autonomy and responsiveness', *University of New South Wales Law Journal*, 2002, vol. 25, 690–92.

12 See Law Reform Commission (NSW), 'Legal Profession Act 1987: A further review of complaints against lawyers', 2002; Law Reform Commission (NSW), 'Report 99 (2001) Complaints against lawyers: An interim report'. Available from: <www.lawlink.nsw.gov.au/lrc.nsf/pages/r99chp1> (accessed 20 November 2009); Office of the Legal Services Commissioner (NSW), 'Submission in response to the NSW Attorney General's Department Issues Paper'. Available from: <www.lawlink.nsw.gov.au/lawlink/olsc/

ll_olsc.nsf/pages/OLSC_december2001> (accessed 20 November 2009); Legal Profession Act 2004 (NSW) (repealing Legal Profession Act 1987) (NSW).

13 Legal Profession Act 2004 (NSW), ss. 494(2)(b), (d).

14 ibid., ss. 514–16. See also Office of the Legal Services Commissioner, *2006–07 Annual Report*, pp. 12–13 (reporting that Mediation and Investigation Officers resolved 1,066 of 1,560 consumer disputes; three resolved through formal mediation; Inquiry Line Officers resolved 230 telephone mediations before filing of formal complaint).

15 Mark, 'The Office of the Legal Services Commissioner', 14.

16 ibid., note 20, s 517, 2008.

17 ibid., 14–15.

18 Mark, 'The Office of the Legal Services Commissioner', 15.

19 Compare Parker and Evans, *Inside Lawyers' Ethics*, pp. 54–55 (stating 'vast majority' of conduct claims referred back) and Mark, 'The Office of the Legal Services Commissioner', 15 (approximating that OLSC handles 75 per cent of investigations, with 25 per cent handled by professional associations, subject to monitoring by OLSC).

20 Parker and Evans, *Inside Lawyers' Ethics*, p. 55.

21 See, for example, Office of the Legal Services Commissioner (NSW), 'Submission'.

22 Legal Profession Act 2004 (NSW), ss. 539, 573(3).

23 ibid., s. 540(2).

24 ibid., s. 573(5), (6).

25 Legal Profession Act 2004 (NSW), ss. 570–75.

26 Office of the Legal Services Commissioner (NSW), *Fact Sheet 11, Negligence*. Available from: <www.lawlink.nsw.gov.au/lawlink/olsc/ll_olsc.nsf/pages/OLSC_factsheet11> (accessed 20 March 2009). Section 540(2)(c) of the Legal Profession Act 2004 (NSW) authorizes the Commissioner or Council to issue a compensation order as provided in 4.9; section 573 provides the Tribunal may refer the matter back to either one for issuance of a compensation order, after finding unsatisfactory conduct or professional misconduct.

27 Mark, 'The Office of the Legal Services Commissioner', 16 (Consumer, Trader and Tenancy Tribunal is available for claims under $25,000).

28 L. Levin, 'Building a better lawyer discipline system: the Queensland experience', *Legal Ethics*, 2006, vol. 9, 191–93.

29 See the Legal Profession Act 2007 (Qld), ss. 440–41. See also J. Briton, *Queensland Legal Services Commissioner 2007–08 Annual Report 7*, pp. 18–20. Available from: <www.lsc.qld.gov.au/AnnualReports/Annual_Report – 07–08_Legal_Services_Commission.pdf> (accessed 20 November 2009).

30 See the Legal Profession Act 2007 (Qld), ss. 442, 464–67; L. Levin, 'Building a better lawyer discipline system', 199.

31 Legal Profession Act 2007 (Qld), s. 418 ('Unsatisfactory professional conduct includes conduct of an Australian legal practitioner happening in connection with the practice of law that falls short of the standard of competence and diligence that a member of the public is entitled to expect of a reasonably competent Australian legal practitioner.').

32 ibid., ss. 419, 420 (defining professional misconduct and conduct that could also be characterized as unsatisfactory professional conduct).

33 Legal Services Commission, 'Complaints'. Available from: <www.lsc.qld.gov.au/30.htm#What_the_Commission_does_not_do> (accessed 20 November 2009).

34 Levin, 'Building a better lawyer discipline system', 200–201, 204–5.

35 Legal Profession Act 2007 (Qld), ss. 456, 458, 464–67.

36 J. Briton and S. McLean, 'Incorporated legal practices: Dragging the regulation of the legal profession into the modern era', *Legal Ethics*, 2008, vol. 11, 241.

37 Legal Profession Amendment Act 2000 (NSW), s. 47(E), carried forward in Legal Profession Act 2004 (NSW), s. 140(3).

38 C. Parker, S. Mark and T. Gordon, 'Research report: Assessing the impact of management-based regulation on NSW incorporated legal practices', 2008. Available

from: <www.lawlink.nsw.gov.au/lawlink/olsc/ll_olsc.nsf/vwFiles/Research_Report_ ILPs. pdf/$file/Research_Report_ILPs.pdf> (accessed on 20 November 2009).

39 ibid., Executive Summary.

40 S. Mark, quoted by C. Butner, 'Incorporation boosts profitability: OLSC', *Lawyers Weekly*, 19 October 2007.

41 ibid., table 4 (showing 37 per cent of self-assessed ILPs have one legal practitioner; 21 per cent have two practitioners, and 16 per cent have three to five practitioners).

42 C. Parker, A. Evans, L. Haller, S. LeMire and R. Mortenson, 'The ethical infra-structure of legal practice in larger law firms: Values, policy and behaviour', *University of New South Wales Law Review*, 2008, vol. 31, 160, 174–75.

43 Legal Profession Act 2004 (NSW), ss. 140, 168.

44 Parker et al., 'Research report', Executive Summary.

45 Parker and Evans, *Inside Lawyers' Ethics*, pp. 48–49.

46 Legal Profession Model Laws Project, Introductory note 1 (identifying as core provi-sions that require textual uniformity), 4.2.1 (Unsatisfactory professional conduct); 4.2.2(1) (Professional misconduct); 4.2.3 (Conduct capable of constituting unsatisfac-tory professional conduct or professional misconduct).

47 Briton, *Queensland Legal Services Commissioner*.

48 Law Council of Australia, 'Prime Minister clears path for a truly national profession', media release, 4 February 2009. Available from: <www.lawcouncil.asn.au/media/ news-article.cfm?article=3EBD2ECC-1E4F-17FA-D28A-70E0048FB1C1> (accessed 20 November 2009).

49 Briton and McLean, 'Incorporated legal practices', 10–12.

50 See Parker et al., 'The ethical infrastructure', 169–70, citing empirical work done in the United States, including S. Fortney, 'Soul for sale: An empirical study of associate satisfaction, law firm culture and the effects of billable hour requirements', *University of Missouri-Kansas City Law Review*, 2000, vol. 69, 230; S. Fortney, 'The billable hours derby: Empirical data on the problems and pressure points', *Fordham Urban Law Journal*, 2005, vol. 33, 171; L. Lerman, 'Blue-chip billing: Regulation of billing and expense fraud by lawyers', *Georgetown Journal of Legal Ethics*, 1999, vol. 12, 205; W. Ross, 'Kicking the unethical billing habit', *Rutgers Law Review*, 1998, vol. 50, 1.

51 Briton and McLean, 'Incorporated legal practices', 24–25.

52 ibid.; Parker et al., 'Research report'; Parker et al., 'The ethical infrastructure', 159–60 (citing, among other sources, T. Schneyer, 'Professional discipline for law firms?', *Cornell Law Review*, 1991, vol. 77, 1; E. Chambliss and D. B. Wilkins, 'A new framework for law firm discipline', *Georgetown Journal of Legal Ethics*, 2003, vol. 16, 355).

53 Briton and McLean, 'Incorporated legal practices', citing Chambliss and Wilkins, 'A new framework', 366.

54 M. Moran, *The British Regulatory State: High Modernism and Hyper-Innovation*, Oxford: Oxford University Press, 2002, pp. 84–85.

55 Lord Chancellor's Department, The Work and Organization of the Legal Profession, 1989, Cm 570, at 16 (recommending Ombudsman office, among other things).

56 Courts and Legal Services Act 1990, c. 41 ss. 21–26 (Eng.)

57 M. Partington, *Introduction to The English Legal System*, Oxford: Oxford University Press, 2006, p. 256.

58 Legal Services Ombudsman, *Annual Report*, 2002, p. 5.

59 ibid., p. 13.

60 Sir David Clementi, *Review of the Regulatory Framework for Legal Services in England and Wales, A Consultation Paper*, 7 March 2004 (hereafter, Clementi Consultation).

61 J. Flood, 'Will there be fallout from Clementi? The global repercussions for the legal profession after the UK Legal Services Act 2007', 8 Jan. Monet/Robert Schuman Paper Series (No. 6), April 2008, 2–5.

62 Ibid., at 2.

63 Sir David Clementi, *Review of the Regulatory Framework for Legal Services in England and*

Wales, Final Report, December 2004, pp. 8–10. Available from: <www.legal-services-review.org.uk> (accessed 20 November 2009).

64 Legal Services Act 2007 (c. 29) (Eng.). Available from: <www.opsi.gov.uk/acts/acts2007/ukpga_20070029_en_1>, and Legal Services Act Explanatory Notes. Available from: <www.opsi.gov.uk/acts/acts2007/en/ukpgaen_20070029_en.pdf> (accessed 20 November 2009).

65 J. Maute, 'Alice's Adventures in Wonderland: Preliminary reflections on the history of the split English legal profession and the fusion debate (1000–1900 AD)', *Fordham Law Review*, 2003, vol. 71, 1364.

66 Lord Chancellor's Department, *The Work and Organization of the Legal Profession*, 1989, Cm. 570.

67 J. Maute, 'Revolutionary changes to the English legal profession or much ado about nothing?', *Journal of the Professional Lawyer*, 2006, vol. 17, 2006, 7.

68 M. Zander, 'The Thatcher government's onslaught on the lawyers: Who won?', *International Lawyer*, 1990, vol. 24, 764–65.

69 N. Lawson, *The View from No. 11: Britain's Longest-Serving Cabinet Member Recalls the Triumphs and Disappointments of the Thatcher Era*, London: Doubleday, 1992, pp. 621–22.

70 Courts and Legal Services Act 1990, c. 41, s. 17 (Eng.) (hereafter CLSA).

71 ibid., Sch. 2, s. 20.

72 ibid., Sch. 2, s. 5(3).

73 ibid., ss. 29–31.

74 CLSA, ss. 22–24.

75 R. James and M. Seneviratne, 'The Legal Services Ombudsman: Form versus function?', *Modern Law Review*, 1995, vol. 58, 193–95, 206–7.

76 V. Lewis, *Complaints Against Solicitors: the Complainants' View: Lay Complainants' Experiences and Perceptions of the Solicitors Complaints Bureau and Solicitors' In-House Complaints Procedures*, London: Law Society Management and Planning Directorate, 1996, pp. x–xi, 16–29.

77 ibid., p. 33.

78 ibid., pp. 36–52.

79 James and Seneviratne, 'The Legal Services Ombudsman', 193–95.

80 ibid.

81 Access to Justice Act 1999, ch. 22 (Eng.). Available from: <www.opsi.gov.uk/acts/acts2007/ukpga_20070029_en_1> (accessed 20 November 2009).

82 ibid., s. 35; M. Zander, *Cases and Materials on the English Legal System*, 9th edn, London: Lexis/Nexis, 2003, pp. 757–59.

83 K. Malleson, *The Legal System*, 3rd edn, Oxford: Oxford University Press, 2007, pp. 180–81.

84 ibid.

85 Access to Justice Act 1999, ch. 22 (Eng.), ss. 36–37, 44.

86 Malleson, *The Legal System*, p. 188 (at time of 2003 publication, there were approximately 10,000 barristers and 90,000 solicitors).

87 Legal Services Ombudsman, *Annual Report*, 2000, p. 6 (stating that in the 10 years since its inception, the LSO had undertaken 9,456 complaints about solicitors and 1,036 complaints about barristers).

88 ibid. (stating LSO satisfaction with 94 per cent of cases handled by the Bar Council compared with only 57 per cent of those handled by the Law Society).

89 Access to Justice Act 1999, ch. 22 (Eng.), s. 49(4), (5).

90 ibid., ss. 51–52; M. Partington, *Introduction to the English Legal System*, 3rd edn, Oxford: Oxford University Press, 2006, p. 256.

91 F. Gibb, 'Law Society fined £250,000 over complaints procedure', *Times Online*, 17 May 2006.

92 Legal Services Ombudsman, *Annual Report*, 2005, p. 19 (referring to government White Paper, 'The Future of Legal Services: Putting the Consumer First', prepared in preparation to submitting its proposed Legal Services Bill to Parliament).

93   Clementi Consultation.
94   Robert Baldwin et al., *Scoping Study for the Regulatory Review of Legal Services*, March 2003, p. 85.
95   Legal Services Review website: <www.legal-services-review.org.uk>.
96   Clementi Consultation, pp. 2–5.
97   ibid., 25. See also Council of the Bars and Law Societies of the European Union, *CCBE Response to Clementi Consultation Document*. Available from: <www.ccbe.eu/fileadmin/user_upload/NTCdocument/ccbe_response_clemen1_1183706107.pdf> (accessed 20 November 2009); Council of the Bars and Law Societies of the European Union, *CCBE Position on Regulatory and Representative Functions of Bars*. Available from: <www.ccbe.eu/fileadmin/user_upload/NTCdocument/ccbe_position_on_reg1_118 2254709.pdf> (accessed 20 November 2009).
98   ibid., pp. 36–42.
99   ibid., Chapter B.
100 Clementi, *Review of the Regulatory Framework*.
101 ibid., pp. 66–67.
102 ibid., p. 67.
103 ibid., pp. 112–13, 124–28, 138–39.
104 Department for Constitutional Affairs, *Draft Legal Services Bill, Explanatory Notes and Regulatory Impact Assessment*, 2006, Cm. 6839 (hereafter DLSB). Available online at: <www.official-documents.gov.uk/document/cm68/6839/6839.pdf> (accessed 20 November 2009).
105 ibid., Part 1 (regulatory objectives), Part 2 (creating Legal Services Board), Part 3 (Reserved Legal Activities), cll. 15–16 (regulatory functions defined to include setting qualification regulations, licensing rules and arrangements to authorize persons to carry out reserved legal activities, establish practice, conduct and discipline rules, disciplinary arrangements over regulated persons), Part 4 (Regulation of Approved Regulators), cll. 22–23.
106 ibid., Part 6, cl. 92ff. See also, cl. 127 (excluding approved regulators from making provision for redress); cl. 128 (abolishing the office of Legal Services Complaints Commissioner and Legal Services Ombudsman).
107 ibid., cl. 127.
108 ibid., cl. 102(4).
109 See, for example, 'Law Society will keep place as top legal body, vows chief', *Birmingham Post*, 27 May 2005 (stating that the Law Society pre-empted the Clementi Report recommendations, to provide for separate functions from 2008). 'Solicitors Regulation Authority, newly created entity, describes its functions, focus group findings on consumers views of solicitor regulation, and announcing new consultations open for comments', see Solicitor Regulation Authority website: <www.sra.org.uk/consumers/consumers.page> (accessed 20 November 2009).
110 C. Whelan, 'The paradox of professionalism: Global law practice means business', *Pennsylvania State International Law Review*, 2008, vol. 28, 486–87.
111 ibid., p. 488 (discussing independence concerns of Flemish Bar and Law Society of Zimbabwe).
112 The Legal Profession and Legal Aid (Scotland) Act 2007 (asp 5) established a Scottish Legal Complaint Commission to deal with all service complaints starting 1 October 2008; all conduct complaints will be referred without investigation to the Bar or Law Society. The Legal Services Ombudsman (Eire) Act, enacted 10 March 2009, creates the office of the Legal Services Ombudsman charged with oversight of complaint handling by the Bar Council and Law Society and reporting annually on the adequacy of both professions' admissions policies. The Irish statute appears to create a Legal Services Ombudsman similar to that repealed by the new Legal Services Act 2007 (UK).
113 Whelan, 'The paradox of professionalism', 488–91.

114 Legal Services Act 2007 (UK), Sch. 1, ss. 1–2.
115 ibid., s. 3.
116 ibid., Pt. 3, s. 3(3).
117 ibid., s. 30.
118 ibid., ss. 12–19.
119 ibid., ss. 20–21, 27–45.
120 ibid., ss. 49–50.
121 ibid., ss. 32, 41, 49(1)–(4).
122 ibid., ss. 8–11.
123 ibid., ss. 57–61.
124 ibid., ss. 6, 118–22 (Board oversight over OLC).
125 ibid., Ch. 29, s 113.
126 ibid., s 126(1).
127 ibid., ss. 112, 128, 131.
128 ibid., ss. 137, 138(1).
129 ibid., s. 137(5).
130 ibid., ss. 113(2)(b).
131 ibid., ss. 133(4).
132 ibid., s. 134.
133 ibid., s. 140.
134 ibid., ss. 141–42.
135 ibid., s. 136.
136 Legal Services Board, *Business Plan 2009/10*. Available from: <www.
    legalservicesboard.org.uk/news_publications/publications/pdf/business_plan_2009_
    10.pdf> (accessed 20 November 2009).
137 Chief Ombudsman Adam Sampson and the new board members assumed responsi-
    bilities on 1 July 2009.
138 For example, Elizabeth France served as Chief Ombudsman and executive of
    Ombudsman Service Ltd (TOSL), providing an ombudsman service for telecom-
    munications, energy and surveyors. See <www.legalservicesboard.org.uk/about_us/
    office_for_legal_complaints/olc_board/elizabeth_france.htm>   (accessed   20
    November 2009). Mary Seneviratne has published extensively about the ombudsman
    role and operations.
139 D. Edmonds, speech given at the Institute of Legal Cashiers and Administrators
    Annual Luncheon, 23 September 2009. Available from: <www.legalservicesboard. org.
    uk/news_publications/speeches_presentations/2009/pdf/speech230909.pdf>
    (accessed 20 November 2009).
140 ibid.
141 The Law Society has established an independent entity, the Legal Complaints Service
    for complaint handling in the interim until the OLC Ombudsman scheme takes over.
142 'New faces at Law Society to drive change', media release, 4 December 2007.
    Available   from: <www.epolitix.com/stakeholder-websites/press-releases/press-
    release-details / newsarticle / new-faces-at-law-society-to-drive-change / sites / law-
    society> (accessed 20 November 2009); Legal Regulation Review. Available from:
    <www.legalregulationreview.com> (closed on 9 April 2009 with report to follow
    autumn 2009); Review of the Regulation of Corporate Legal Work. Available
    from: <www.legalregulationreview.com/files/report_smedleyfinal.pdf> (accessed 20
    November 2009).
143 Model Rules of Professional Conduct, Preamble [11](ABA 2007).
144 See, for example, M. Devlin, 'The development of lawyer disciplinary procedures in
    the United States', *Georgetown Journal of Legal Ethics*, 1994, vol. 4, 918, 928–32. See also
    C. Wolfram, *Modern Legal Ethics*, St Paul, MN: West Publishing Co., 1986, pp. 33–34
    (stating that: 'In fact, courts serve as the largely passive sounding boards or disap-
    provers of initiatives that are taken by lawyers operating through bar associations'

and that, regardless of functional differences between mandatory and voluntary bars, 'bar associations exercise pervasive influence over bar admission and discipline'). Reforms after the American Bar Association 1992, *Lawyer Regulation For a New Century, Report of the Commission on Evaluation of Disciplinary Enforcement* (hereafter 'McKay Report'), Appendix B. Available from: <www.abanet.org/cpr/reports/mckay_report.html> (accessed 20 November 2009), note 23, may have lessened the extent to which lawyers' involvement in the regulatory process was 'merely as representatives of the profession'; '[i]n recent years ... there has been noticeable movement toward lessening the self-regulation features ... [with] the bodies making disciplinary recommendations through appointment by the state courts ... [while references to passive supervision by supreme court courts remain accurate, one] should not infer that the task of supervision is always being exercised by lawyers acting solely in their private capacity.' A. Kaufman and D. Wilkins, *Problems in Professional Responsibility for a Changing Profession*, Durham, NC: Carolina Academic Press, 2009, p. 631.

145 See generally, F. Zacharias, 'The "self-regulation" misnomer', in K. Tranter et al. (eds), *Reaffirming Legal Ethics*, London: Routledge, 2009 (arguing to replace misnomer with more accurate terms, distinguishing between self-regulation as individual self-restraint, collective self-monitoring or self-policing, external non-judicial institutions authorized by statute or administrative regulation, judicial implementation of civil (and criminal?) law). Notable examples of external agency regulation are the Internal Revenue Service, Office of Thrift Supervision, and Securities and Exchange Commission. See T. Schneyer, 'How things have changed: Contrasting the regulatory environments of the Canons and the Model Rules', *Journal of the Professional Lawyer*, 2008, vol. 18, 161.

146 See, for example, ABA Standing Committee on Client Protection, *State by State Adoption of ABA Client Protection Programs* (11 June 2007) (indicating that 23 states provide mediation of non-fee disputes, 12 states have mandatory fee arbitration and 37 require notification of trust account overdrafts). Available from: <www.abanet.org/cpr/clientpro/statebystate_cp_programs.pdf> (accessed 20 November 2009).

147 See, for example, Devlin, 'The development of lawyer disciplinary procedures', 918, 928–32. See also Wolfram, *Modern Legal Ethics*, pp. 33–34 (stating that '[i]n fact, courts serve as the largely passive sounding boards or disapprovers of initiatives that are taken by lawyers operating through bar associations' and that, regardless of functional differences between mandatory and voluntary bars, 'bar associations exercise pervasive influence over bar admission and discipline'); *In re Attorney Discipline System*, 967 P. 2d 49 (Cal. 1998); *In re Shannon*, 876 P. 2d 548, 570 (Ariz. 1994) (noting that the state judiciary's authority to regulate the practice of law is universally accepted and dates back to the thirteenth century).

148 See *Restatement of the Law Governing Lawyers* s1 cmt.c. (noting that, while some state courts maintain their constitutional power, regulating lawyers is exclusive and required by separation of powers, some decisions invoke principles of comity in giving effect to legislation or regulations extending to lawyers).

149 See, for example, *Petition of New Hampshire Bar Ass'n*, 855 A.2d 450 (NH 2004) (finding unconstitutional a state statute requiring a bar association to conduct and be bound by membership referendum on unification; the statute directly conflicts with long-standing court ordered unification); *In re Examination of the Washington State Bar Ass'n*, 548 P.2d 310 (Wash. 1976) (reaffirming exclusive and inherent power of a state Supreme Court to admit, enrol, disbar and discipline attorneys; holding that the unified Bar was not a state agency or department subject to audit of revenues pursuant to legislative authority granted state auditor). See also Q. Johnstone, 'An overview of the legal profession in the United States, how that profession recently has been changing, and its future prospects', *Quinnipiac Law Review*, 2008, vol. 26, 749 at n. 40 (noting that many state courts claim superior regulatory authority over lawyers, either under inherent authority or as expressly conferred in the state constitution).

150 See, for example, *People ex rel. Chicago Bar Ass'n v. Goodman*, 8 N.E. 2d 941, cert. den. 302 U.S. 728, reh. den. 302 U.S. 777; *In re Integration of Nebraska State Bar Association*, 275 N.W. 265 (Neb. S. Ct. 1937); *Washington State Bar Ass'n v. State*, 890 P. 2d 1047 (Wash. 1995).

151 See L. Lerman and P. Schrag, *Ethical Problems in the Practice of Law*, Aspen: Wolters Kluwer, 2008, pp. 25–26; American Bar Association, *Division for Bar Services*. Available from: <www.abanet.org/barserv/stlobar.html> (accessed 20 November 2009) (US map showing 18 states with voluntary state bars, and all remaining jurisdictions with unified bars); American Bar Association, *Chart on Unified Bars* (listing 32 unified bar states plus the unified District of Columbia Bar, and 18 non-unified bar states) (17 September 2007). See also Devlin, 'The development of lawyer disciplinary procedures', 933–34 (stating that, of the 33 unified bar jurisdictions, 12 maintain a separate lawyer disciplinary agency; in the 18 non-unified, or voluntary bar states, lawyers are regulated by the highest state court, administered through an agency of the court).

152 Q. Johnstone, 'Bar associations: policies and performance', *Yale Law and Policy Review*, 1996, vol. 15, 197; L. Rector, 'Compelled financial support of a Bar association and the Attorney's First Amendment rights: A theoretical analysis', *Nebraska Law Review*, 1996, vol. 66, 763–64 (indicating when various state Bar associations became unified and the type of authority invoked to accomplish this). For cases invoking inherent power doctrine, see *In re Integration of State Bar of Oklahoma*, 95 P.2d 113, 115 (Okla. 1939) (granting a petition to integrate, or unify, the Oklahoma State Bar Association, pursuant to the inherent power and exclusive final authority of the court, which included 'inherent right of the court to surround itself with honest assistants who are sympathetic and will unite with it in the proper administration of justice'); *In re Integration of the Nebraska State Bar Ass'n*, 275 NW 265 (Neb. 1937) (exercising sound discretion of inherent power to approve the formation of integrated (unified) bar association; more effective and efficient regulation would result from a cooperating bench and bar, provided that the court retains final and exclusive authority over the admission and discipline of lawyers). See also *ABA/BNA Lawyers' Manual on Professional Conduct* ss. 201: 101–4 (24 July 1996).

153 Dissenting members may have limited claim to refunded bar dues: *Keller v State Bar of California*, 496 US 1 (1990).

154 ABA, *Chart* (identifying the 12 unified bars that do not oversee lawyer discipline as Hawaii, Louisiana, Michigan, Missouri, Montana, Nebraska, New Hampshire, New Mexico, North Dakota, Rhode Island, South Carolina and Wisconsin).

155 ABA, *Map* (identifying as regional cluster of voluntary bar states, including Maine, Vermont, Massachusetts, New York, New Jersey, Delaware, Pennsylvania, Ohio, Indiana, Illinois, Iowa and Minnesota, with non-contiguous Tennessee, Arkansas, Kansas and Colorado). Among the North Atlantic states, only New Hampshire and Rhode Island have unified bars. The historical and political reasons for this distribution are beyond the scope of this work.

156 T. Schneyer, 'The incoherence of the unified bar concept: generalizing from the Wisconsin case', *American Bar Foundation Research Journal*, 1983, vol. 1.

157 J. Pribek, 'Bar experts discuss merits of mandatory, voluntary bars', *Wisconsin Law Journal*, 13 July 2005 (discussing failed legislative efforts for moves to voluntary bar in Florida and New Hampshire, pending effort in Wisconsin); J. Zemlicka, 'Mandatory membership debate in Wisconsin heats up prior to committee meeting', *Wisconsin Law Journal*, 25 August 2008 (WLNR 16671510). See also Oklahoma Bar Association, 'E-News special legislative edition', email (19 February 2009): email to members on proposed legislation that would (a) make bar membership voluntary, and (b) amend the state constitution requiring that the bar Association submit to legislature for approval any proposed rules of professional conduct, admission to practice, rules of judicial conduct and state court rules. Both measures died in committee without coming up for a vote.

158 Wolfram, *Modern Legal Ethics*, p. 79. Fred Zacharias asserts that the orientation of disciplinary agencies (as client-centred; lawyer-centred; profession-centred; or process-centred) impacts their choice of goals (for example, remedy for private or public harms, punishment, deterrence) and the need to assess and prioritize their goals. F. Zacharias, 'The purpose of lawyer discipline', *William and Mary Law Review*, 2003, vol. 45, 681, 693–98.

159 *Restatement (Third) of the Law Governing Lawyers* s 1 cmt. d (2000).

160 American Bar Association Special Committee on Evaluation of Disciplinary Enforcement (Tom C. Clark, Chairman), *Problems and Recommendations in Disciplinary Enforcement* (Final Draft, June 1970), p. 1. See also, V. Johnson, 'Justice Tom C. Clark's legacy in the field of legal ethics', *Journal of the Legal Profession*, 2004–5, vol. 29, 33 (discussing substantial advances in legal ethics and professionalism over the last 35 years).

161 E. Steele and R. Nimmer, 'Lawyers, clients, and professional regulation', *American Bar Foundation Research Journal*, 1976, 942 (reporting a 203 per cent increase in the rate of disciplinary expenditures, from the 1968–69 rate of $5.85 per lawyer to the 1974–75 rate of $17.73 per lawyer; the consumer price index increased by 43 per cent during that period). See also Steele and Nimmer, 'Lawyers', 925, 946–62, 1009–13 (discussing client complaints and limited Bar response in terms of creating dispute resolution formats).

162 See, for example, D. Rhode, *In the Interests of Justice: Reforming the Legal Profession*, Oxford: Oxford University Press, 2000, pp. 158–63; A. Blumenthal, 'Attorney self-regulation, consumer protection, and the future of the legal profession', *Kansas Journal of Law and Public Policy*, 1993–94, vol. 3, 6; F. Marks and D. Cathcart, 'Discipline within the legal profession: Is it self regulation?', *University of Illinois Law Forum*, 1974, 193; S. Martyn, 'Lawyer competence and lawyer discipline: Beyond the Bar?', *Georgetown Law Journal*, 1980–81, vol. 69, 705; B. Garth, 'Rethinking the legal profession's approach to collective self-improvement: Competence and the consumer perspective', *Wisconsin Law Review*, 1983, 639. See also, P. Hannaford, 'What complainants really expect of lawyer disciplinary agencies: Lessons from the Virginia State Bar Complainant Satisfaction Survey', *Journal of the Professional Lawyer*, 1996, vol. 3, 1–7 (most disciplinary complaints concern 'the fundamentals of human relationships: communication, courtesy and forthright dealings with one's clients, the courts and opposing counsel'. Quoting Michael Rigsby, Bar Counsel for Virginia State Bar; an empirical survey of complainants revealed that those who viewed the process as 'a means to prompt respondents to react' to their demands were 'quite satisfied', yielding 3.82 average on a five-point scale; complainants who expected the agency 'to investigate suspected lawyer misconduct' were least satisfied, with an average rating of 2.09, perhaps reflecting their perspective that the process does not treat 'both the complainant and the respondent in a manner that is objectively fair'; those complainants who expected the agency 'to impose sanctions on respondents' ranked overall satisfaction as 2.46, with differences based on the severity of sanction imposed; 3.52 average for those resulting in mild sanctions and 3.13 for severe sanctions, likely influenced by other factors, such as thoroughness of investigation and overall fairness of outcome). See also D. Rhode, 'Institutionalizing ethics', *Case Western Reserve Law Review*, 1995, 694–95. (Besides resource constraints that lead agencies to decline jurisdiction over abuses for which there is theoretically a civil remedy available, 'industry capture' of the process grants the profession almost exclusive control over the process.)

163 McKay Report, Appendix B. See generally, Devlin, 'The development of lawyer disciplinary procedures', 931–33 (discussing the history of lawyer discipline and highlighting key recommendations of the McKay Commission: recommending the highest level judiciary's control rather than that of elected Bar officials; central intake; random audits of trust accounts; and, 'perhaps the most controversial ... to make disciplinary matters public from the time of the complainant's initial contact with the agency'). Devlin, 'The development of lawyer disciplinary procedures', 931.

164 McKay Report, Appendix C.
165 ibid., Appendix D, Complete Text of Recommendations as Adopted by the House of Delegates (February 1992) (hereafter ABA McKay Recommendations).
166 ibid., including recommendations 3.1(f), (g), 4, 9, 10, 12. See ABA Commission on Lawyer Assistance Programs, *Directory of CoLAP Programs*. Available from: <www.abanet.org/legalservices/colap/lapdirectory.html> (accessed 20 November 2009); B. Melendez, *The Affiliate, YLD (2000–2001), An Alternative to Traditional Discipline for Minor Misconduct: Disciplinary Diversion* (stating that about one-third of surveyed jurisdictions had adopted or were experimenting with diversion programmes in the four years since the ABA amendment to the ABA Model Rule for Disciplinary Enforcement, Model Rule 11(G) provided for alternatives to discipline). Available from: <www.abanet.org/yld/affiliate/jan98/23-3-5.html> (accessed 20 November 2009).
167 Results of an informal survey in 2003 by the National Organization of Bar Counsel indicated that at least 14 states reported having some type of central intake system. See National Organization of Bar Counsel, *Chart, Survey of States: Central Intake Systems* (undated, copy with author).
168 See, for example, ABA Standing Committee on Client Protection, *State by State Adoption of ABA Client Protection Programs* (11 June 2007) (indicating that 23 states provided mediation of non-fee disputes; 12 states had mandatory fee arbitration and 37 required notification of trust account overdrafts). Available from: <www.abanet.org/cpr/clientpro/statebystate_cp_programs.pdf> (accessed 20 November 2009).
169 See, for example, National Organization of Bar Counsel, *Chart* (21 of 32 Unified Bar States and the District of Columbia oversee lawyer discipline). See also T. Schneyer, 'The incoherence of the unified bar concept: generalizing from the Wisconsin case', *American Bar Foundation Research Journal*, 1983, vol. 1 (finding states with unified bars slower than voluntary bar states to implement regulatory programmes benefiting consumers); B. Smith, 'The limits of compulsory professionalism: How the unified bar harms the legal profession', *Florida State University Law Review*, 1994, vol. 22, 35 (claiming that voluntary bar states are at the 'forefront of consumer oriented legal reform' and that compulsory membership is divisive to the profession). Smith, 'The limits', 37.
170 ABA MRLDE 16 and ABA McKay Recommendation 7, and ABA Center for Professional Responsibility Chart on Access to Disciplinary Proceedings (showing that 36 jurisdictions allow public access after probable cause finding; only three jurisdictions allow public access either upon finding of probable cause or dismissal of probable cause; only Oregon provides that initial complaints are open to public inspection on request). Cf. L. Levin, 'The case for less secrecy in lawyer discipline', *Georgetown Journal of Legal Ethics*, 2001, vol. 20, 1: 49–50 (arguing for earlier public access to information, after initial screening decision and shortly after complaint is docketed, and 'to learn ... that a lawyer had a complaint against him summarily dismissed (as well as the reasons for dismissal), that he received a minor sanction, that he agreed to diversion, or that there was a probable cause determination'); S. Krane, 'Meet the Gundersons', *New York State Bar Journal*, 2001, vol. 73, 5 (stating that two-thirds of states open disciplinary proceedings, usually after probable cause determination, and criticizing continued secrecy in New York as unnecessary to protect the reputation of lawyers who are formally charged, but later cleared by dismissal or private censure).
171 T. Morgan, 'Real world pressures on professionalism', *University of Arkansas at Little Rock Law Review*, 2001, vol. 23, 420. See McKay Report, p. 18. See also A. Blumenthal, 'Attorney self-regulation, consumer protection, and the future of the legal profession', *Kansas Journal of Law and Public Policy*, 1993–94, vol. 3, 6 (discussing potential dramatic reform to a 'consumer-oriented disciplinary system' that might 'change from self-regulation to government regulation [which] could have significant and dire consequences for the role of the attorney in our legal system and for our entire society'). Blumenthal, 'Attorney self-regulation', 11, 15.

172 Morgan, 'Real world', 420.
173 Telephone Interview with James J. Grogan, Deputy Administrator and Chief Counsel, Attorney Registration and Disciplinary Commission of the Supreme Court of Illinois in Chicago, IL, 13 August 2008.
174 See 2006 ABA Survey on Lawyer Discipline Systems (SOLD), Charts I, IV; M. Frisch, 'No stone left unturned: The failure of attorney self-regulation in the District of Columbia', *Georgetown Journal of Legal Ethics*, 2005, vol. 18, 325 (reporting egregious delays and outcomes 'rife with favoritism').
175 See T. Schneyer, 'How things have changed: Contrasting the regulatory environments of the canons and the model rules', *Journal of the Professional Lawyer*, 2008, vol. 18, 185–87 (author's emphasis added). See also Paton, 'Between a rock and a hard place', 89 (dramatic regulatory changes resulting from confluence of 'scandal, strong political leadership and intense public scrutiny of lawyer conduct').
176 R. Mallen and J. Smith, *Legal Malpractice Vol. 1*, St Paul: West Books, 2007, pp. 19, 23; S. Rosner, 'A decade of professionalism', *Journal of the Professional Lawyer*, 1995, vol. 6, 2, citing R. Creamer, *Law Firm Limited Liability Entities*, APRL Midyear Meeting Materials (1995).
177 American Bar Association Standing Committee on Lawyers' Professional Liability, *Profile of Legal Malpractice Claims 2000–2003* (2005) (hereafter 2000–2003 Profile), at tables 7 and 7A, p. 12, and summary at p. 16 (showing an increase of 0.14 per cent in claims in the period 1995–2003 where over $250,000 in indemnity was paid to claimants, and a 'slight increase' over a 10-year period where claims settled for over $2 million in indemnity). See also Mallen and Smith, *Legal Malpractice*, pp. 23, 66 (suggesting a 60 per cent increase in claims exceeding $2 million since 1996).
178 Mallen and Smith, *Legal Malpractice*, p. 23; 2000–2003 Profile, p. 3 (explaining the limited utility of national malpractice claims data conducted by malpractice insurer groups, including significant variations among states; numbers only address insured lawyers and lack of information on claims against uninsured lawyers; there is also a spotty response by some carriers about claims and a caveat that no conclusions were drawn about the relative riskiness of different practice areas). The Standing Committee issued prior studies in 1985, 1995 and 1999. ibid. at 1. Data collection is underway for the next edition. Insurance carriers limit public availability of data on claims frequency, defence and indemnity costs because they consider proprietary the data used in underwriting and rate-setting. See also M. Ramos, 'Legal malpractice: Reforming lawyers and law professors', *Tulane Law Review*, 1995–96, vol. 70, 2584 at n. 2 (quoting R. O'Malley, of the Attorneys' Liability Assurance Society stating that in 1992 there were expenditures of $3–4 billion a year for payouts, lost reserves, settlements and defence costs; this was 'at least five or six times' the cost 10 years earlier; M. Ramos, 'Legal malpractice: the profession's dirty little secret', *Vanderbilt Law Review*, 1994, vol. 47, 1679–82 (discussing the explosion in legal malpractice since the 1980s, with increased numbers of claims and severity as tip of the iceberg).
179 Ramos, 'Legal malpractice: Reforming lawyers', 2589. (The author admits that, during his extensive malpractice defence practice in California during the 1980s, he routinely 'conspired with lawyer-clients, plaintiffs' lawyers, plaintiffs, judges and insurance carriers by entering into confidential settlement agreements', leaving no public document showing fact of claim or settlement terms.)
180 2000–2003 Profile, table 1, p. 6 (reporting 29,637 claims made in the 2003 study, compared with 29,227 claims in the 1985 study; textual summary showing 5.86 per cent increase in claims against personal injury defence lawyers). See also *ABA/BNA Lawyers' Manual on Professional Conduct*, 24 Current Reports 114 (5 March 2008) (panellists noted 'mushrooming' claims against insurance defence counsel, with actions by insured that often revealed 'shocking neglect ... perhaps stemming from a basic

misunderstanding of client identity' and other suits lodged by insurers, excess insurers and reinsurers).

181 2000–2003 Profile, at 6.

182 ibid., table 5, pp. 10, 17 (47 per cent substantive legal errors; 28 per cent administrative errors).

183 ibid., p. 17.

184 See J. Maute, 'Scrutinizing lawyer advertising and solicitation rules under commercial speech and antitrust doctrines', *Hastings Constitutional Law Quarterly*, 1985, vol. 13, 487–535; Mallen and Smith, *Legal Malpractice*, p. 22.

185 Mallen and Smith, *Legal Malpractice*, pp. 54–55.

186 Ramos, 'Legal malpractice: reforming lawyers', 2602.

187 See B. Barton, 'An institutional analysis of lawyer regulation: Who should control lawyer regulation – Courts, legislatures, or the market?', *Georgia Law Review*, 2003, vol. 37, 1178–82, 1185–1204, 1209, 1246–47 (discussing preferential treatment given to lawyers by judges who came from their ranks; the high risk of industry capture; under-funding of disciplinary discipline, with institutional analysis leading 'inexorably to the conclusion that state supreme courts should not be in charge. These justices are too busy, too connected and sympathetic to lawyers, and too inaccessible to the public to do any more than allow bar associations and lawyers almost total control of the system. Legislative control, whether by state legislatures or Congress, will not eliminate the powerful influence of lawyers, but it will allow a healthy dose of public influence to enter the picture and may begin to reform the system'), 1246.

188 See S. Fortney and V. Johnson, *Legal Malpractice Law: Problems and Prevention*, Minneapolis: Thompson West, 2008, pp. 8–9 (discussing various reasons for expansion). Whether arbitration of fee disputes and malpractice claims provide meaningful recourse to clients is beyond the scope of this work. Some scholars and courts have raised concerns about the fairness of pre-dispute arbitration clauses, and about whether the private forum may reflect industry bias. See J. Dzienkowski, 'Legal malpractice and the multistate law firm: Supervision of multistate offices; firms as limited liability partnerships; and pre-dispute agreements to arbitrate client malpractice claims', *South Texas Law Review*, 1995, vol. 36, 995–96; L. Russo, 'The consequences of arbitrating a legal malpractice claim: Rebuilding faith in the legal profession', *Hofstra Law Review*, 2006, vol. 35, 327; *In re Akin Gump Strauss Hauer & Feld, LLP*, 252 SW 3d 480 (Tex. App. – Hous (14 Dist.) (2008) (upholding trial court confirmation of arbitration award between lawyers and sophisticated company, and denying lawyers' petition for mandamus to remand back to original arbitration panel); *LaFleur v Law Offices of Anthony G. Buzbee, PC*, 960 So.2d 105 (1st Cir. 2007) (holding unenforceable pre-dispute mandatory arbitration provision in retainer agreement with injured maritime worker). *Compare Schatz v Allen Matkins Leck Gamble & Mallory LLP* (2009) 87 Cal. Rptr.3d 700 (Cal.) (upholding pre-dispute arbitration agreement in retainer).

189 See, for example, J. Leubsdorf, 'Legal malpractice and professional responsibility', *Rutgers Law Review*, 1995, vol. 48, 101 (urging further development of legal malpractice doctrine beyond negligence law, to become integral part of system of legal regulation); N. Moore, 'Expanding duties of attorneys to "non-clients": Reconceptualizing the attorney–client relationship in entity representation and other inherently ambiguous situations', *South Carolina Law Review*, 1994, vol. 45, 659; Rhode, 'Institutionalizing ethics', 665, 695 (discussing the 'mismatch between client needs and regulatory responses'); ABA Standing Committee on Lawyers' Professional Liability, *Lawyer's Desk Guide to Legal Malpractice VIII* (1992).

190 See, for example, *Abramson v Wildman* 184 Md. App. 189, 964A.26730 (allowing restitution for fees paid based on a provision in the retainer agreement promising to 'be both sensitive and professionally responsive' to the client's situation in a custody dispute).

191 K. Kunzke and S. Anderson, 'They crash and you burn: When the stock market

falls, you can count on malpractice risk to rise' (May 2002). Available from: <www.abanet.org/legalservices/lpl/downloads/journalmay02.pdf> (accessed 20 November 2009).

192 See generally A. Davis, 'Legal ethics and risk management: Complementary visions of lawyer regulation', *Georgetown Journal of Legal Ethics*, 2008, vol. 21, 95 (developing the claim that law firm risk management enhances careful ethical deliberation by individual lawyers); S. Fortney and J. Hanna, 'Fortifying a law firm's ethical infrastructure: Avoiding legal malpractice claims based on conflicts of interest', *St Mary's Law Journal*, 2002, vol. 33, 669; M. Bassingthwaighte, 'Keep malpractice and disciplinary problems at bay', *Trial*, 2008, vol. 44, 34. See also Ramos, 'Legal malpractice: Reforming lawyers', 2601.

193 See Conference Report, 2008 Legal Malpractice and Risk Management Conference, reprinted in *ABA/BNA Lawyers' Manual on Professional Conduct*, 24 Current Reports 118 (5 March 2008) (speakers encouraging firms to state and implement core values; have firm's risk managers annually review claims history and look for common risk patterns; conduct in-house continuing education; involve top firm management; monitor for signs of trouble, including rogue or isolated lawyers and large outstanding receivables; conduct 'due diligence' before bringing in lateral associates or partners; and encourage periodic, random firm reviews); M. Skolnick, 'Lessons from recent Utah legal malpractice cases', *Utah BJ*, 21, 2008, 28.

194 See, for example, D. Moss, 'Going bare: Practicing without malpractice insurance', *ABAJ*, 1987, vol. 73, 82 (reporting statewide surveys indicating that at least 20 per cent of lawyers are uninsured, and many others 'who don't go bare may be wearing only a bikini'). See also J. Fischer, 'External controls over the American Bar', *Georgetown Journal of Legal Ethics*, 2008, vol. 19, 59, 64 n. 23 (reporting that 83 per cent of Illinois lawyers in private practice are insured; about 60 per cent of Pennsylvania lawyers are insured; about 90 per cent of Virginia lawyers carry insurance; and in other states the range is from 50–70 per cent of private practitioners carrying insurance). A knowledgeable observer put the number of Oklahoma uninsured lawyers at over 50 per cent. Email from Steve Dobbs to author confirming results of unscientific, anecdotal survey (on file with author).

195 McKay Report, note 23 above, Recommendation 18.

196 ABA Chart, State Implementation on Insurance Disclosure (as of November 16, 2009). Available from: <www.abanet.org/cpr/clientpro/malprac_disc_chart.pdf> (accessed 4 December 2009). (stating that Oregon requires all lawyers to maintain professional liability insurance).

197 See Ramos, 'Legal malpractice: The profession', 1728–30. It appears that Oregon's mandatory coverage through a state-administered fund works reasonably well. Non-practising lawyers and patent attorneys are exempt from the requirement of at least $300,000 in coverage. See N. Cunitz, 'Mandatory malpractice insurance for lawyers: Is there a possibility of public protection without compulsion?', *Georgetown Journal of Legal Ethics*, 1995, vol. 8, 651 (stating that the fund had substantial reserves and that there was 'not a notable increase in claims').

198 In August 2004, the ABA House of Delegates adopted a 'Model Court Rule on Insurance Disclosure'. Available from <www.abanet.org/cpr/clientpro/malprac_disc_rule.pdf> (accessed 29 November 2009). For the status of adoption by the states, see ABA Standing Committee on Client Protection, *State Implementation of ABA Model Court Rule on Insurance Disclosure (as of April 19, 2010)*. Available from: <www.abanet.org/cpr/clientpro/malprac_disc_chart.pdf> (accessed June 21, 2010 (hereafter, ABA Chart, State Implementation on Insurance Disclosure). See also *ABA/BNA Lawyers' Manual on Professional Conduct*, 25 Current Reports 200 (15 April 2009) (discussing opposing views on insurance disclosure rules, and listing Connecticut, Arkansas, Florida and Kentucky as having rejected mandatory disclosure rules).

199 ABA Chart, State Implementation on Insurance Disclosure. Four additional states

are considering adoption of the ABA Model Rule on Insurance Disclosure. Eighteen jurisdictions allow public access to the disclosure of malpractice coverage contained in annual registration statement; seven jurisdictions require disclosure directly to the client. See also, E. Wald, 'Taking attorney–client communications (and therefore clients) seriously', *University of San Francisco Law Review*, 2008, vol. 42, 791, n. 213 (23 jurisdictions contemplated adopting ABA proposed revisions, resulting in a split, described above).

200 See generally A. Paterson, 'Professionalism and the legal services market', *International Journal of Legal Profession*, 1996, vol. 3, 149–58 (discussing renegotiation in terms of professionalism); C. Whelan, 'The paradox of professionalism', 492 (concluding emerging UK view that legal services can be viewed more like a business than profession and better regulated by the market than self-regulation); R. Pearce, 'The professionalism paradigm shift: Why discarding professional ideology will improve the conduct and the reputation of the Bar', *New York University Law Review*, 1995, vol. 70, 1229: 1266 ('The reinterpretation of business as a worthy endeavour, together with the acknowledgment that law practice has the characteristics of a business, suggest a new understanding of the framework for the delivery of legal services').

201 For example, after Alaska became a state, Alaska courts had the freedom to decide cases on a clean slate, unimpaired by precedent from older states.

202 See, for example, B. Rabe, 'North American federalism and climate change policy: American state and Canadian provincial policy development', *Widener Law Journal*, 2004, vol. 14, 152, 164 (urging 'accountable devolution' of federal standards to states with measurable accountability); A. Harrell, 'Commentary: The case for nonuniformity in state law', *Consumer Finance Law Quarterly Report*, 1997, 322–26 (discussing the history of states' service as incubators for legal and financial reforms dating back to the beginning of the republic).

203 US Central Intelligence Agency, *The World Factbook 2007*, pp. 38–39; Law Council of Australia, *Snapshot of the Legal Profession*, September 2004.

204 See generally B. Bryson, *In a Sunburned Country*, New York: Broadway Books, 2000. See also S. Mark, 'Technology and compliance auditing – The future of legal regulation', paper presented at Third International Legal Ethics Conference, Gold Coast, Australia, (13–16 July 2008) (opening quote from Peter Drucker: 'The best way to predict the future is to invent it.').

205 A. Pinnington and J. Gray, 'The global restructuring of legal services work? A study of the internationalization of Australian law firms', *International Journal of the Legal Profession*, 2007, vol. 14, 150–53, 160–66.

206 S. Mark, 'Views from an Australian regulator', paper presented at Chicago conference 'The Future is Here: Globalisation and the Regulation of the Legal Profession', American Bar Association Center for Professional Responsibility and Standing Committee on Professional Discipline and Georgetown Center for the Study of the Legal Profession Present, Chicago, IL, 27 May 2009, pp. 1, 3. Available from: <www.law.georgetown.edu/news/documents/CCJ-2009-WebMaterials-final.doc> (accessed 20 November 2009).

207 See generally M. Schwarzschild, 'Class, national character, and the Bar reforms in Britain: Will there always be an England?', *Connecticut Journal of International Law*, 1994, vol. 9, 188–219 (discussing how 'class colors almost everything in England ... and [while] not completely interchangeable with wealth and power' is also reflected in the legal professions and views toward litigation).

208 US Constitution, Art. 1 s1, X Amendment.

209 See generally L. Terry, 'GATS applicability to transnational lawyering and its potential impact on US state regulation of lawyers', *Vanderbilt Journal of Transnational Law*, 2001, vol. 34, 989.

210 L. Terry, 'The European Commission project regarding competition in professional services', *Northwestern Journal of International Law and Business*, 2009, vol. 29, 1–2, 18.

211 Treaty Establishing the European Community art. 249 Mar. 25, 1957, 2002 OJ (C325) 249 (authorizing Parliament to issue binding directives 'as to the result to be achieved, upon each Member State to which it is addressed, but shall leave to the national authorities the choice of form and methods').

212 See Treaty Establishing the European Community art. 5, Nov. 10, 1997, 1997 OJ (C 340) 5, discussed in K. Abbott and D. Snidal, 'Strengthening international regulation through transnational new governance', *Vanderbilt Journal of Transnational Law*, 2009, vol. 42, 538 at n. 166.

213 Terry, 'The European Commission', 17–18. See also Directive 98/5/EC (16 Feb. 1998), L77/36 Official Journal of the European Communities.

214 Terry, 'The European Commission', 18–26, discussing Case C-309/99, *Wouters v Nederlandse Orde van Advocaten*, 2002 ECR I-1577, 2002 ECJ CELEX LEXIS 681 (Feb. 19, 2002); Case C-35/99 *Arduino*, [2002] ECR I-1529 (2 February 2002).

215 See, for example, A. Hamilton, J. Madison and J. Jay, *The Federalist Papers, No. 46* (James Madison); E. Veasey, 'What would Madison think? The irony of the twists and turns of federalism', *Delaware Journal of Corporate Law*, 2009, vol. 34, 46–53 (discussing the Sarbanes–Oxley Act and other 'federal incursions into the states' traditional domain [in which] this division of responsibilities survived as a fragile ecosystem more or less intact for over seventy years').

216 E. Cohen, 'Chief Justices, Others, consider ideas on regulating lawyers in global setting', *Lawyers Manual of Professional Conduct*, 25 June 2009, p. 300 (quoting remarks of Utah Supreme Court Chief Justice Christine M. Durham, president-elect of the Conference of Chief Justices).

217 ibid.

218 H. Jackson, 'Learning from Eddy: A meditation upon organizational reform of financial supervision in Europe', *Perspectives in Company Law and Financial Regulation* (Michel Tison, et al., eds), Cambridge: Cambridge University Press, 2009, pp. 523–39.

219 See Zacharias, 'The self-regulation misnomer'; L. Terry, National Conference of Bar Counsel CLE materials, 'Should Rule 5.1 be used more proactively?' Plenary presentation to the National Organization of Bar Counsel (9 August 2008) (on file with author). Terry urged state regulators to implement this modest proposal based on the New South Wales and Queensland self-assessment mechanisms relating to 10 areas, including negligence, communication, delay, file transfers, billing practices, conflicts, record management, undertakings, supervision and trust accounts. See also: <www.lawlink.nsw.gov.au/lawlink/olsc/ll_olsc.nsf/pages/OLSC_tenobjectives> (accessed 29 November 2009).

3   Our common future: the imperative for contextual ethics in a connected world

Vivien Holmes and Simon Rice [1]

3.1 Introduction

The late twentieth century phenomenon of global connectedness, driven by technology and capital, offers possibilities for development and peace – and poses threats to security and the environment – on a scale we are still trying to comprehend. In our intricately connected contemporary world, lawyers must firmly and clearly restate their ethics, making them relevant to an environment where borders and boundaries no longer reliably define the limits of cause, effect and accountability.

There have long been challenges to the standard conception of legal ethics as 'neutral partisanship', on the basis that it appears to enable lawyers to avoid moral accountability for their actions. However, these critiques now have additional force in a world where the consequences of lawyers' actions – for good or bad – can reverberate around the globe. Lawyers' capacity to facilitate harm, and the concomitant power they have to avoid or mitigate it, take on significantly greater importance when the effects of conduct can spread so widely and quickly, as illustrated by such diverse examples as environmental pollution and the global financial crisis.

In this chapter we argue that lawyers must recognize this new context of legal practice, and must adopt models of lawyering that enable them to contribute positively to their globalized world. We focus on the intersection between two seemingly separate topics: a globalized world facing enormous challenges to its future, and legal ethics.

First we outline the connected nature of the contemporary world, and consequently the connected nature of contemporary legal practice. We then describe the conventional roles of lawyers, and emphasize the often-overlooked fact that transactional and advisory lawyers are under the same ethical obligations as lawyers in the more popularly familiar role of court advocate. We highlight transactional and advisory work as the area of lawyering which most usually takes lawyers across borders and into globalized legal practice.

Three case studies of lawyers' facilitation of harmful corporate conduct provide a context for the discussion that follows, about the failure of the standard conception of legal ethics to engage lawyers in the needs of a connected world, and about the risk that zealous pursuit of clients' interests can lead to lawyers' complicity in the occurrence of harm. Those case studies form a basis for analysing lawyers' perceived role as gatekeepers for their clients' conduct, and we note the predictability but inadequacy of regulatory responses to recurring incidents of lawyers' failure in that role.

We then outline the standard conception of lawyers' practice ethics, and consider one of the many available alternative approaches – contextual lawyering – which encourages lawyers to take account of the context in which they act. We propose that contextual lawyering has greater potential than neutral partisanship to enable lawyers to avoid causing harm, that it is a preferable conception of lawyers' ethics generally, and that it is a necessary one for globalized legal practice – particularly in light of the weak role of the state as regulator of transnational activity.

Finally we consider the practice of contextual ethics in a globalized world, and review our three case studies to see how lawyers' practice according to contextual ethics could have played out differently. We conclude by acknowledging the difficulty of establishing and sustaining this alternative legal practice ethic, and propose that contextual ethics needs to be encouraged and maintained through reflective practice.

3.2 Our connected world

3.2.1 *Intricate connectedness*

The interconnectedness of all life has been recognized for millennia.[2] What is new is the number and speed of our interconnections.

New technologies have enabled increasingly numerous and rapid interactions across the globe, particularly in trade and investment, but also between people on the move – whether for business, tourism, emigration or mass migration in the face of disaster or conflict. The idea that anyone is separated by only six degrees from anyone else in the world now has scientific support.[3]

The heightened speed and visibility of connectedness are at the heart of contemporary globalisation: a 'multidimensional financial, social and cultural phenomenon ... [caused by] the occurrence within a short period of time of unprecedented advances in telecommunications, transportation and information retrieval systems as well as the political upheavals that replaced communist and socialist regimes with democratic systems of governments and capitalist economic policies'.[4]

The 2008–09 global financial crisis is one of many recent examples of the world's connectedness. It began locally with sub-prime mortgage loans going 'bad' in the United States; however, soon economies in Eastern and Western Europe, Russia, South America, Asia, Africa, Australasia and the Pacific found they had to deal with the repercussions of those loans. In the economy of jobs and livelihoods, those repercussions saw an escalation in the number of the world's unemployed, and of working poor living on less than US$ 2 a day.[5]

3.2.2 Our common future

The world's interconnectedness means that humanity necessarily shares a common future, and it is a future that faces significant challenges. Sachs believes that the world's current ecological, demographic[6] and economic trajectory is unsustainable, and that 'if we continue with "business as usual" we will hit social and ecological crises with calamitous results'.[7] Many agree with his analysis.[8] Discussing our ecological and social trajectory, and summarizing what is now widely accepted science,[9] Flannery concludes that:

> Humanity is now suspended between the tipping point [when greenhouse gas concentration is sufficient to cause catastrophic climate change] and the point of no return [when that concentration of greenhouse gas has been in place long enough to give rise to irreversible processes] and only the most strenuous efforts on our part are capable of returning us to safe ground.[10]

The defining challenge of the twenty-first century will be to accept that this interconnectedness exposes us all to the same ecological and social challenges: we need 'to face the reality that humanity shares a *common fate ... on a crowded planet*'.[11] To similar effect, Preston says that 'what is non-negotiable in the twenty-first century is that our perspective, our worldview, our understanding must have global dimensions ... I speak of our response as individuals, although the character of global citizenship may also be expected of corporate actors'.[12] Recognizing that we face an interconnected future should be a matter of '[e]nlightened self interest ... whether our starting point is ... philosophy or whether it is hard-headed commerce'.[13]

Sommerville reminds us that we ignore our interconnections at our peril: 'Common humanity and universal responsibility link us'. She points out, however, that 'much of the time we act as if this is not the case – we are in denial as individuals and societies. In the past, our denial harmed those whose plight we ignored. Today it harms everyone, which is why we, the deniers, can no longer afford it – if indeed we ever could'.[14] Similarly, the directors of the United Nations Millennium Project note that, while observations about our common humanity are not new, 'the consequences of failure to realize their importance may be much more serious in the future than in the past'.[15]

The Millennium Project highlights both the ecological and social challenges facing the world, and the importance of accepting our interconnectedness when addressing those challenges. The Millennium Project has identified 15 'Global Challenges for Humanity'[16] which are 'transnational in nature and transinstitutional in solution'.[17] Thus the challenge of sustainable development is no more or less important than the challenge of global ethics: they are interdependent, and 'require collaborative action among governments, international organizations, corporations, universities, and NGOs'.[18]

The last of the Millennium Project's 15 challenges is 'How can ethical considerations become more routinely incorporated into global decisions?' The need to incorporate routinely ethical considerations into decisions with global effect arises quite simply because 'globalization and advanced technology allow fewer people to do more damage and in less time ... or alternatively, enable more people to do more good than ever before'.[19]

What, then, is the place of lawyers in this connected world? Lawyers advise on and facilitate many decisions made by states and corporations that have a global effect, and that relate in some way to the 15 Global Challenges. Lawyers are among those people enabled by globalization and advanced technology to do more damage, or good, in less time than ever before. The actions of lawyers and their clients both exacerbate and mitigate the significant challenges to humanity's future. Because the work of lawyers can have repercussions well beyond their home jurisdiction, the need arises for global ethical considerations to play a part in lawyers' work.

We turn to look at the nature of legal practice generally in a connected world before focusing on the transactional and advisory work of lawyers, and the particular ethical challenges thrown up by that type of legal work.

3.2.3 *Legal practice in a connected world*

Lawyers traditionally have conducted their work locally, confined to the bounds of a state and even, in some states such as Australia, within provincial parts of the state. While law remains largely tied to its state-defined jurisdictional bounds, the global commerce and international relations of a connected world mean that, increasingly, the transactions, the subject matter, the parties and the lawyers themselves are outside the lawyers' home jurisdiction. State borders and jurisdictional boundaries no longer confine the conduct or consequences of legal practice, and many legal transactions today are transnational in both character and consequence.[20] Whether a lawyer is practising commercial law in Montreal, litigation in Mumbai or administrative law in Melbourne, the interconnectedness of today's world means that their clients' conduct and its effects can reach around the globe.[21]

The number of lawyers who work internationally and transnationally is growing.[22] Globalization has taken ordinary private legal activity across borders and into a connected world.[23] The movement of capital, goods and people around the world is accompanied by process, documentation and rules that enable, and give predictability to, these commercial and social transactions. As a result, the business of lawyers is now, more than ever, writ large on the international stage;[24] lawyers are intimately and perhaps essentially involved in conduct with international effect and consequences.

Even lawyers who practise in domestic firms on domestic issues under domestic law often deal with matters that traverse national jurisdictional boundaries, simply because the parties themselves are in different jurisdictions. Examples include commercial activity, where a local manufacturer commissions the production of component parts in another state, and relationship breakdown, where the division of jointly owned property on separation requires the sale of overseas assets. For many lawyers today, the practice of law can now radiate from a local to a global context and back again 'with great speed'.[25]

Most of the legal work that has a global reach is transactional and advisory, and in the following section we discuss that type of legal work and its particular ethical challenges.

3.3 Lawyers' globalized practice

3.3.1 Lawyers' roles

The popular conception of the lawyer-as-litigator (on their feet, in court, arguing) is, of course, a misconception. It is certainly the most dramatic and easily represented of lawyers' roles, and it is the role that is most usually the basis of regulation of lawyers' ethical conduct. Yet the litigator's role, more broadly and realistically understood, extends to dispute resolution generally (such as negotiation) and requires the performance of a wide range of prosaic office-based tasks.

More commonly, however, lawyers provide advice, and facilitate and document transactions. Advice is usually about the meaning of a law or legal process and its effect on the client's proposed conduct, or on a dispute in which the client is involved; a transaction is usually an exchange of some sort between a client and another party. We do not mean to provide an exhaustive list of lawyerly activities, but merely to highlight that lawyers' principal roles in a liberal democracy play out not only in the courts for purposes of litigation, but also, and predominantly, in the office, for purposes of advice and transactions.

As a general proposition, a lawyer is instructed by a client to advise and to represent the interests of the client – although the lawyer can have many roles, and the corresponding client many identities. Conventionally, lawyers are in private practice for profit, licensed by the state to hold themselves out as lawyers and to charge a fee for service; the lawyer's client is a private individual, a private entity, a public entity (including the state), or any grouping of individuals or entities. More broadly, a lawyer is an 'in-house lawyer' or 'corporate counsel' or government lawyer, who advises and represents the interests of his or her corporate employer[26] or the state.[27] There are also lawyers who have, or believe they have, no direct client: cause lawyers, public-interest lawyers or 'legislative lawyers',[28] who represent interests rather than people or entities. As Ziv acknowledges, the represented interests are invariably manifest in a person or entity, even if the actual accountability of the lawyer to the client is somewhat 'attenuated'.[29]

3.3.2 A focus on transactional and advisory lawyering

As we noted above, despite this range of lawyers' roles, it is adversarial litigation that is commonly the site for both illustrating and analysing the ethics of lawyering. A lawyer in litigation, particularly in a criminal matter, is the apotheosis of the zealous advocate – a fearless representative of the client's interests, committed on the client's behalf to establishing or denying a claim or a charge – and it is in adversarial court proceedings that the tension between a lawyer's duties to the client and duties to the court is most clearly on show; Nicolson and Webb remark that 'much of professional legal ethics takes its cue from the adversarial system and the advocate's role'.[30]

Looking at lawyers' practice in a court setting does indeed highlight aspects of lawyers' ethics that are much less apparent in the more usual office environment of legal practice. The dynamics of litigation illustrate the tension between competing duties almost literally, when the demands of the court and notions of 'justice' may be at odds with the position a lawyer wishes to take on behalf of her client – for example, in pursuing a line of questioning, tendering evidence, requiring the production of certain material or making a claim of privilege. A consequence of this focus on the vivid and familiar dynamics of the courtroom to illustrate lawyers' ethics is to downplay, if not to completely sideline, the ethical issues that arise in the far more common lawyers' practice of transactional work and advice. Regan observes that transactional and advisory lawyers are a group of lawyers 'largely neglected in ethics rules and whose activities generally are shielded from public view'.[31]

The absence in transactional and advisory legal practice of such clear illustrations of competing ethical duties both reduces the appeal of that type of legal practice as a vehicle for explaining those duties, and obscures the fact that the same competing duties can be at play. But legal practice, and in particular global legal practice, is very substantially transactional and advisory, so that any discussion of the ethics of legal practice must take account of the particular features of that form of lawyering.

Transactional and advisory lawyering is not necessarily less adversarial, nor does it necessarily demand less zealousness, than court advocacy. Luban's view that the lawyer as adviser or counsellor is not in a role of one-sided partisanship,[32] and Parker and Evans' description of a lawyer who is advising a client in a transactional matter as a 'counsellor' rather than as an advocate,[33] do not fully recognize the oppositional nature of many legal transactions. While it is probably true that parties engage in transactions or arrangements to establish 'relationships ... founded largely on consensual lines in which co-operation benefits both sides',[34] and that '[t]he best way to achieve this ... is to structure relationships so that the parties benefit from the relationship, feel that it is fair and trust one another',[35] parties to transactions may nevertheless be oppositional, if not actually adversarial, in protecting their own interests. Commercial arrangements are achieved through negotiation precisely because there are different, if not competing, interests at stake.

Transactional and advisory legal work – commercial, personal or administrative – within a rule-of-law democracy is just as bounded by the requirements of ethical practice as the court-based work that is used to illustrate those ethics. In drafting a tender or advising on a commercial arrangement, a lawyer is no less an 'officer of the court' than is his or her litigator colleague. The commercial lawyer is as obliged as that colleague to be truthful, to not be party to illegal conduct, and to uphold the law.

But although the duties are the same, the usual environment of transactional and advisory practice is different from the advocacy environment on which conventional legal ethics are largely based. Unlike in litigation, where lawyers conduct their business under the scrutiny of the very institution to which they owe their duty, transactional and advisory lawyers are not under direct scrutiny. As a result, they *appear* to be, and *may feel that they are*, less restrained by external duties in pursuing their clients' interests. Because lawyers' duties 'to the court' are not manifest in transactional and advisory practice in the same way as they are in court-based practice, they can seem largely irrelevant to achieving what are effectively private interests: 'For many, the vestigial nature of the duty to the court is taken for granted and hardly ever has to be thought about. It is like an appendix – irrelevant to the normal digestion of legal work but occasionally liable to flare up'.[36]

In transactional and advisory practice, there is no formal or systematic check on whether a lawyer has facilitated a transaction that was achieved through misrepresentation, or is in breach of the law. In fact, it may suit all parties to a transaction to both misrepresent fact and evade law – an example would be understating the value of a sale to reduce or evade stamp duty. The possibility that the lawyer will later be held to account for their part in facilitating such a transaction does not necessarily prevent the conduct, and can be treated by a lawyer as a risk factor to be weighed in commercial terms.

3.3.3 *Transactional and advisory legal practice beyond regulation*

An important aspect of global legal practice is that it increasingly operates, or has effect, outside the reach of liberal democratic rule of law. The connectedness of the world is such that the transactional or advisory lawyer in Mumbai, Melbourne or Montreal can be involved in matters concerning activity in, for example, developing states, states under dictatorships or martial law, or states in political transition.

Lawyers increasingly are working at least at the margins, if not beyond the reach, of effective professional regulation, and on matters where the client's conduct is outside the conventional framework of public and social accountability: 'globalization ... has undermined the power of nation states. States' regulatory power and authority have been put under pressure from ... transnational markets ... from communications and transport technologies which can move ideas, goods, money and people across national boundaries with relative ease and great speed'.[37] Daly put it simply as long ago as 1997: 'The essential characteristic of a global organization is that it has divorced markets from nation-states'.[38]

The connected nature of the world is such that lawyers may find their practice extending to social and political environments that do not recognize, at least effectively, the rule of law that underpins the conventional ethical conception of lawyering, which we discuss in detail below.[39] At worst, lawyers and their clients are active in proverbial cowboy territory, where there are very weak rules,[40] or effectively no rules, to constrain conduct that causes harm, or to prevent a lawyer facilitating harm. Indeed, it may be that the states in which such conduct takes place actively encourage it,[41] perhaps for the short-term financial gain that will flow to those in power despite harm done to the community or environment. Two of the case studies we discuss below – AWB and BTC – exemplify this situation.

When our connected world takes legal practice in this direction, lawyers may find themselves acting as a 'mini-legislators',[42] engaged in 'private law-making – creating law from the ground up'.[43] We must anticipate that professional responsibility in globalized legal practice can be very weakly regulated, putting some lawyers beyond the effective reach of the conventional formal and informal means of guiding and regulating professional behaviour, such as training, professional rules and enforcement, and local culture and ethos.[44] As a result, 'the globalized bar, in particular the expatriate segments of it, do not take part in ... activities [organized by lawyer associations, such as continuing legal education and promotion of law reform and pro bono work], and can be regarded as ... de-professionalized'.[45] The idea of the global lawyer 'carries with it the danger of professional statelessness, a condition in which lawyers over time become dissociated from the legal profession's fundamental values, such as lawyer independence'.[46] As well, 'law firms are handing over work to individuals who are not subject to the disciplinary authority of state or local bar associations, may have limited legal training, and do not necessarily have any legal obligation to abide by [the law firms' domestic] laws and ethical rules applicable to lawyers'.[47]

The phenomenon of increasingly globalized legal practice has generated fresh discussion of legal professional ethics, including debate over possible international codes of ethics.[48] While acknowledging the importance of such a debate, our focus is on resolving an issue that will persist despite any such code(s), and which becomes more acute as the conduct and effect of legal practice continues to expand beyond the reach of state-sanctioned codes: whether there is a place in lawyers' professional ethics for a lawyer's own morality, and for lawyers to act as agents of 'justice' in a broad sense.[49]

As we have argued above, a globalized world expands significantly the effect of lawyers' conduct on behalf of their clients. To the extent that a client's conduct has the potential to cause social and ecological harm, the lawyer risks complicity in causing that harm. This prompts us to ask whether the ethical paradigm that commonly guides lawyers' practice either facilitates or works against lawyers playing a positive role to address the challenges humanity faces. In the following section, we consider three case studies where lawyers' work contributed to far-reaching consequences and, in at least two of the cases, demonstrable and far-reaching harm.

3.4 Case studies

We have chosen three very different case studies to ground our discussion of legal ethics: the much-discussed financial collapse of the US energy corporation Enron, which resulted in widespread harm that was predominantly confined to the United States; the AWB scandal, which saw the Australian wheat exporter bankroll Saddam Hussein's regime even as the United States and Australia were preparing to invade Iraq; and the Baku-Tbilisi-Ceyhan (BTC) pipeline negotiations, the ramifications of which will be felt 'not only by the communities living along the pipeline's [lengthy] path, but also by their counterparts around the globe'.[50]

3.4.1 Enron

Enron was at one stage the seventh largest corporation in the United States. A summary of the facts of the Enron collapse risks 'wildly over-simplifying an extraordinarily complex saga'[51] but, drawing on Rhode and Paton's 'factual backdrop',[52] Regan's very detailed (and illustrated) account[53] and Parker and Evans's summary,[54] we will take the risk.

Enron traded in energy sources such as natural gas, and in the infrastructure that supports the production and supply of those energy sources. To cope with an increasing problem of financial liquidity in its business in the mid-1990s, Enron created corporate entities with which it could engage in financially risky transactions. The entities and transactions were either not disclosed in Enron's own financial statements or, if disclosed, the disclosure was contrived for its effect on the financial statement rather than made for a legitimate accounting purpose.

When establishing the entities and deciding whether and how to disclose them and their transactions, Enron relied on advice from, among others, its in-house lawyers and externally retained legal advisers. In 2001 the nature of the dealings – and the grossly inflated value of Enron's worth – were exposed, and Enron's house of cards crashed.

Our focus is on the conduct of Enron's lawyers. Rhode and Paton consider that, in Enron's corporate and financial contrivances, 'too many lawyers were part of the problem, rather than part of the solution'.[55] Regan's account shows how lawyers – both in-house counsel and external lawyers – were involved at almost every step of Enron's deceit: they advised on the formal rule compliance of transactions that were in fact of a different character,[56] they documented[57] and negotiated[58] transactions that appear to have been intended for improper purposes, and they advised on steps taken to evade disclosure requirements.[59]

As a result of the Enron collapse, 'more than 4000 employees lost their jobs [and] thousands of investors lost their life savings as $70 billion in wealth vanished. Confidence in Corporate America plunged [and] ... the accounting firm [Arthur Andersen] imploded in less than a year when its other clients fled after public exposure of the firm's alleged role'.[60]

3.4.2 AWB

AWB Ltd was the holding company in the AWB group of companies that evolved from the Australian Wheat Board,[61] and at the relevant time the sole marketer of Australian wheat overseas. From 1996 the AWB sold wheat to Iraq under the United Nations (UN) Oil-for-Food Programme. That programme had been established to soften the effects of UN sanctions against Iraq, by allowing Iraq to sell oil and use the revenue received to purchase food and other humanitarian goods. Under the programme, Iraqi oil revenue was held in a UN escrow account. Funds for UN-approved Iraqi purchases were paid to vendors out of the UN account.

In 1999, AWB (along with some other suppliers of wheat to Iraq) accepted an Iraqi-imposed condition on its wheat sales: Iraq insisted that, with each wheat delivery, AWB pay 'fees' to Iraq, purportedly for transportation of the wheat from seaports to inland silos. AWB invoiced the UN Oil-for-Food Programme for the cost of the wheat and 'transport' fees, and then paid these fees to Iraq. Such fees were in fact 'kickbacks' of hard currency to Iraq, and so were in breach of the UN sanctions and contrary to Australian government policy. To get around this, AWB crafted the invoices it submitted to the UN escrow account so that they did not reflect the true arrangements between AWB and Iraq. In this way, AWB facilitated Iraq's access to large amounts of hard currency: between November 1999 and March 2003 it paid approximately US$224 million in 'fees' to the Iraqi regime.[62]

By taking advantage of the Oil-for-Food Programme in this way, Saddam Hussein's regime was able to obtain hard currency to prepare for a war that might otherwise have been avoidable.[63] Further, the regime used money earmarked for desperately needed humanitarian goods for its own corrupt purposes.[64] In a 2008 civil lawsuit filed in the United States against 94 companies, including AWB,[65] the Iraqi government alleged that: 'Billions of dollars were lost [from the UN escrow account], all of which were directly translatable into food, medicine and other humanitarian goods that were supposed to reach the Iraqi people'.[66] The suit claimed that: 'The resulting damage in human suffering caused to the Republic of Iraq and to the people of Iraq is virtually incalculable'.[67]

Again we focus on the conduct of the lawyers as a context for our following discussion of lawyers' ethics. While the kickbacks were initially designed and implemented without the assistance of AWB's in-house lawyers, when AWB's legal division became aware of the arrangement, it did not advise against it but facilitated its continuation and cover-up because to have interfered with the arrangement would have put Australian wheat sales at risk. In his report on AWB's role in the kickback scheme, Commissioner Cole criticized 'so called' legal advice that was in fact an attempt to hide from the UNAWB payments to Iraq and to make it 'at least arguable' that the transactions did not breach UN sanctions.[68] He also found that internal and external counsel knew about a separate sham agreement designed to extract further monies from the UN account, but did not advise against it.[69]

The AWB lawyers practised law in downtown Melbourne, but their legal work supported a corrupt scheme with global adverse ramifications. As well as the dire consequences for the Iraqi people, AWB lost its reputation, shareholders lost half the value of their investment, millions of dollars of Australian trade with Iraq was forfeited, and a shadow was cast over Australia's reputation in international trade.[70] On one view, the AWB scandal was instrumental in Australia's slipping out of the top 10 least corrupt countries, as measured by Transparency International's 2007 Corruption Perceptions Index.[71]

3.4.3 *The Baku–Tbilisi–Ceyhan (BTC) pipeline*

Our third case study is the conceiving, negotiation, construction and operation of a 'mega-development',[72] the BTC pipeline.[73] Operated by an international consortium of energy companies,[74] the pipeline carries oil more than 1,600 kilometres, from under the Caspian Sea to the Mediterranean Sea, for export to Western markets.[75] The pipeline crosses Azerbaijan, Georgia and Turkey, each of which has agreed to the free passage of the pipeline under a series of 'host government agreements' with the consortium, and an intergovernmental treaty.[76]

Private law firms acting for the transnational consortium companies and host states crafted the pipeline's legal structure over many years. While some have hailed the pipeline as a 'model of highest standards, responsible corporate behaviour and the positive influence of [international financial institutions'] participation in projects',[77] there has been sustained criticism of it from communities along the pipeline and international observers, who see the legal architecture of BTC as privileging protection for the transnational corporations over human rights, state sovereignty and environmental concerns.[78] Indeed, it appears that the risk of adverse consequences of the BTC mega-development are 'well beyond manageable by the sorts of technocratic efforts' of the consortium,[79] and 'the reality is that BTC impacts upon highly marginalized communities' in ways that cannot be controlled.[80]

When crafting the legal architecture to underpin the BTC pipeline (described as the 'contract of the century'),[81] the BTC consortium lawyers used 'concepts and authority from international law where convenient and discard[ed] others where not'.[82] For example, the principle of 'freedom of transit of petroleum' does not exist in international law, but this did not prevent the team of transnational lawyers making the 'doctrinal leap' to create it without reference to plausible precedent.[83] The lawyers represented the interests of the mega-development in 'weakened facilitative host states without due critical attention',[84] and their handiwork has significant adverse repercussions for the communities living along the pipeline, for citizens of the host states and, because of its precedent value, for pipeline communities around the globe.[85] For example, the intergovernmental treaty between the Azerbaijan Republic, Georgia and the Republic of Turkey ensures 'the principle of freedom of transit of petroleum' by restricting future regulatory law developments, expediting the expropriation of land needed for the pipeline, and indemnifying the consortium from liability for human rights violations resulting from pipeline security measures.[86]

The BTC consortium lawyers were more than mere advisers and facilitators – no doubt conscious of the concerns of the pipeline communities about the economic, human rights and environmental impacts of the pipeline, they nonetheless created a legal architecture that 'exemplifies if not surpasses traditional mega-development arrangements in its potential to curtail pipeline-affected communities' avenues of redress'.[87]

3.5 Lawyers as gatekeepers

In the inquiries, reports, recriminations and soul-searching generated by events such as the Enron collapse and the AWB transactions, it is common – and understandable – that people ask: 'Where were the lawyers?'[88] and 'How could the legal profession let this happen?'[89] As the adverse ramifications of the BTC pipeline are felt by the communities living along the pipeline and more widely, similar questions are being asked of the design of that project.[90] People see lawyers as 'gatekeepers of their corporate clients' conduct'[91] because, to all appearances, 'lawyers are positioned to be suspicious of and to discourage the misconduct [that corporate] transactions can disguise'.[92] Commentators do not argue that lawyers were solely or even principally responsible for these events, but they recognize that lawyers were involved as advisers and facilitators.[93]

As tempting as it is to ask 'Why didn't the lawyers act as gatekeepers?' there are good reasons for pausing, and considering first the environment within which the lawyers were working and the effect it may have had on them. How reasonable *is* it to expect lawyers to act as gatekeepers?

Along with cognitive psychology,[94] a relatively recent and promising area of research – identity theory[95] – offers insights as to why lawyers behave as they do when confronted with clients' outright unethical behaviour (as in the case of AWB), clearly questionable behaviour (as in the case of Enron) or short-term interests that threaten to damage the rule of law, fundamental rights or the environment (as in the case of BTC). Identity theory emphasizes the significance of a lawyer's organizational work environment to their ethical decision-making.

Regan's analysis of the conduct of the Enron lawyers, for example, focuses on their working environment to give 'an appreciation of the circumstances in which a given set of lawyers operated',[96] enabling us to 'imagine the world as these lawyers may have seen it as the events unfolded'.[97] Regan suggests that the essentially problematic nature of the Enron lawyers' conduct – a willingness to settle for formal over substantive compliance[98] – was supported by three rationalizations: deference to other experts; refuge in narrowly defined responsibility; and deference to a client's business judgments.[99] He notes that such rationalizations will thrive in a 'deal-making culture that bristles at any obstacle to moving forward'.[100]

Similarly, in relation to AWB, Hall and Holmes comment that in the 'cutthroat commercial world in which AWB operated, economic rationalizations clearly dominated decision making by AWB officers, including lawyers, and that those rationalizations strongly influenced the in-house lawyers' decision making'.[101] AWB's 'trade at all costs' culture permeated the AWB legal department and compromised its objectivity and independence.[102]

While the activities of both Enron and AWB have been the subject of independent inquiry, through which we have a detailed account of the lawyers' roles, there has not been any such inquiry into BTC, nor any apparent need or call for one. As Regan pointed out in relation to Enron, without the advantage of an external review: 'gaining an appreciation of the circumstances in which a given set of lawyers operated can be difficult, because it requires access to details about the texture of practice that often are unavailable'.[103] We do not have 'access to details about the texture of practice' of the BTC consortium lawyers, and so cannot analyse the decisions they made to structure the pipeline deal as they did. We can, however, note the circumstances in which those lawyers were operating: they worked outside the jurisdictions in which the effects of their work would be felt; they exercised considerable if not decisive influence on the conduct of the BTC business; and they did so while working with 'weakened facilitative host states'.[104]

3.6 Lawyers' accountability

When harm is done, and there are recriminations, the remedy is often a simple positivist one: rules are changed or introduced, and enforcement is pursued with vigour. The Enron collapse resulted in the Sarbanes-Oxley Act of 2002,[105] and Wald's proposed response to lawyers' complicity in the collapse was that 'reform efforts should focus on stricter enforcement of the existing rules'.[106] Campbell and Gaetke's proposed response of 'certain structural changes in corporate governance'[107] is in reality only more, and differently worded, rules to spell out more clearly the obligations and duties expected of lawyers.

But rule-based responses are no more likely to be effective in the future than they have been in the past. Koniak notes that the statute books already contained laws prohibiting most, if not all, of the damaging conduct engaged in by Enron that was facilitated by its lawyers.[108] Lawyers' blinkered focus on their clients' interests, and over-identification with those interests, are phenomena unlikely to respond to rules alone: 'no amount of legislation is going to save us from the foibles of human nature'.[109] If lawyers' practice is 'dominated by a moral consciousness that encourages endless rationalization and wilful blindness, then the deterrent effect [of rules] is likely to be minimal'.[110] Pepper agrees that: 'moral questions are often too complex and multifaceted to lend themselves to rule-bound solutions'.[111]

Compounding the limited effectiveness of rules as a means of ensuring ethical practice, we made the point above that globalized legal practice goes to the edge of, if not outside, the effective reach of professional legal regulation. The globalized world is not especially amenable to regulation by state-based legal rules. The challenge, therefore, is to build not professional rules, but professional *cultures*[112] from within which we can reasonably expect a lawyer to not participate in, or facilitate, wrongdoing, and to act to avoid it occurring. An essential ingredient of such cultures is a conception of legal ethics that counters lawyers' inclination to identify so closely with their clients' interests that they disregard harm caused to others. In the following section we explore the alternative ethical models available to practising lawyers, and discuss which of them contributes most towards equipping lawyers to play a gatekeeping role.

3.7 Models of lawyers' ethics

3.7.1 *The standard conception of neutral partisanship*

Within the adversary system of law, the standard conception[113] of the lawyer's role is one of 'neutral partisanship',[114] a term that incorporates both the partisanship of a lawyer's zealous advocacy for their client, and the neutrality of the lawyer's position in relation to the justice and morality of the client's cause.[115] Nicolson and Webb summarize the common justifications for neutral partisanship: 'it is essential to the adversary system; it promotes human dignity, autonomy and equality; and it upholds the institutions of the liberal state'.[116]

Picking up on the last of these, Dare explains neutral partisanship with an 'appeal to pluralism'.[117] In pluralist communities, he says, the institutions of law – parliament and the courts – mediate between the broad range of community views on fundamental questions such as 'what constitutes human flourishing, what basic goals are intrinsically most worthy of pursuit, and what is the best way for individuals to live their lives'.[118] The institutions of law, Dare argues, are 'designed and intended to mediate between the diverse range of views of what ought to be done'.[119]

In the same vein, Wendel explains neutral partisanship 'in terms of the *legitimacy* of institutions and their associated roles'.[120] He invokes 'the legitimacy of legal institutions and procedures',[121] and argues that the legal system and its associated institutions, when operating within a 'reasonably just political system',[122] are designed to handle 'the predicament of people living together in a community who disagree about what integrity and moral agency require'.[123] He extends the institutions' legitimacy to lawyers, arguing for 'the special institutional role of lawyers as custodians of law',[124] and presumably Dare would agree. Wendel distinguishes this 'authority of law' argument from the 'highly client-focused' standard conception,[125] but in truth the distinction is in the justification, not the essential nature of the legal ethical stance argued for.

This reliance on the authority of state institutions, including lawyers, suggests a broadly positivist streak[126] to the justifications for neutral partisanship.[127] Wendel makes clear that his is an explicitly positivist stance (albeit a 'soft' or inclusive one, where laws' moral value can derive from their source)[128] when he proposes that 'the most general obligation of all lawyers is to exhibit fidelity to enacted, positive law ... [lawyers] are constrained to refer to the output of procedures that have been established for resolving competing claims about justice'.[129]

In summary, neutral partisanship requires lawyers to perform their roles 'irrespective of considerations of morality [such as] ... whether or not [their conduct] ensures truth or justice, whether their clients are oppressed or oppressing, and whether this protects or violates civil liberties'.[130] It is up to the institutions of the state under rule of law, not the individual lawyer, to decide which interests will receive legal protection, and what legal rights should be allocated to whom. Lawyers who decide not to pursue their clients' legal entitlements, despite instructions to do so, privilege their own moral view over their clients' and so 'undercut the procedures that allow the advocates of plurality of views to live in common community'.[131] A lawyer's view about the justness of a law is 'just that – her own view',[132] which must defer to institutions and procedures for dealing with that sort of disagreement'.[133] Precisely because neutral partisan lawyers operate within, and defer to, the institutions of the state under the rule of law, says Dare, their conduct is 'grounded in fundamental moral concerns'.[134] Similarly, Wendel sees positive law as having its own 'moral goodness'[135] when it has been enacted according to 'rule of law values such as generality, impartiality, and publicity'.[136]

As we suggested above, the 'rule of law rationale' that underpins the standard conception of ethics falls away when a lawyer's work is in jurisdictions where the rule of law does not operate robustly. A lawyer cannot justify acting on a client's instructions simply because those instructions are 'legal', or even 'not illegal', in circumstances where institutions of the state cannot be relied on 'to mediate between the diverse range of views of what ought to be done'. However, even when discussion is confined to legal practice within rule of law democracies, and institutions can be so relied on, the standard conception of lawyers' ethics has its critics. We explore the work of some of those critics now, and suggest that the alternative ethical paradigms they offer hold more promise than the standard conception does for supporting lawyers' ethical decisions in a connected world.

3.7.2 A contextual critique of neutral partisanship

Unsurprisingly, the standard conception of neutral partisanship has been the subject of consistent critique from a range of perspectives.[137] Alternative ethical models for legal practice include an 'ethics of care'[138] from both feminist[139] and Christian[140] perspectives, and a 'personal integrity' approach based on classical virtue ethics.[141] But, as Tranter and Corbin point out: 'Most critics of the standard conception advocate for a "contextual" account of lawyer ethical conduct'.[142] This recognizes the lawyer as a moral agent, having to make moral decisions in particular practice contexts. A contextual approach is not a radical rejection of neutral partisanship; as we point out below, those who promote a contextual approach acknowledge the legitimacy and usefulness of neutral partisanship in some circumstances. We focus on it because it is an approach to lawyers' ethics that would operate to reduce the risk of globalized legal practice contributing to clients' harmful conduct, and is at the same time a realistically attainable alternative to neutral partisanship.

The contextual approach begins as a moral critique of the standard conception of lawyer's ethics. It takes a less optimistic and less benign view of the moral virtue of the institutions of the liberal state and rule of law, and adopts an essentially realist perspective.[143] Critics of neutral partisanship from this moral perspective reject the view that justice will necessarily be done by law (even when made with 'rule of law values such as generality, impartiality, and publicity',[144]) and by the state's institutions (even in a liberal democratic state). Rather, they 'suggest that deep-seated social inequality governs the major western economies and that to rely on rule of law ... as an ethical guideline is naive, or worse, complicit in the perpetuation of that inequality'.[145] Nicolson, for example, criticizes the conventional faith in legal institutions as ignoring 'the unequal access of different social groups to the making and application of law, and the fact that law is already imbued with the values and interests of those who historically have held power in society ... [and ignoring] the fact that most members of the community are excluded from decision-making and that law tends to reflect vested rather than community interests'.[146] His view is that 'the liberal institutions of government do not work sufficiently efficiently, fairly and democratically to justify lawyers being required to leave all moral and political decisions to the holders of formal power'.[147]

Nicolson and Webb take this moral criticism beyond the liberal institutions of government to the lawyers themselves, and object to the 'lawyer amorality'[148] that is at the heart of the standard conception of lawyers' ethics.[149] Lawyers' amorality leads, they say, to 'anaesthetization of moral conscience'[150] and allows 'far too many dishonest and unfair lawyer tactics, with detrimental consequences to opponents, third parties ... and to the general public'.[151] In Nicolson and Webb's view, lawyers 'are always morally responsible' for their conduct, and lawyers 'are not entitled to quieten their own moral conscience by taking refuge in the argument that pursuit of this role is a moral act in itself'.[152] Similarly, Rhode considers that an advocate should not 'simply retreat into some fixed conception of role that denies moral accountability for public consequences or unduly privileges clients' and lawyers' own interests',[153] but should work within a framework which, '[a]t its most basic level ... requires lawyers to accept personal responsibility for the moral consequences of their professional actions'.[154]

The moral critics of neutral partisanship do not, however, completely reject it as a model of lawyering, and it is through this concession that the moral critique is refined to become a critique based on context. They concede that it is perhaps a necessary approach in criminal defence work,[155] and that more generally it is a default approach – 'the starting point for ethical practice in most ordinary situations'[156] – from which there may be discretionary departures – for example, to avoid engaging in immoral ends or means,[157] to promote law's ideals and values,[158] to avoid violating the rights of others[159] or to accord with common morality.[160] Boon suggests that, even for cause lawyers, neutral partisanship is the 'recourse' stance, from which they depart, 'blurring the bounds of neutrality and partisanship when they must', but perhaps no more than 'any other lawyer, for whom a full range of moral duties is constantly in play'.[161]

The point of departure from neutral partisanship (Boon's 'blurring the bounds') is the time (that 'must come')[162] 'when the dictates of individual conscience should outweigh even the strongest of institutional arguments and the apparent belief that in the long run it is better to trust the system to get the right outcomes than to seek such outcomes in each individual case'.[163] Commentators differ about the circumstances warranting departure, and about the degree of divergence required from neutral partisanship, and so the question of context arises. As Boon acknowledges, a 'full range of moral duties is constantly in play' for lawyers, and for that reason lawyers routinely compromise 'the boundaries of neutrality and partisanship'. Indeed, this suggests that the point of departure may be very early on in the lawyer–client relationship, so much so that a lawyer's own morality might *always* be a factor in the way they perform their role. Boon's concession that all lawyers blur the boundaries of neutrality and partisanship 'where they must'[164] highlights the weakness of the conventional neutral partisanship paradigm: it is tenable only if there are no forces at play other than the client's instructions and the expectations of the legal system. It fails when lawyers must negotiate other moral duties, such as a duty to third parties/society. And when it fails, then what?

Rhode's answer is to propose an alternative framework that takes account of context, requiring 'lawyers to assess their obligations in light of all the societal interests in issue in particular practice contexts'.[165] She makes the realist nature of her approach clear when she exhorts lawyers to 'consider the social contexts of their [legal practice] choices ... [and to] assess their actions against a realistic backdrop, in which wealth, power, and information are unequally distributed, not all interests are adequately represented, and most matters will never reach a neutral tribunal'.[166] In a direct response to the optimistic reliance on the institutions of the liberal state and rule of law, Rhode's assessment is that: 'The less confidence that attorneys have in the justice system's capacity to deliver justice in a particular case, the greater their own responsibility to attempt some corrective'.[167]

Rhode's approach obliges a lawyer to have regard to moral issues as they arise in context; Nicolson and Webb similarly refer to a 'contextually sensitive moral activism',[168] which requires lawyers to 'take into account the real life situation of their clients, including all their needs, desires and interests, and the possible impact of their actions on third parties, the general public and the environment'.[169] Against this, they argue, the influences that underlie neutral partisanship in turn undermine lawyers' ability to play a 'truly positive social role'.[170]

Of course, both neutral partisanship and contextual lawyering advocate in principle for a moral dimension to lawyering – who, after all, would say that lawyers ought to act immorally? However, they find their morality in different places. Proponents of neutral partisanship have an optimistic faith in the moral capacity of the rule of law and its institutions to do justice, while opponents are less optimistic. In practice, the difference will in part be illustrated by the scope of 'allowable' zeal on behalf of clients – neutral partisanship permits a lawyer's zeal to take their conduct (on behalf of their client) to the bounds of what is permitted by law, while contextual lawyering requires a lawyer to exercise judgment as to how far their conduct (on behalf of the client and within the law) ought to go. Parker and Evans anticipate that a moral dimension to lawyering will move lawyers to 'critically examine their own inclinations and commitments in each situation in terms of what justice requires'.[171]

But when a practice context causes a lawyer to depart from neutral partisanship, and to exercise judgment as to how far their conduct ought to go, they do not do so without restraint. A client is not then at the mercy of a lawyer's own idiosyncratic moral view, and the lawyer's judgment is made 'on the basis of principle (not personal opinion)'.[172] For Nicolson and Webb, there remain in place four underlying principles that maintain the conventional lawyer–client relationship: loyalty (a duty to uphold a client's interest), tempered by integrity (acceptance of moral responsibility for action taken on behalf of clients); candour between lawyer and client, and between lawyer and third party where not incompatible with the duty of loyalty; and informed consent from the client.[173] Rhode too sets some bounds on contextual lawyering, proposing that lawyers '[seek] ways of advancing justice without violating formal prohibitions',[174] and Parker and Evans acknowledge that moral activism in lawyering 'does not discount the importance of loyalty and confidentiality to clients as an important part of the way justice is usually achieved in our legal system'.[175]

Defenders of neutral partisanship suggest that contextual lawyering is a form of moral activism that allows a lawyer to pursue 'an imperative other than a client's goals', as Boon puts it.[176] The clear implication in this criticism is that contextual lawyering assumes that the lawyer will take on, with some confidence, the role of making moral judgments. But when Nicolson refers to 'moral activism',[177] he means moral reflection, not an overbearing morally driven intervention. Contextual lawyering requires only an alert and conscious appreciation of the context in which practice decisions are made; it 'forces lawyers to keep morality at the forefront of their minds'.[178] In practice, the point for a morally alert practitioner is that they are presented with the opportunity to decide how best to respond to challenges posed by the client's proposed conduct. They engage in what for Pepper is a 'fuller conversation', an 'exploration' and a '[d]ialogue' that lead to both a 'meaningful moral life for the lawyer and [a] meaningful moral connection between lawyer and client'.[179]

A transactional and advisory lawyer, alert to the context of contemporary legal practice, will be conscious that they practise in a globalized world which faces very significant challenges to its future. The lawyer will be aware of the possibility that their actions on behalf of clients could result in significant harm or good, far beyond the jurisdiction in which they are based. In the next section, we consider how a contextual ethic of lawyering may have alerted the lawyers in our three case studies to the harm they were involved in facilitating.

3.8 Practising contextual ethics

3.8.1 Practising in global context

As the case studies of Enron, AWB and BTC demonstrate, there are significant pressures on lawyers to identify (both consciously and unconsciously) with the perceived interests of their clients. Hall and Holmes suggest[180] that the neutral partisanship paradigm is too often used by lawyers to justify both this identification ('I'm just doing my job of zealously pursuing my client's interests') and the consequent sidelining of moral responsibility. Rather than working as a brake on unethical behaviour, the neutral partisanship paradigm can be used to rationalize unethical decisions and so undermine lawyers' ability to play a 'truly positive social role'.[181]

Lipshaw[182] comments on humans' capacity to mistake a comfortable stance on an issue – one that is agreed by like-minded colleagues – with what is right. The only check on this tendency, he posits, is openness to other points of view. The neutral partisanship paradigm militates against such openness – partisanship is not conducive to listening to other points of view; Langevoort suggests that 'individual lawyers will never be resistant to commitment-generated biases unless and until they see their relationship with a client as something different from a commitment'.[183]

In contrast, a contextual approach to practice encourages a lawyer to step back from a single-minded commitment to the client's interests alone, to weigh up competing values (including her own) before advising on a transaction, and to formulate her advice in a way that brings these competing values to the client's attention. Pitts proposes a contextual approach even in characterizing the 'client', and consequently the client's interests. He suggests that what he calls the 'true client' is properly seen as 'the corporation as a whole including shareholders and other stakeholders, as opposed to merely managers and directors'. Accordingly, a lawyer 'may and should advance the long-term and broader interests of the true client ... without damaging the rule of law, fundamental rights, the environment, or the extended enterprise'.[184]

If Enron's lawyers had kept in mind their 'true client', they would have had the opportunity to consider more deeply the implications of settling for legal form over economic substance in the transactions they facilitated. They are more likely to have ensured that they understood the purposes behind those transactions, rather than being content to defer to the judgment of others, such as the accountants. And they would have been less willing to characterize certain issues as calling only for business judgment, rather than for a stronger judgment from themselves as to legality.[185] These considerations may, in turn, have led to 'whistleblowing' before the Enron house of cards tumbled.

Similarly, if AWB's lawyers had worked within a contextual ethics paradigm, they would have given some thought to the implications for the global community of facilitating both the breach of UN sanctions and the receipt by the Iraqi regime of millions of dollars in hard currency. They would have considered also the repercussions of AWB's actions for its reputation and its long-term sustainability as a corporation. Such considerations are likely to have led them to advise against the kickback scheme.

Reyes describes the transnational lawyers on the BTC project as working 'behind closed doors in conjunction with the international oil companies and host statesmen'.[186] It is easy to imagine how this milieu limited the lawyers' consideration of the economic, human rights and environmental concerns expressed at the time by the pipeline communities, and of the potential impact their legal work would have on the development of public international law, and consequently on other communities who will be affected by similar future ventures. Lawyers working with a more contextual ethic may well have opened the 'closed doors', given more consideration to the interests adversely affected by their work, and discussed those interests more robustly with their clients.

3.8.2 *The challenges of engaging in contextual ethical practice*

Contextual lawyering is not proposed as an ethic of practice only for lawyers who *want* to make, or feel they *ought* to make, moral judgments; it is proposed as an ethical approach that is necessary for *all* lawyers. Contextual lawyering is not easy, and many lawyers will find it difficult – or at least troublesome – to have to grapple with moral issues, but this does not excuse them from the moral obligation to do so.

Advocates for a contextual lawyering ethic say little about how it will be achieved or maintained, even though Nicolson and Webb refer to the need for lawyers to have 'the capacity for a more sophisticated form of reasoning which recognizes the centrality of ethical sensitivity and "judgment" '.[187] Nicolson and Webb recognize that a 'sea change in lawyer attitudes' will not be brought about 'solely through changes to the content and form of current regulatory norms',[188] but their relatively brief account of how to instil a contextual lawyering ethic is similar to the more extensive account Rhode gives of systemic strategies: education, rules and regulation, accountability measures, market mechanisms, and so on,[189] while Luban focuses in particular on clinical legal education as a place for inculcating legal ethics,[190] and Parker and Evans rely generally on legal education.[191] As Rhode warns: 'To proselytize for heightened moral sensitivity is always easier than to instil it'.[192] What should be possible, however, is to encourage in lawyers a capacity for reflective practice.

3.9 Reflective practice

Webb's account of 'ethical decision-making' describes neatly what the practice of contextual lawyering requires: perceptive ability (with both cognitive and affective capacities), judgmental capacity, motivation to give priority to ethical concerns over other considerations, and the capacity to act out ethical thought.[193] Webb goes on to discuss in detail the type of legal education necessary to ground a moral approach to lawyering, and Boon usefully categorizes the challenges legal education faces in this task: reinforcing resistance to practice cultures, inculcating habits of ethical problem-solving and strengthening professionalism.

Discussing the same issue by reference to values, Maugham and Webb observe that:

> Often we don't think of our decision [as involving choice between our own competing values], which is why we sometimes end up with all sorts of niggling doubts or complaints after the event: it turns out that the decision we made was not a good one because it was actually inconsistent with the things we really value ... Identifying the values that we hold about particular areas of our lives, and assessing which of our values are most important to us ... is a powerful way of ensuring that our behaviour is congruent ... with our attitudes and values.[194]

This suggests to us that reflective practice is essential to lawyers' ability to engage in and maintain contextual lawyering. To redirect lawyers' ethical practice will involve introducing them to, or reminding them of, the art of reflective practice – the 'essence of professionalism'[195] – which requires practitioners to engage in 'reflective conversations with their situations'.[196] An essential focus of reflection is values: the lawyer needs to ask 'What are my values, and how do they sit with what I am being asked to do?' or, as Schon puts it, 'How should I live my life?'[197]

In commenting on evidence in the AWB inquiry, Commissioner Cole noted the failure of significant players to stand back and ask the simple question 'Is this right?'[198] In a similar vein, an earlier inquiry into the financial collapse of an Australian insurance company had suggested that:

> professional advisers [which includes lawyers], need to identify and examine what they regard as the basic moral underpinning of their system of values. They must then apply those tenets in the decision-making process ... In an ideal world the protagonists would begin the process by asking: is this right? That would be the first question, rather than: how far can the prescriptive dictates be stretched? The end of the process must, of course, be in accord with the prescriptive dictates, but it will have been informed by a consideration of whether it is morally right.[199]

If reflective practice – the practice of stepping back and asking 'Is this right?' – is important for lawyers working within a rule of law democracy, how much more so is it for lawyers working at the margins of, or beyond, effective rule of law or professional regulation? In such 'professional statelessness',[200] where the regulatory framework is weak or absent, lawyers have only, or principally, themselves and their own resources to draw on in deciding how to act ethically. Ethical decision-making is in the lawyers' hands – literally in their heads – and they must look within themselves, their professional training and the social context in which they are acting for guidance. In these circumstances, reflective practice is essential.

3.10 Conclusion

In this chapter, we have described two defining phenomena of the contemporary world: its connected nature and its challenged future. In our connected world, the influence that transactional and advisory lawyers have over the conduct of their clients means that they are in a powerful position to affect, for better or worse, the global impact of the clients' conduct.

We offer three case studies to illustrate how local conduct can have widespread and distant consequences, and how lawyers play an influential role in that conduct. In the case of Enron, lawyers advised and facilitated conduct that caused harm and loss to thousands of people in the United States, rocked the stock exchange, brought down an international firm, and led to prosecutions. In the case of AWB, lawyers advised on and facilitated conduct that breached UN sanctions and supported an oppressive regime on the other side of the world. And in the case of BTC, lawyers have constructed a venture that privileges protection of transnational corporations over human rights, state sovereignty and the environment. We suggest how these case studies might have played out differently had the lawyers worked within a contextual legal ethic. At the same time, we acknowledge the difficulty of instilling and sustaining an alternative legal ethic, and propose that reflective practice is essential if lawyers are to take responsibility for their own conduct.

Our thesis in this chapter is simply stated. The world is connected as never before, and humanity's future is challenged as never before. In this context, the world needs lawyers to recognize the global effect of their conduct, and to take responsibility for it. This need becomes greater as legal practice increasingly operates away from, or outside, both formal regulation and 'rule of law' legal institutions. While an ethic of neutral partisanship allows lawyers to avoid taking this responsibility, a contextual approach to legal ethics preserves and respects the lawyer–client relationship while requiring lawyers to take moral responsibility for the consequences of their legal work. The world cannot afford lawyers to do otherwise.

Notes

1 A version of this chapter was first presented at the Third International Legal Ethics Conference in Queensland on 13–16 July 2008. Later versions were presented at a Baker and McKenzie seminar in Sydney on 2 December 2008 and at the Centre for Commercial Law's Hartnell Colloquium at the at the ANU College of Law in Canberra on 31 July 2009. We are grateful to Adrian Evans for his support and helpful discussions, to the anonymous commentator on drafts of this chapter, and to Trevor Moses for research assistance.

2 See, for example, K. Armstrong, *The Great Transformation: The Beginning of Our Religious Traditions*, New York: Knopf, 2006, Ch. 8.

3 See, for example, D. Watts, *Six Degrees: The Science of a Connected Age*, New York: W.W. Norton, 2003.

4 M. Daly, 'The cultural, ethical, and legal challenges in lawyering for a global organization: The role of the general counsel', *Emory Law Journal*, 1999, vol. 46, 1058 n. 2 and extensive references cited there.

5 International Labour Organization, 'ILO says job losses are increasing due to economic crisis', press release, 28 May 2009. Available from: <www.ilo.org/global/About_the_ILO/Media_and_public_information/Press_releases/lang – en/WCMS_106525/index.htm> (accessed 7 October 2009).

6 The global population is 6.8 billion (July 2009) and expected to reach 9.2 billion by 2050: J. Glenn, T. Gordon and E. Florescu, *Executive Summary – 2009: State of the Future*, p. 4. Available from: <www.millennium-project.org/millennium/SOF2009-English.pdf> (accessed 7 October 2009).

7 J. Sachs, *Common Wealth: Economics for a Crowded Planet*, Melbourne: Allen Lane, 2008, p. 5.

8 See Glenn, Gordon and Florescu, *2009: State of the Future*, p. 1; D. Spratt and P. Sutton, *Climate Code Red: The Case for Emergency Action*, Melbourne: Scribe, 2008; Intergovernmental Panel on Climate Change, *Climate Change 2007: Synthesis Report. Summary for Policy Makers 2*. Available from: <www.ipcc.ch/publications_and_data/publications_ipcc_fourth_assessment_report_synthesis_report.htm> (accessed 25 October 2009).

9 But contra, see I. Plimer, *Heaven and Earth. Global Warming: The Missing Science*, Melbourne: Connor Court Publishing, 2009.

10 T. Flannery, 'Now or never: A sustainable future for Australia?', *Quarterly Essay*, 2008, vol. 31, 25.

11 Sachs, *Common Wealth*, p. 3 (emphasis in original).
12 N. Preston, 'Ethics sans frontiers: The vocation of global citizenship', speech delivered at the 2006 Aquinas Lecture, Australian Catholic University, Brisbane Campus, 8 September 2006. Available from: <http://dlibrary.acu.edu.au/research/theology/ejournal/aejt_8/preston.htm> (accessed 7 October 2009).
13 Ibid.
14 M. Somerville, *The Ethical Imagination: Journeys of the Human Spirit*, Melbourne: Melbourne University Press, 2007, p. 1.
15 The Millennium Project, *Global Challenges Facing Humanity*. Available from: <www.millennium-project.org/millennium/Global_Challenges/chall-15.html> (accessed 7 October 2009).
16 These are: sustainable development; clean water; population and resources; democratization; long-term perspectives; global convergence of IT; rich-poor gap; health issues; capacity to decide; peace and conflict; status of women; transnational organized crime; energy; science and technology; and global ethics: The Millennium Project, *Global Challenges for Humanity: Excerpt from 2009 State of the Future*. Available from: <www.millennium-project.org/millennium/challeng.html> (accessed 7 October 2009).
17 Ibid.
18 Ibid.
19 The Millennium Project, *Global Challenges Facing Humanity*.
20 International Legal Education and Training Committee of the International Legal Services Advisory Council for the Australian Government, *Internationalisation of the Australian Law Degree* (2004), p. 5. Available from: <www.ilsac.gov.au/www/ilsac/RWPAttach.nsf/VAP/(712B446AA84F124A6F0833A09BD304C8)~Internationalisation+of+the+Australian+law+degree.pdf/$file/Internationalisation+of+the+Australian+law+degree.pdf> (accessed 20 October 2009).
21 Similarly diverse geographic connections are suggested in H. Kritzer, 'The professions are dead, long live the professions: Legal practice in a postprofessional world', *Law and Society Review*, 1999, vol. 33, 731.
22 P. Bekker et al., *Report of the Task Force on International Professional Responsibility*, The American Society of International Law, 2007. Available from <www.asil.org/pdfs/taskforcereport.pdf> (accessed 7 October 2009).
23 This is so even if the globalized legal profession is better described as an example of 'globalized localism': H. Arthurs, 'A global code of legal ethics for the transnational legal field', *Legal Ethics*, 1999, vol. 2, 68.
24 See generally Kritzer, 'The professions are dead'.
25 M. Pfeifer and J. Drolshammer, 'Introduction: On the way to a globalized practice of law?!', *European Journal of Law Reform*, 2000, vol. 2, 393.
26 See also the definition of in-house counsel and related terms in Daly, 'The cultural, ethical, and legal challenges', 1057 at n. 1 and n. 3.
27 See the discussion of the 'complexity' of the idea of a client for a government-employed lawyer in W. Wendel, 'Legal ethics and the separation of law and morals', *Cornell Law Review*, 2005–6, vol. 91, 71 at n. 9 and references there.
28 N. Ziv, 'Cause lawyers, clients, and the state: Congress as a forum for cause lawyering during the enactment of the *Americans with Disabilities Act*', in A. Sarat and S. Scheingold (eds), *Cause Lawyering and the State in a Global Era*, New York: Oxford University Press, 2001, p. 217.
29 Ibid., p. 214.
30 D. Nicolson and J. Webb, *Professional Legal Ethics: Critical Interrogations*, New York: Oxford University Press, 1999, p. 166, a point also made in the Canadian context by A. Dodek, 'Canadian legal ethics: Ready for the twenty-first century at last', *Osgoode Hall Law Journal*, 2008, vol. 46, 44.
31 M. Regan, 'Teaching Enron', *Fordham Law Review*, 2005–6, vol. 74, 1140–41.
32 D. Luban, 'Tales of terror: Lessons for lawyers from the "war on terrorism" ', in

K. Tranter, F. Bartlett, L. Corbin, R. Mortensen and M. Robertson (eds) *Reaffirming Legal Ethics: Taking Stock and New Ideas*, Routledge, London, pp. 56–73.

33 C. Parker and A. Evans, *Inside Lawyers' Ethics*, Melbourne: Cambridge University Press, 2007, p. 225.

34 C. Sampford and S. Condlin, 'Educating lawyers for changing process', in C. Sampford, S. Blencowe and S. Condlin (eds), *Educating Lawyers for a Less Adversarial System*, Sydney: Federation Press, 1999, p. 174.

35 Ibid., p. 175.

36 Ibid., pp. 180–81.

37 C. Whelan, 'Ethics beyond the horizon: Why regulate the global practice of law?', *Vanderbilt Journal of Transnational Law*, 2001, vol. 34, 941–42, quoting Arthurs, 'A global code of legal ethics for the transnational legal field', 61.

38 Daly, 'The cultural, ethical, and legal challenges', 1111.

39 Kinley reports the 2008 estimate of the United Nations' Commission on Legal Empowerment of the Poor that 'some 4 billion people worldwide live outside the rule of law': D. Kinley, *Civilising Globalisation: Human Rights and the Global Economy*, Cambridge: Cambridge University Press, 2009, p. 216.

40 Daly, 'The cultural, ethical, and legal challenges', 1090–93.

41 Kinley, *Civilising Globalisation*, p. 189.

42 Luban, 'Tales of terror', p. 10.

43 Whelan, 'Ethics beyond the horizon', 946.

44 Daly, 'The cultural, ethical, and legal challenges'.

45 Detlev Vagts, 'The impact of globalization on the legal profession', *European Journal of Law Reform*, 2000, vol. 2, 411.

46 Daly, 'The cultural, ethical, and legal challenges', 1111.

47 J. Ham, 'Ethical considerations relating to outsourcing of legal services by law firms to foreign service provides: perspectives from the United States', *Pennsylvania State International Law Review*, 2008, vol. 27, 323.

48 For example, Arthurs, 'A global code of legal ethics'; Whelan, 'Ethics beyond the horizon'; C. Whelan, 'The paradox of professionalism: global law practice means business', *Penn State International Law Review*, 2008, vol. 27, 465.

49 J. Pitts III, 'Business, human rights, and the environment: The role of the lawyer in CSR and ethical globalisation', *Berkeley Journal of International Law*, 2008, vol. 26, 491.

50 A. Reyes, 'Protecting the "Freedom of Transit of Petroleum": Transnational Lawyers Making (Up) International Law in the Caspian', *Berkeley Journal of International Law*, 2006, vol. 24, 842–43.

51 D. Rhode and P. Paton, 'Lawyers, ethics and Enron', *Stanford Journal of Law, Business and Finance*, 2002–3, vol. 8, 13.

52 Ibid., 13–17.

53 Regan, 'Teaching Enron'.

54 Parker and Evans, *Inside Lawyers' Ethics*, pp. 177–78.

55 Rhode and Paton, 'Lawyers, ethics and Enron', 9.

56 Regan, 'Teaching Enron', 1162–66, 1172–76.

57 Ibid., 1186–88, 1195–99, 1213–17, 1240–41.

58 Ibid., 1186–88, 1205–10.

59 Ibid., 1220–25; 1238–40.

60 Rhode and Paton, 'Lawyers, ethics and Enron', 9–10.

61 Commonwealth of Australia, *The Inquiry into Certain Australian Companies in Relation to the UN Oil-for-Food Programme, Final Report*, 2006, vol. 2, pp. 1–2 (paras 9.1–9.8).

62 Ibid., vol. 1, p. xxi.

63 Caroline Overington, *Kickback: Inside the Australian Wheat Board Scandal*, Sydney: Allen & Unwin, 2007, p. 178.

64 Ibid., p. 117.

65 *The Republic of Iraq v AWB et al.*, 2008 Civil Action 59517 (SDNY), Original Complaint filed 27 June 2008, para. 5. Available from: <www.awb.com.au/NR/rdonlyres/ DC29E8CD-992B-4412-BF12-F8CD7CD7BF95/0/Original_Complaint_filed_ 270608. pdf> (accessed 7 October 2009).

66 *The Republic of Iraq v AWB*, Original Complaint, para. 5.

67 Ibid.

68 Commonwealth of Australia, *The Inquiry into Certain Australian Companies*, vol. 1, pp. lviii–lix.

69 Ibid., vol. 3 (27.424). See also vol. 1, p. lxi: 'The recasting of the [sham Tigris] transaction was done on the advice of, or with the concurrence of, internal and external lawyers for AWB'.

70 Ibid., vol. 1, p. xi.

71 On a scale from 0 (worst) to 10 (best), Australia was rated 8.5, down from 8.6 the previous year, significantly losing two places in the rankings, from ninth to eleventh: Michael Ahrens, executive director of Transparency International Australia, 'AWB scandal takes its toll, says corruption watchdog', TI Australia Press Release, 27 September 2007.

72 A term of art describing 'a class of large-scale, high-risk projects that exploit energy or other natural resources of typically resource-rich capital poor countries ... usually organized by consortia of transnational corporations in cooperation with state authorities, and financed by a combination of private investors, bank loans and financial institutions': Reyes, 'Protecting the "freedom of transit of petroleum" ', 845–46 at n. 13 and references cited there.

73 Also called the Baku–Tbilisi–Ceyham Main Export Pipeline (MEP): ibid., 844 at n. 5.

74 Shareholders (and their country of origin) in the BTC consortium are BP (UK), SOCAR (Azerbaijan), Unocal (USA), Statoil (Norway), TPAO (Turkey), Eni (Italy), Total (France), Itochu (Japan), INPEX (Japan), ConocoPhillips (USA) and Amerada Hess (USA): ibid., 843 at n. 5.

75 Ibid., 843; see also Pitts, 'Business, human rights, and the environment', 487, where the author seems to approve of the BTC's incorporation of voluntary CSR standards.

76 Reyes, 'Protecting the "Freedom of Transit of Petroleum" ', 844.

77 Green Alternatives et al., 'Baku–Tbilisi–Ceyhan Oil Pipeline human rights, social and environmental impacts Georgia and Turkey sections', Preliminary Report of Fact Finding Mission 16–21 September 2005, Ch. 7. Available from: <www.bakuceyhan.org.uk/ publications/FFM_sep_05.pdf> (accessed 23 October 2009); and see the account of 'transparency, accountability, community consultation and involvement, and environmental and social safeguards' in the project design: T. Carroll, 'Pipelines, participatory development and the reshaping of the Caucasus', Centre on Asia and Globalisation Working Paper 007, August 2009, p. 10.

78 See, for example, the Civil Society Analyses, and the reports of, among others, the International NGO Fact Finding Mission: Bank Information Centre, 'Baku–Tbilisi– Ceyhan (BTC) Pipeline Project'. Available from: <www.bicusa.org/en/Project. Resources.3.aspx> (accessed 19 October 2009). See also reports of the Committee of Oil Industry Workers' Rights Protection, and of the International Crisis Group, in Carroll, 'Pipelines, participatory development and the reshaping of the Caucasus', pp. 15–16.

79 Carroll, 'Pipelines, participatory development and the reshaping of the Caucasus', p. 13.

80 Ibid., p. 14.

81 Ibid., p. 6.

82 Reyes, 'Protecting the "Freedom of Transit of Petroleum" ', 880.

83 Ibid., 869; Reyes notes that one danger of incorporation of such a principle into an intergovernmental treaty is that the treaty in turn may help to create international law, since customary international law is created incrementally as state practices emerge.

84 Ibid., 880.
85 Ibid., 843.
86 Ibid., 844 (references omitted).
87 Ibid., 848 at n. 26.
88 D. Langevoort, 'Where were the Lawyers? A behavioural inquiry into lawyers' responsibility for clients' fraud', *Vanderbilt Law Review*, 1993, vol. 46, 76.
89 E. Wald, 'Lawyers and corporate scandals', *Legal Ethics*, 2004, vol. 7, 59.
90 Reyes, 'Protecting the "Freedom of Transit of Petroleum"', 847–48; 879–80.
91 R. Campbell Jr and E. Gaetke, 'The ethical obligation of transactional lawyers to act as gatekeepers', *Rutgers Law Review*, 2003–4, vol. 56, 9.
92 Ibid., 10.
93 Sargent lists 'basic types' of the 'varieties of complicity' of lawyers in corporate wrongdoing: M. Sargent, 'Lawyers in the moral maze', *Villanova Law Review*, 2004, vol. 49, 868–70.
94 See, for example, J. Haidt, 'The emotional dog and its rational tail: A social intuitionist approach to moral judgement', *Psychological Review*, 2001, vol. 108, 814; M. Regan, 'Moral intuitions and organizational culture', *St Louis University Law Journal*, 2006–7, vol. 51, 941.
95 See, for example, Langevoort, 'Where were the lawyers?'; Sargent, 'Lawyers in the moral maze'; H. Gunz and S. Gunz, 'Hired professional to hired gun: An identity theory approach to understanding the ethical behaviour of professionals in non-professional organizations', *Human Relations*, 2007, vol. 60; C. Robertson, 'Judgement, identity and independence', Case Western Reserve School of Law Research Paper Series in Legal Studies no. 11, April 2009.
96 Regan, 'Teaching Enron', 1141.
97 Ibid., 1142.
98 For example, ibid., 1179–80, 1189.
99 Ibid., 1172.
100 Ibid.
101 K. Hall and V. Holmes, 'The power of rationalisation to influence lawyers' decisions to act unethically', *Legal Ethics*, 2008, vol. 11, 151.
102 Ibid., 152.
103 Regan, 'Teaching Enron', 1141.
104 Reyes, 'Protecting the "Freedom of Transit of Petroleum"', 880.
105 Public Law 107–204, 116 Stat. 745; described as a measure to offset greed: N. Rapoport, 'The curious incident of the law firm that did nothing in the night-time (reviewing Milton C. Regan Jr, *Eat What You Kill: The Fall of a Wall Street Lawyer*)', *Legal Ethics*, 2007, vol. 10, 102.
106 Wald, 'Lawyers and corporate scandals', 84.
107 Campbell and Gaetke, 'The ethical obligation', 14.
108 S. Koniak, 'Corporate fraud: See lawyers', *Harvard Journal of Law and Public Policy*, 2003, vol. 26, 227.
109 Rapoport, 'The curious incident', 100.
110 Sargent, 'Lawyers in the moral maze', 884, although he does suggest that nothing may be as effective in changing lawyers' behaviour as 'a more stringent liability regime': 885.
111 S. Pepper, 'Counselling at the limits of the law: An exercise in the jurisprudence and ethics of lawyering', *Yale Law Journal*, 1994–95, vol. 104, 1607, 1610.
112 Pepper calls this the cultivation of 'moral habits': ibid., 1608; to the same effect, see D. Nicolson, 'The theoretical turn in professional legal ethics', *Legal Ethics*, 2004, vol. 7, 20.
113 The term 'standard conception' is used 'following David Luban [in] *Lawyers and Justice: An Ethical Study*': K. Economides and J. Webb, 'Editorial – Now we are six: The quest for ethical certainty in an uncertain world', *Legal Ethics*, 2004, vol. 7, 1 at n. 4, and see

the discussion in K. Tranter and L. Corbin, 'Lawyers, clients and friends: A case study of the vexed nature of friendship and lawyering', *Legal Ethics*, 2008, vol. 11, 73–77; it is also called the 'dominant view' or the 'libertarian–positivist' view: see W. Wendel, 'Civil obedience', *Columbia Law Review*, 2004, vol. 104, 464 at n. 4 and references cited there; and the discussion in S. Peppet, 'Lawyers' bargaining ethics, contract, and collaboration: The end of the legal profession and the beginning of professional pluralism', *Iowa Law Review*, 2004–5, vol. 90, 500–503.

114 See, for example, D. Luban (ed.), *The Ethics of Lawyers*, New York: New York University Press, 1994; Nicolson and Webb, *Professional Legal Ethics*, p. 162.

115 Nicolson and Webb, *Professional Legal Ethics*, pp. 162–65.

116 Ibid., pp. 182–83.

117 T. Dare, 'Mere-zeal, hyper-zeal and the ethical obligations of lawyers', *Legal Ethics*, 2004, vol. 7, 29.

118 Ibid., 38.

119 Ibid., 27.

120 W. Wendel, 'Legal advising and the rule of law', in K. Tranter, F. Bartlett, L. Corbin, R. Mortensen and M. Robertson (eds) *Reaffirming Legal Ethics*, Routledge, London, pp. 45–55.

121 Wendel, 'Legal advising and the rule of law', 10.

122 Ibid., 11.

123 Ibid., 4.

124 Wendel, 'Legal ethics and the separation of law and morals', 114.

125 Wendel, 'Civil obedience', 364.

126 Although '[g]lib talk of "positivist" accounts of law is dangerous, given the growing diversity of positivist positions in legal theory': L. McDonald, 'Positivism and the rule of law: Questioning the connection', *Australian Journal of Legal Philosophy*, 2001, vol. 26, 94 at n. 4.

127 See W. Simon, 'The ideology of advocacy: Procedural justice and professional ethics', *Wisconsin Law Review*, 1978, vol. 29, 41; and in Luban, *The Ethics of Lawyers*, pp. 179, 190; and see Anand's critique of Simon and Luban, and his epistemological defence of the rule of law as a source of legal ethics: R. Anand, 'Toward an interpretive theory of legal ethics', *Rutgers Law Review*, 2005–6, vol. 58.

128 Wendel, 'Legal ethics and the separation of law and morals', 102.

129 Wendel, 'Legal advising and the rule of law', 10; and see Wendel, 'Civil obedience', 376–89; ibid., 86–98, 100–109.

130 Nicolson and Webb, *Professional Legal Ethics*, pp. 180–81.

131 Dare, 'Mere-zeal, hyper-zeal', 31.

132 Wendel, 'Legal advising and the rule of law', 6.

133 Ibid., and see Wendel, 'Legal ethics and the separation of law and morals', 127.

134 Dare, 'Mere-zeal, hyper-zeal', 38.

135 Wendel, 'Legal advising and the rule of law', 11.

136 Ibid., 17.

137 For a survey of principal critiques of the standard conception of lawyers' ethics, see Peppet, 'Lawyers' bargaining', 504–14.

138 See, for example, Parker and Evans, *Inside Lawyers' Ethics*, pp. 31–37.

139 See, for example, the discussion in R. Mortensen, 'The lawyer as parent: Sympathy, care and character in lawyers' ethics', *Legal Ethics*, 2009, vol. 12, 14, citing in particular the work of Carrie Menkel-Meadow and Carol Gilligan.

140 See, for example, the discussion of Thomas Shaffer's idea of 'parentalism' in Mortensen, 'The lawyer as parent', 7–9.

141 See, for example, the discussion of the work of Thomas Shaffer and Robert Cochran in Tranter and Corbin, 'Lawyers, clients and friends', 79–81.

142 Ibid., 82.

143 Pepper contrasts the 'traditional understanding' of lawyers' ethics with a 'realist' view: Pepper, 'Counselling at the limits of the law', 1554.
144 Wendel, 'Legal advising and the rule of law'.
145 Parker and Evans, *Inside Lawyers' Ethics*, p. 245.
146 D. Nicolson, 'Afterword: In defence of contextually sensitive moral activism', *Legal Ethics*, 2004, vol. 7, 270.
147 Ibid., 274.
148 Nicolson and Webb, *Professional Legal Ethics*, p. 209.
149 See, for example, Wendel, 'Legal ethics and the separation of law and morals', 72.
150 Nicolson and Webb, *Professional Legal Ethics*, p. 224.
151 Ibid., p. 240.
152 Ibid., p. 213.
153 D. Rhode, *In the Interests of Justice*, New York: Oxford University Press, 2000, p. 67.
154 Ibid., pp. 66–67.
155 Nicolson and Webb, *Professional Legal Ethics*, pp. 194–97; Rhode, *In the Interests of Justice*, p. 72; but see Nicolson's clarification of this 'defeasible presumption': Nicolson, 'Afterword: In defence of contextually sensitive moral activism', 275.
156 Parker and Evans, *Inside Lawyers' Ethics*, p. 22.
157 Per authors cited in Nicolson and Webb, *Professional Legal Ethics*, p. 215 at n. 13.
158 Per William Simon and other authors cited in ibid., p. 220 at n. 34.
159 Per A. Goldman, *The Moral Foundations of Professional Ethics*, Lanham, MD: Rowman & Littlefield, 1980; cited in ibid., pp. 220–21.
160 Per David Luban in the works cited in Nicolson and Webb, *Professional Legal Ethics*, pp. 222–23.
161 A. Boon, 'Cause lawyers and the alternative ethical paradigm: Ideology and transgression', *Legal Ethics*, 2004, vol. 7, 267.
162 Nicolson, 'Afterword', 274.
163 Ibid.
164 Boon, 'Cause lawyers and the alternative ethical paradigm', 267.
165 Rhode, *In the Interests of Justice*, p. 67; see also Simon who, at a more general level, proposes that lawyers exercise judgment and discretion to do justice: W. Simon, 'Ethical discretion in lawyering', *Harvard Law Review*, 1987–88, vol. 101, 1083.
166 Rhode, *In the Interests of Justice*, p. 67.
167 Ibid.
168 Nicolson, 'Afterword', 269.
169 Nicolson and Webb, *Professional Legal Ethics*, p. 280.
170 Ibid., p. 223.
171 Parker and Evans, *Inside Lawyers' Ethics*, p. 169.
172 Ibid.
173 Nicolson and Webb, *Professional Legal Ethics*, p. 281.
174 Rhode, *In the Interests of Justice*, p. 77.
175 Parker and Evans, *Inside Lawyers' Ethics*, p. 169.
176 Boon, 'Cause lawyers and the alternative ethical paradigm', 267.
177 Nicolson, 'Afterword', 269.
178 Ibid., 272.
179 Peppet, 'Counseling at the limits of the law', 1564.
180 Hall and Holmes, 'The power of rationalisation', 137.
181 Nicolson and Webb, *Professional Legal Ethics*, p. 223.
182 J. Lipshaw, 'Law as rationalization: Getting beyond reason to business ethics', *University of Toledo Law Review*, 2006, vol. 37, 1020.
183 Langevoort, 'Where were the lawyers?' 114 at n. 156.
184 Pitts, 'Business, human rights and the environment', 500–501.
185 Regan, 'Teaching Enron', 1243–47.

186 Keyes, 'Protecting the "Freedom of Transit of Petroleum",' 848.
187 Nicolson and Webb, *Professional Legal Ethics*, pp. 286–87.
188 Ibid., p. 286.
189 Ibid., pp. 286–92; Rhode, *In the Interests of Justice*, Chs 6–8; D. Rhode, 'Ethical perspectives on legal practice', *Stanford Law Review*, 1985, vol. 37, 639–43 in Luban, *The Ethics of Lawyers*, pp. 447–51.
190 See chapters by Robert Condlin, Norman Redlich and John Ferrin in D. Luban (ed.), *The Good Lawyer: Lawyers' Roles and Lawyers' Ethics*, Lanham, MD: Rowman & Littlefield, 1984, Part 5.
191 Parker and Evans, *Inside Lawyers' Ethics*, p. 254.
192 Rhode, *In the Interests of Justice*, Chs 6–8; Rhode, 'Ethical perspectives on legal practice', 647, cited in Luban (ed.), *The Ethics of Lawyers*, 455.
193 J. Webb, 'Ethics for lawyers or ethics for citizens: New directions for legal education', *Journal of Law and Society*, 1998, vol. 25, 140.
194 C. Maughan and J. Webb, *Lawyering Skills and the Legal Process*, Cambridge: Cambridge University Press, 2005, p. 156.
195 D. Schon, *The Reflective Practitioner*, New York: Basic Books, 1983, p. 141.
196 Ibid.
197 Ibid.
198 Commonwealth of Australia, *The Inquiry into certain Australian Companies*, vol. 1, p. xii.
199 Commonwealth of Australia, *The Failure of HIH Insurance*, 2003, Vol. 1: A Corporate Collapse and its Lessons, p. lxiv.
200 Daly, 'The cultural, ethical, and legal challenges in lawyering for a global organization', 1111.

4   The emperor's new clothes: from Atticus Finch to Denny Crane

Paula Baron

> It is in the name of the father that we must recognize the support of the symbolic function which, from the dawn of history, has identified his person with the figure of the law.
>
> Jacques Lacan, *Ecrits* (1977), p. 67

> Bored? How can I be bored? I'm Denny Crane. Even the sound of my name fascinates. More, Sydney. More about me.
>
> Denny Crane, *Boston Legal*, season 2, episode 23, 'Race ipsa'

4.1 Introduction

Popular culture is proving to be a rich field for socio-legal scholarship. It has generated, in particular, a considerable amount of literature in the area of ethics. Fictional depictions allow us 'to explore the dimensions of lawyers' choices, both at the micro-level of a particular choice in legal practice and in the larger sense of how to "live a good life" as a lawyer and as a human being'.[1] In this regard, few characters can equal the influence of Atticus Finch in *To Kill a Mockingbird*.[2] He has been described as a 'moral archetype' that engenders 'continuing reverence';[3] a lawyer of 'uncompromising integrity and unquestioned skill';[4] a model of integrity;[5] a lawyer hero.[6] He would appear to stand in stark contrast to Denny Crane of *Boston Legal*, a character who could be described as highly unethical, licentious, aggressive, egoistic and possibly senile. Perhaps unsurprisingly, Crane does not feature large in the literature of legal ethics.

There is, of course, a difference of genres to be taken into account here. Finch is a dramatic character, Crane a comedic one. Nonetheless, the character of Crane has attracted some anxiety, particularly from some members of the US legal profession, for the negative image of lawyers and lawyering that he represents.

Conventional accounts would tend to place the figures of Finch and Crane within a general trend from positive to negative representations of lawyers that has occurred since the 1970s. This is a trend that has attracted some attention in academic literature and in legal professional publications. It has generated calls for more positive depictions of lawyers and for more effective public relations work on the part of the profession to improve the public perception of lawyers.

The purpose of this chapter is to offer a different reading of these two characters, based in psychoanalytic theory. Rather than highlighting their differences, psychoanalytic theory would pay attention to some intriguing similarities. On this reading, Finch and Crane are not so much opposed as two sides of the same coin. They provide insight into the links in Freudian and Lacanian theory between the law and fatherhood.

Through this psychoanalytic reading, I hope to reveal some underlying reasons for the movement from Finch to Crane in the popular imagination, and to show why it is that this movement provokes such anxiety. These reasons tend to be structural, located both within the inherent duality of the father and what has been described as the decline of the paternal function. If this is the case, the increasingly negative depictions of lawyers in popular culture cannot be remedied by simply providing positive images of lawyers in the media or by the profession collectively undertaking more effective public relations. Moreover, these reasons suggest that the ethical uncertainty that currently faces the profession is also structural and likely to continue.

This reading locates itself within the body of literature that examines the relationship between law and popular culture.[7] It follows on from a relatively small body of legal literature that explores, explicitly, the links between fatherhood and the law from a psychoanalytic perspective. For instance, Austin Sarat has provided interpretations of *The Sweet Hereafter*[8] and *A Perfect World*,[9] in which he explores the themes of fatherhood and law; and David Caudill has examined the relationship between the father, the law and psychosis.[10]

4.2 Popular culture and legal ethics

> Is there any place a law and society scholar will not go to understand law in its magnificent variety, complexity and uncertainty?
>
> Austin Sarat, 'Imagining the law of the father' (2004)

For socio-legal scholars, fictional narratives have long provided a rich source of understandings about law. Examination of fictional narratives can offer the 'promise of curing the deficiencies of formal law through highlighting alternative, less dominant voices and perspectives ... through the mechanism of empathy'. This is so because 'narrative often achieves its desired effects by appealing directly to readers' ability to identify emotionally and psychologically with the viewpoint expressed'.[11]

An examination of fictional narratives is not confined to 'literature' as narrowly defined, but encompasses those representations and narratives in popular culture.[12] Attention to popular culture in legal academic literature originates in the work of Macaulay[13] and Friedman[14] in the late 1980s. Friedman's work, 'Law, lawyers and popular culture', published in 1989, is widely viewed as establishing the field of law and popular culture, which 'concerns itself with how the legal system is connected to the imaginary life of [American] society'.[15] Friedman defined popular culture as 'the norms and values held by ordinary people, or at any rate, by non-intellectuals, as opposed to high culture, the culture of intellectuals and the intelligentsia'.[16] He defined popular legal culture as 'books, songs, movies, plays, television shows which are about law or lawyers and which are aimed at a general audience'.[17] To Friedman, law and popular culture had a mutually influencing effect: while legal culture – that is, popular opinions about law – had the potential to shape the law itself, popular legal culture had the potential to shape opinion.[18] Popular legal culture could 'illuminate the porous, permeable boundary between law – a legal domain – and almost every other ostensibly non-legal domain'.[19] This was in contrast to the orthodox view of law as an autonomous domain, bound by doctrine.[20] Popular legal culture is one of a number of powerful globalizing forces linking parochial national legal systems on the basis of commonly held values and beliefs concerned with matters such as authority, identity and choice.[21] The aim of the scholars in this tradition is not the traditional orthodoxy of seeking to fix or reform law:

> but to observe, analyze, understand, and converse with ... the consumers of the legal system. Their goal is not to shore up the legitimacy of law or its institutions, so much as it is to understand why law and its systems function the way they do in particular moments and circumstances.[22]

Academic examination of popular culture is increasing.[23] There is general acknowledgement that popular culture can provide not only insight into the understandings of law and the legal system in the popular imagination – what has been called 'legal consciousness'[24] – but also can reveal a jurisprudence of popular culture.[25]

Popular culture has proved to be a particularly rich source of material for scholars interested in legal ethics. This is because works of popular culture can illuminate the consequences of ethical choice. Atkinson writes that if abstract normative discourse, such as law and ethics, provide maps of what lies ahead:

> literature can show us what it is like to go one way or the other. It can show us what it is like to be the kind of person who affirms one set of values over another, to live in a world where certain potential human capacities and relationships, on the part of some people or all, chronically are left unrealised.[26]

In a similar vein, Menkel-Meadow observes that fictional narratives have been seen as valuable to explore the issue of lawyers' choices, both at the level of individual choice and in the larger sense of how to live life as a 'good lawyer'.[27] Simon, while expressing some caution as to the nature of works of popular culture, also acknowledges the benefits of an analysis of these works to further our understanding of legal ethics.[28] He writes:

> As ethical discourse, these works suffer from a preoccupation with extreme situations, a tendency to oversimplify the dangers and difficulties of

independent ethical decisionmaking, and an unreflective suspicion of institutions. Nevertheless, as social data, the works are useful in indicating how different popular moral understanding may be from established professional norms. And in their insistence on the limitations of categorical norms and constituted authority, they are a valid corrective to biases of professional responsibility doctrine.

The literature relating to popular culture and legal ethics reveals a widespread consensus. This is that the depiction of lawyers in popular culture – particularly cinema – has become increasingly negative over time. Asimow observes that negative representations of lawyers and law firms have been a characteristic of the majority of films involving law since the 1970s, and that this trend is an accurate reflection of public opinion of lawyers.[29] Other commentators have observed that 'the negative image of lawyers could hardly get worse';[30] that '[m]ythic heroes like Atticus Finch have been replaced by the anti-hero lawyer';[31] and that there is an increasing vilification of lawyers in popular culture,[32] with lawyers portrayed as greedy, inept or non-communicative.[33] McAuliffe observes that it is difficult to recall any recent movie that has portrayed lawyers in a positive light and that television depictions of lawyers are even bleaker.[34] Is this trend towards the negative depiction of lawyers in popular culture indicative of the fall from grace of the legal profession in the popular imagination?

4.3 From Atticus Finch to Denny Crane

I'm no idealist to believe firmly in the integrity of our courts and of our jury system – that's no ideal to me. That is a living, working reality! Now I am confident that you gentlemen will review, without passion, the evidence that you have heard, come to a decision and restore this man to his family. In the name of God, do your duty.
... I punched Jem. What'd he say?
'In the name of God, believe him,' I think that's what he said.

To Kill a Mockingbird, pp. 209–10

Of course we believe you. We even believe the part about the car being stolen. We believe it all, Ronald. That's why you pay us.

Denny Crane, *Boston Legal*, season 2, episode 8, 'The ass fat jungle'

The fictional characters of Atticus Finch and Denny Crane are considered illustrative of the general trend identified in the literature towards increasingly negative representations of lawyers. *To Kill a Mockingbird* has generated a substantial body of literature in the area of legal ethics. The author describes the character as 'a man of absolute integrity with as much good will and humour as he is just and humane'. Hyland claims that there is 'no more famous portrayal of a heroic lawyer than Atticus Finch'.[35] Lubet observes that the fictional Finch has done more than any real-life lawyer for the self-image and public perception of the legal profession,[36] serving in the public imagination as the 'ultimate lawyer'.[37] Both the novel and the film have been considered inspirational, motivating many people to enter the profession.[38]

Writers vary in their explanations of why *To Kill a Mockingbird* occupies such an iconic status.[39] Althouse describes Atticus Finch as a role model for those entering the legal profession who are concerned that they will lose themselves in an oppressive legal culture.[40] Finch's virtues, in her view, are his acceptance of duty, his moderation and a willingness to work within the system.[41] He has found a way to live as a good person in a flawed society.[42] Powell finds Finch's heroism in the ability to act so as to uphold principle, particularly in the face of public disapproval.[43] Similarly, Garcia claims that Finch's strength is his commitment to standing up for the oppressed.[44] Menkel-Meadow maintains that lawyer heroes, including Finch, are characterized by their commitment to principles and to justice, usually at significant personal risk.[45] Perrin believes that Finch's strength is his profound respect for the client, which Perrin is keen to point out is not the same as blind loyalty to the client.[46]

Others have stated that the novel has influenced professional integrity through its ability to invoke empathy.[47] Failing argues that it is Finch's 'aloneness' that strikes a chord with members of the legal profession. Members of the legal profession, she maintains, consistently seek to distance themselves from their firms and their colleagues by their capacity for reflection and their passion for social justice.[48] Practising lawyers have seen Finch as a role model for his 'gentlemanly' behaviour, belief in fair play, kindness, humility and respect for truth.[49] In the public's eyes, too, Finch is highly regarded, with the American Film Institute naming Finch as the number one in its list of the greatest motion picture heroes of all time.[50]

This admiration for Finch has given way to some criticism in recent years, and I shall return to this point later in the chapter. Nevertheless, Finch retains an iconic status and still serves as a model of integrity in many quarters.

In contrast, *Boston Legal's* Denny Crane, the founding partner and rainmaker in the firm Crane, Pool and Schmidt, is a decidedly unethical character. He is described on the network's website in the following terms:

> An outrageous, egotistical, unwavering conservative with self-diagnosed Mad Cow Disease, the one-of-a-kind Denny Crane is always eager to trumpet his achievements, his sexual conquests, and of course, his name.
>
> Despite his age, his declining memory, and the fact that his 'penis only works on medication', Denny still shows flashes of the brilliance that made him a living legend, and he is as committed as ever to his hobbies: fishing, drinking Scotch, smoking cigars, operating firearms, evading jail time, and of course, wooing women. Denny's past paramours include multiple ex-wives, a dwarf and her mother, a woman with a peg leg, a Barbra Streisand impersonator, and his one true love: Shirley Schmidt.
>
> With his 'name on the door' and his best friend Alan Shore by his side, he remains the one and only ... Denny Crane.[51]

There is some acknowledgement in the literature of the negative depictions of lawyers in *Boston Legal*. Berenson notes that television shows such as *The Practice* presented relatively positive depictions of lawyers, but *Boston Legal* reverses that trend.[52] Asimow also notes the movement from *Perry Mason* to *Boston Legal*, observing that the latter (among other contemporary representations of lawyers in popular culture) shows the adversary system to be fallible, not necessarily producing truth and justice. Innocent people are sometimes convicted; and, conversely, the guilty sometimes walk free. Lawyers deliberately blame people they know to be innocent to create reasonable doubt; their ethical practices are situational; the lawyers have personal and relationship problems and they are trying to earn 'big bucks (or at least a decent living)'.[53] *Boston Legal* has also attracted some attention from members of the legal profession. McAuliffe observes that he takes some comfort from the fact that an alphabetical list of fictional lawyers would place Atticus Finch before Alan Shore,[54] though he goes on to note that he suspects this is not the order in which the contemporary viewing public would place them. Watson identifies *Boston Legal*, among certain other television shows, as portraying lawyers as 'self-important, self-promoting, unethical, and dishonest'.[55] Clifford writes that he was disappointed in the character of Denny Crane for following the general pattern of negative depictions of lawyers in popular culture:

> From sticking a lit cigar in his ear, to blatantly hitting on female associates or turning down a gay Santa discrimination case because it brings up bitter memories of his kilt-wearing father are far from the reality that I know in law offices across the country.[56]

Keenan observes that, although it is unlikely most lawyers have an interest in fictional accounts of lawyering, many non-lawyers do. He watched *Boston Legal*:

> whose senior partner is William Shatner, who went from Captain Kirk to the lead partner in a Boston law firm. The episode was the most preposterous thing I have ever seen. It was fiction beyond a screenwriter's wildest dreams. Shatner was more believable when he wore a polyester jumpsuit and barked out commands to Sulu.[57]

Of course, it could be argued here that Keenan and Clifford, among others, just don't get the joke. Crane is intentionally larger than life, a comedic character. Yet Caudill observes that, even when lawyers find representations of law and lawyers in film unrealistic, members of the public tend to view these representations as credible. These depictions thus delineate the limitations and possibilities for law in contemporary society.[58] McAuliffe, too, argues that, although lawyers may discount such representations because they bear little or no relationship to reality, members of the public do not share the experience of the practising profession and may think that this is the way lawyers and other members of the justice system actually behave.[59]

If this is the case, negative representations of lawyers, such as Denny Crane, must be taken seriously as a reflection of the public perception. Hyland, for instance, argues that: 'The cinematic lawyer must be analyzed both seriously and critically as such portrayals are an important social datum which has significant consequences for the legal system'.[60] Asimow agrees that works of popular culture tend to reflect (albeit often in a distorted form) 'popular attitudes, misconceptions, and myths'. On this basis alone, he considers popular culture a worthy object of study.[61] There is some empirical evidence that supports the view that negative depictions of lawyers and their ethics in popular culture reflect actual perceptions among the public. The American Bar Association, in its 2002 survey of public perceptions of lawyers, found that the public were of the view that 'lawyers are greedy; lawyers are manipulative; lawyers are corrupt; and that the legal profession does a poor job of policing itself'.[62] This followed a number of other polls administered since the 1990s that have reflected a significant loss of prestige and respect accorded to lawyers.[63] As Asimow has pointed out, 'popular culture reflects attitudes and myths that are already deeply rooted in the common psyche'.[64]

Some commentators, such as Asimow, go further to suggest these popular representations may serve not merely to reflect but to *shape* public perception. This being the case, these representations are not only an important social datum into the public's view of lawyers, but they also have real consequences.[65] These include a negative impact on the self-esteem of law students; a tendency of lawyers to devalue their work, leading to career dissatisfaction and stress; and a distrust of lawyers on the part of the public involved in the legal system, such as clients and jurors.[66] Representations of lawyers in popular culture may also influence the future of the profession. Spikes in applications to US law schools have been seen to coincide with popular legal shows on television, including *LA Law* in the 1980s, *Law and Order* in the 1990s and, more recently and perhaps most ironically, *Boston Legal*.[67]

Given these linkages between representations and real-world perceptions and effects, there has been considerable anxiety expressed about negative portrayals of lawyers. Explanations and solutions for the phenomenon have been suggested.

In terms of explanation, Sadvari points to the demystification of the role and powers of lawyers as leading to a loss of respect for lawyers in public opinion:

> The more television, movies and books feature lawyers as all too fallible and more interested in material success (and sex), the less respect lawyers get. Perry Mason, the all round hero, has been transformed into Denny Crane, the sleaze ball has-been.[68]

Hyland argues that an attitude of suspicion and resentment towards lawyers arises from the alienation of the public to lawyers.[69] Asimow offers some very practical reasons as to why lawyers are held in such low regard by the public: lawyers will always be distrusted, partly because their task is to play 'whatever role and manipulate whatever law a client's interest demands'; lawyers tend to represent the rich and powerful and this breeds resentment; criminal practice is the most public function of lawyers and the need to follow process may not accord with the public's notion of justice; the public tend to associate lawyers with personal negative experiences, such as divorce.[70] He also identifies a number of factors acknowledged in the literature as contributing to the decline of lawyers in the public esteem: these include factors relating to lawyers themselves (rising incomes, increasing numbers of lawyers and increasing litigation, highly publicized trials); factors relating to changes in society (increases in divorce, crime and bankruptcy, increase in government regulation, increased public distrust in institutions and power centres, changes in mass communication); factors relating to the litigation process (perception that cost, delay and complexity have increased); lawyer advertising; bad public relations; and negative stereotypes of lawyers as human beings.[71] Nevertheless, he is of the view that negative representations of lawyers in popular culture since the 1970s have 'reinforced and deepened those feelings'.[72]

Based upon these explanations, calls have been made for more positive representations of lawyers in popular culture and better public relations on the part of lawyers and the legal profession to counter the negative stereotypes.[73] But is a public relations campaign likely to address the issue?

A rather different reading of the causes of negative representations of lawyers in popular culture is given by Epstein. In a thoughtful paper, he observes that 'there is something about American television's representations of attorneys that places them at the crossroads of contestation in popular culture'.[74] This 'something', he argues, is that 'they exploit cultural tensions that exist as the boundaries between public and private spheres break down in American society'.[75] He argues that:

> Although some in the legal establishment may argue that the public looks upon good and bad lawyers differently, it is my belief that all popular lawyer representations are potential sites of conflict and resistance, regardless of the stated agenda of the lawyer or the value placed on the lawyer image by audiences or critics.[76]

Epstein is of the view that this is because the administration of justice is associated simultaneously with liberating ideologies of Enlightenment, such as liberty, and modernity's dark side of repression and control. He cites with approval (though acknowledging a false dichotomy in) the words of Attorney Charles Rosenberg, a legal adviser for *LA Law*, who maintains that Americans have a 'schizophrenic fascination' with lawyers.[77] This is because 'the inherent contradiction of a liberating and repressive Modernity, I would argue, is inscribed on the representation of the lawyer'.[78]

Epstein identifies the pervasive representation of the 'lawyer-statesman' ideal, a modernist concept that was engaged in the nineteenth century and that privileged lawyers as 'manly, rational and emotionally aloof and [which] placed that lawyer in a sphere that was exclusively public and masculine'.[79] He argues that in television shows where the legal process is represented as androcentric public space, the lawyer-statesman is the lawyer for the people, but where the legal process is not represented as exclusively public space, the lawyer-statesman is used to 'subvert or parody the rationality and insularity of legal process'.[80] Epstein notes that while the lawyer-statesman ideal is a myth, it is a powerful one that privileges male power in the law and male lawyers. Despite the reality that male privilege has begun to erode and the public–private spheres are eliding, the myth continues to be highly influential in popular culture.[81]

These observations lead Epstein to observe that the predecessors to *Boston Legal*, *Ally McBeal* and *The Practice*, although a comedy and a drama respectively, are 'two sides of the same coin' – that is, 'serialized legal programs that erase distinctions between private emotion and public duty'.[82] They in fact subvert the concept of the lawyer-statesman through the conflation of public and private space. He observes that television dramas that focus upon hard-working women attorneys do not succeed in popular culture. This is because: 'Carnivalesque parody flourishes as a liberating force from the repressive Modern ideology that law is a masculine domain in which male lawyers are the most powerful'.[83]

Epstein's ideas are not identical, but move closer to, a psychoanalytic reading of the movement in representation from Atticus Finch to Denny Crane.

4.4 Two sides of the same coin

> Radically different as the second father – the father of the law – may be from the savage first father, they are hardly unacquainted.
>
> Peter Fitzpatrick

> The current president of the United States is George Walker Bush, son to George Herbert Walker Bush, whose father was the late United States Senator Prescott Bush, who, as an undergraduate at Yale, once wrestled my father in the nude. But that's a story for another day. Let's stick to the issues at hand. Denny Crane.
>
> Denny Crane, *Boston Legal*, season 1, episode 6, 'Truth be told'

It is the contention of this chapter that it is certain similarities, rather than the differences, between Finch and Crane that are significant. These similarities offer insight from a psychoanalytic perspective not only into the movement from Finch to Crane in terms of representation in popular culture, but into the nature of law and legal ethics.

4.4.1 Lawyer as father

Sarat has pointed to the 'ubiquitous presence of tropes of fatherhood in popular cultural iconography about law',[84] arguing that fatherhood is 'one of the key terms through which law is mythologized and through which fantasies and anxieties about law are expressed'.[85]

Issues of fatherhood are significant in the fictional lives of both Atticus Finch and Denny Crane, and intertwine with their professional lives as lawyers. *To Kill a Mockingbird* has been described as a celebration of 'lawyerly paternalism':[86] 'Atticus is the ideal father, the perfect prototype for the projections of paternalistic religions'.[87] 'For many lawyers and would-be lawyers, Atticus Finch represents the classic model of how to pursue a career and raise a family (as a single parent, no less) with grace and integrity.'[88] Indeed, the author characterizes the novel as a love letter to her own father, Amasa Lee, upon whom the character of Atticus Finch was based.[89]

In the case of Denny Crane, issues of fatherhood are also significant, although Denny's conduct is more questionable. Denny's father was also a lawyer. Indeed, he was a lawyer who disapproved of Denny's unethical practices. Crane admits to euthanizing his father, who he claims was demented (the murder of the father is, of course, a central theme in psychoanalytic understandings of law, as is discussed below). Denny is also believed to be father to Donny Crane, an illegitimate son to a woman who is not named. Although it is revealed that Denny is not Donny's biological father, he assumes the symbolic role of father, regarding Donny as his son. In a significant conversation between them, Donny recounts how he went looking for his biological father:

DONNY CRANE: He lives in Maine. He works on a cranberry bog. Good man. Wears waders. Most days he's up to his knees in water and little red fruits.
DENNY CRANE: Sounds like a very moist man.
DONNY CRANE: (laughs) He's not you. Not the man I imagined growing up. Not the man I pictured in my mind when I was studying at law school.
DENNY CRANE: So you're all alone?
DONNY CRANE: (nods) Yepper. So? Any interest in being my fake father again?
DENNY CRANE: I never stopped being your fake father, son.[90]

In fact, the symbolic role of father is very important to Crane. His role at Crane, Poole and Schmidt is also quasi-paternal. He is the 'old man' of the firm and, as he is fond of saying, 'his name is on the door'. His relationship with Alan Shore is also paternal in nature.

The linkages between fatherhood and paternity are central to Freudian and Lacanian psychoanalytic theory. As Caudill has pointed out, Lacan's work is full of interrelated themes about law: patriarchy, religion, the Name-of-the-Father as a master-signifier, the distinction between the symbolic and the real father (so aptly illustrated by the conversation between Donny and Denny above), Freud's mythical father murdered by the primal horde and the network of law and culture that binds all subjects. As he points out, Lacan's theory 'culminates in an account of the function of law *as*, and not simply *in*, culture and language'.[91] These themes are ubiquitous in Lacanian theory because it is the father who institutes law in the social sense; and it is the father who institutes law in the individual through the exercise of the co-called 'paternal function'.[92]

Freud's myth[93] of the primal horde in *Totem and Taboo* is the explanation for the institution of law in societies. The now-familiar story is that the primal horde of sons cooperates to kill and cannibalize the original, all-powerful father who had held a sexual monopoly over the females of the group. The sons, struck by remorse and conscious that they, in turn, could be overthrown, established totems (representations of the deposed father) and taboos (prohibitions against murder and incest), binding themselves 'to be ruled henceforth by the moral, internalized workings of a law attributed to the now-dead Father'.[94] Thus, MacCannell argues 'law is no more and no less than the persistent struggle against the brutal fantasies that accompany its installation in the subject of the unconscious';[95] while for Goodrich, law is the speech of the father or, more technically, speech 'in the name of the father'.[96] The establishment of law, then, is characterized by the ambivalent relationship to the original father (what Lacan calls the symbolic father) – that is, a mixture of triumph and remorse. At the same time, there is no 'simple opposition between the archaic Father and the Symbolic Father. The two co-exist in the same subject.'[97]

In the individual sense, it is the father's prohibition of the all-encompassing relationship between mother and child that institutes law. The exercise of what Lacan termed 'the paternal function' – that is, the intervention of a third into the mother–child dyad – drives the child to the realization that it cannot be the mother's *jouissance*. *Jouissance* is often translated from the French as enjoyment, but it denotes something more:

> *Jouissance* is a legal term – in latin *usufructus* – referring to the right to enjoy the use of a thing, as opposed to owning it. The *jouissance* of the Other, therefore, refers to the subject's experience of being for the Other an object of enjoyment, of use or abuse, in contrast to being the object of the Other's desire.[98]

The child can, however, be the mother's desire by situating itself in the Symbolic order – that is, the domain of law, culture and language. Once the child realizes this, he or she tries to determine what it is about the third party that makes he, she or it desirable so the child can become that. This is done by recognizing what it is the mother wants symbolically – be that wealth, or status or power – and attaining that.[99] Thus, the individual develops objects and goals he or she feels driven to pursue, such as 'grades, diplomas, success, marriage, children – all the things usually associated with anxiety in neurosis'.[100] Many of our 'socially valorized' pursuits can be thought of as belonging to the Other – that is, objects of the Other's demand.[101] Although the exercise of the paternal function (ordinarily, although not necessarily, exercised by the real father) ushers the child into the social order, the child hates the father as a rival and oppressor for enforcing the incest prohibition. Like the relationship with the original primal father, the individual retains an ambivalent attitude to the father, marked by love and hate.[102]

Lacan had many names for the paternal function, including the 'Name-of-the Father', the concept that the function of the father is symbolic and based in patriarchy. This, too, is a theme common to both Finch and Crane. In *To Kill a Mockingbird*, the genealogy of the Finches is traced in the first chapter from the 'founding father' of the clan, Simon Finch, 'a fur-trapping apothecary from Cornwall' who established the family homestead at Finch's Landing.[103] This narrative device establishes Finch in a specific social structure. As Goodrich has pointed out, 'the social order is an order or law of prescribed places that the phantasm of an identity, a place, and a role in the social inculcates in the subject'.[104]

In *Boston Legal*, Crane's 'name is on the door' of Crane, Pool and Schmidt, and he repeats his own name in conversation (and in his sleep) – a ritualistic self-invocation of the Name-of-the-Father that serves to remind others of his place in the social order (and serves as a defence against the madness he fears).[105] The ubiquitous symbol of phallic power, the gun,[106] also features strongly in the stories of both Finch and Crane. Finch's shooting of the rabid dog[107] is symbolic of his phallic power, but it is a carefully controlled power. In the case of Crane, guns are also a symbol of phallic power, but power largely out of control: 'Do you think it's a sign of Alzheimer's if you can't remember how many people you've shot?', Crane asks.[108]

At one level, the very different reactions to the characters of Finch and Crane from members of the profession and from scholars may be attributed to what Sarat has termed the 'complex structure of desire and anxiety' that attaches to both law and fatherhood.[109] We both love the protection of law and fathers, but fear their power.[110] Both the father and the law thus have a dual nature: the all-powerful, all-wise, protecting parent; and the harsh tyrant who exercises power wilfully, cruelly and wantonly.[111] If we take pleasure in projecting onto Finch our longing for the 'good father' and 'good law', we also take delight in undermining the father of the law[112] enjoying the 'carnivalesque parody', to use Epstein's words, of Crane.

4.4.2 Father as lawyer

The link between lawyering and fathering is not only that the father institutes law, but that lawyers perform the paternal function for their clients. Clients seek the assistance of a lawyer because of concerns about their Symbolic relations[113] – that is, some conflict in the Symbolic realm (e.g. the alleged commission of a crime) – and/or because of a desire they wish to pursue within the realms of the Symbolic (the purchase of a house, for instance, or the creation of a company). As Kruse, writing from a very different perspective, points out, 'clients come to lawyers, not to get answers to routine legal questions, but to get help solving problems that are deeply embedded within particular contexts'.[114] These are, in Lacanian terms, anxieties generated by the individual's relation to the Symbolic order of language, sexuality and law. In response to these anxieties, the client seeks an answer. As Schroeder points out, the client's question to the Symbolic order, taken up by the lawyer, is that of the hysteric – what do you want of me?[115]

> The agent addresses the big Other with the hysteric's question, 'Che Voui?' when one negotiates a contract, or seeks to comply with the law (by, for

example, applying for a license), this question is asked in an inquisitive, but not accusatory voice: 'What do you want from me?' in the sense of 'What do I need to do to comply?' or 'What do you want from me in exchange for what I want from you?'. In litigation, however, the question takes on its more aggressive form of the accusation of castration. The status quo is wanting and therefore, should be changed.[116]

Žižek observes that the hysteric's question 'Che voui?' is 'to unearth the meaning of the opaque events in which I am forced to participate'. Each subject is 'originally decentered, part of an opaque network whose meaning and logic elude [his/her] control'.[117] The lawyer's role in procuring an answer to the hysterical question is inherently paternal: both castrating and pacifying. As Fink notes: 'The symbolic – the law – divides things up, providing a kind of distributive justice: this is yours, that is mine'.[118] Carlson observes that law's function is to symbolize an act: once the act is symbolized – made subject to the rule of law – the trauma disappears.[119] This is done through language. Just as the paternal function provides a fundamental linkage between 'signifier and signified, between language and meaning',[120] so the lawyer places the client's conflict within language and law. Similarly, Sarat observes:

> Law turns random events into accidents with causes, blameworthy agents, structures of responsibility ... In law, Craft contends ... 'the unpredictability of actual life is forced into an order that identifies cause and effect, innocence and blameworthiness.' Law provides the solace of a simplifying narrative. While many criticize law for its distancing, formal quality, for flattening the experience of dread, of loss, of mourning, Craft ... praises law for precisely this quality, for providing dignity in the face of pain and suffering, for providing coherence in the face of disorder.[121]

Indeed, this is symbolically recognized in *To Kill a Mockingbird* where, in the final chapter, Scout is lulled to sleep by her father's words.[122] In *Boston Legal*, many episodes conclude with Crane and Shore on the balcony of the firm's offices, pacified and engaging in friendly conversation, drinking scotch and smoking cigars.[123]

Clients seek out *lawyers* to resolve their relations with the Symbolic order because the Symbolic order itself bestows upon lawyers a specific and privileged position in relation to it. The granting of the privileges and powers of legal practice explicitly holds the lawyer out as 'the one who knows'. This is particularly significant in Lacanian psychoanalysis because it is the definition of transference. That is, the subject, by speaking, addresses his or herself to the Other assumed to know the truth: 'As soon as the subject who is supposed to know exists somewhere ... there is transference'.[124] Ordinarily, this means that the client will perceive the lawyer to stand in an authoritarian, quasi-parental relationship, rather than an equal and hence rivalrous one. The presence of such transference has been acknowledged by writers outside the psychoanalytic context. For instance, Binder and Price observe that clients 'are remarkably sensitive to, and easily swayed by, what they guess their lawyer thinks is best for them',[125] and will often make decisions based on what they think their lawyer wants them to do. Similarly, Vischer observes that: 'As the gatekeepers to a public sphere that is not especially amenable to the entry of personal moral claims, attorneys' responsibility for the question, "Is it legal?" often expands to de facto responsibility for the question, "Is it right?" '[126] Without a concept of transference, this phenomenon can seem mysterious. Thus Kruse, for instance, observes that: 'The question thus becomes, not whether the lawyer influences the client's decision-making, but how and why the lawyer wields that influence'.[127]

As a side note, if lawyering is linked so strongly to the paternal function and to phallic power, what are the implications for women in the law? As Boyarin has observed: 'The assumption that speech is a matter of separation rather than connection, overlaid on the assumption that Father separates the child from Mother, in effect assigns nature and animality to Mother, language and law to Father ...'[128] Despite this view of the inherently paternalistic nature of the paternal function, and by implication lawyering, it should be pointed out that Lacan is not of the view that the paternal function is always, or should be, played by a man.[129] In Lacanian theory, women are quite capable of exercising the paternal function. Although Lacanian theory acknowledges the significance of gender, this relates to the way the subject positions him or herself vis-à-vis the Symbolic order. It is not a theory that posits an essentialist dichotomy between men and women. Thus, although the Lacanian view would support the emphasis upon the relationship between client and lawyer, the exercise of the paternal function is essentially 'castrating' in the Lacanian sense, rather than a relationship characterized by an 'ethics of care'.[130] However, the unconscious confusion between the paternal function and the 'real' or even the imagined father would explain the phenomenon noted by Epstein and others that television dramas focusing on hard-working women lawyers do not succeed.

To summarize, the similarities between Finch and Crane reveal the links between law and fatherhood. The very different reactions to these characters can be explained by the inherent ambivalence held towards the father, symbolic and real. At the same time, the progression in representation from Finch to Crane (and, incidentally, the 'fall from grace' of Finch exhibited more recently in scholarly writings on *To Kill a Mockingbird*) has an additional significance. This is related to what has been termed the decline of the paternal function.

4.5 From Atticus Finch to Denny Crane: reprise

> Jean Louise, Jean Louise, stand up. Your father's passing.
>
> Rev Sykes, *To Kill a Mockingbird*, p. 216

> DONNY CRANE: He's mocking me ... Dad, he's mocking me!
> DENNY CRANE: You're a Crane. Get used to it.
>
> *Boston Legal*, season 1, episode 3, 'Catch and release'

The decline of paternal symbolic authority was noted by Lacan but has been explored in more detail by the philosopher Žižek.[131] Žižek calls this phenomenon variously the 'crisis of Oedipus'; the 'decline of Oedipus'; and the 'decline of the paternal function'. What is meant by these terms is the decline of paternal symbolic authority, which derives in turn from trust in the Symbolic Order itself: 'the big Other's non-existence has attained a much more radical dimension: what is increasingly undermined is precisely the symbolic *trust* which persists against all sceptical data'.[132] Žižek gives the example of the judge who may, in reality, be a 'corrupt weakling' but because the law speaks through him, is accorded respect. When people see not the representative of the law, but the actual (wanting) human being itself, the authority of that figure is increasingly undermined. This loss of paternal authority is not the same as the gap that exists between the symbolic function of the father and the person who is its representative (the issue that Sarat acknowledges). Rather, it is the symbolic function *itself* that is increasingly undermined.[133]

This decline is linked to the fact that the two functions of the father, ordinarily separated in other societies, were united in one figure in the modern bourgeois nuclear family. That is, the father embodied both the pacifying ego ideal and the ferocious superego, the agent of prohibition.[134] This conflation of the real and the symbolic father meant that symbolic authority was more and more smeared by the mark of obscenity, and thus undermined. In Žižek's view, the Oedipus complex can function normally and accomplish its job of the child's integration into the Symbolic Order only insofar as this dual identity remains concealed. The moment it is revealed, the figure of paternal authority[135] potentially turns into an obscene *jouisseur*. Thus Žižek notes that with the decline of Oedipus comes the return of such figures:

> When the 'pacifying' symbolic authority is suspended, the only way to avoid the debilitating deadlock of desire, its inherent impossibility, is to locate the cause of its inaccessibility in a despotic figure which stands for the primordial *jouisseur*: we cannot enjoy because *he* appropriates all enjoyment.[136]

I have already highlighted the 'pacifying' effect of the law and noted that this effect is acknowledged in both *To Kill a Mockingbird* and *Boston Legal*. What is worth noting here is that, if pacification occurs through sleep – nature – in the former, it occurs through Scotch and cigars – culture – in the latter.

What Crane represents, and Finch does not, is obscene enjoyment. Crane is, in many ways, the contemporary incarnation of the primordial *jouisseur*, his enjoyment obscene, whether in relation to sex ('For what it's worth, I like chubby girls. I like chubby sex');[137] aggression ('Hey, hey, hey, hey, come on. With all that's going on in the world today, who among us hasn't at least once wanted to take an axe to a priest?'); the law ('I have an erection. It's a good sign. Let the trial begin. I'm ready');[138] or food ('Alan, you know, one thing you sometimes forget is, no matter how hard your day, no matter how tough your choices, how complex your ethical decisions – you always get to choose what you want for lunch').[139] Žižek has written:

> 'ridiculous, childish, foolish, stupid, silly, ludicrous, bizarre, grotesque, crazy, repulsive, burlesque, profane, superstitious, shameless, outrageous, revolting, tiresome, dangerous, barbarous, brutal, cruel, coarse, rapacious, vindictive, riotous, licentious, mad' – are not all these words eventually so many synonyms for *jouissance*?[140]

It is this obscene enjoyment that contributes to the 'carnivalesque' nature of Crane, and that so effectively represents the undermining of symbolic authority. What we see in Crane is not Finch's enforcement of law, but the appropriation and enjoyment of the desire that underpins the law. As Douzinas has pointed out, while law is closely tied to the structure of desire, 'the object of desire is always kept at a certain distance, as it is both proximate and barred'.[141] The performance of the paternal function requires repression. The professional need to maintain this repression, to maintain the necessary distance, can be deadening, turning the lawyer into 'an emotionally incompetent ... withdrawn, abstracted and frequently lost soul'.[142] I noted earlier Garcia's observation that Finch is popular among practising lawyers because they identify with his distance, his aloneness. Crane has no such distance. It is not so much Crane's transgressions as his *enjoyment* of those transgressions that raises the ire of critics. What, in fact, is ethics but the refusal to engage in *jouissance*, to enjoy the other as object?

Significantly, the decline of paternal authority signifies not only the rise of the *jouisseur* but an increase in ethical uncertainty. Žižek notes that a tendency for the lack of the big Other to be compensated for by 'ethical committees'. In so doing, 'small big others' are created, 'on to which the subject transposes his responsibility and from which he expects to receive a formula that will resolve his deadlock'.[143] This is because there is no longer a single reference point (either in nature or tradition) for conduct in which we place our trust. In Žižek's view, this uncertainty is both structural and unavoidable. Thus the considerable debates around legal ethics can be seen to reflect the loss of paternal authority more generally in the Symbolic Order.

One illustration of this is the way in which some recent literature casts doubt about the iconic status of Finch. Atkinson acknowledges that legal scholarship abounds with glowing references to Finch, and 'the current professionalism movement has canonized him as something of a patron saint'.[144] However, Atkinson finds the figure of Atticus troubling, his virtues the product of social and economic stratification that imposes the obligation to lift others up: 'Before we liberate them, they need us; afterward, they should be thankful to us'.[145] The virtuous are only those who are, or who become, 'folks like us';[146] the wrongdoers are 'poor whites'.[147] He observes that the attitudes of the novel show 'serious signs of wear, not just as permanent standards but even as standards appropriate to [Atticus's] own time'.[148] Similarly, Holcombe argues that the film 'obscures the very questions of class and race that underlie its mythic reputation, relying on a portrait of America as a place in which racism and hatred are incidental to social and political inequality'.[149] Lubet argues that Finch defended Tom Robinson, 'neither in the name of truth nor in disregard of it. He defended Tom Robinson in a way he hoped might work'.[150] Martinez observes that many lawyers have an 'Atticus Finch complex'. This is a firm belief in access to the legal system for all – a lack of which, she claims, not only offends the lawyer because of potential harm to the client but diminishes the lawyer's role.[151]

These are legitimate criticisms, and they reflect changes in societal norms; importantly, however, from the psychoanalytic perspective, such criticisms reflect doubt about the exercise of paternal authority and a lack of trust in the person who exercises it. Further, this loss is intensely anxiety provoking for both lawyer and client. Žižek argues that, although each individual in contemporary society is free to make decisions, including ethical decisions, there is never enough information available to determine whether the *right* decision is being made. The compulsion to decide freely is anything but liberating. Rather, it is an 'anxiety-provoking obscene gamble'.[152] Each of us is held accountable for decisions that we are forced to make without sufficient knowledge of the situation.[153] Moreover, this anxiety is exacerbated by the fact that, as the paternal function declines, clients are more likely to see lawyers not as authoritative figures, but as rivalrous ones.[154] Thus the lawyer is no longer perceived to be 'the one who knows' but as an equal – and a rival. Žižek argues that this loss of the symbolic function of the father means that subjects never really mature so that 'we are dealing today with individuals in their thirties and forties who remain, in terms of their psychic economy, "immature" adolescents competing with their fathers'.[155] Thus the place of moral authority from which the lawyer might wish to speak is fundamentally undermined.[156]

4.6 Conclusion

> the proof that the dimension of Law does not cover the entire field of ethics resides in the very fact that there are two laws, the public symbolic Law and its obscene superego underside ...
>
> Slajov Žižek, 'Ideology between fiction and fantasy', p. 1511

Much anxiety attends the increasingly negative representations of lawyers in popular culture. In one sense, anxiety that attends the loss of the 'statesman-lawyer' can be seen as mourning for the loss of the 'good' father, the pacifying father of Atticus Finch: the father who is 'manly, rational and emotionally aloof'.[157] Disapproval that attends the rise of 'bad' lawyers, including Denny Crane, can be seen as fear of the irrational, unfair, powerful, 'bad' father. But there is enjoyment here too, as we ridicule the father through the person of the lawyer. We also acknowledge – albeit often unconsciously – the decline in the paternal function, with its pacifying, even deadening, certainty. On an individual level, ethically, as lawyers, we can choose to be the ethical Finch rather than the unethical Crane, to repress rather than enjoy. The conduct of the 'good' lawyer, however, will remain contentious and many, alarmed by this, will seek to impose responsibility for this choice upon the ethics committees of the profession. Finally, the psychoanalytic reading of Finch and Crane suggests that no amount of good public relations or calls for positive representations of lawyers will conceal the acknowledgement, in the public psyche, that Symbolic authority has declined. It is increasingly apparent, although perhaps not always consciously obvious, that the emperor has no clothes.

Notes

1 C. Menkel-Meadow, 'Telling stories in school: Using case studies and stories to teach legal ethics', *Fordham Law Review*, 2000, vol. 69, 798.
2 H. Lee, *To Kill a Mockingbird*, London: William Heinemann, 1960.
3 S. Lubet, 'Reply to comments on "Reconstructing Atticus Finch"', *Michigan Law Review*, 1999, vol. 97, 1382–83.
4 L. T. Perrin, 'The perplexing problem of client perjury', *Fordham Law Review*, 2007, vol. 76, 1709.
5 A. Althouse, 'Reconstructing Atticus Finch? A response to Professor Lubet', *Michigan Law Review*, 1999, vol. 97, 1364.
6 C. Menkel-Meadow, 'Can they do that? Legal ethics in popular culture: Of characters and acts', *UCLA Law Review*, 2001, vol. 48, 1315.
7 Outlined below.
8 A. Sarat, 'Imagining the law of the Father: Loss, dread and mourning in the sweet hereafter', *Law and Society Review*, 2000, vol. 34, 3–46.
9 A. Sarat, 'Living in a Copernican universe: Law and fatherhood in a perfect world', *New York Law School Law Review*, 1999–2000, vol. 43, 843–74; also published as 'Rethinking law and fatherhood: Male subjectivity in the film *A Perfect World*', *Genders*. Available from: <www.gender.org.lockss.Genders1999.html> (accessed 8 July 2008).
10 D. Caudill, ' "Name-of-the-father" and the logic of psychosis: Lacan's law and ours', *Legal Studies Forum*, 1992, vol. 16(4), 20–41.
11 Note, 'Being Atticus Finch: The professional role of empathy in *To Kill a Mockingbird*', *Harvard Law Review*, 2004, vol. 117, 1684.
12 Hyland defines popular culture to include 'books, songs, movies, plays, television shows, and similar mediums, as well as those works of imagination whose intended audience is the public as a whole. A society's legal culture also includes books, songs, movies, plays, and television shows that involve law or lawyers which are aimed at the general public': W. G. Hyland Jr, 'Creative malpractice: The cinematic lawyer', *Texas Review of Entertainment and Sports Law*, 2008, vol. 9, 236.
13 S. Macaulay, 'Popular legal culture: An introduction', *Yale Law Journal*, 1989, 98, 1545–58.
14 L. M. Friedman, 'Law, lawyers and popular culture', *Yale Law Journal*, 1989, vol. 98, 1579–1606.
15 J. Carrillo, 'Links and choices: Popular legal culture in the work of Lawrence M. Friedman', *Southern California Interdisciplinary Law Journal*, 2007, vol. 17, 11.
16 Friedman, 'Law', 1579.
17 Ibid., 1580.
18 Carrillo, 'Links', 12.
19 Ibid., 14.
20 Ibid., 15.
21 Ibid., 18–19.

22 Ibid., 20.

23 D. S. Caudill, 'Idealized images of science in law: The expert witness in trial movies', *Saint John's Law Review*, 2008, vol. 82, 921–22. So far as its status as a sub-discipline of law is concerned, Caudill notes that the practice may be identified as law and film studies; as part of the law and literature movement; as a primary focus of law and popular culture studies, or as existing under the umbrella of law, culture and the humanities.

24 A. Sarat and W. L. F. Felstiner, 'Lawyers and legal consciousness: Law talk in the divorce lawyer's office', *Yale Law Journal*, 1989, vol. 98, 1665–88.

25 W. MacNeil, *Lex Populi*, Stanford: Stanford University Press, 2007.

26 R. Atkinson, 'Liberating lawyers: Divergent parallels in *Intruder in the Dust* and *To Kill a Mockingbird*', *Duke Law Journal*, 1999, vol. 9, 723.

27 Menkel-Meadow, 'Telling stories', 798.

28 W. Simon, 'Moral pluck: legal ethics in popular culture', *Columbia Law Review*, 2001, vol. 101, 421.

29 M. Asimow, 'Bad lawyers in the movies', *Nova Law Review*, 2000, vol. 24, 535.

30 Caudill, 'Idealized images', 927.

31 Hyland, 'Creative malpractice', 237.

32 P. L. Garcia, 'Did you hear the one about the lawyer?', *Texas Bar Journal*, 2007, vol. 70, 960–61.

33 R. A. Clifford, 'Popular media paints unrealistic portrait of lawyers (… and what we can do about it)', *Chicago Bar Association Record*, 2005, 267–70.

34 D. J. McAuliffe, 'Real world lawyers', *Arizona Attorney*, 2007, October, 6.

35 Hyland, 'Creative malpractice', 237.

36 S. Lubet, 'Reconstructing Atticus Finch', *Michigan Law Review*, 1999, vol. 97, 1339–84.

37 Ibid., 1340.

38 See further T. L. Shaffer, 'The moral theology of Atticus Finch', *University of Pittsburgh Law Review*, 1981, vol. 42, 181–224; C. Johnson, 'The secret courts of men's hearts: Code and law in Harper Lee's *To Kill a Mockingbird*', *Studies in American Fiction*, 1991, vol. 19, 129–39; and generally, C. Johnson, 'Symposium: *To Kill a Mockingbird*', *Alabama Law Review*, 1994, vol. 45, 389–584. Practising lawyers, as well as academics, have acknowledged the character of Finch as being inspirational. See, for example, B. Haltom, 'But seriously folks! Gregory Peck was perfect for the role', *Tennessee Bar Journal*, 2007, vol. 43, 34. Simon, 'Moral pluck', 2, notes that Kenneth Starr invoked Finch as an ethical role model in a speech to a South Carolina Bar Association during the Clinton impeachment crisis. See also J. A. Stein, 'Atticus Finch, LLP – formerly PC, formerly LLC'. Available from: <www.dcbar.org/for_lawyers/washington_lawyer/may_2002/spectator.cfm> (accessed 14 June 2006).

39 Note, 'Being Atticus', p. 1685. That status is conferred on the movie, as well as the book. See, for instance, M. Holcombe, '*To Kill a Mockingbird*', *Film Quarterly*, 2002, vol. 55, 35–36, who notes that the film 'is actually not, in purely technical terms, a cinematic masterpiece' but derives its impact from a 'convergence of powerful feelings of nostalgia and the movie's standing as … a "social problem" film'.

40 Althouse, 'Reconstructing Atticus', 1364.

41 Ibid., 1365.

42 Ibid., 1369.

43 B. V. Powell, 'A reaction: "Stand up, your father [a lawyer] is passing" ', *Michigan Law Review*, 1999, vol. 97, 1373–75.

44 Garcia, 'Did you hear?', 960.

45 Menkel-Meadow, 'Can they do that?', 1315.

46 Perrin, 'The perplexing problem', 1729.

47 Note, 'Being Atticus', 1682.

48 M. A. Failinger, 'Gentleman as hero: Atticus Finch and the lonely path', *Journal of Law and Religion*, 1993–94, vol. 10, 308.

49 W. Gross, 'To save a mockingbird', *Orange County Lawyer*, 2008, 18.
50 S. A. Goldman, 'In defense of the damned', *Ohio State Journal of Criminal Law*, 2007–8, vol. 5, 611–28.
51 ABC, *Boston Legal*. Available from: <http://abc.go.com/primetime/bostonlegal/index?pn=bios#t=character&d=30236> (accessed 8 July 2008).
52 S. K. Berenson, 'Passion is no ordinary word', *Albany Law Review*, 2008, vol. 71, 171, note 38.
53 M. Asimow, 'Popular culture and the adversary system', *Loyola of Los Angeles Law Review*, 2007, vol. 40, 678.
54 McAuliffe, 'Real world', 6.
55 T. J. Watson, 'Improving lawyers' image starts with client relations', *Wisconsin Lawyer*, 2007, vol. 80, 23.
56 Clifford, 'Popular media', 267.
57 M. Keenan, 'We knew the real killer before the first commercial break', *Journal of the Kansas Bar Association*, 2006, vol. 9, 9.
58 Caudill, 'Idealised images', 923.
59 McAuliffe, 'Real world', 6.
60 Hyland, 'Real world', 231.
61 Asimow, 'Bad lawyers', 550.
62 American Bar Association, *Public Perceptions of Lawyers: Consumer Research Findings*, 2002, cited in Caudill, 'Idealised images', 927, note 28.
63 Asimow, 'Bad lawyers', 535.
64 Ibid., 549.
65 Ibid., 535.
66 Ibid., 541–42.
67 M. Finnemore, 'She knows the score', *Oregon State Bar Bulletin*, 2006, 35.
68 G. Sadvari, 'Review: *The New Lawyer: How Settlement is Transforming the Practice of Law*, Vancouver: UBC Press, 2008 Julie Macfarlane', *Queen's Law Journal*, 2008, vol. 33, 635–38.
69 Hyland, 'Creative malpractice', 237.
70 Asimow, 'Bad lawyers', 536–37.
71 Ibid., 544–49.
72 Ibid., 582.
73 See, for instance, McAuliffe, 'Real world', note 6.
74 M. M. Epstein, 'For and against the people: Television's prosecutor image and the cultural power of the legal profession', *University of Toledo Law Review*, 2002–3, vol. 34, 817–46.
75 Ibid., 818.
76 Ibid., 820.
77 Ibid., 823.
78 Ibid., 824.
79 Ibid., 817.
80 Ibid., 817–18.
81 Ibid., 846.
82 Ibid., 839.
83 Ibid., 845.
84 Sarat, 'Living in a Copernican', notes 8, 9.
85 Ibid., note 3.
86 Atkinson, 'Liberating lawyers', 601.
87 Ibid., 691.
88 Note, 'Being Atticus', 1688.
89 Atkinson 'Liberating lawyers', 726.
90 *Boston Legal*, season 2, episode 5, 'Squid pro quo'.
91 Caudill, 'Name of the Father', 422.

92 That is to say, Lacan's schema was descriptive rather than normative. Lacan and Freud were of the view that the Oedipus process is universal, but this is not to say that it is always experienced within the Western nuclear family form. For discussions of the way in which the nuclear family form is historically and culturally specific, see for instance, J. Butler, *Gender Trouble: Feminism and the Subversion of Identity*, New York: Routledge, 1990, p. 36; R. Collier, *Masculinity, Law and the Family*, London: Routledge, 1995, p. 185; J. Mitchell, *Psychoanalysis and Feminism*, New York: Pantheon, 1974, pp. 378–79; S. E. Dalton, 'From presumed fathers to lesbian mothers: Sex discrimination and the legal construction of parenthood', *Michigan Journal of Gender and Law*, 2003, vol. 9, 322.

93 Much discussion has surrounded the problem of whether the primal horde is a myth or an actual occurrence. As J. Boyarin, 'Another Abraham: Jewishness and the Law of the Father', *Yale Journal of Law and the Humanities*, 1997, vol. 9, 350 observes, 'the psychoanalytic foundational fiction of the origin of the law and civilization is tormented by the dilemma of positing simultaneously that its origin myth "really happened" and that its "memory" is instituted as an unconscious explanation of unnatural restraints on individual will'.

94 Boyarin, 'Another Abraham', 362.

95 J. F. MacCannell, 'Between the two fears', *Cardozo Law Review*, 2003, vol. 24, 2408.

96 P. Goodrich, 'Maladies of the legal soul: Psychoanalysis and interpretation in law', *Washington and Lee Law Review*, 1997, vol. 54, 1044.

97 MacCannell, 'Between the two', 2408.

98 J. F. Guervich, 'The *jouissance* of the Other and the prohibition of incest: A Lacanian perspective', *Other Voices*, 1999, vol. 1. Available from: <www.othervoices.org/1.3/jfg/other.html> (accessed 2 June 2006).

99 B. Fink, *A Clinical Introduction to Lacanian Psychoanalysis: Theory and Technique*, Cambridge, MA: Harvard University Press, 1997, p. 249.

100 G. Wilson, 'MLAlienation', Special Session, MLA Convention, Toronto, 28 December 1997. Available from: <www.langlab.wayne.edu/MLAlienation/GWilsonMLA97.html> (accessed 14 June 2006).

101 Wilson, 'MLAlienation'. Hence Lacan's often-quoted dictum that desire is the desire of the Other.

102 The myth of the primal horde and the Oedipus myth, are, of course, closely connected. As Boyarin, 'Another Abraham', p. 369 has observed: 'The founding repression, which results in the illusion of the totemic Father, is an exceptional moment that is at the same time "called for", anticipated as necessary for progress. The causality works backwards and forwards; the genealogy in which ontogeny recapitulates phylogeny is mirrored by a teleology in which phylogeny anticipates ontology'.

103 Lee, *To Kill a Mockingbird*, p. 9.

104 Goodrich, 'Maladies', 1038.

105 On this point, see D. Carlson, 'The traumatic dimension in law', *Cardozo Law Review*, 2003, vol. 24, 2292: 'A final merger with the Real is "ceasing-to-be" – negative becoming, or psychosis. The subject resists this descent into darkness by striving to recognize itself symbolically. To distinguish itself and thereby to stave off death, the subject must body forth and find its shape in the symbolic. There the subject finds the public materials out of which it can build a "fantasy" – the narrative in which the subject has positive existence to others'.

106 Guns function as phallic symbols so effectively because they are external to the body. As S. Žižek, 'Ideology between fiction and fantasy', *Cardozo Law Review*, 1995, vol. 16, 1521 has observed: 'Insofar as phallus qua signifier designates the agency of symbolic authority, its crucial feature therefore resides in the fact that it is not "mine," the organ of a living subject, but a place at which a foreign power intervenes and inscribes itself onto my body, a place at which the big Other acts through me – in

short, the fact that phallus is a signifier means above all that it is structurally an organ without a body, somehow "detached" from my body'.

107 Lee, *To Kill a Mockingbird*, p. 102.
108 *Boston Legal*, season 2, episode 23, 'Race ipsa'.
109 Sarat, 'Imagining the Law', 16.
110 Ibid., 16.
111 Ibid., 39–40.
112 Ibid., 41.
113 Fink, *A Clinical Introduction*, p. 33: 'What are symbolic relations? One simple way of viewing them is as one's relation to the Law, to the law laid down by one's parents, one's teachers, one's religion and one's country'.
114 K. R. Kruse, 'Fortress in the sand: The plural values of client-centred representation', *Clinical Law Review*, 2006, vol. 12, 374.
115 J. Schroeder, 'Can lawyers be cured? Eternal recurrence and the Lacanian death drive', *Cardozo Law Review*, 2003, vol. 24, 961, 962.
116 Ibid., 962.
117 Žižek, 'Ideology', 1529, note 27.
118 Fink, *A Clinical Introduction*, p. 98.
119 Carlson, 'The traumatic dimension', 2306.
120 Fink, *A Clinical Introduction*, p. 111.
121 Sarat, 'Imagining the law', 25, note 68.
122 Lee, *To Kill a Mockingbird*, p. 284: 'I willed myself to stay awake, but the rain was so soft and the room was so warm and his voice was so deep and his knee was so snug that I slept'.
123 See, for instance, season 1, episode 9, 'A greater good'.
124 J. Lacan, *The Four Fundamental Concepts of Psycho-analysis*, Harmondsworth: Penguin, 1973, p. 232. Although transference is a specific and pivotal phenomenon within psychoanalysis as a therapy, Lacan was clear that it can occur outside that context. At p. 233 he states: 'Whenever this function may be, for the subject, embodied in some individual, whether or not the analyst, the transference ... is established'.
125 Quoted by Kruse, 'Fortress in the sand', 379.
126 R. K. Vischer, 'Legal advice as moral perspective', *Georgetown Journal of Legal Ethics*, 2006, vol. 19, 272–73.
127 Kruse, 'Fortress in the sand', 388.
128 Boyarin, 'Another Abraham', 366.
129 Fink, *A Clinical Introduction*, p. 79 writes: 'The paternal function is not the function played by the individual's father, regardless of his particular style and personality, the role he plays in the family circle, and so on. A flesh-and-blood father does not immediately and automatically fulfil the paternal function, nor does the absence of a real, live father in any way automatically ensure the non-existence of the paternal function. This function may be fulfilled despite the early death or disappearance of the father due to war or divorce; it may be fulfilled by another man who becomes a "father figure"; and it may be fulfilled in other ways as well'.
130 The genesis for the ethics of care was C. Gilligan, *A Different Voice*, Cambridge, MA: Harvard University Press, 1982, which challenged 'justice-based' approaches to moral discussion as inherently masculine and rights-based and suggested that women tend to demonstrate an ethic of care based on responsiveness, relationship and prevention of harm.
131 S. Žižek, *The Ticklish Subject: The Absent Centre of Political Ontology*, London: Verso, 1999, pp. 313–400.
132 Ibid., 332.
133 For an acknowledgement of the loss of paternal function as reflected in popular culture, see MacCannell, 'Between the two fears', 2393, in which she analyses Thompson's *Cape Fear* and the Martin Scorsese remake of that film. She argues that

where Thompson's film deals with the return of the obscene father, by the time of the Scorsese remake, 'the power of any sort of Father has been radically curtailed – and so has the Law's. Scorsese's film presents a superegoic world in which the fall of the Father is complete: it pictures everyone as already freed from the Father and devoid of illusions about the effectiveness of Symbolic Law'.

134 Žižek, *The Ticklish Subject*, p. 313.
135 MacCannell, 'Between the two fears', 2406 notes the decline of Oedipus and its link to a regime of rights: 'The regime of legal "freedom" is one tinged with the aura of a right to *jouissance*. The sense of a "right to ..." seems to authorize the expansion of drive beyond the ability to contain it by tried-and-true Symbolic, Fatherly means'.
136 Ibid., 315.
137 *Boston Legal*, season 2, episode 5, 'From men to boys'.
138 *Boston Legal*, season 2, episode 10, 'Legal deficits'.
139 *Boston Legal*, season 2, episode 22, 'Ivan the incorrigible'.
140 Žižek, 'Ideology', 1516.
141 C. Douzinas, 'Law's birth and Antigone's death: On ontological and psychological ethics', *Cardozo Law Review*, 1995, vol. 16, 1330.
142 Goodrich, 'Maladies', 1050.
143 Žižek, *The Ticklish Subject*, p. 334. He is writing here with specific reference to internet communities, but the principle is very applicable to legal ethics.
144 Atkinson, 'Liberating lawyers', 604. He observes that in fact the majority of scholarship in relation to Atticus Finch had been primarily in the work of two legal scholars, rather than literary scholars.
145 Ibid., 608.
146 Ibid., 655.
147 Ibid., 672.
148 Ibid., 724.
149 Holcombe, '*To Kill a Mockingbird*', 36.
150 Lubet, 'Reconstructing Atticus', 1350.
151 J. S. Martinez, 'Process and substance in the "war on terror"', *Columbia Law Review*, 2008, vol. 108, 1013–92. She concedes, however, that the complex ultimately probably does more good than harm.
152 Žižek, *The Ticklish Subject*, p. 337.
153 Ibid.
154 This can be observed in the literature as well, particularly from those writers who emphasize client 'empowerment' and the creation of more equal relationships between lawyer and client. See further Kruse, 'Fortress in the sand', 371–72.
155 Žižek, *The Ticklish Subject*, p. 334.
156 This is also the case for judges, a phenomenon that has been readily observable in jurisdictions such as Australia and, to a lesser extent, New Zealand, where judges in recent years have received relatively unprecedented attacks upon their decision-making.
157 Epstein, 'For and against', 817.

5 Doing good by stealth: professional ethics and moral choices in *The Verdict* and *Regarding Henry*

Rachel Spencer

5.1 Introduction: the lawyer as protagonist

That the legal profession is dimly regarded is not news.[1] Law graduates are joining a profession that enjoys neither popularity nor esteem. Strident and unnerving messages about lawyers are being sent through the popular media. This chapter analyses the messages and ideals suggested by two popular Hollywood films about lawyers and the legal system, *The Verdict* and *Regarding Henry*.

Before providing an analysis of the two films, it is important to explore the concept of the lawyer as protagonist. The fact of the protagonist being a lawyer in each of these films is critical to the films' study of the human condition, and of existentialist choice. The non-lawyer's perception of morality and ethics is highlighted by the choices made by each of these lawyers. Yet the breach of legal professional ethics as understood by legal practitioners is not disclosed to the layperson in either film. Further, neither protagonist undertakes any kind of legal ethical reasoning. Societal morality is shown as separate and incontrovertibly apart from legal ethics. The message in both films is starkly simple: it is not possible to be both a good person and a good lawyer.

Lawyers represent the law. They advise on matters touched by the law; they interpret the law. So they have a responsibility towards the law. This is where the popular perception of lawyers falls foul of the public's ideal representative of the law. The integrity of the legal process must be upheld and maintained by lawyers. The irony is that in maintaining the integrity of the process, the lawyer is criticized. For maintaining client confidentiality, the lawyer is criticized. For insisting on the right of an accused to a fair trial, the lawyer is criticized. For representing a client who is despised by society, the lawyer is criticized. For maintaining a professional distance, the lawyer is criticized.

Asimow believes that casting lawyers as protagonists is purely commercial, because: 'If lawyers are *already* loathed by the likely consumers of a new film, then the odds for commercial success for a film about loathsome lawyers are better than the odds on films putting down French teachers, rabbis or grandmothers'.[2] Using lawyers to convey a message concerning making choices about how to live one's life employs a deeper message. The lawyer represents justice, a concept that is deeply seated in all human beings. From the time when a child first laments that 'it's not fair', each individual member of society develops an attraction to analysing the fairness or justice of a situation. One need not have studied jurisprudence to have an opinion about whether a situation has been dealt with fairly or justly. So the appeal of a film about the struggle between 'right' and 'wrong' can only be increased when the protagonist is the very symbol of justice itself.

Whether their prevalence is because of commercial reality or because the lawyer represents a unique archetype, the 'loathsome lawyer' film cannot be ignored, especially if one accepts Asimow's theory that 'works of popular culture tend to (not only) reflect ... popular attitudes, misconceptions, and myths'[3] but also influence public opinion and shape attitudes because the images and emotional responses to a well-scripted and well-acted film will endure in a viewer's memory and be reinforced with each new 'loathsome lawyer' story. Simon argues that 'popular culture is a source of evidence about popular moral understanding'.[4] The depiction of loathsome characters as lawyers is a wake-up call to all lawyers. We should all be asking ourselves how we can individually and collectively improve our image.

The decision of authors and scriptwriters to depict characters as lawyers, rather than members of some other profession, merits careful observation and is a reminder of the lawyer's privileged position in society. J. J. Abrams[5] and David Mamet[6] show how easily that position can be abused and the fact that legal ethics provide plentiful plot points in filmic narrative. Unfortunately, what they do not show is the existence of alternative choices. They do not highlight the rules of discovery. They do not articulate the obligation of a lawyer to act upon instructions. They do not reflect the requirement that a lawyer must be a fit and proper person to be an officer of the court.

Asimow has asserted that 'the trend in filmed portrayal of lawyers accurately reflects public opinion', but has also speculated that 'negative filmed images can lead public opinion as well as follow it'.[7] Of primary concern is that the filmed portrayal of lawyers can mislead the public in relation to ethical legal practice. In *The Verdict* and *Regarding Henry*, the depiction of the ethical choices available to lawyers is inaccurate and incomplete, thereby leading audiences to conclude that there can be no such thing as successful ethical legal practice. Asimow is justifiably concerned about 'the venomously negative public perception of the profession',[8] which is only further entrenched by inaccurate portrayals of the reality of practising law in popular movies.

The protagonists in *The Verdict* (Frank Galvin, played by Paul Newman) and *Regarding Henry* (Henry Turner, played by Harrison Ford) refute Greenfield's argument that lawyers are generally given favourable treatment in American films. He argues that there is a general theme of the lawyer being portrayed as ethically superior to those around him: 'Being able to see beyond the immediate problem to see a broader picture sets our hero aside both inside and outside of the community'.[9] Neither Frank Galvin (*The Verdict*) nor Henry Turner (*Regarding Henry*) fits into this category at the beginning of either film; however, they do by the end of the films – at the expense of ethical conduct. Despite breaking the law and breaching professional ethics (in the case of Galvin) and defying client instructions (in the case of Turner), both emerge as morally superior characters by the final scene. In both films, however, the protagonist acts against the wishes of others in the profession. They become heroes despite their status as lawyers, not because of it.

Henry Turner and Frank Galvin have completely different personalities. Henry is rich, powerful, flamboyant and a clever lawyer. He would probably despise Frank, the alcoholic ambulance chaser. Asimow points out that these characters (as portrayed before the 'change' in each film) represent the popular view of what lawyers are really like, 'except in the unlikely event that fate gives them a personality transplant'.[10]

The scriptwriter has cast Henry as a member of a profession that is skilled with words, because learning to read again and discovering vocabulary is part of his rehabilitation as a new person. It is integral to the development of his relationship with his daughter and his wife, and his discovery of the shallowness of the relationships. Literacy is the key to his discovery that not only was his wife having an extra-marital affair with a colleague, but also that he was involved in an extra-marital liaison with another colleague. This use of language as a narrative tool could have been embedded in a variety of character types. Henry could have been an English teacher, a historian, a philosopher or a playwright. However, making him a lawyer puts him in the echelons of power, and draws on public perceptions of lawyers as devious and untrustworthy.[11] Galvin's use of language is not as pointed, nor is it an integral part of the narrative. While the loss of linguistic skill is a key element of the 'fall' of the main character in *Regarding Henry*, it is the loss of self-respect and self-esteem that characterises the 'fall' of Frank Galvin in *The Verdict*. Galvin's alcoholism is not treated compassionately; he is cast as devious and despicable. Yet he and Henry Turner share a common attribute: both disregard common decency in order to make a living. Henry, while handsome and fashionably dressed, is rude, arrogant and professionally unethical. Frank Galvin, on the other hand, is dishevelled and often drunk; he is late for meetings with clients and appears to be generally incompetent.

Both *The Verdict* and *Regarding Henry* analyse the traits of lawyers that are often expressed in lawyer jokes.[12] Overton is of the view that 'the complaints expressed in lawyer jokes reflect genuine public concerns'.[13] Overton suggests that jokes about lawyers can be divided into five societal grievances against lawyers: that they are devious and untrustworthy; they are obsessed with money; their behaviour is contemptible; they are incomprehensible, boring and frequently useless; and, finally, that there are too many of them.[14]

Galvin has a reputation as an 'ambulance chaser' – a lawyer who has a habit of pursuing complaints that should never go to court.[15] The early images of Galvin handing out his card at funerals, leaving bogus messages on his door and spending more time in the bar than at his desk cement his image as devious, untrustworthy, obsessed with money and, above all, contemptible.

Henry Turner is depicted first as obsessed with money and contemptible. Then, as the narrative unfolds, he is shocked to discover that before he was shot and suffered a brain injury, he was also devious and untrustworthy. As Henry finds out more about the person he used to be, he too defies the lawyer joke stereotype. Henry's transformation into a childlike, artless creature throws into stark relief the archetype he once was. The new Henry is kind, thoughtful, even loveable, unrecognizable from the tyrant he was before. The audience is drawn to this warm, caring individual who reinforces the viewer's notion of lawyers as uncaring and cold when his former colleagues reveal their own contemptible attitudes. The message of the movie is, 'Why would he ever want to go back to that life of fakery and deception?' The vast majority of viewers watching the film, as Asimow points out, are eager to accept 'radically negative statements about law and lawyers when served up along with a good story'.[16]

Greenfield considered the role of screen lawyers and 'the extent to which they might go outside the formal process of law to ensure that the right result is achieved'.[17] He mentions the 'causal link between what the public sees (the cultural representation) and the effect of such representation'.[18] Importantly also, Greenfield notes that the majority of popular films about lawyers are American.[19] The international film industry is dominated by the Hollywood production houses, and a large number of movies about lawyers are about the US legal system.

There is a wide literature on the lawyer depicted as a hero.[20] Greenfield describes Galvin as 'the modern-day example of the heroic lawyer who delivers justice, yet he is imbued with personal deficiencies such as his heavy drinking'.[21] Henry Turner becomes heroic when he turns his back on unethical practice, notwithstanding his newly acquired personal deficiencies (loss of confidence, illiteracy and memory loss).

The Verdict's scriptwriter, David Mamet, focuses on the theme that 'things change'.[22] This idea is interlaced throughout the film: Galvin's good luck changes, his solitary life changes, his attitude to his client changes, and finally *he* changes. Similarly in *Regarding Henry*, life changes for everyone: for Henry, his wife, his lover, his daughter, his partners and the plaintiffs, his former opponents. Basing a plot on the idea of change from 'bad person' to 'good person' is classic, but it takes on a new dimension when the protagonist is a lawyer, because the ethical dimension cannot be ignored.

5.2 Civil litigation as the basis of narrative

Fictional accounts of lawyers are more often than not about criminal law. Crime provides all the necessary elements of drama: tension, conflict, suspense and finally resolution. Crime not only sells newspapers, it also sells novels – especially when the story invites the public to analyse the ethics and morality of lawyers. Asimow notes that 'lawyers are doomed to be unloved because criminal practice is their most public function'.[23] Stories involving the law capture the public's desire for a good narrative: sadness, tragedy, loss, pain and redemption. However, there are some notable exceptions to the criminal lawyer as the protagonist. It has been said that John Grisham's *The Firm* elevated the tax lawyer to the hero status enjoyed by Atticus Finch[24] and Perry Mason.[25] *The Castle*[26] brought constitutional law into the lounge rooms of viewers who may never before have heard of it.[27]

Filmmakers have used civil trials as the basis of many fictional narratives. Examples include *I'm No Angel* (1933), *Class Action* (1991), *Philadelphia* (1993), *Brilliant Lies* (1996), *A Civil Action* (1999), *Liar Liar* (1997), *The Castle* (1997), *Erin Brockovich* (2000) and *Two Weeks' Notice* (2002).[28] While civil litigation can appear to be less exciting than crime, lawyers involved in this area of practice know that it can be fraught with emotion for the parties involved – particularly personal injury practice. A common theme in films about personal injury litigation is the innocent individual fighting the unscrupulous or cavalier corporation. Dramatic energy is often highlighted by the role of the lawyers – usually 'unpleasant or unhappy human beings you wouldn't want as friends'[29] or 'bad professionals you wouldn't admire or want as your lawyer'.[30]

The Verdict[31] and *Regarding Henry* are both about personal injury litigation involving medical negligence. They depict the legal profession as shallow, grasping and unpleasant. The medical profession receives equally unfavourable treatment in both films. Frank Galvin and Henry Turner are loners – the latter because of his intolerance for others, the former because of his incompetence but also because of his mistrust of others. As well as sharing similar subject-matter, both films can be said to illustrate a popular perception of lawyers and their role in the justice system.

5.2.1 *The Verdict*

In *The Verdict*, Frank Galvin acts for a young woman who is now severely brain-damaged and in a permanent coma because of medical negligence. Galvin receives instructions from the client's sister and her husband. The defendants are numerous, although they are collectively depicted as only one: a hospital, two medical specialists and the Catholic Church[32] (which owns the hospital). In reality, these defendants would all be represented separately, but the film uses their number to highlight the contrast with Galvin. Galvin works alone out of a 'seedy, disorganized small office'.[33] A simple sign on his door, 'Francis P. Galvin, Attorney at Law', announces his simplicity and his solitude (and provides a hint about the nexus of the narrative with his namesake, Saint Francis of Assisi). The defendants have a team of corrupt lawyers whose vast, glamorous offices symbolize their seemingly unlimited resources. The judge is biased. 'Everything he [Galvin] is up against is enormous.'[34] These are the ingredients of a classic David and Goliath tale.

Galvin is aware of his lack of status. When he leaves his office to go to a bar, he types a fake note from a non-existent secretary ('Judge Geary called. Lunch tomorrow? Back soon. Clare'), and sticks it on his door. When he comes back late from lunch and finds the client waiting for him, he feigns surprise that the door is locked. Then he lies to the client again, saying: 'Sorry we have to meet out here but I've got this case coming up in court in a couple of days and the place is full of paper'. He thus misrepresents himself as having another, more palatial office somewhere else and gives the impression that he is a busy lawyer with other clients.

Galvin has already once been the unwitting victim of corruption, having discovered that a partner in the firm for which he worked had bribed a juror to make sure Galvin won a case. After threatening to tell the judge, he was himself indicted and imprisoned for jury tampering. Upon then agreeing that he had 'made a mistake', the charges against him were dropped and he was released from jail. The firm terminated his employment and his wife divorced him. Thus began his lapse into alcoholism.

Galvin's ability to win this case for his client appears doomed, but Lumet and Mamet engage our empathy for him. They portray him against a backdrop of snow, bleak skies and dingy bars, and we know the dull colours that follow his trajectory through the narrative can only be lifted by something he does himself. Lawyers watching this film can see that settling this case as soon as possible would be in the best interests of his clients and also for himself. But when Galvin takes photographs of the woman for whom he is acting, this is a significant plot point in the film. 'This is where he starts to believe that there is something more at stake here, more than just the money. She becomes real to him.'[35] This is an example of what Simon means when he speaks of ethics within practical lawyering. Rules of professional conduct set out neatly on paper are easily recited. Mamet's script thrusts the rules in our faces and demands that we, as lawyers, analyse ourselves and our role in society.

Frank Galvin is initially portrayed as incompetent and morally bankrupt. He is arguably not a fit and proper person to be a lawyer. His judgment is clouded by excessive consumption of alcohol. His tasteless behaviour (handing his card out to strangers at funerals) is likely to bring the profession into disrepute. He is incompetent in the way he handles his work. For example, he has had a file for eighteen months and has done no work on it, having sent only one letter to the client in that time. In fact, he does not recognize his only client's name. His lack of attention exemplifies a lack of client-centred practice (but sadly reflects the reality of experience for many personal injury litigants).[36] He flies into a drunken rage. He ignores his clients' instructions to settle. He commits several offences by breaking into a letter box to track down the telephone number of a witness. He lies to the friend of a witness to trick her into giving him information. He lies to the witness by fraudulently misrepresenting himself to find out her whereabouts. He lies to another witness, saying: 'Sorry I didn't get back to you. The case got postponed ... We've had a change of strategy'. On learning of his lover's treachery, he reacts violently, knocking her down. In reality, such ongoing professional misconduct would probably result in him being struck off, or at least suspended from practice.

Some textbooks on ethics raise the issue of accepting a settlement offer on behalf of a client and the client complaining because it is not enough. In *The Verdict*, the opposite happens – Galvin refuses a settlement offer that is much higher than the clients had suggested they wanted. Galvin knows that by accepting the defendant's offer of $210,000, he would keep $70,000 – a large amount in 1982 – certainly large enough to revive his ailing legal practice. In fact, his risks are substantial; he admits that he only has one client. The plaintiff's claim is for

$600,000. The Archdiocese wants to settle the case to avoid publicity. The Bishop says to Galvin that:

> It's a question of continuing values. St Catherine's – to do the good that she must do in the community – has to maintain the position that she holds in the community. So we have a question of balance: on the one hand, the reputation – and so the effectiveness – of our hospital and two of her important doctors and, on the other hand, the rights of your client. Nothing, of course, can begin to make it right. But we must do what we can. We must do all we can ... We must try to make it right.

Galvin's duty is to act in the best interests of his client. Again, conflicts emerge. The 'real' client is unable to provide instructions. The clients' best interests are to accept the offer of $210,00, so they would receive $140,000 and Galvin would earn $70,000. This is nearly three times what the clients actually wanted ($50,000). Galvin is presented as having a genuine choice over whether or not to accept the offer from the defendants. The appropriate response from the other side would have been, 'Go and get instructions', at which point the movie might have ended because Galvin would have had two very happy clients!

Yet, in accepting this offer – which is more than his clients have asked for – he also recognizes that:

> no one will know the truth ... [t]hat that poor girl put her trust in the hands of two men who took her life, she's in a coma, her life is gone. She has no family, she has no home, she's tied to a machine, she has no friends – and the people who should care for her: her doctors, and you, and me, have been bought off to look the other way. We have been paid to look the other way.

This is the moment in the film where Galvin must struggle between professional ethics (informing his clients of the offer and then acting upon instructions) and his own personal morality. 'I can't take it,' he realizes. 'If I take it, if I take that money I'm lost. I'm just going to be a rich ambulance chaser ... I can't do it. I can't take it.'

This decision is a turning point. Galvin says, 'I can't take your money', thus defying the popular image of greedy lawyer and depriving the lawyer joke of its punchline. But he is only able to do this by defying the laws of lawyering. He breaches ethical standards in order to reject the image of the greedy lawyer.

There is a nod to reality when the client (the husband) threatens to have Galvin disbarred for turning down the offer. Mr Doneghy says: 'You ruined my life, Mister ... Me and my wife ... and I am going to ruin yours ... You don't have to go out there to see that girl. We been going four years ... Four years ... my wife's been crying herself to sleep what they, what, what they did to her sister.'

Galvin replies, 'I swear I wouldn't have turned the offer down unless I thought that I could win the case ... I'm going to win this case ... Mist ... Mr Doneghy

... I'm going to the jury with a solid case, a famous doctor as an expert witness, and I'm going to win $800,000.'

This enrages the client even more. 'What you thought!? What you thought ... I'm a working man, I'm trying to get my wife out of town, we hired you, we're paying you, I got to find out from the other side they offered two hundred ... You guys, you guys, you're all the same. The Doctors at the hospital, you ... it's "What I'm going to do for you"; but you screw up it's "We did the best that we could. I am dreadfully sorry ... " And people like me live with your mistakes the rest of our lives.'

Galvin tells his client: 'I'm going to do the best that I can for you and your sister. I know how much it means to you and it means that much to me too.' This is arguably an inappropriate comment, as it suggests emotional involvement. On the other hand, Galvin may be demonstrating the 'ethics of care' approach (see below).[37] In any event, the portrayal of Galvin as a hero for this behaviour ignores the choices that he could and should have made earlier. He could and should have prepared the matter for trial much earlier than he did. If he had done that, he might not have been so aggressive with the first nurse witness and may have been able to find the other witness who was critical to the case, without resorting to illegality. He should not have discussed the case with his lover, a woman he hardly knew. But the audience sitting in the dark cinema sees a desperate lawyer trying to fight injustice and therefore doing 'the right thing'. Asimow points out that 'most people think that justice means finding the truth regardless of the adversarial system, procedural technicalities, statutory loopholes, police or prosecutorial misconduct, or lawyers' tricks'.[38]

Griffin notes that 'the standard criticism of the lawyer's amoral role' is 'that it is *too* client-centred because it neglects other concerns about, for example, common morality, social values, or the public interest'.[39] In Galvin's situation, he can see that exposing the negligence of the doctors is in the public interest, but to do this is contrary to his client's wishes. Indeed, in the client's view, 'You ruined my life Mister.' If Galvin accedes to his client's wishes and accepts the settlement offer, he neglects common morality, social values and the public interest. He is damned if he does, damned if he does not.

Further confusion arises for the general public watching this film because they recognize that the defendants are unethical in their practice as well. They coach witnesses. They plant a spy with Galvin to relay confidential information about the plaintiff's case. They 'get rid of' an expert witness who had agreed to give evidence against their clients because he wanted to 'do the right thing – isn't that why you are doing it?'. However, he too can be bought, giving credence to the nurse Mary Rooney's allegation that 'You guys are all the same. You don't care who gets hurt. You're a bunch of whores. You'd do anything for a dollar. You got no loyalty ... no nothing ... ' But 'doing the right thing' becomes the motivation for Galvin to persist. It appears that all lawyers are corrupt and the legal system is ineffective, so Galvin's risk-taking is not only admirable but necessary.

Mamet has included all possible sources of morality in his script: lawyers, courts and a biased judge (representing societal morality and the system of justice); the Catholic Church (representing divine law and a higher notion of justice);

the client's notion of fairness; and the jury (the seeker of truth). Each of these representations of morality, as they affect the comatose client, offers a different view of what is 'just' in the situation. The lawyer's code of ethics says: 'I must act upon my clients' instructions, and therefore accept the offer. This is acting in the best interests of my client'. The defendants acknowledge that 'nothing can bring the girl back', but they offer an amount that they 'thought was just'. It actually was an amount that would hush the matter up and avoid the publicity of a trial as the matter had been diagnosed as a 'nuisance suit'. The biased judge warns that the matter should settle. The client's view is that justice would be receiving enough money to enable the injured sister to be housed in a more comfortable facility, and enabling them to start a new life in Tucson. Galvin the ambulance chaser knows that accepting the settlement offer will clear his debts and enable him to start again. The voice of conscience demands that the injustice and the truth about the negligence should be revealed, even though this cannot help the young woman whose life has been destroyed. These intertwining conflicts create the dramatic tension required. The title of the film suggests that the latter voice is the loudest in the end.

Galvin is desperate at this point. He has been unable to have the case adjourned, his crucial medical witnesses have vanished and the defendants' offer has been withdrawn. But he also seems to be completely destroying any chance of getting other witnesses to cooperate. Mamet's script portrays corruption as 'ubiquitous and inevitable'.[40] At this point in the narrative, Galvin has the audience's sympathy. The audience's motive to keep watching is to see that he does whatever it takes to beat the other side. It has become personal. When he finally tracks down the witness he needs (by theft, fraud and deception), he asks her not 'Will you help my client?' but 'Will you help me?'

Later, Galvin says to Laura: 'The weak, the weak have got to have somebody to fight for them. Isn't that the truth?' And then: 'That's why the court exists. The court doesn't exist to give them justice, eh? But to give them a chance at justice'. The irony behind these speeches is that he is speaking to the person whose role it is to betray him. Laura is working for the solicitors who act for the defendants. She is supplying information to the other side about the plaintiff's case. Neither Galvin nor the viewer knows this yet. When her treachery is revealed, the lay observer sees this as yet another obstacle that Galvin in the role of hero must overcome, and further cements the notion that all lawyers are corrupt. From a technical legal perspective, Galvin should not have discussed the case with her at all. After all, she is a stranger he met in a bar. He has breached his duty of confidentiality to his client by discussing the matter with her. This layer of ethical responsibility is not raised in the film – most likely because it would cloud the plot, if not rendering it unworkable. If he had not told her about the witness, she would not have told the defence team and then there would have been no need to find another expert witness; they would have won anyway. But that makes a boring film! Dramatic tension is achieved by misrepresenting the way legal ethics work. Galvin rejects the suggestion that they apply for a mistrial because of Laura. He does not tell the clients about this turn of events. He does not ask for their instructions. So, in ignoring the technical ethical rules, the script becomes believable to the lay moviegoer.

Simon argues that 'the dominant conception of the lawyer's professional responsibilities weakens the connection between the practical tasks of lawyering and the values of justice that lawyers believe provide the moral foundations of their role'.[41] So, in Galvin's eyes, in practical terms he does what it takes to ensure that justice will prevail, despite his earlier incompetence. The ends justify the means. Breaking the law (by breaking into a witness's letter box) and breaching professional ethics (by lying to a witness about his identity, failing to obtain instructions and failing to convey an offer of settlement) are portrayed as justified because the truth has been revealed and the plaintiff wins a huge damages award.

Our initial impressions of Galvin are that he is negligent and uncaring. Once he decides that if he accepts the settlement money he is 'lost', Galvin throws himself into the role of zealous advocate. However, in doing so he ignores what have been described as the two principles of legal ethics: 'partisanship and moral non-accountability, which comprise the "standard" or "dominant" conception of the lawyer's role'.[42] Perlman has explained partisanship as the necessity for lawyers to 'undertake all lawful actions that best serve their clients' interests, even if those actions are antithetical to the interests of justice or morality in particular cases'.[43] Galvin goes beyond this definition. He decides for himself what his clients' best interests are and deliberately either ignores their instructions or chooses not to obtain them. In order to achieve his goal of unearthing the truth, he also commits criminal offences, including breaking into a witness's letter box, opening her mail and stealing her bill. Further, he lies to a witness and misleads her into giving away details of the whereabouts of her friend who is a crucial witness. He then lies on the telephone to that witness in order to mislead her into revealing where she works. Finally, he breaches confidentiality by discussing the case with Laura.

Galvin believes that his personal redemption will be achieved by following what he believes to be an honourable course of action. His choice, however, is in defiance of his clients' instructions and is professionally unethical in a number of ways. He commits offences and breaches professional ethics in order to do what he believes is the right thing, and what the lay observer might accept to be an appropriate course of action in order to achieve a just end.

5.2.2 *Regarding Henry*

Regarding Henry[44] is also about a medical negligence case. Henry Turner acts for the defendant hospital. The opening scene is a wide-angle shot of the majesty and grandeur of the Supreme Court and the power that it represents. Henry personi-fies that power and all that the legal system encompasses. He is conservative, a workaholic, and expects to be listened to whether he is speaking to a jury, his secretary, his daughter or a shop assistant. Henry is at ease and always in control. He is at the pinnacle of professional success. The opening scene is similar to that in *The Verdict*: it is snowing. But unlike the bleakness of the wintry scenes in *The*

Verdict, this movie opens with opulence and self-assurance. While Frank Galvin shields himself from the cold with whisky, Henry Turner turns up the collar of his cashmere coat and defies the wind to slow him down.

Henry is articulate, quick witted and ruthless. He has been able to discount the plaintiff's evidence by withholding a document that proves its truth (that the plaintiff told nursing staff at the hospital he was a diabetic). This is critical evidence in favour of the plaintiff because the case will be decided on Mr Matthews' word that he did in fact tell the nursing staff against East Shore Hospital's contention that he did not. Henry is a clever wordsmith who is accustomed to his bidding being done. He loses the power of speech after being shot during the purchase of cigarettes late in the evening after attending a glitzy party. His struggle to regain his ability to communicate is central to the film. In his new state as an artless creature, he discovers and is appalled by the person he used to be. The script offers him only one option to redeem himself as a human being: he must abandon his career as a lawyer.

Personally, Henry is as flawed as Frank Galvin. He is selfishly incapable of recognizing the needs of others. His daughter aches for his attention and praise. He cheats on his wife, on whom he relies to remember the names of his shallow acquaintances. He is driven by professional and financial success. He is rude, aggressive, wealthy, arrogant and accustomed to getting his own way. He barks orders at his secretary, his relationship with his daughter is based on her understanding of 'the work ethic', and his relationship with his beautiful fur-swathed wife is one of convenience. He appears to derive pleasure only from his work, and then only if he wins – which we are led to believe he often does. He is immaculately dressed and lives in a palatial New York City apartment. He only uses manners with people who he thinks can be useful for him. He ignores the doorman at his apartment and he is unable to apologize to his daughter for upsetting her. The world has to see it his way or there is no point having your eyes open. We know that he has engaged in at least one act of unethical conduct (failing to make proper discovery on behalf of his client) and the implication is that he would have done this more than once. His firm accepts and encourages this unethical behaviour.

After his dismissal as Prime Minister of Australia by Governor-General Sir John Kerr in 1975, Gough Whitlam famously declared: 'Well may we say "God save the Queen", because nothing will save the Governor-General.' Similar sentiments are implied at the beginning of *Regarding Henry*. As the camera pans from the 'In God we trust' plaque on the wall, we hear Henry Turner's confident, articulate address to the jury.[45] In God we trust, because we cannot trust anyone else – especially not Henry Turner. Implicitly, we cannot trust any lawyer and we cannot trust the legal system to deliver justice.

Is Henry a fit and proper person to be a lawyer? It has been said that: 'The real test of ethical behaviour is when a lawyer's personal values and attitudes must respond to ethical situations which arise unexpectedly and spontaneously in practice ... from a range of sources – clients, the commercial environment of legal practice, or even from peers or employers'.[46] Henry is pressured by his partners and his clients to act unethically for financial reasons. Only a bullet to the head enables him to recognize the immorality of this, with childlike innocence and clarity. The moral of the story is that it is better to be a good person, even if unemployed, than to be rich, clever and corrupt. The flaw in the tale is that these are offered as the only choices. The message is that to be a lawyer, one has to be corrupt to succeed. The option of financial success combined with matrimonial harmony and ethical practice is portrayed as unattainable.

There are several assumptions that lawyers must make in analysing the ethical issues in *Regarding Henry*. First, we assume that the document has been concealed from the plaintiff and not disclosed in the discovery process. We assume that it is not a privileged document,[47] that the document is genuine and that it can assist the plaintiff's case and will harm the defence case. As an officer of the court, Henry Turner was obliged (pre-trial) to advise his client that the document was discoverable. If the client refused to provide instructions to discover the document, Henry was obliged to cease to act, or the client would have had to make an offer to the plaintiff with a view to settling the matter. Now that the case has been tried and resolved in a court, the relevant law must determine whether the matter can be retried in the light of fresh evidence or whether an appeal is warranted. 'What we did was wrong,' he tells his partner.

'What we did is paying for our lunch,' the partner replies.

The 'old' Henry might have laughed at this response. The new Henry is deeply troubled. The audience is led to believe that in acting in the best interests of his client, Henry was obliged to engage in this deceptive behaviour. This is misleading because it is likely that the rules of discovery would have led to the disclosure of this document, and the case would most likely have then settled in the plaintiff's favour. The scriptwriters have sacrificed the reality of legal ethics for the excitement and dramatic tension created by an incorrect portrayal of the way lawyers operate.

This behaviour can be contrasted with the way the character loses cognitive function and his memory. The audience is encouraged to prefer his childlike innocence over the earlier sophisticated deviousness. As further untruths are disclosed, the audience is encouraged to distrust the legal system. Henry's former life is uncovered as a tangle of lies and deceit, into which his unethical and untrustworthy legal practice was inextricably entwined. When Henry discovers that his wife was having an affair with a work colleague – his best friend – he is devastated. When he discovers that he too was having an affair with a work colleague, he is completely confused. He does not like who he was. As his cognitive function improves, he learns to read and he is again able to communicate, life becomes even more complicated for him. Being a lawyer becomes intrinsically integrated with being a contemptible character. His colleagues are painted as equally despicable and untrustworthy by association with his past.

After Henry discovers that the Matthews' case was handled unfairly, his partners do not allow him access to any more of his old files. The film ends after he visits Mr and Mrs Matthews at their home (having found the address in the file) and gives them the document that will prove the defendant's negligence and eventually win the case for them. The film does not explore the complications of a retrial or an appeal, but the implication is that now the Matthews can win the compensation they deserve and that the truth will be revealed about the negligence of the doctors. Nor does the film mention that, in finally providing a copy of the document, Henry should not have directly approached the plaintiff but should have approached the plaintiff's solicitor. This is much the same as the evidence given by the witness against the hospital in *The Verdict*. Even though the evidence is disallowed, justice for the innocent ultimately prevails, as if in answer to Galvin's plea to the jury to 'believe in ourselves ... [a]nd act with justice'.

In the same way that Frank Galvin undergoes a transformation, Henry explains to Mrs Matthews, upon handing her the critical document: 'I changed.' The audience knows the whole story of how he changed, but just as Galvin changed from being an ambulance chaser into someone who believed in fighting for the truth (like his namesake, Saint Francis of Assisi), Henry also seeks 'truth' as the ultimate goal. These notions of truth are superficial at best, given the inauthenticity of the presentation of the adversarial process, but they do provide a convenient denouement to the dramatic tension. Simon has noted that: 'Popular culture is a source of evidence about popular moral understanding'.[48] The shaping of the narrative in each of these films evidences popular understanding about the adversarial system, and popular distrust of the adversarial system's ability to provide justice.

Perhaps the most disappointing aspect of the way professional ethics are seen to collide with personal morality is that Henry decides he 'can't be a lawyer any more'. This decision is not because of his memory loss or his diminished intellectual capacity; it is a moral decision. A far more preferable resolution would have been Henry setting up his own practice, where he represents clients according to his newly discovered sense of morality and ethics. It is disappointing – and indeed alarming – to recognize that Hollywood's answer to these ethical dilemmas is to cease the practice of law entirely, as if it is not possible to be an ethical lawyer.

5.3 Ethical framework

While producing enjoyable entertainment, the scriptwriters and producers of *Regarding Henry* and *The Verdict* have ignored the ethical framework within which lawyers must operate. They have had to do this in order to create the required dramatic tension for a visually and emotionally appealing work. Both characters inhabit worlds devoid of human warmth and moral integrity. Both characters appear to belong to a profession which requires a 'win at all costs' attitude. Neither film makes any reference to the fact that a lawyer must abide by an ethical code of conduct. Neither film alerts the viewing public to the notion that a lawyer is an officer of the court.

Both films explore the idea that violating the rules is sometimes the right thing to do,[49] because: 'Following the rules would [mean] deference to an abstract (categorical) principle at the cost of concrete injustice'.[50] Both films show lawyers exhibiting 'role transgressions (which) seem to arise from plausible moral judgments ... [a] combination of moral and tactical acuity [that Simon calls] Moral Pluck'.[51] Simon has traced 'moral pluck' through the novels of John Grisham and the television series *LA Law* and *The Practice*. He uses this expression to define 'a combination of resourcefulness and transgression in the service of basic but informal values'.[52] Both Henry Turner and Frank Galvin technically breach ethical rules, and engage in improper – even unlawful – conduct. However, that conduct that gives them hero status because they ultimately disclose that injustice has occurred and even greater evil has been committed by others. Their transgressions appear mild and justified in light of the great good that has ultimately been achieved.

Lewis and Kyrou describe the Galvin situation as 'doing good by stealth'. They advise that:

> At all times you must avoid getting yourself into trouble by trying to do good by stealth ... Some practitioners take this course of action because they want to intermingle their egos with the client's cause of action. Somehow the practitioner measures his or her own abilities by the results achieved on behalf of the client.[53]

Frank Galvin decides to right what he sees as an indisputable wrong that has been done to his client who cannot speak for herself, but he confuses his own need for redemption with the interests of his client. Henry Turner also wants to right the wrong that he has caused to someone else. Both of these are examples of 'moral pluck', a 'combination of transgression and resourcefulness in the vindication of justice'.[54] So is their behaviour unethical?

As a starting point, it is necessary to think about the definition of ethics. It has been suggested that ethics is 'the science of human morals or of right human conduct'.[55] 'Legal ethics' suggests the concept of right conduct, of duty, of human goodness or virtue.[56] Boston said that:

> Philosophically considered, it seems to me that legal ethics is the result of the application by thinkers, more or less profound, of the principles of philosophy of right conduct, to the specific problems, which experience has shown, confront the lawyer, in the prosecution of his professional duties.[57]

Lamb and Littrich define 'ethics' as 'the term applied to the moral philosophy or moral principles adopted as a code or framework of behaviour in a particular context'.[58] It is useful to adopt their definition of 'legal ethics' as 'the particular ethical principles adopted by the legal profession'.[59] The question of whether 'ethics' is the same as 'morality' has been debated at length. For example, Rhode and Luban have argued that:

> legal ethics cuts more deeply than legal regulation; it concerns the fundamentals of moral lives as lawyers. As Socrates noted about the subject of

ethics, 'it is not about just any question, but about the way one should live' ... These two aspects of legal ethics cannot be separated ... legal codes of personal conduct that ignore the moral commitments of the people they govern are doomed to irrelevance. On the other hand, a purely philosophical study of legal ethics that ignores the institutional and doctrinal basis of law practice cannot succeed.[60]

Lamb and Littrich conclude that the 'observance of an ethical framework is the choice between alternatives, exercised by the interpretation and discretion of the individual making that choice – not, "what can I get away with?" but "what should I do?"'[61] Both Frank Galvin and Henry Turner are represented as having choices to make, but the scriptwriters do not disclose what the real choices are. Frank's choice is not to decide whether or not to accept the defendant's offer (as shown in the film) but to decide what the appropriate advice to his clients must be in relation to the offer. He should have discussed with them the options of accepting the offer or going to trial and attempting to reveal the negligence of the doctors. His decline of the offer marks the turning point in the film, and represents a first step on his own personal road to redemption; however, it is also his first major breach of professional ethics. He is more interested in relieving his own conscience rather than making the lives of his clients more bearable. By ignoring the interests of his clients, he puts his own interests ahead of those of his clients. In order to act in the best interests of one's client (one of the fundamental ethical principles of lawyering), a lawyer must first of all act upon the client's instructions. In *The Verdict*, if Galvin had taken instructions to accept the offer, taken his contingency fee and settled the case, he would have been acting ethically and within the requirements of professional conduct. Yet he would not have acted morally, knowing that an injustice had been done. Further, Mamet's script indicates that this action was not the 'right' thing to do. 'If I take it [the offer], I am lost,' he says. This is portrayed as noble and admirable, notwithstanding the fact that by rejecting the offer, he risks losing the trial. The risk is high. He is unprepared, he has only one expert witness who is likely to be discredited, and he has no witnesses who were present at the relevant time who can prove any negligence. If he loses the trial, his clients will be liable to pay the other side's substantial costs, they will be unable to move to the new life they dream of, and the plaintiff will remain in an inhospitable, uncaring institution. If the offer is accepted, they can move the plaintiff to a better, more caring environment, they can move to a new life and their legal bills will be paid. Galvin's own personal salvation is irretrievably connected to whether or not he wins this case, creating a monstrous conflict of interest. In real life, this would be untenable. In Hollywood, such conflict delivers Academy Award nominations.[62]

Similarly, when the 'new' Henry discovers that he, as the 'former' Henry, hid a document from the plaintiff (that would have resolved the dispute), he provides the plaintiff with a copy. The audience is left believing that this was a betrayal of his own client and a betrayal of his partners.[63] Even though the client failed to admit any negligence, and indeed concealed evidence of negligence, the lay observer is led to believe that if the client wants to hide evidence, the lawyer has to follow those instructions. Admittedly, Henry ought to have notified the client that he was in fact going to give it to the plaintiff, but what the scriptwriter fails to tell the audience is that Henry is legally and ethically bound to do so under the rules of discovery, and should have done so when he first became aware of its existence. Henry breached his duty to the court by failing to observe the rules and failing to protect the integrity of the evidence.[64] He withholds a document that he knows to exist, and which therefore should have been discovered well before trial.[65] The narrative reveals the choice he finally makes about having withheld this information.

Both Henry Turner and Frank Galvin fit within the public perception of lawyers who, as a profession, are 'more despised than ever before'.[66] Both characters are morally unattractive, although this prevents neither of them from successfully seducing women. Both films have extremely popular Hollywood leading men cast as the lawyers. Notably, they are older, attractive men who are instantly recognizable from earlier roles. It has been suggested that 'the public cynically winks at the moral failings of people they find attractive'.[67] This does raise the question of whether the actions of Henry and Frank would have been translated as admirably if less physically attractive man were cast in those roles. In Galvin there are shades of Butch Cassidy, the likeable outlaw.[68] Despite our initial misgivings about a lawyer who preys on bereaved people to solicit clients, it is difficult not to warm to Galvin by the end of the film. Similarly, Henry exhibits elements of Han Solo, the character in the *Star Wars* series of films, which made Harrison Ford a star. Han Solo's personality is revealed in his name. Like Han Solo, Turner is also a loner whose actions are based on his own best interests. When circumstances force him to reach out to others, he discovers that his own fulfilment lies in respecting the interests of others.

Notably, none of the lawyers in these films is portrayed favourably – except perhaps Mickey, Galvin's colleague and mentor. Galvin's opposing counsel is particularly unsavoury.[69] Ed Concannon is 'not paid to do his best, but [he is] paid to win'. His tactics include ensuring favourable media coverage of his client, bribing a defence witness not to give evidence and planting a spy with Galvin in the form of the traditional *film noir femme fatale*, also a lawyer. Laura pretends to be seduced by Galvin in order to spy for Concannon. Arguably, it is Laura who presents as the most unfit for practice out of all the legal practitioners in *The Verdict*.

Neither of these films acknowledges that working within an ethical framework involves more than observing professional conduct rules. Ethical behaviour:

> is a pervasive part of all legal practice, engaging the lawyer's attention intellectually, morally and emotionally. Lawyers need to adopt an ethical stance as a component of competence, because ethical issues can arise when they are least expected, not from a clear breach of the rules but in situations where value-laden choices have to be made.[70]

Lawyers have a duty of candour – they must be open, frank and honest in the disclosure of both facts and law before the court. Has Galvin misled the court in relation to the facts? No. He has not presented any evidence that is false or misleading.[71] Henry has breached this duty. Henry has failed to act appropriately as an officer of the court by concealing a document, and has thereby misled the court and the jury.

Galvin has failed to act in the best interests of his client. He has also breached his duty to obey his client's instructions. He has knowingly acted without authority, and is likely to be found guilty of unprofessional conduct.[72] He has 'substituted [his] own judgment for the specific instructions of [his] clients, believing that this is more likely to operate in the client's best interest'.[73] However, Lewis and Kyrou point out that 'it is no defence to a claim against [a lawyer] for acting contrary to instructions that [the lawyer] was doing what [he] thought was right for the client'.[74]

Greenfield notes that the 'bending of procedural rules or those relating to client conduct is a commonplace means of revealing the independence, from both the law and the legal community, of our screen hero'.[75] Galvin appears to be acting in the best interests of the clients 'at the expense of formal rules'.[76] Henry Turner is not acting in the best interests of his client, but he abandons formal rules in the interests of greater justice.

In addition to breaches of lawyering rules, both Frank Galvin and Henry Turner have failed to apply ethical reasoning to their actions. Rhode and Luban have commented that 'legal ethics cuts more deeply than legal regulation; it concerns the fundamentals of moral lives as lawyers. As Socrates noted about the subject of ethics "it is not about just any question, but about the way one should live"'.[77] Parker and Evans suggest that there are four strands of ethical reasoning available to lawyers: adversarial advocacy; responsible lawyering; moral activism; and ethics of care.[78] Henry could have applied Parker and Evans' ethical reasoning to his situation (before the trial in the opening scene and before he was shot and subject to a personality overhaul).

His first option might have been to apply the traditional concept of adversarial advocate. If he had chosen this path, he would still have been obliged to disclose the document. The scriptwriter might have maintained the 'shark' persona by having Henry employ a tactic used by lawyers that is strictly in compliance with the rules but still morally bereft – that is, he might have 'hidden' the document among a multitude of discovered documents, with a view to the plaintiff never actually finding it. Such an action might technically have been legitimate but still morally and ethically reprehensible.

Henry's second option was to apply the ethics of the 'responsible lawyer': trustee of the legal system and officer of the court. His duty as an advocate for his hospital client is tempered by his duty to ensure compliance with the spirit of the law. He would have made it clear to the court that the document existed. Alternatively, he could have applied the 'moral activist' approach, seeking to counsel the hospital client on the morally right thing to do (accept responsibility and pay compensation to the plaintiff). In any event, he would have advised the client that he was obliged to disclose the document. The final ethical option would have been the 'ethics of care' model. This is, in fact, the option on which he decides at the end of the film. He decides that 'preserving relationships and avoiding harm are more important than impersonal justice'.[79] He ignores the interests of his client completely and discloses the document to the plaintiff.[80]

Similarly, if Galvin had applied Parker and Evans' ethical reasoning to his situation, he might have applied the traditional concept of adversarial advocate, or the 'responsible lawyer' approach. He would have notified his clients about the offer, and explained the potential consequences of accepting or not accepting it. He would have been better prepared for the trial. Alternatively, he could have applied the 'moral activist' approach, seeking to encourage his client to persist with the litigation, notwithstanding the high risk. Like Henry, the final ethical option for Frank could have been the 'ethics of care' model. Again, this is in fact the option on which he decides at the end of the film. He comes to the conclusion that 'preserving relationships and avoiding harm are more important than impersonal justice'.[81] Frank also ignores the interests of his clients, in the interests of what Simon has entitled 'moral pluck'.[82]

Brennan J, in *Waterford v Commonwealth*,[83] expressed the widely accepted view that:

> the legal adviser must be ... independent, in order that the personal loyalties, duties or interests of the adviser should not influence the legal advice that he gives or the fairness of his conduct of litigation on behalf of his client. If a legal adviser is ... unable to be professionally detached in giving advice or in conducting litigation, there is an unacceptable risk that the purpose for which [legal professional] privilege is granted will be subverted.

A lawyer:

> must be independent of [the] client in the sense that the legal services provide[d] reflect ... professional judgment and are not compromised to suit the interests of [the] client. While, of course, [the lawyer] should take into account [the] client's views and interests, in providing legal services to [the] client, [the lawyer] must not depart from what [he or she] consider[s] to be the legally and ethically correct position in response to self-interest or pressure from [their] client or a third party.[84]

Both Galvin and Turner lose sight of this need to be independent, but their actions are portrayed as laudable.

One of the themes of *The Verdict* is what Simon describes as the 'moral anxiety' of the role of the lawyer.[85] Simon explains that the traditional criticism of lawyers as expressed by the non-lawyer through popular culture is that 'lawyers in their conventional practice contribute knowingly to injustice'.[86] In *The Verdict*, Galvin refuses to contribute knowingly to injustice – he refuses to settle the case. In *Regarding Henry*, Henry also refuses to contribute knowingly to injustice once he knows that is has occurred.

Galvin's desire to win the case is no longer dependent on the needs or instructions of the client. It has become his ticket to personal redemption. His colleague Mickey is pragmatic about Galvin's refusal of the offer: 'Are you nuts? What are you going to do, bring her back to life? ... You won it. When they give you the money, that means that you won. We don't want to go to court – is this getting to you?' But Galvin no longer sees the situation as the dispassionate attorney. He is no longer the amoral technician:[87] 'I have to try this case. I have to do it, Mick. I've got to stand up for that girl. I need your help ... Will you help me?'

Simon argues that: 'No social role encourages such ambitious moral aspirations as the lawyer's, and no social role so consistently disappoints the aspirations it encourages'.[88] Is Galvin one of those lawyers whose moral aspirations have been disappointed? Is he now striving to fulfil the aspirations of youth before it is too late? Galvin is haunted by his past. His desperation to break away from it overrides his professional judgment. So he behaves unprofessionally, even criminally, but the viewer can see that this is for a worthy goal. As is often the case in popular culture, 'the way to virtue involves transgression and resourcefulness'.[89]

As Lamb and Littrich point out: 'The real test of ethical behaviour is when a lawyer's personal values and attitudes must respond to ethical situations which arise unexpectedly and spontaneously in practice. Confrontation with real ethical dilemmas may reveal an inconsistency between professional obligation and personal values'.[90] This type of ethical analysis is not revealed in either film, and Simon notes that it is often overlooked in popular culture in favour of the more popularly admired moral pluck.[91]

If Henry had acted in accordance with professional ethical standards, he could have achieved the same outcome. The film suggests that the firm prefers a corrupt, unethical approach, and would have hindered his attempts to do the right thing. In addition Henry may be unaware of his ability to turn to the relevant regulatory authorities for guidance and assistance (because of his reduced intellectual capacity and amnesia), but the existence of such assistance is withheld from the viewer. Frank Galvin appears to be so swamped by corruption that abiding by conformist moralism will not achieve any justice for anyone. Indeed, Simon points out that professional conduct rules 'tend to require mechanical judgment or literal application'.[92] Simon also notes that 'popular culture is utopian about the possibilities of individual initiative'.[93]

Simon notes that Hollywood's approving portrayals of lawyers use a recurring theme of lawyer vigilantism where lawyers' criminal behaviour is portrayed as admirable.[94] Hollywood suggests that: 'Popular respect for law may *require* lawyers to violate the positive law'.[95] In *Regarding Henry*, Henry helps the plaintiff by providing the vital document. This is appropriate in his role as an officer of the court and is what he should have done in the first place, but he does not inform his client that he is doing so. He is certainly acting against the wishes of his partners (and presumably his clients), but the script would have us believe that what he is doing is a professional transgression. Henry Turner is held up to be a hero for this transgression and the legal system is portrayed as the villain.

Both films contain strong messages about ethics being more than a duty to society, but as also relevant to character and personal integrity.[96] While neither *Regarding Henry* nor *The Verdict* provides an especially poignant example of professional ethical reasoning, they do both illustrate interpretations of moral reasoning as a means of personal redemption. It is worth mentioning the parallels between Francis Galvin, Attorney at Law and Saint Francis of Assisi; the appellation of the character cannot simply be coincidental. In this interpretation of the life of Saint Francis, who preached repentance as a way of life and devoted himself to a life of poverty, Frank (Francis) Galvin rejects an opportunity to solve his financial problems. His rejection of the easy way out (accepting the offer) is his own personal repentance, his only means of personal salvation. He is therefore accused of heresy (professional misconduct), but ultimately canonized for his desire to uncover the truth and his deep sense of personal responsibility towards his fellow human beings. Redemption in a religious context is strongly reinforced by Galvin's final soliloquy to the jury. He expresses not only an explanation for his actions but also the theme of the film:

You know, so much of the time we're lost. We say, 'Please, God, tell us what is right. Tell us what's true. There is no justice. The rich win, the poor are powerless ... ' We become tired of hearing people lie. After a time we become dead. A little dead. We start thinking of ourselves as victims ... And we become victims ... And we become weak ... and doubt ourselves, and doubt our institutions ... and doubt our beliefs ... We doubt the law[97] ... but today you are the law ... And not some book and not the lawyers, or the marble statues and the trappings of the court ... all that they are is symbols ...
Of our desire to be just ...
All that they are, in effect, is a prayer ...
... a fervent, and a frightened prayer. In my religion we say, 'Act as if you had faith, and faith will be given to you' ...
If ... if we would have faith in justice, we must only believe in ourselves.
And act with justice ...
And I believe that there is justice in our hearts ...[98]

Greenfield suggests that this 'appeal to the jury's sense of justice' is necessary 'to override the deficiencies in his own case',[99] but it is more than that. It echoes popular desire for visibly effective justice. The public is not buying the idea that the legal system in its current form is capable of delivering justice. The DVD cover of *The Verdict* states that Galvin 'courageously decides to refuse a settlement'.[100] Through the eyes of the lay observer, Galvin's breach of professional ethics is admirable because it demonstrates his 'moral courage'. Could the film have been as good if Mamet's script had been guided by the rules of professional conduct? Frank Galvin's path to redemption as a human being is the same as Henry's. It is a rejection of corruption and a desire for fairness. Lawyers should be alarmed that their profession is seen in popular culture as a detour from that path.

The message in both movies is that, having breached professional ethics, the two characters are morally redeemed. In Henry's case, he has to abandon the profession completely in order to achieve ultimate salvation.

5.4 Conclusion

If a lawyer is driven to act unethically in a quest ultimately to do good and achieve justice, is this ever justifiable? Conversely, can a lawyer ever do good by acting according to professional ethical principles? Is the only way to redemption to do something that is either illegal or unethical? To the layperson watching *The Verdict* and *Regarding Henry*, these questions have bleak answers.

As lawyers (before their transformation into 'redeemed human beings'), Frank Galvin and Henry Turner present a grim face. Both face moral choices. In both films, these choices are presented as inseparable from their professional ethics. As Asimow points out:

> There are many plausible reasons why the public despises our profession, but it's just possible that negative lawyer films of the 1980s and 1990s reinforced and deepened those feelings. For these reasons we should pay attention to and care about the way lawyers are shown in film.[101]

Both *Regarding Henry* and *The Verdict* offer bleak views of the lawyer as an instrument of the justice system. Neither inspires confidence in the general public to trust lawyers, nor in lawyers that their role is valued. It all makes for a good narrative, but it misleads the layperson into believing that lawyers' ethics are in permanent conflict with societal morality. The film makers either tell deliberate untruths about lawyers' ethical duties or they choose to misrepresent them because it adds to the dramatic tension. Perpetuating stereotypes allows the archetypal lawyer to provide the internal conflict that is essential for a successful film. The lawyer might be either the ambulance-chasing sole practitioner, or the arrogant, greedy, self-opinionated top-end law firm partner – the end result is the same: go against the tide of what your colleagues say, ignore legal ethical requirements and you will not only redeem yourself as a person but you will become an honourable member of society. Continue as a lawyer, thinking like a lawyer, and you remain despicable.

The film makers are 'trying to create a situation in which justice and humanity require a departure from conventional role expectations, and to portray [the lawyer characters] as admirable for daring such a departure'.[102] That the conventional role expectation of a lawyer is popularly regarded as removed from justice and humanity should be of concern to all lawyers, law students and law teachers.

Acknowledgement

An earlier version of this chapter was presented at the Third International Ethics Conference, Gold Coast, Australia, in July 2008.

Notes

1 A point discussed in detail by Baron in this volume (see Chapter 4).
2 M. Asimow, 'Bad lawyers in the movies', *Nova Law Review*, 2000, vol. 24, 549.
3 Ibid., 550.
4 W. H. Simon, 'Moral pluck: Legal ethics in popular culture', *Columbia Law Review*, 2001, vol. 101, 422.
5 Scriptwriter, *Regarding Henry*, Paramount Pictures, 1991.
6 Scriptwriter, *The Verdict*, Twentieth Century Fox, 1982.
7 Asimow, 'Bad lawyers in the movies', 534.
8 Ibid., 541.
9 S. Greenfield, 'Hero or villain? Cinematic lawyers and the delivery of justice', *Journal of Law and Society*, 2001, vol. 28, 33.
10 Asimow, 'Bad lawyers in the movies', 564, n. 143.
11 See T. W. Overton, 'Lawyers, light bulbs and dead snakes: The lawyer joke as societal text', *UCLA Law Review*, 1995, vol. 42, 1069, 1099.
12 For an example of the lawyer joke stereotype presented as humour, see *Liar Liar*, Universal Pictures and Imagine Entertainment, directed by Tom Shadyak, 2003.
13 Overton, 'Lawyers, light bulbs and dead snakes', 1090.
14 Ibid., 1082–85.
15 R. Rabin, 'Lawyer bashing has moved into prime time', *Newsday* (New York City edition), 1 July 1993, cited in Overton, 'Lawyers, light bulbs and dead snakes', n. 12.
16 Asimow, 'Bad lawyers in the movies', 553.
17 Greenfield, 'Hero or villain?'
18 Ibid., 26.
19 Ibid.
20 Ibid., 27–29.
21 Ibid., 28.
22 Sidney Lumet, director, voice-over 'extra' on *The Verdict* DVD, Twentieth Century Fox Home Entertainment, 2002.
23 Asimow, 'Bad lawyers in the movies', 536.
24 Harper Lee, *To Kill a Mockingbird*, 1960; film adaptation by director Robert Mulligan, 1962, starring Gregory Peck.
25 E. M. Jensen, 'The heroic nature of tax lawyers', *University of Pennsylvania Law Review*, 1991, vol. 140, 367.
26 *The Castle*, 1997, director Rob Sitch.
27 For a comprehensive analysis of *The Castle* as an exposé of the inherent contradictions in the decision in *Mabo and Others v The State of Queensland (No. 2)* (1992) 107 ALR 1 and 'the panic, moral or otherwise, generated by the [*Wik*] case' (*Wik Peoples v The State of Queensland* (1996) 141 CLR 129) see W. P. MacNeil, *Lex Populi*, Stanford: Stanford University Press, 2007, pp. 116–31.
28 For a comprehensive list of films depicting trials produced up to 2000, see K. Laster, *The Drama of the Courtroom*, Sydney: Federation Press, 2000.
29 Asimow, 'Bad lawyers in the movies', 533.
30 Ibid.
31 For law students and newly graduating lawyers, the impact of *The Verdict* is not dulled by the fact that it is now somewhat dated. For example, the film opens to the sound of a pinball machine. In this age of electronic recreation, this sound is not so readily recognized any more. The pinball machine becomes a motif throughout the film: as Galvin's life improves, so does his score. Dated though this motif is, its effect is still powerful.
32 Lumet notes in his DVD commentary that Boston, the city in which this story is set, 'has a strong religious feel about it. The Church has a predominant role in the life of the city and its politics'.

33 David Mamet, *The Verdict*, Screenplay, 26 May 2008. Available from <www.dailyscript.com/scripts/the-verdict-script.html> (accessed 29 November 2009).
34 Sidney Lumet, director, voice-over 'extra' on *The Verdict* DVD, Twentieth Century Fox Home Entertainment, 2002.
35 Ibid.
36 L. Griffin, 'What do clients want? A client's theory of professionalism', *Emory Law Journal*, 2003, vol. 52, 1087.
37 C. Parker and A. Evans, *Inside Lawyers' Ethics*, Cambridge: Cambridge University Press, 2007.
38 Asimow, 'Bad lawyers in the movies', 536.
39 Griffin, 'What do clients want?', 1088.
40 W. H. Simon, *The Practice of Justice*, Cambridge, MA: Harvard University Press, 1998, p. 94.
41 Ibid., 2.
42 See D. Luban, *Lawyers and Justice: An Ethical Study*, Princeton, NJ: Princeton University Press, 1988, pp. 50–55, 154–57.
43 A. M. Perlman, 'A career choice critique of legal ethics theory', *Seton Hall Law Review*, 2001, vol. 31, pp. 829, 846.
44 The title itself is a quirky play on legalese: many lawyers commence letters by using the abbreviation 'Re'.
45 Conversely, *The Verdict* ends with the address to the jury.
46 Lamb and Littrich, *Lawyers in Australia*, Sydney: Federation Press, 2007, p. 186.
47 If it were privileged, this would raise other issues about privilege and public interest.
48 Simon, 'Moral pluck', 422.
49 Ibid., 421.
50 Ibid.
51 Ibid., 436.
52 Ibid.
53 G. D. Lewis, E. J. Kyrou and A. M. Dinelli, *Handy Hints on Legal Practice*, 3rd edn, Sydney: Thomson Law Book Co., 2004, p. 26.
54 Simon, 'Moral pluck'.
55 K. F. O'Leary, *Structuring a Course in Legal Ethics*, Australasian Professional Legal Education Council (APLEC) Conference Papers 1982, p. 1.
56 Ibid.
57 C. A. Boston, 'The source and formulation of ethical precepts', *Central Law Journal*, 1914, vol. 78, 400.
58 Lamb and Littrich, *Lawyers in Australia*, p. 183.
59 Ibid.
60 D. L. Rhode and D. Luban, *Legal Ethics*, New York: Foundation Press, 1995, p. 3 cited in Lamb and Littrich, *Lawyers in Australia*, p. 183.
61 Ibid., p. 184.
62 *The Verdict* was nominated for Best Picture in 1982. Richard Attenborough's *Ghandi* won the Oscar. Paul Newman in *The Verdict* was nominated for best actor in a leading role; Ben Kingsley in *Ghandi* won the Oscar. Other nominations in relation to *The Verdict* were for James Mason (best supporting actor), Sidney Lumet (director) and David Mamet (screenplay).
63 It is interesting to note that *Regarding Henry* was made before the case of *Cowell (Estate of McCabe Deceased) v British American Tobacco Australia Services Ltd* 2007 VSCA 301. Arguably, media attention surrounding the advice given by lawyers Clayton Utz in relation to their client's 'Document Retention Policy' has now increased public awareness of the role played by lawyers in relation to discoverable documents.
64 See G. E. Dal Pont, *Lawyers' Professional Responsibility*, 3rd edn, Sydney: Thomson Law Book Co., p. 390.
65 In reality, this would probably have forced his client to settle.

66 Asimow, 'Bad lawyers in the movies', 537.
67 Simon, 'Moral pluck', 441, citing R. A. Posner, *An Affair of State: The Investigation, Impeachment and Trial of President Clinton 92–3* (1999).
68 Paul Newman starred in *Butch Cassidy and the Sundance Kid*, 1969, Twentieth Century Fox, winner of four Academy awards in 1970.
69 James Mason won an Academy award for best supporting actor in this role.
70 Lamb and Littrich, *Lawyers in Australia*, p. 186.
71 Lewis, Kyrou and Dinelli, *Handy Hints on Legal Practice*, p. 30.
72 *Wheatley v Bastow* (1855) 7 De GM & G 558; 44 ER 218, cited in ibid., p. 24.
73 Lewis, Kyrou and Dinelli, *Handy Hints on Legal Practice*, p. 24.
74 Ibid.
75 Greenfield, 'Hero or villain?', p. 36.
76 Ibid.
77 Rhode and Luban, *Legal Ethics*, p. 3.
78 Parker and Evans, *Inside Lawyers' Ethics*, p. 23.
79 Ibid.
80 Ibid.
81 Ibid.
82 Simon, 'Moral pluck', 421.
83 (1986) 163 CLR 54 at 70 cited in Lewis, Kyrou and Dinelli, *Handy Hints on Legal Practice*, p. 35.
84 Lewis, Kyrou and Dinelli, *Handy Hints on Legal Practice*, pp. 35–36.
85 Simon, *The Practice of Justice*, pp. 1–2.
86 Ibid., p. 4.
87 See R. Wasserstrom, 'Lawyers as professionals: some moral issues', *Human Rights*, 1995, vol. 5, 1.
88 Simon, *The Practice of Justice*, p. 1.
89 Simon, 'Moral pluck', 429.
90 Lamb and Littrich, *Lawyers in Australia*, p. 186.
91 Simon, 'Moral pluck'.
92 Ibid., 423.
93 Ibid.
94 Simon, *The Practice of Justice*, p. 23.
95 Ibid., p. 95.
96 Simon, 'Moral pluck', 442.
97 This is the wording from the film. The screenplay at this point says, 'we say for example, "The law is a sham ... there is no law ... I was a fool for having believed there was"': David Mamet, *The Verdict*, Screenplay, 26 May 2008. Available from <www.dailyscript.com/scripts/the-verdict-script.html> (accessed 29 November 2009), p. 109.
98 Mamet, *The Verdict*, Screenplay, pp. 108–9.
99 Greenfield, 'Hero or villain?', p. 36.
100 *The Verdict* DVD cover, Twentieth Century Fox Home Entertainment, 2002.
101 Asimow, 'Bad lawyers in the movies', 583.
102 Simon, 'Moral pluck', 431.

6 Solicitors as imagined masculine, family mediators as fictive feminine and the hybridization of divorce solicitors

Lisa Webley

6.1 Introduction

This chapter provides an analysis of the evolving nature of family lawyering and family mediation in divorce matters in England and Wales, and looks at some of the professional identity implications raised by it. The study upon which this chapter is based employed a ground theory method to analyse the cues that professional bodies transmit to their members via training, accreditation, best practice and professional code requirements. The data were derived from publicly available professional body documents that set out mandatory and advisory standards and policies. The study examined the extent to which the professional bodies transmit messages of adversarialism and/or consensus-based approaches to their members, in the light of statements made by policy-makers and legislators during the passage of the Family Law Bill in the United Kingdom in the mid-1990s. Further, the research addressed the nature of professional identity for each of the professional groupings, as constructed through the messages delivered by the professional bodies, employing the lens of 'imagined masculine' and 'fictive feminine' as developed by Thornton in relation to approach and identity. The labels represent a bundle of attributes and values loosely associated with adversarial and mutualist traditions, which may also be linked to dispute-resolution traditions. The research provides an analysis of some of the similarities and differences between the messages transmitted by the Law Society and the UK College of Mediators and the implications of those messages. Finally, the research examined the extent to which the higher profile of family mediation has impacted the way in which the Law Society of England and Wales interprets professional role and ethics in relation to solicitors.

6.2 Background to the study

Prior to the Family Law Act 1996, there was little public knowledge in England and Wales about family mediation.[1] Information and debate were restricted to practitioners in the field and a small group of academics who worked within family policy, family justice and family law. Most couples who were involved in divorce either conducted their case themselves[2] or sought advice and/or assistance from a solicitor – one for each of them as they were not permitted to instruct one solicitor to represent their joint interests. That remains the dominant pattern, even though attendance at an initial family mediation session is now compulsory for any individual in receipt of legal aid to conduct their divorce.

Genn's study noted that 92 per cent of respondents who were divorcing or separating indicated that they had taken legal advice, of which 82 per cent saw a solicitor. Sixty-one per cent saw a solicitor as their first port of call for advice.[3] Solicitors remain dominant within this context. The courts are still involved in divorce issues, notwithstanding the move towards alternative dispute settlement or the relative ease with which a couple may now obtain a divorce. Aside from the declaration of the end of the marriage – the *decrees nisi* and *absolute*, Genn found that 56 per cent of respondents with divorce or separation problems had a court decision or order, by far the highest percentage of all forms of civil justice legal issues considered in her study.[4] This may be attributable to the need to involve the courts in order for the marriage to be legally terminated, but it may also be because people expect to involve the courts in divorce matters, or seek the imprimatur of the courts by turning individual agreements into court orders via the use of consent orders.[5]

Official statistics indicate that there has been a decline in ancillary financial relief orders that determine the financial issues in relation to the marriage, even though this is one of the more legally complex areas to be considered on divorce.[6] Yet the courts are not called upon to adjudicate on ancillary issues in the majority of divorce cases, although when consent orders are added to other forms of order, the role of the court appears more extensive. The use of the courts and the role of the law as a validating and enforcement mechanism remain central to divorce, even if many of the orders made are with the consent of the divorcing couple, rather than as a result of court adjudication.

Although the court is now rarely involved in a substantive way as regards the divorce itself, during the passage of the Family Law Bill in 1995, this aspect of divorce overshadowed much of the debate. Lord Phillimore's comments are instructive in this regard:

> The vast majority of divorces are on the basis of behaviour and adultery.[7] Only a handful of defended divorces take place and very few of those are successfully defended. It is a sterile exercise. As was said by my noble friend Lady Faithfull, it is a traumatic experience for the children. The present existence of fault in the law does not make it more difficult in practice to obtain a divorce. It exists on paper but in practice it serves little effect to restrain a divorce . . . Therefore, the fault serves only to increase bitterness and acrimony . . . Another consequence of a defended divorce under the present law is the increased expense to the considerable detriment of the family and children.[8]

The debate elided the fault-based system of divorce, adversarialism, the role of the court and lawyers' role within the process. The traditional notion of an adversarial trial in open court with witnesses is a rarity in divorce matters, even though the rhetoric around the Family Law Bill suggested otherwise. Little attention was paid to the reality of divorce for many couples, with undue focus being placed on fault and defended petitions and perceptions of lawyer adversarialism for which there was little empirical evidence (and some counter-evidence) from studies undertaken in England and Wales.[9]

The Family Law Act 1996 increased the profile of family mediation for divorcing couples. Some individuals had been making use of mediation services prior to the Act, and family mediation services were well established in some parts of the country from the 1980s, even if they were relatively little used in most mainstream divorce cases. Mediators had also been associated with a different way of resolving disputes. Traditionally, solicitors have been perceived to be partisan advisers and advocates, and mediators viewed as dispute-settlement facilitators. The difference in professional approach has been tied in with the court-based versus non-court-based modes of dispute settlement, even though some family mediators have been annexed to courts and worked as part of court-run family mediation schemes. The privatization of divorce from court-adjudicated outcomes to negotiated settlements has promoted a reconsideration of the most appropriate mode of dispute settlement for divorce matters. Family mediators have highlighted that their mode of dispute settlement is well adapted to meeting the needs of people attempting to negotiate an agreement. Other commentators, including some solicitors, have sought to distinguish between the mode of dispute settlement and the role of the law in reaching the outcome. Some lawyers have opposed the introduction of legally aided family mediation,[10] as may be expected when a virtual monopoly comes under threat, while others appeared to welcome it with reservations.[11] Much of the concern has centred on the perception that law should play a central role in settlements and that agreements made outside a legal framework can breed long-term inequality, particularly for women.[12] This is the point from which much of the confusion in the debate stems – the conflation of professional approach, mode of dispute settlement and the role of law in reaching a settlement. Professional identity is also confused in the process.

Whether the charge of adversarialism is a true reflection of the professional bodies' attitudes to a professional approach will be considered later; however, it is certainly the case that there is an impression of adversarialism linked to solicitor practice. Even 40 per cent of the Family Mediation Association members (who traditionally operate a co-mediation strategy of one lawyer mediator with one non-lawyer mediator), when asked whether the move towards mediation in the Family Law Act 1996 would make a difference to the way in which solicitors conducted the divorce process, stated that solicitors would become 'less adversarial'.[13] However, the spectre of law is still evident and available where private justice cannot be reached between the parties. And it could be argued that the law is present even in negotiated agreements.[14] The confusion around professional approach, mode of dispute settlement and the role of the law is also now being heightened by professionals dual-qualifying as both solicitors and family mediators.

6.3 Method

A great deal of research has been conducted on divorce, family solicitors and family mediators and their roles in the process of divorce.[15] Previous studies have tended to focus either on the role that family solicitors or family mediators perform in process terms, or on the outcome of their intervention. Others have looked at family mediation or family solicitors but have not compared the two directly.[16] Some have carried out extensive empirical studies on what family mediators or family solicitors do, and this study has drawn upon these findings.[17] However, none appears to have looked at the training, accreditation and codes of conduct of divorce solicitors and family mediators in England and Wales to examine what these indicate about adversarial or consensus-based approaches to dispute settlement on divorce.

It is accepted that there will be as many professional approaches as there will be professionals working as solicitors and family mediators in England and Wales. With this in mind, the study focused on the macro level – the national professional level – namely the standards set by the Law Society of England and Wales (Law Society) and the UK College of Mediators (UK College). The research examined what cues the professional bodies give to their members, and what these indicate about the professionally acceptable best-practice approaches to the work of solicitors and of mediators in divorce disputes. It is admitted that this does not capture the subtleties of individual practice; however, it also controls for the quirks of individual professionals. Equally, the signals that the professional bodies transmit to their members may not be picked up by their members, or may be thwarted or misinterpreted. That is accepted too, although it is submitted that the professions subconsciously or consciously inculcate certain values into the profession in relation to acceptable approaches to the professional project, even if some members may not be as influenced by this as others.

For the purposes of the research, training was defined as the training required in order to permit admittance as initial or trainee members of the profession. The professional bodies control, at least in part, the content of and standards associated with initial training courses, even if they do not provide the courses themselves. There are some difficulties with this method. Solicitors do not specialize prior to beginning legal practice and therefore generic courses for would-be solicitors have been considered alongside family-specific courses for family mediators. This is not ideal; however, it reflects the reality of professionally ascribed training in this context. In addition, a number of other assumptions have been made. It has been assumed for the purposes of this study that those entering family mediation training and professional training to be a solicitor had already successfully obtained an undergraduate degree or equivalent other qualification. It is admitted that a large proportion of entrants into the solicitor's profession do so after completing an undergraduate LLB degree course rather than through the non-qualifying law degree route followed by the Graduate Diploma in Law (GDL) course (often known as the CPE course or the conversion course).[18] However, there is no equivalent subject-specific degree programme for family mediators with which to compare a law degree programme, and the GDL coupled with the Legal Practice Course (LPC) appeared to be the most appropriate comparator to family mediation foundation training. Further, the GDL and the LLB are both required to cover the seven foundations of legal knowledge, so a core component of legal education may be found in both courses, even though there are a number of important differences between them.

The documentation on the accreditation requirements or the post-entry training and supervision requirements for full membership of the solicitor's profession (to reach 'Solicitor of the Supreme Court of England and Wales' status) and of the family mediation profession (to reach full membership of the UK College of Mediators or practitioner members of the Family Mediation Panel of the Law Society of England and Wales) was also examined. Once again, the underlying assumption for this method of analysis has been that mandatory professional requirements will have an impact on the way in which professionals approach their work. In addition, the accreditation requirements have also been considered for solicitors who wish to be accredited as family law specialists by the Law Society. This specialist group is subject to detailed higher level testing to ensure that individuals meet a quality threshold in family law matters. All must first qualify as solicitors.

Finally, the study also considered the codes of practice and additional specialist codes for solicitors, accredited family law solicitors and family mediators. All practising solicitors are required to follow the solicitors' code of conduct, the Guide to the Professional Conduct of Solicitors, and family law solicitors who apply for accredited family law status must comply with the Family Law Protocol. Solicitors who carry out family mediation are encouraged to meet the requirements of the voluntary code of conduct on family mediation, the Code of Practice for Family Mediators. Family mediators who are members of the UK College are required to meet the requirements of the College Code of Practice for Family Mediators.

The research involved a grounded theory analysis of the training documentation published by the Law Society and the UK College in respect of solicitors, accredited family solicitor specialists and family mediators regulated by the Law Society and the UK College. The grounded theory method requires the researcher to read each document, line by line, and note down any conceptual categories encountered.[19] Each document is considered in sequence, and categories that are repeated are retained, with those that find no traction within later documents discarded. All documents published by the professional bodies in respect of training, accreditation, best-practice guidance and the codes of conduct that were extant as at 31 December 2006 were analysed. Over time, the categories solidified and links began to appear between them; these are known as theoretical concepts. As the data cycles progressed, links also began to emerge between the theoretical categories, which developed into a grounded theory that appeared to explain the association between the theoretical categories. The analysis ended at the point when saturation had occurred and the researcher believed she had a solid theory that brought together the theoretical concepts, which in turn explained and brought together the conceptual categories. In view of the relatively short length of this chapter, it is not possible to demonstrate the detail of the conceptual category generation, nor indeed much of the detail in relation to conceptual categories; however, it is hoped that the overview of research findings and its discussion in the light of the 'fictive feminine' and the 'imagined masculine' will prove useful nonetheless. The findings reveal some of the theoretical and practice-based similarities and differences between the different professional groupings, which have implications for the way in which we define professionalism and identity.

At this point, some may be asking why a gender lens was chosen as a proxy for identity. Why not simply describe what has been found without recourse to these gender-based labels? The study did not begin as an attempt to consider professional approach and professional identity with reference to gender assumptions. However, during the study the author and Liz Duff were asked to undertake research on the reasons why women solicitors were leaving the solicitor's profession in England and Wales at a far greater rate than male solicitors.[20] The gender dimension arose during focus group interviews with women solicitors, who noted some of their disenchantment with legal practice related to rigid views on what constituted being 'a good lawyer', which skills were recognized and which were required but ignored. Not all women solicitors felt the same, as one would expect, and some noted that different areas of law appeared to operate differently, as did different types of firm. This led to an examination of approach and identity, and links began to appear with the study on training, accreditation and ethical conduct and good practice, about messages sent by the legal profession to its members in the context of divorce matters.

Why limit the scope of the research to divorce and why not include other forms of relationship breakdown instead? Similar issues arise for cohabiting non-married couples as for married couples: child contact and residence, child support, property and finance. As O'Donovan points out,[21] there are varying and various forms of families, few of which fulfil the idealized nuclear, married family conception of 'family', and therefore divorce is only part of a larger issue of family breakdown and of professional intervention in instances of family breakdown. However, family policies and family law privilege marriage over other forms of family union, and ascribe formalities and legal consequences to this type of relationship that are not apparent in others. It is argued by Eekelaar that there are three kinds of assumptions behind family law: predictive assumptions based on what the law considers is likely to happen, normative assumptions about what people – or at least the majority of people – believe ought to happen and value assumptions through which policy-makers and the law indicate what ought to happen.[22] Law regulates marriage in a way it does not for other family groupings,[23] relying heavily on normative and value assumptions both at the inception of marriage and on divorce. These constrain and support divorcing couples in a way that does not immediately impact on non-married couples.

The next section will provide a brief summary of the findings in relation to the three data sources. The following section will consider professional identity for solicitors, family law specialist solicitors, Law Society-regulated family mediators and UK College family mediators. The final section will provide some brief conclusions.

6.4 Summary of findings in relation to training, accreditation and codes of conduct

This section sets out the research findings regarding the messages sent to the respective professionals by their professional bodies through training, accreditation and codes of conduct.

6.4.1 Training

The documentation indicated that the training for would-be solicitors seeks to broaden and deepen students' legal knowledge. It also aims to develop the skills needed in order to be able to use substantive knowledge effectively. Skills development is focused on those interpersonal skills required to enhance the solicitor–client relationship, although there is no evidence of overt skills training in how to enable a client in making decisions that assist in giving effective instructions to the solicitor. This is interesting, as it appears to be at odds with the reality of family legal practice as discussed in the literature, which has found that solicitors try to steer their clients towards appropriate settlements and to raise or lower their expectations, while taking into account the needs of any dependants, such as children.[24] The lack of negotiation skills training (in formal training courses), and the inclusion of advocacy and litigation skills, provides some evidence for the proposition that solicitors are trained to practise in the shadow of litigation, even if they do not regularly take cases on to court.

Family mediator training, on the other hand, appears to reinforce, and if necessary inculcate, key values and principles within students. It is training in values and skills rather than knowledge-based training. Facilitation skills are prized, presumably as the key to assist clients to reach their own decisions. The documentation revealed no evidence of training in a normative structure through which clients may be assisted to reach an 'appropriate' agreement for UK College family mediators. Impartiality is emphasized. There is evidence within the professional documentation to support the proposition that family mediators adopt a consensus-based approach to practice; however, the documentation is vague, particularly for UK College family mediators, about when a mediator must intervene to prevent a prima facie consensual settlement that is manifestly unfair for one of the parties or for the children. This goes to the heart of the distinction between information giving and advising, which is one of the major distinctions between family mediation and solicitor approaches to divorce.

6.4.2 Accreditation

The analysis demonstrated that both professional bodies exercise continued control of their membership following entry into the profession. The accreditation requirements set by the Law Society and the UK College reflect their view of their role. The documentation suggests that the Law Society regards its role as that of a gatekeeper, ensuring that those who wish to receive the status of full member, regardless of whether they wish to be a solicitor or a Law Society mediator, meet a minimum standard of competence to be assessed in detail against specific outcome-based criteria. Once a professional is admitted to full membership, scrutiny of competence is left to the profession itself – the Law Society does not require further evidence of competence. The exception to this is specialist accreditation to the Family Law Panel (at Member and Advanced Member levels). Those solicitors who wish to attain specialist status must resubmit to assessment every five years, which involves an element of reflective practice. As much of the assessment is knowledge-based, and the law changes at a rapid rate, it could be argued that resubmission to assessment is a necessary condition of continued specialist status and the continued endorsement of the Law Society, although resubmission to assessment is not within usual Law Society practice for non-specialist solicitors. Family Law Panel members are required to have the characteristics of solicitors but also to adopt a conciliatory approach to family law matters, including alternative modes of resolving disputes (if appropriate), which brings their professional approach closer to the approach that has been identified as consensus based rather than adversarial. Having said that, Family Law Panel members appear to maintain their partisan stance, but attempt to broker a settlement that they and their clients consider to be appropriate.

The UK College appears to regard its role as a continuing one, more as the supervisor of its members than as a gatekeeper. This may reflect the fact that the UK College is of relatively recent inception and it oversees a relatively new profession without a large, established and competitive market.[25] Accreditation requirements for family mediators are set at a relatively low level in some respects – professional experience is measured in hours rather than in days, but again this may reflect the lack of an established market, rather than an unwillingness to set stringent standards. Instead, the UK College compensates for this low experience requirement with ongoing surveillance of members, including peer observation of the family mediator and the need for professional endorsement by a professional practice consultant.

6.4.3 Codes of conduct

The categories derived from the codes of conduct and best-practice requirements indicate the relative importance placed by solicitors on the role of legal norms within divorce matters. This in turn has an impact on the way in which solicitors advise their clients on appropriate settlement alternatives, as the solicitor should provide information then advice. To some extent, even family mediators

recognize legal norms as a guide to a range of appropriate settlement arrangements. UK College family mediators consider law to be one of a set of normative
frameworks that the clients may access to assist them in reaching a decision. The
UK College stresses the importance of facilitative approaches to mediation in
which it is for the clients to seek value-laden views – advice from a solicitor or
others – rather than for the family mediator to provide those views. The family
mediator will provide the legal information that is appropriate to the clients in
certain circumstances.

The Law Society code for family mediation adopts a halfway approach: law is
the final layer of protection. It requires Law Society family mediators to put
clients on notice if they are reaching an agreement that is not one that a court
would normally reach in their situation. But it leaves the clients free to go ahead
with the arrangement after being reminded that they should seek legal advice
before finalizing the agreement. This provides a degree of protection to the clients
as it may mitigate the effects of reaching (or being persuaded to reach) an agreement on the basis of inadequate knowledge of one's legal entitlement, assuming
that the Law Society family mediator has a full enough knowledge of the client's
situation to permit them to provide an assessment of divergence of any agreement from the legal standard.

The basis for decision-making is viewed differently by solicitors and family
mediators – the former view decision-making in the context of the law (even for
Law Society family mediators), while the latter view decision-making in the context of consensus, whether or not it conforms to legal entitlement. Solicitors have
the final role of championing the client's case through the formal legal process if
necessary, but the Family Law Protocol makes it clear that their role is not the role
of an adversary, using whatever tactics they may legally employ in order to obtain
the best deal for their client. Their role is to encourage, cajole and if necessary
intervene to get clients to behave as responsibly as possible towards their families.
This takes the solicitor away from the model of 'hired gun' for the client towards a
conciliator with knowledge of the law, of many previous divorces and of how to
navigate the client through a difficult time. This is an interesting development in
the role of the solicitor – influenced, some would say, by the emergence of family
mediation and the ethics of mediation.

6.5 Professional approach, professional identity: 'fictive feminine', 'imagined masculine' and the hybridization of divorce solicitors

What did the analysis indicate about the signals that the professional bodies
transmit about being a solicitor, an accredited family law solicitor and a family
mediator regulated by the Law Society and/or by the UK College of Mediators?
The starting point for this study was the rhetoric surrounding adversarial and
consensus-based approaches to dispute settlement in a legal context with regard to
solicitors and family mediators. However, there is a psychological, sociological and
criminological literature on adversarialism. This literature links adversarialism

and mutualism (a more developed form of consensus-based decision-making) to gender and gender traits. The literature links adversarialism to a traditional conceptualization of the masculine identity[26] and mutualism to a traditional conception of a feminine identity.[27] Naturally, 'masculine' and 'feminine' are highly contested terms, and appear to reduce the debate to a binary divide that appears to elide sex and gender and to divide attributes and proclivities between them. Thornton provides an extremely useful overview of the difficulties associated with the terms. She argues that 'feminine' is used to denote a:

> cluster of values conventionally ascribed to women, including care, corporeality, emotion, dependence and docility. Some of these terms have negative and disempowering connotations, and are the antithesis of notions of freedom, independence and autonomy. To stress the constructivist meaning of the feminine and to avoid its conflation with biological women, which all too often occurs within legal and other discourses, I used the term 'fictive feminine'.[28]

There remain some difficulties with the term 'fictive feminine', not least the charge of gender essentialism; however, as used by Thornton, it is a label for a conception of feminine rather than to describe women, femininity or feminism. It is a shorthand expression of the depiction of the feminine in Western literature, even if there may be legitimate debate about whether the depiction is distorted and even fallacious. Thornton has labelled conceptions of the masculine within the same tradition as the 'imagined masculine', thus:

> contrast the term with the 'imagined masculine' which includes a cluster of characteristics likely to be ascribed to [benchmark] men and which carry more positive connotations – such as rationality, objectivity, independence, and strength. Within the Western intellectual traditional, these imagined values of masculinity and femininity have come to be associated with public and private and, in turn, with law and non-law binarisms that are themselves open to question.[29]

Thornton further argues that other values associated with the 'fictive feminine' are 'community, consultation, conciliation, compassion, consideration and care'[30] in contrast to those of the 'imagined masculine' that encompass 'competitiveness, adversarialism, and commitment to a cold and uncompromising vision of justice that extols means-ends rationality'.[31] Consequently, she argues that 'fictive feminine' values are premised on mutualism – cooperation, equality and comparison – and 'imagined masculine' are premised on adversarialism – competitiveness, assertion of rights and individualism. Interestingly, different strands of feminism have interpreted the challenge of the 'feminine' in different ways: some have sought to capitalize on the caring dimensions of this theory to promote a feminist ethic of care, such as that argued by Gilligan,[32] while others, such as MacKinnon, have been deeply critical of this approach, as it can be used to elide women with child-rearing and care for men as an inherent biological char-acteristic.[33] Others, too, have provided detailed discussion of the traditional conceptions of masculinist and feminist traits in a professional context.[34] It is important to note that women and men will have aspects of the 'imagined mascu-line' and the 'fictive feminine' within them, and therefore the charge of essential-ism need not derail the theory in this context. They are being used here as labels for conceptions rather than labels for women and for men, and are evidence of dominant gender identity rather than biology. It is noted that gender, biology and identity are often considered to be synonymous in many contexts within society, thus forming a nexus leading to the potential for profound discrimination, but for reasons of space this issue will not be considered any further here.

Adversarialism and mutualism are also conceptions of interaction and decision-making that have different starting points.[35] The literature explains that adver-sarialism is reliant on autonomy, on objectivity and on the assertion of a right against another's position, as well as being outcome focused, whereas mutualism relies on notions of mutual respect, cooperation and interrelationships, and mutual trust and development, being process focused.[36] These features have been mirrored in the professional and academic literature on the use of law and the use of mediation, although less explicitly in relation to mutualism. The findings in this study reintegrate the theory of adversarialism and a weaker form of mutual-ism (consensus-based decision-making) with their gendered conceptions, as the theory underpinning adversarialism and consensus explains the core theory that emerged from the data. The next section will take each of these professional groups in turn and provide an explanation of what the professional bodies' docu-mentation has revealed about professional identity, with reference to the 'imagined masculine' and 'fictive feminine' traits that have been associated with adversarialism and consensus.

The next four subsections consider professional identity as constructed for non-specialist solicitors (those that have trained as solicitors but have not sought train-ing and accreditation as specialist family law solicitors), accredited family law solicitors, family mediators regulated by the Law Society, and lastly family medi-ators regulated by the UK College of Mediators. Each subsection paints a portrait of the professional as defined by the professional body, and as such provides an insight into the professional's apparent traits, skills and values.

6.5.1 Professional identity as constructed by the professional body: non-specialist solicitors

The documentation has revealed that the Law Society of England and Wales transmits the message that a non-specialist accredited solicitor's identity is more closely associated with the 'imagined masculine' rather than 'fictive feminine' characteristics or traits. An archetypal 'non-specialist' solicitor embodies mastery of a large body of knowledge and is emotionally controlled – there is little emphasis on emotional intelligence or on active empathy; instead, the solicitor is to be distanced and impersonal.[37] The distanced professional stance, in contrast to a more personally involved one, is reinforced by the way in which solicitors are taught law and how they are trained to critique and apply it.[38] There is a reliance on a non-empathic skills base, with the exception of relating skills required in order to secure information needed to formulate advice.[39] Such a solicitor is expected to be an outcome-oriented problem solver, someone who is potentially adversarial but only when that is what is required in order to attain an appropriate outcome for the client. To achieve this, the solicitor is expected to be firm but fair, partisan and pragmatic, as evidenced by the codes of conduct and best-practice statements indicating when a solicitor must insist on certain conditions being met by the client or the client's former spouse or legal representative, if the retainer is not to be terminated by the solicitor. This archetypal professional is also deemed to be financially and business minded,[40] as well as a reflective practitioner (during the training and accreditation stages), as this is required to enhance competence and to retain professional standing. In short, the non-specialist solicitor is the traditional, effective, noble professional.[41]

6.5.2 Professional identity as constructed by the professional body: accredited family law solicitors

The accredited family law solicitor, the specialist, is considered to be a step apart from the non-specialist solicitor although she has similar traits. The differences stem from the way in which the family law solicitor is trained to relate to the client and the client's family law matter. The accreditation and best-practice documentation suggest that accredited family law solicitors begin their professional life by following the persona of the distanced male solicitor but then put on a thin 'emotionally understanding' cloak over this identity. The cloak obscures but does not obliterate the 'imagined masculine' traits, but instead displays a more 'feminine' identity to the client.[42] This archetype presents as a realistic negotiator, who aims to achieve a fair settlement for the family rather than solely for the client. Decision-making is as consensual as is possible between the solicitors for both clients, but the family law solicitor is also an expectation manager, particularly for her own client, as there are some inherent value assumptions about what is right (although it is hoped that 'right' and 'legal' dovetail). Consequently, the 'masculine' has not been lost entirely. The solicitor is also partisan on the one hand while keeping an eye on the collective unit on the other (the individual should not profit to the real detriment of related others). And the solicitor is expected to be able to foresee consequences for non-clients and focus the client on those. She should be emotionally understanding yet sufficiently emotionally distanced in order to retain professionalism.[43] The solicitor's professionalism extends to multi-agency working when necessary, which is consistent with collegial working practices.[44] She should also be able to balance multiple interconnected issues and yet be able to separate these issues when required. Such a solicitor is still fundamentally outcome oriented (with the use of litigation if required), while taking into account the impact of the current process and the long-term consequences of the process and the outcome once the solicitor has ceased to act. In sum, the accredited family solicitor is a newly feminized professional who retains the skeleton of her original 'imagined masculine' identity with emotional add-ons, who has a greater overview, but who is also consequently potentially less authoritative, as authority and empathy are often considered to be contradictory.[45]

6.5.3 Professional identity as constructed by the professional body: Law Society family mediator

A Law Society-trained family mediator has first been through training as a solicitor and has adopted the identity of the 'imagined masculine' professional. Mediators are required to wear a thick humanizing cloak that all but obscures their original identity and allows them to be emotionally enlightened negotiation facilitators. The professional body assumes emotional aptitude and an ability to be impartial and facilitative, but it does not require the professional to believe in the values espoused by the family mediation movement. One could speculate that this is because belief in these values runs contrary to a traditionally masculinist view of professionalism that is born out of Western liberalism.[46] Inclination to mediate is the key rather than a belief in family mediation as a process of transformation and empowerment for the clients. The Law Society appears to recognize that family mediators may need training by way of resocialization in emotional intelligence (some may say, rather uncharitably, emotional literacy).[47] Family mediation is viewed as a process rather than a profession – process training is provided as well as the theoretical underpinning, but it is taught in a way that requires the solicitor to understand decision-making in an emotional context on the assumption that this is distinct from rational decision-making.[48] Law Society family mediators never lose their solicitor identity, and so are trained to be ever vigilant that the cloak may slip and reveal this to their mediation clients. This cloak assists with neutrality, and professionals must constantly remind themselves of the need to be non-partisan; the problem-solver must remember to be a facilitator. This raises an interesting paradox, as rationality and impartiality are generally associated with the 'imagined masculine' even though empathy and facilitation are more closely associated with the 'fictive feminine'.[49] However, there are circumstances under which the Law Society family mediator is required to remove the cloak – when power imbalances between the clients are too great, or where the agreement that is being reached would offend against fundamental legal principles aimed at the protection of the clients. The Law Society family mediator thus always retains the solicitor identity underneath, including the solicitor's legal normative framework.

6.5.4 Professional identity as constructed by the professional body: UK College family mediator

The UK College-trained family mediator must have some of the markers of the family mediator identity before being permitted to undertake training. She must then adopt the full family mediator identity and maintain it with active adherence to a family mediator's beliefs and values. This mediator is a true facilitator, and in some circumstances may also be a transformer – the person who shows their clients how to change the way in which they interact and negotiate between themselves and with others. UK College mediators are inherently impartial – unlike Law Society-trained family mediators, who must remind themselves of the need to be impartial when acting as mediators. They are provided with the knowledge that is necessary to be effective family mediators, but all knowledge is of equal importance – for example, legal knowledge is given similar weight to the knowledge related to how to involve children in mediation sessions. Knowledge transmission is also very limited, although present. UK College family mediators remain reflective with regard to their professional development, although the UK College does warn family mediators to beware of the influence of their previous professional identity – belief in family mediation may be so strong that it overwrites previous identities. This is reinforced through professional practice consultancy through which experienced family mediators oversee, assist and in part supervise other family mediators in their professional development. This is in keeping with feminized professions, in which there is often greater supervision of members as, it has been argued, the greater the feminization the more likelihood that members are viewed as less authoritative and thus in need of greater supervision.[50] UK College family mediators are flexible yet process controlling, empathic and transformative, yet firm in the face of inappropriate behaviour. They encourage consensual decision-making, and may suggest that clients gain outside advice before they reach a final agreement – there is a deferral to outside authority on the one hand, while preserving the identity of the family mediation profession, which encompasses collegiality and loyalty. The mediator should aim as far as possible to maintain a relative power balance between the separating couple, but there are virtually no circumstances under which she should challenge the client's agreement unless the safety of one of the clients or a child is in danger, as there is no single normative framework against which an agreement is to be judged. The clients are the guardians of the norms, which are personal to them, and the family mediator is the guardian of the process and its integrity. Thus the UK College family mediator embodies many of the characteristics associated with the 'fictive feminine', and is the most closely associated with this conception than the other professional groupings.

6.6 Conclusions

What have we learned as a result of this study? It appears that the Law Society promotes the traditional professional, distanced identity that prizes problem solving and emotional distance through its generalist training, accreditation requirements and code of conduct. However, as family mediation has attracted more attention, so has the role of empathy along with the skills of facilitation. The Law Society has attempted subtly to re-engineer the professional identity of family law solicitors to make it more feminized, more consensus oriented and less adversarial, even if adversarialism is less evident within the training, accreditation and codes of conduct for all solicitors than the literature would suggest. It is by no means certain whether this has come from a genuine desire to seek greater feminization or a cynical desire to promote professional capture of the family mediation field by its members. As the Law Society has ostensibly embraced more traditionally feminized characteristics within the professional project, it has also felt the need to monitor accredited family solicitor expertise on a periodic basis. This may be purely a function of the expert status accorded to accredited family solicitors, rather than the concern to monitor feminized professionals more closely than the more usual distanced professional, although this is unclear. The Law Society family mediator appears to be a further extension of the feminized professional, rather than a believer in the family mediation project as the UK College requires of its family mediators. The UK College's documentation appears to suggest an apparent obliteration of a family mediator's previous professional identity. It selects for, and further inculcates, a belief in family mediation values, even though family mediation is viewed by the Law Society as a process-oriented profession rather than a substantive one. For the Law Society, family mediation is a skills-based tool rather than a value-driven process distinct from the law and court involvement.

The messages transmitted by the Law Society to its solicitors have yet to filter down to the public, even if they have been evidenced within the profession by a number of empirical studies that have examined solicitors and family solicitors in some detail. The messages transmitted by the UK College to family mediators have also been transmitted to the public and have been picked up in the media, in political debates and in the academic literature. As little large-scale observational empirical research has been undertaken on family mediation and on family mediation sessions in England and Wales, it is difficult to know whether the messages sent by the professional body are shared and embraced by its professionals. That is an area for further study.

The Law Society appears to have adopted the 'feminine' traits and approaches that it considers constructive in the family law arena, and the UK College has embraced many of them wholeheartedly. Indeed, the Law Society had already begun to signal its support for these values, even at the time when its members were being chastised publicly for their perceived adversarialism. It is clear that both professional bodies in a family context appear to be converging on a feminized conception of the professional, which shuns latent adversarialism and prizes cooperation and settlement for the good of children and long-term parenting arrangements. There may be fewer differences between family law solicitors and family mediators with respect to their professional approach than between non-specialist solicitors and family mediators, but the distinction between a legal normative framework for family law solicitors and no clear normative framework for family mediators persists.

Acknowledgements

Much of this material formed part of the author's Ph.D. research, completed in 2007. A much more detailed exposition of the findings may be found in

L.C. Webley, Adversarialism and Consensus? The Professions' Construction of Solicitor and Family Mediator Identity and Role (QuidPro forthcoming 2010).

Notes

1 Haynes illustrated this point around the time of the passage of the Family Law Bill 1995 by reference to where family mediation services were indexed in the *Yellow Pages* (or equivalent) in each city he visited on his speaking tours. He reported that family mediation services were often wrongly indexed and advertised in the meditation section, leading him to conclude that few people understood what mediation was nor had spotted and reported the error. For details, see the introduction of J. Haynes, *The Fundamentals of Family Mediation*, New York: Albany State University and New York Press, 1994.

2 The Solicitors Family Law Association Divorce Procedure Fact Sheet. Available from: <www.sfla.org.uk/factsheetdisplay.php?id=18> (accessed 20 October 2009). The SFLA has subsequently been renamed Resolution.

3 H. Genn, *Paths to Justice: What Do People Think About Going To Law?* Oxford: Hart Publishing, 1999, 115.

4 Ibid.

5 As suggested by G. Douglas, 'Resolving family disputes', Nuffield Seminars in Civil Justice, Seminar 4, 4 March 2002, 5.

6 Judicial statistics indicate that during 2005 there were 151,654 divorce petitions lodged, which resulted in 142,393 *decrees absolute*. See *Judicial Statistics 2005*, London: Department for Constitutional Affairs, 2006, 60–62. There were over 50,000 ancillary relief consent orders, the largest number of court orders other than *decrees nisi* and *absolute*. These orders are made at the request of the divorcing couple. In relation to court orders made by the judiciary, there were 15,468 maintenance orders in respect of children, although most child maintenance issues since April 1993 have been dealt with by the Child Support Agency. There were also 4,721 orders for periodical payments, 9,470 lump sum orders, 10,940 property adjustment orders, 2,943 pension sharing or attachment orders and 50,140 other ancillary relief consent orders. *Judicial Statistics 2005*, London: Department for Constitutional Affairs, 2006, Tables 5.5 and 5.7, pp. 73–74.

7 Lord Phillimore quotes the figure of 75 per cent earlier on in his speech.

8 Lord Phillimore, *Hansard* (HL), 11 January 1996, cols. 338 and 339.

9 See, for example, R. Ingelby, 'The solicitor as intermediary', in R. Dingwall and J. Eekelaar (eds), *Divorce Mediation and the Legal Process*, New York, Oxford: Oxford University Press, 1988.

10 See L. Tsang, 'Separating the issues – Mediation is no longer seen as sounding the death knell for family lawyers as it appeared to do when the Family Law Bill was published in 1995', *Law Society Gazette*, general news section, 21 July 1999; cf. S. Ward, 'Some of the issues topping the conference agenda, as solicitors congregate to discuss "Fitting the Profession for the Future"', *Law Society Gazette*, 8 October 1997, general news section.

11 'Fault Lines Rock Act', *Law Society Gazette*, 1 February 2001, 26.

12 For a discussion, see L. C. Webley, *A Review of the Literature on Family Mediation in England and Wales, France, Ireland, Scotland and the United States*, London: Lord Chancellor's Advisory Committee on Legal Education and Conduct, 1998, 86–90. On mediator neutrality, see further, for example, R. Field, 'Mediation praxis: The myths and realities of the intersection of mediator neutrality and the process of redressing power imbalances', Fifth National Mediation Conference, Australia, 2000. Available from: <www.apmec.unisa.edu.au/events/conference2000/field.pdf> (accessed 20 October

2009); and K. Douglas and R. Field, 'Looking for answers to mediation's neutrality dilemma in therapeutic jurisprudence', *ELaw Journal* 2006, vol. 13(2), 177.

13 P. McCarthy and J. Walker, 'Mediation and divorce – The FMA view', *Family Law*, February 1996, 112.

14 R. H. Mnookin and L. Kornhauser, 'Bargaining in the shadow of the law: The case of divorce', *Yale Law Journal*, 1979, vol. 88(5), 50.

15 See for family solicitors' skills: A. Sherr, H. Lewis-Ruttley and L. Webley, *A Training Skills Analysis for Family Lawyers*, London: Institute of Advanced Legal Studies, 1995. See J. Haynes, *The Fundamentals of Family Mediation*; and S. Roberts, 'Three models of family mediation', in R. Dingwall and J. Eekelaar (eds), *Divorce Mediation and the Legal Process*, Oxford: Clarendon Press, 1988, 144–49 in relation to family mediators.

16 See G. Davis et al., *Monitoring Publicly Funded Family Mediation: Final Report to the Legal Services Commission*, Legal Services Commission, 2000 for a detailed consideration of family mediators in the context of legal aid work.

17 See J. Eekelaar, M. Maclean and S. Beinart, *Family Lawyers: The Divorce Work of Solicitors*, Oxford: Hart Publishing, 2000 for a detailed consideration of the role and approach of family law solicitors; see also Ingelby, 'The solicitor as intermediary'; and see G. Davis, *Partisans and Mediators: The Resolution of Divorce Disputes*, Oxford: Clarendon Press, 1988, for a comparison of solicitors and mediators in the context of divorce, researched at a micro level.

18 The Law Society's Annual Statistical Review 2006 notes that the GDL route is the second most frequently adopted route into the profession, after the LLB route, of seven possible routes.

19 A. Strauss and J. Corbin, *Basics of Qualitative Research: Techniques and Procedures for Developing Grounded Theory*, 2nd edn, Thousand Oaks, CA: Sage, 1998, 44–45; See B. G. Glaser, 'Constructivist grounded theory?', *Qualitative Sozialforschung/Forum: Qualitative Social Research* (online journal), 2002, vol. 3(3). Available from <www.qualitative-research.net/fqs/fqs-eng.htm> (accessed 20 October 2009); cf. K. Charmaz, 'Grounded theory: Objectives and constructivist methods', in N. K. Denzin and Y. S. Lincoln (eds), *Handbook of Qualitative Research*, 2nd edn, Thousand Oaks, CA: Sage, 2000, 509–35; B. D. Haig, 'Grounded theory as scientific method', *Philosophy of Education*, 1995. Available from <www.edu.uiuc.edu/EPS/PES-yearbook95_docs/haig.html> (accessed 20 October 2009). See further B. M. Kinach, 'Grounded theory as scientific method: Haig-inspired reflections on educational research methodology', *Philosophy of Education*, 1995. Available from <www.edu.uiuc.edu/EPS/PES-Yearbook/95_docs/kinach. html> (accessed 20 October 2009). See also M. B. Miles, 'Qualitative data as an attractive nuisance: The problem of analysis', *Administrative Science Quarterly*, 1979, vol. 24, 590.

20 See L. Webley and L. Duff, 'Women solicitors as a barometer for problems within the legal profession – time to put values before profits?', *Journal of Law & Society*, 2007, vol. 34(3), 374–402.

21 K. O'Donovan, *Family Law Matters*, London: Pluto Press, 1993, 30–33.

22 J. Eekelaar, 'Uncovering social obligations: Family law and the responsible citizen', in M. Maclean (ed.), *Making Law for Families*, Oxford: Hart Publishing, 2000, 9.

23 Although with the introduction of civil partnerships, this is set to change for same-sex relationships that have been put on a legal footing through the Civil Partnership Act 2004.

24 See J. Eekelaar, M. Maclean and S. Beinart, *Family Lawyers: The Divorce Work of Solicitors*, Oxford: Hart Publishing, 2000.

25 For a discussion of professionalization and the development of professions, see for example H. L. Wilensky, 'The professionalization of everyone?', *American Journal of Sociology*, 1964, vol. 70(2), 137; M. Larson, 'The rise of professionalism: A sociological analysis, Berkeley, CA: University of California Press, 1977; R. L. Abel, 'The rise of professionalism', *British Journal of Law and Society*, 1979, vol. 6, 82.

26 See, for example, M. Karlberg, 'The power of discourse and the discourse of power: Pursuing peace through discourse intervention', *International Journal of Peace Studies*, 2005, vol. 10(1), 1, discussing the link between adversarialism, conflict, competition and power, which obscure mutualism and its importance. This draws upon 'power as domination' discourse: Machiavelli, Weber, Bourdieu as well as feminist critiques of the 'power as domination model' and the development of a 'power with model' that characterizes mutualism: 'Together, mutualistic power relations and adversarial power relations constitute two parallel and mutually exclusive relational categories' (p. 9).

27 Thornton draws upon Gilligan's discussion from *In a Different Voice: Psychological Theory and Women's Development*, Cambridge, MA: Harvard University Press, 1982, positing that the reason why feminist lawyers have found work within legal practice so difficult is associated with extreme adversarialism in legal practice. However, Gilligan's theory has been criticized due to concerns of gender essentialism. M. Thornton, ' "Otherness" on the bench: How merit is gendered', *Sydney Law Review*, 2007, vol. 29, 396.

28 M. Thornton, 'Towards embodied justice: Wrestling with legal ethics in the age of the "new corporatism" ', *Melbourne University Law Review*, 1999, vol. 28, in *IV Femina, Feminine, Feminist*.

29 Ibid.

30 Ibid.

31 Ibid.

32 See, for example, C. Gilligan, *In a Different Voice: Psychological Theory and Women's Development*, Cambridge, MA: Harvard University Press, 1982; N. Noddings, *Caring: A Feminine Approach to Ethics and Moral Education*, Berkeley, CA: University of California Press, 1984; and T. Cockburn, 'Children and the feminist ethic of care', *Childhood*, 2005, vol. 12(1), 71.

33 C. MacKinnon, *Feminism Unmodified: Discourses on Life and Law*, Cambridge MA: Harvard University Press, 1987, 39, discussed by Thornton.

34 See, for example, Webley and Duff, 'Women solicitors as a barometer', 374. For a discussion of the traditional definitions of gender and the difficulty of essentialism, see N. Dowd, 'Resisting essentialism and hierarchy: A critique of work/family strategies for women lawyers', *Harvard Blackletter Law Journal*, 2000, vol. 16, 815; C. Menkel-Meadow, 'The comparative sociology of women lawyers: The "feminization" of the legal profession', *Osgoode Hall Law Journal*, 1986, vol. 24, 987. For a critique in relation to masculinities, see R. Collier, 'Reflections on the relationship between law and masculinities: Rethinking the "man question" in legal studies', *Current Legal Problems*, 2003, vol. 56, 354. See further for a critique, H. Sommerlad, ' "Becoming" a lawyer: gender and the processes of professional identity', in E. Sheehy and S. McIntyre (eds) *Calling for Change; Women, Law and the Legal Profession*, Ottawa: University of Ottawa Press, 2006.

35 For a discussion in a different context, see G. Barak, 'A reciprocal approach to peace-making criminology: Between adversarialism and mutualism', *Theoretical Criminology* 2005, vol. 9(2), 131.

36 Mutualism, feminism and the ethic of care have been linked, as have adversarialism, objectivity and autonomy, which are identified as masculine traits. For a helpful summary of the debate on this point, see T. Cockburn, 'Children and the feminist ethic of care', *Childhood*, 2005, vol. 12, 73, who cites the work of Curtin, Plumwood, Gilligan and Code in this respect.

37 R. Collier, 'The changing university and the (legal) academic career – Rethinking the relationship between women, men and the "private life" of the law school', *Legal Studies*, 2002, vol. 22, 3–4, discussing reconceptualizing gender and the traditional understanding of the masculine.

38 See C. Menkel-Meadow, 'Can a law teacher avoid teaching legal ethics?', *Journal of Legal Education*, 1991, vol. 41, 7. See further C. Menkel-Meadow, 'Portia in a different voice: speculations on a woman's lawyering process', *Berkeley Women's Law Journal*, 1985, vol. 1, 39. See further K. Economides, 'Cynical legal studies', in J. Cooper and

L. G. Trubek (eds), *Educating for Justice: Social Values and Legal Education*, Aldershot: Ashgate, 1997, 26.

39 R. Kanter, 'Reflections in women and the legal profession: A sociological perspective', *Harvard Women's Law Journal*, 1978, vol. 1, 1. See further E. Gorman, 'Work uncertainty and the promotion of professional women: The case of law firm partnership', *Social Forces*, 2000, vol. 8, 865.

40 C. Seron, 'Managing entrepreneurial legal services: The transformation of small firm practice', in R. L. Nelson, D. Trubek and R. Solomon (eds), *Lawyers' Ideals/Lawyers' Practices: Transformation in the American Legal Profession*, Ithaca: Cornell University Press, 1992, 71; P. Patton, 'Women lawyers, their status, influence, and retention in the legal profession', *William and Mary Journal of Women and the Law*, 2004–5, vol. 11, 182–83, for a discussion of the sociological literature on entrepreneurialism, the masculine and the feminine.

41 See C. McGlynn, 'The business of equality in the solicitors' profession', *Modern Law Review* 2000, vol. 63, 442 for a discussion of apparent gender neutrality and the masculine in relation to the profession, and further D. Rhode, 'The profession and its discontents', *Ohio State Journal* 2000, vol. 61, 8–9.

42 For a discussion of gender differences, skills and leadership, see S. Hegelsen, *The Female Advantage: Women's Ways of Leadership*, New York: Doubleday, 1990.

43 D. Rhode, *The Unfinished Agenda: Women and the Legal Profession, The ABA Report on Women in the Profession*, 2001, 6, discussing her research finding that feminine characteristics and the characteristics expected of successful solicitors – assertiveness and competitiveness – are often perceived to be in contradiction although these characteristics are more associated with commercial rather than family law practice. For a discussion of the changing face of masculinity and the profession, see Collier, 'The changing university'.

44 See Webley and Duff, 'Women solicitors as a barometer'; Hegelsen, *The Female Advantage*.

45 For a discussion of cultural capital and how these traits are viewed within the profession, see H. Sommerlad and P. Sanderson, *Gender Choice and Commitment: Women Solicitors in England and Wales and the Struggle for Equal Status*, Aldershot: Ashgate, 1998. See further R. Kanter, 'Reflections on women and the legal profession: A sociological perspective', *Harvard Women's Law Journal*, 1978, vol. 1, 1. See Collier, 'The changing university', p. 10: 'assessment of women against a normative "ideal" employee, a figure understood simultaneously (and somewhat paradoxically) to be both distinctively gendered (as male/masculine: assertive, rational, competent, unemotional and so on); and, equally, to be somehow gender-neutral in terms of the commitment and dependencies which are seen as "outwith" the field of paid employment'.

46 See discussion in Thornton, ' "Otherness" on the bench', 396.

47 This may be what the profession considers necessary, whereas many studies in relation to women solicitors suggest that many women (and perhaps also men) have these skills and traits already, although they feel forced to repress them in a working environment if they wish to advance within the profession at the rate associated with those solicitors who display more 'masculinist' traits. See for a discussion Webley and Duff, 'Women solicitors as a barometer'. See further S. Hegelsen, *The Female Advantage*.

48 R. Collier, 'The changing university'.

49 For a discussion, see Webley and Duff, 'Women solicitors as a barometer'.

50 See M. Thornton, *Dissonance and Distrust – Women and the Legal Profession*, Oxford: Oxford University Press, 1996. See further, Thornton, ' "Otherness" on the bench'.

7 Stein's ethic of care: an alternative perspective to reflections on women lawyering

Elizabeth Gachenga

7.1 Introduction

Numerous studies have been undertaken in various jurisdictions around the world on the effect that the increase in the number of women in the legal profession has had on the profession. Despite the current intellectual trend among feminist scholars to use theoretical frameworks with caution, most of these studies are conceptualized within the framework of Gilligan's notion of the 'different voice'. Gilligan identifies the 'ethic of care' as one of the main contributions to this 'different voice'. This chapter attempts to dialogue with the current literature on the subject using a novel conceptual framework, an ethic of care founded on the philosophy of Edith Stein. Stein did not explicitly develop an ethic of care, nor did she propose a feminist theory. However, this chapter infers from her philosophy of the human person and her reflections on woman, a foundation for an ethic of care that can serve as the basis for revisiting the discourse on the effect of the increase in the number of women working in the legal profession.

7.2 Foundations for an ethic of care

The question of the effect of the entry of more women into the legal profession has been the subject of discussion among feminist scholars in many jurisdictions the world over.[1] Over time, this has come to be articulated as: 'Does the legal profession change women or do women change the legal profession?'[2] Most reflections and empirical studies on the impact of women in the legal profession are contextualized within a conceptual framework whose roots can be traced to Gilligan's work on moral psychology.

Gilligan is generally credited with the popularization of the ethic of care and its presentation as an alternative moral system. She discusses the conception of care in the course of her work on women's moral development.[3] Gilligan began with the premise that morality is gendered. This was based on her observation of the thinking of some proponents of Western ethical theories. Gilligan's work was specifically aimed at counteracting the prevailing theory on psychological development created by Kohlberg.[4] In her view, Kohlberg's work was filled with prejudicial findings regarding the moral development of the different sexes. As a reaction, Gilligan challenged the theory and embarked on a woman-centred approach to ethics. She challenged the Freudian notion of woman's moral inferiority.[5] Her entire work sought to disprove Freud and Kohlberg by highlighting the moral experience of women. Despite the disclaimer in her work, Gilligan's conclusions seem to suggest that justice and care are gendered concepts and that justice is the language of the male, whereas care is that of the female.[6]

The assumption is that men and women are different, and thus there are certain features that are characteristic to women. These feminine features include empathy, compassion and sensitivity, which lead women to be attentive to voices other than their own.[7] Gilligan faults traditional Western moral theories for their tendency to ignore, trivialize or demean character traits culturally associated with women.[8] In her efforts to undo the male bias in ethical theories based on justice, she seems to promote a female-biased ethical theory that only admits care as the foundation of a moral system.[9]

The contraposition of care and justice led to attacks on this initial work, as well as on subsequent works by feminist scholars relying on Gilligan. In response to the critics, Gilligan clarifies that it was not her intention to present the care perspective as biologically determined or unique to women.[10] Despite this disclaimer, the conclusions in her work seem to support the idea that women do, in fact, demonstrate the care perspective in their approach to moral problems while men do not. Further, this care perspective seemed to be lauded as the better foundation for a moral order.

Apart from the above criticism on the presentation of care as the foundation of the moral order and the perception of care as gendered, Gilligan's works also came under other attacks from within feminist circles. These attacks have taken various forms in the course of feminist scholarship. First, some feminists have faulted Gilligan for commencing from the assumption that it is possible to speak of 'woman' as a general concept applying to all individual women.[11] In third-wave feminism, such an assumption is dubbed as essentialist. 'Essentialism' in this context is described as the adoption of a theoretical framework that fails to recognize diversity among women and that falsely generalizes or reifies femininity.[12] Moi cautions against essentialism and, adopting the thought of Simone de Beauvoir, points out the dangers of reducing women to their 'femininity' or the 'general humanity'. She argues that every woman – like every other human being – is in a concrete situation.[13] Rhode seems to be alluding to this danger of essentialism when, in the context of studying the impact of women on the legal profession in the United States, she draws attention to the pitfall of homogenizing on the basis of experience drawn from some women.[14]

Other feminists have criticized Gilligan's glorification of the 'ethic of care' on the grounds that it encourages the continued repression of women by keeping women in situations that do not empower them. Bartky, for instance, argues that experience shows that the tendency of women to care disempowers them and so should not be praised.[15] She argues that, despite the argument by some women that their dedication to activities in which they exercise care brings satisfaction, this is merely a sense of subjective empowerment that is distinct from the objective reality of having power.[16]

Despite the criticisms, the ethic of care as conceptualized by Gilligan has been used in determining the impact that women will have in society. Menkel-Meadow was among the first to use Gilligan's theory as a framework for the analysis of women's expected impact on the legal profession. In her initial speculation on women's lawyering, she sought to determine whether the female voice of relationship, care and connection leads to a different form of law practice.[17] Using Gilligan's analogy of Portia, a character in Shakespeare's *The Merchant of Venice*, to represent the 'different voice' in lawyering practice, Menkel-Meadow tried to speculate on the effect that Portia would have in the legal profession. She anticipated that it would perhaps be in the client–lawyer relationship that the difference in lawyering practice by women lawyers would have the greatest impact.[18] This observation is consistent with Gilligan's identification of the tendency of women to be concerned about the person as a whole, which would lead them to include other considerations apart from the objective legal problem as presented by the client. Menkel-Meadow anticipated a contribution from women lawyers in the demystification of law and the legal profession. According to her, women would be more likely to work with clients on lay advocacy projects, and be more open to advising clients on the possibility of self-representation.[19]

Using the theory of Gilligan, Menkel-Meadow observed that the capacity of the woman 'to take the part of the other and submerge the self' would facilitate their comprehending their client and reduce the risk of dominating the client and assuming they know the client's best interests. She anticipates that women lawyers, due to their greater sensitivity to altruism and empathy, would have a more comprehensive understanding of clients' needs. She distinguishes this mode of acting from that of female lawyers' male counterparts, who make 'assumptions about the primacy of economic and efficiency considerations', thus ignoring other factors that may be relevant to the client.[20]

Further, Menkel-Meadow considers the possibility of a distinction in legal representation resulting from the fact that women lawyers would be operating within a different structure. Assuming the feminine form of reasoning developed by Gilligan, she anticipates that women lawyers may prepare and plan for their cases differently. Due to their appreciation of the particular circumstances, and their detachment from abstract and universal judgments, women may have an advantage in situations where a case is peculiar and thus not comparable with the precedents.[21]

Menkel-Meadow also suggests that women may create different ethical codes due to the fact that they use different considerations in making moral judgments. She foresees the possibility of women resorting less to the adversarial approach to resolve disputes, particularly where there is a likelihood that the other party would be hurt or a meritorious claim would be defeated. Further, she considers the possibility of women being more conscious of the duty to reveal a client's wrong-doing if it causes harm to another. Menkel-Meadow goes as far as to suggest that the ethic of care and affiliation practised by women lawyers may have implications for the rules of conflict of interest, and result in a different conception of client loyalty.[22]

Various empirical studies have been undertaken to test the hypothesis of Gilligan's conception of an ethic of care as the contribution of women to the moral order, and thus to professions, and Menkel-Meadow's speculation on the impact of women on the legal profession. The conception of the different voice has formed the basis of the questions that continue to be at the heart of the investigations of the effect of more female entrants into law. These questions include: Will women rewrite the rules? Will there emerge distinctively feminine forms of legal practice? Is there any such thing as a distinctively feminine form of legal practice? If so, what distinguishes it from the male form of practice?[23]

7.3 Experience of women lawyering: contribution of an ethic of care?

In most jurisdictions around the world, there has been an increase in the number of women in the legal profession over the last century.[24] As Schultz warns, a superficial glance at the increase in terms of absolute numbers may lead to the mistaken conclusion that the problem of the woman has been resolved and that women have been successful in making an impact on the profession.[25] However, closer and more analytical examinations of the plight of the women in the legal profession across jurisdictions demonstrate complexities that render such a conclusion precipitative.

Demographical studies on the plight of women lawyers conducted in different parts of the world indicate that, despite the initial decisions to admit women into the legal profession, their entry and progression have not been easy. They have had to fight structural and social barriers in the attempt to penetrate a male-dominated field. Thornton's historical analysis of the plight of women lawyers in Queensland bears witness to this.[26] Thornton demonstrates that the adverse conditions in which women found themselves after admission into the profession greatly undermined the anticipated 'feminization' of the legal culture understood as the introduction of stereotypically feminine forms of relating to each other – for example, more caring.[27] Boigeol corroborates this observation, indicating that after admittance women discover that in order to be successful, the academic capital they have must be complemented by social capital.[28] Olgiati confirms that the same difficulties were experienced by women lawyers in Italy.[29] The entry of more women into the profession does not automatically imply their influence on the profession, as they could be within it – but as outsiders. As Hunter graphically describes it, women may simply succumb to the pressure of becoming honorary 'blokes', so as not to be marginalized.[30]

Empirical studies further demonstrate that, even after successful entry, there are a myriad of factors that affect the capacity of women to influence the profession. Women in many jurisdictions continue to be 'fringe dwellers' in the profession – either by choice or because of external pressures – and thus exert only a minimal influence on the profession.[31] Whereas male lawyers tend to dominate in commercial and property work, women remain in areas of perceived 'little prestige and financial gain but heavy emotional labour'.[32] While conceding that these areas are dominated by women, the classification of these areas of legal practice as being of little prestige and financial clout is arguable, although such an argument falls outside the scope of the present chapter. Even in these areas associated with characteristics for which women have a competitive advantage over men, the question as to whether they fare better in these areas or exhibit an ethic of care is still not clear. De Groot, collecting data from the Netherlands, suggests that women are less likely to be involved in disciplinary complaints than men.[33] The same has been observed in studies in Queensland. However, as Bartlett concludes, a deeper analysis of the disciplinary complaints profile in Queensland reveals that the fact of fewer complaints against women cannot simply be interpreted to mean women are more ethical. There are many other factors that could – and indeed seem to – explain the reason for the fewer complaints, such as the position, age and seniority of the women advocates in comparison to their male counterparts.[34]

Studies on the effect that the increase in the number of women has had on the legal profession have thus proved more complex than studies on the numbers and placing of women.[35] The attempts to use empirical studies to determine whether women practise law differently, as suggested by Gilligan, have resulted in varied conclusions – sometimes contradictory ones. In France, for instance, an analysis of the way women judges fare leads to the conclusion that female judges are more repressive than their male counterparts.[36] Besides, the study concludes that it is difficult to speak of a homogenous group of women as their sociological profiles differ and these, perhaps more than their gender, affect the way they practise the profession.[37] Despite this observation, some studies – such as Mather's and Bogoch's – have demonstrated that women lawyers show greater concern and more careful listening for their clients in family matters.[38] These latter results to some extent confirm the speculations of Menkel-Meadow, based on Gilligan's different voice. Rhode evaluates the question of how gender structures professional roles using empirical evidence from the United States.[39] She acknowledges that some small-scale studies have shown differences in women lawyering.[40] She does, however, caution against the over-simplification and over-claiming of the gender differences.[41]

The analysis of the empirical results obtained from various jurisdictions regarding the impact of women on the legal profession led Menkel-Meadow to re-examine a decade later the speculations she had made in her 1985 work.[42] In retrospect, she conceded that there is a complexity of factors affecting lawyers, and thus it is difficult to draw conclusions regarding their mode of lawyering on the basis of gender alone. Besides, as she points out in agreement with Epstein, there may be more differences among individuals within a particular gender than the differences across gender.[43] These findings led her to caution against making 'claims for "women" based on universalistic attribution of generalized characteristics of womanhood'.[44]

The results of the empirical studies are thus inconclusive insofar as they determine the extent to which women bring into the profession their feminine features – particularly the ethic of care. The studies nevertheless demonstrate that gender plays a part in the way the law is practised, although it is not the only factor affecting legal practice.[45] It is, rather, intertwined in a multitude of other contextual factors. It is thus difficult to measure or quantify the effect that the entry of more women as an isolated factor has had on lawyering. However, this does not mean that women have made no impact. Traces of this impact are evident, according to Sommerlad, in the consumer revolution that has led to a greater expectation of 'soft skills' from the advocates. Other traces, although not clearly attributable solely to women, are the progressive loss of formal social procedures and the growing emphasis on subjectivity.[46] Further, as Menkel-Meadow observes, there is still a need to listen to the 'different voice' – whether that of women or of minority groups – in the search within legal ethics for the ideal of a 'good lawyer'. Her conclusion justifies the continued relevance of the discussion on the contribution that a marginalized minority can contribute to a conventional legal justice system. This sets the stage for a re-examination of the ethic of care as a contribution of the different voice, but from the perspective of the philosophy of Edith Stein.

7.4 Ethic of care founded on Stein's thought

As stated earlier, Stein did not directly propose an ethic of care. Nevertheless, this work argues that it is possible to found an ethic of care based on Stein's philosophy of the human person and her conception of gender. This chapter argues that this alternative foundation of the ethic of care has advantages over the ethic of care founded on Gilligan, thus justifying a revisiting of the theoretical framework within which the impact of women on the legal profession is evaluated.

7.5 The phenomenological approach

Edith Stein (1891–1942) was a student and disciple of Edmund Husserl, a German philosopher considered the father of the phenomenological movement.[47] Unlike Gilligan, Stein departs from the base of philosophy as opposed to psychology in her reflections on the contribution that women can make to society.[48] She develops a philosophy of the human person in the context of phenomenology.[49] The fact that she builds on philosophy as opposed to psychology will help develop an ethic of care less prone to some of the criticisms levelled at Gilligan's work.

It is difficult to summarize Husserl's phenomenology, given that it transformed considerably during the course of his life. However, he undoubtedly left a legacy insofar as phenomenological methodology as the basis of the study of reality is concerned. In his initial works, Husserl sought to break from the emphasis laid by the particular sciences on the empirical investigation of reality on the grounds that it was not purely abstract and thus would not result in an accurate notion of reality.[50] This is because such investigation of reality was either done in the context of the physical order, oriented to the body, or in the psychological order;

oriented around the mind, memories and emotions of the percipient.[51] He propounded in its place a methodology based on a direct investigation of the essence of reality.[52] His thought turns the focus in philosophy from the perspective of the philosophical subject to the object under study.

Husserl had many followers, who applied his basic thoughts on phenomenology to various aspects of philosophy and social sciences.[53] Stein began her own philosophical journey into the essence of the human person in the context of Husserl's phenomenology. Her first work was a dissertation, *On the Problem of Empathy*. The dissertation was an attempt to continue Husserl's train of thought regarding the subject.[54] Husserl in his classes on 'Nature and Spirit' had, according to Stein, asserted that the objective and exterior world could only be experienced inter-subjectively – that is, by a plurality of knowing individuals engaged in an intellective interchange. This presupposed an act of knowledge involving the experience of another.[55] He referred to this experience of another as '*Einfühlung*', translated as empathy, but did not elaborate further on the precise meaning of the term.[56] He nevertheless asserted that it was only through this process that one could know reality objectively. Stein undertook to investigate the concept of empathy further, using the phenomenological approach. This led her to delve into the human person.

Stein began her dissertation by adopting the phenomenological methodology as a guide in the investigation on empathy, the essence of the human person and more specifically the essence of woman. She asserted that the goal of phenomenology is to clarify and thus find the ultimate basis of all knowledge.[57] In order to achieve this goal, Stein posits that phenomenology must eliminate anything doubtful or preconceived. This justifies her exclusion of scientific results insofar as phenomenology, being the science that seeks to clarify all scientific knowledge, must not itself be grounded on an existing science but rather on itself.[58]

Stein distinguishes phenomenology from psychology. She points out that phenomenology seeks to comprehend the essence of reality in its pure sense, freed from all accidents of appearance. Psychology, on the other hand, presupposes the essence of the thing under study as well as its existence.[59] Phenomenology thus investigates the essence of a reality while psychology, presupposing the reality, investigates its process of realization. She observes that psychological investigation must be led back to the phenomenon, and that therefore in the results of phenomenological investigations we find the criteria for the utility of theories generated from psychological investigations.[60]

Stein's conclusion helps deal with one of the challenges that Gilligan's theory of an ethic of care has faced. Gilligan's theory was derived from psychology and supported by results from a sociological investigation on the subject. Subsequent empirical studies seeking to prove or disprove her theory have resulted in varied conclusions, making it difficult to conclude whether women do indeed bring to the legal profession features characteristic to their gender – particularly the ethic of care.[61]

By investigating the contribution of women to society at the level of philosophy and in the context of phenomenology, Stein removes her theory from the realm of psychology, sociology or empirical investigation. The validity of her conclusions is not to be tested by empirical investigations; rather, these empirical investigations presuppose the conclusions of her phenomenological investigations.[62] The validity of an ethic of care founded on Stein is thus not to be confirmed through empirical investigations, but rather ought to guide such investigations as an underlying assumption. The observation of experiences that seem to contradict the essence of reality would simply imply a deviation as opposed to a disproving of the results of her phenomenological investigation. Applied to the investigation on the impact of women on law, it could be concluded that the fact experience proves that female lawyers do not – at least in some cases – demonstrate an ethic of care in their relations with their clients does not disprove the fact that they have a tendency to care, as it is possible for experience to differ from reality.

7.6 Empathy: the foundation of inter-subjective relations

Stein, like Aristotle, believed that being is intelligible to the human mind. Using the phenomenological approach, the mind is able to grasp the essence of the being by beginning with an analysis of sense perceptions of the object or reality under study.[63] The sense perceptions are then subjected to the rigour of reason. This leads to the intuitive grasp of the essence of the reality studied.[64] Stein uses this methodological approach in her study of humans and their inter-subjective relations, and also uses it in her study of the woman.

Stein set out to determine what exactly happens in an inter-subjective relationship. She elaborated on the notion and act of *Einfühlung* (empathy) in human relations. She was convinced that knowledge of empathy would lead not only to knowledge of the objective reality, as pointed out by Husserl, but more specifically to knowledge of self and knowledge of the other. She explained that knowledge of self is achieved through personal experience, while knowledge of the other is reached through empathy.[65]

For Stein, empathy is an act of cognition.[66] This assertion implies that empathy is not a sense constituted out of experience or an analogical inference on the basis of comparative perceptions, but rather an act of knowing. A grammatical analogy may help to explain the point further. Empathy, for Stein, is an adverb within the cognitive process. She is thus introducing into the philosophy of knowledge a new mode of knowing: empathy.

Stein follows a logical process in arriving at this conclusion. In the course of studying human existence, she observes that there are certain experiences that are not personalized insofar as they are not owned by the subject experiencing them – for instance, the pain one feels for someone who is bereaved. In such an instance, the subject is not the one bereaved yet the subject feels the pain in their person. Stein analyses the mode in which such a subject shares in the experience of someone else. She concludes that the experience (in this case, grief), although not originating from the subject, is as real as any other experience whose source is the subject.[67] The subject identifies with the circumstances of the other person.

The identification occurs not by way of comparison or inference, which could lead to errors and delusion – such as may occur in the course of logical inferences drawn from perception – but rather in an immanent way.[68] She argues that what becomes present to the knowing subject upon the other's expression of grief is the grief of the other per se.

According to Stein, empathy leads the subject actively to go out of self so as to encounter the other person.[69] In this process, an experience that originated from sense content perceived by an individual outside of self results in a real experience within self. Empathy is thus a form of inter-subjective experience that makes possible the constitution of an objective world.[70] The above conception of empathy is particular. It is distinguished from the perception of other philosophers insofar as Stein emphasized that, although we may perceive the experience of the other, we cannot have the other's original experience in the same manner and form that they have it.[71] It can be deduced that the possession of the experience of the other is not an ontological possession but rather a logical one. Just as in the realm of truth, the object known is known in an intentional and not an ontological way.[72] She thus concludes that a person is never one with the other, but rather knowledge of one's structure as a person initiates the knowledge of the other.[73]

Empathy is thus identified as the foundation of inter-subjective relationships. Given the nature of the cognitive act of empathy, it provides the subject knowing with a comprehensive notion of the other's experiences. This holistic knowledge of the other resulting from the cognitive act provides the basis of an ethic of care governing such relations. Her exposition on empathy provides useful insights into the expected effect of the exercise by women of this mode of knowing, which leads them to be more caring.

7.7 Notion of gender in Stein

In the later years of her life, Stein turned her philosophical inquiry to the question of the nature and destiny of women. In her search for the 'essence of woman', she follows the phenomenological method. While appreciating the importance of the findings of empirical sciences such as psychology, sociology and biology, Stein – in keeping with the philosophical method – sought to determine ultimately what is necessary to being, in this case the being of a woman.[74]

In her search for the essence of a woman, Stein began by cautioning against drawing generalizations on the basis of experience or preconceptions, which is not permissible in the context of the phenomenological approach. She argues that the image drawn from such experience may not necessarily be accurate. She thus emphasizes the need to question the source of the ideal notion of woman.[75] In this way, Stein responds to the criticism of those opposed to essentialism. She points out that the risk of exclusion in a universalistic definition of woman occurs if the notion is sourced from experience. However, in the context of phenomenology, the notion of woman is arrived at through a direct investigation of reality that is not dependent upon the observation of a majority of women.

Stein considered woman from an ontological perspective – that is, from the perspective of the science of beings. At the ontological level of being, Stein recognized the various grades of life identified by the classical philosophers, which culminate in the human species.[76] Within the human species, she appreciated the differentiation resulting in the multiplicity of unique individuals. Apart from these differences observable among individuals, she observed another level of differentiation that seemed to cut through the differences among individuals: the differentiation of male and female. The central question in her philosophy of the human person then became the determination of whether woman and man are distinct species, each having an ontologically different essence.[77] Stein addressed the issue of gender differentiation by seeking to establish whether the differences observable between man and woman are structural, or are limited to the body and those psychic functions related to physical organs. This investigation would later have implications in the approach to feminism adopted by Stein.[78] She posited that if the differences are a manifestation of the fact that woman is a distinct species from man, then there are unique feminine characteristics which woman can contribute to all fields of human life.

In the search for the source and nature of differentiation, Stein distinguished between species, gender, type and individual. She identified species as that which is not subject to change except at the ontological level. Turning to the hylomorphic doctrine of Aristotle, she identified the substantial form as the determinant of the species – that is, pertaining to the essence of a being.[79] Stein then distinguished between species and type. The latter, unlike the former, is not unchangeable. In fact, types manifest in individual characteristics can and do change in the process of development of the person. These changes, she observed, occur within the limits set by the species.[80]

Stein's investigation then moved to the next step, which is whether women share an unchangeable feature that would justify their being classified as a species as opposed to a type. She observed that if the distinction between male and female is a distinction of type, then the transformation of one type to another would occur with relative ease. If, on the other hand, male and female constitute a species, then no extent of environmental, cultural or professional factors would result in a change from male to female.[81] Stein argues that whereas the positive sciences can study the factors that condition a being, only philosophy can arrive at the ontological cause or structure of the being.

Applying the philosophical method, she concludes that the human being is actualized as a double species: male and female. She states:

> I am convinced that the species humanity embraces the double species man and woman; that the essence of the complete human being is characterized by this duality; and that the entire structure of the essence demonstrates the specific character. There is a difference, not only in body structure and in particular physiological functions, but also in the entire corporeal life.[82]

Stein thus observed that the essence of the human species is stamped in a binate way, implying that there can be no essential feature lacking in either one. The difference in structure in the double species is at an ontological level and thus not purely at the level of the material body or physiological functions. The very relationship of soul and body which is at the core of the hylomorphic structure of the human species is different in man and woman.[83]

Stein then embarked on an analysis of the person of the woman and of the characteristics that are unique to her. As observed in her conception of gender, she was convinced of the fundamental equality of men and women and as a consequence did not regard the differences in tendencies observed in the different genders as a negation or threat to this fundamental equality. In fact, she started by conceding that men and women have the same basic human traits, with a particular trait predominating in one of the sexes just as another may predominate in an individual.[84] There are nonetheless some tendencies that are distinct in women, and the appreciation of these became her next preoccupation. This perception of femininity is more open to a complementary view of the contribution of the male and the female in society. An ethic of care founded on Stein thus steers clear of the contra-opposition of the values of care and justice in the moral order – something of which the theory of Gilligan has been accused.

Stein argues that the foundation of the differences between women and men lies in the distinct relationship between soul and body in man and woman respectively. Men and women thus differ in their psychic life and in their spiritual faculties of intellect and will.[85] According to Stein, the fundamental difference between men and women, stemming out of this body and soul interaction, is manifest in their search for their goal or end:

> The feminine species expresses a unity and wholeness of the total psychosomatic personality and a harmonious development of faculties. The masculine species strives to enhance individual abilities in order that they may attain their highest achievements.[86]

In her works, Stein seeks to articulate other differences between men and women that flow from this fundamental difference. She observes that the essence of a woman particularly lends itself to the act of cognition that she refers to as empathy. According to Stein, this is because woman tends to what is living, personal and whole, as opposed to what is abstract or lifeless.[87] Woman's bias for the personal leads her to be more perceptive of the experience of the other. Stein does not in any way imply that women are thus incapable of operating at the abstract level, but rather that their strength lies precisely in the living and personal realm. Neither is Stein implying that man is powerless in the realm of personal relations and not capable of caring, but rather that he has a competitive advantage in the abstract analysis of reality. She continues that women characteristically are not content with remaining at the level of the abstract; they seek to relate the conceptual to the world of persons and things, to relate psychology to particular human beings and sociology to the concrete human situations, and even seek to make physics connect with the real world.[88]

Given Stein's sensitivity to personal experience and her appreciation of the uniqueness of each person, it would be inconceivable to conclude that with these statements Stein was shutting out the possibility of individual men and women who demonstrate the opposite of the expected traits. She was merely seeking to draw conclusions that apply at an ontological level. The question then becomes at what point the line should be drawn so as to determine certain features as belonging to the unchangeable core and others as falling within the characteristics proper to type and thus not bound to a particular gender.

Stein notes that, due to human freedom, the development of tendencies possessed at an ontological level depends on the individual. This may explain why some women may be less sensitive than particular men. Further, she points out that each individual – whether male or female – has a destiny or objective in life. The traits of an individual, she argues, are adapted to the individual's destiny or calling in life. She observes, for instance, that whereas marriage and motherhood are the primary calling or objective in life for the majority of women, this is not necessarily true for every individual. Some women, she argues, may be called to singular cultural achievements resulting in an adaptation of their feminine tendencies to suit this way of life.[89] The individual's destiny or goal therefore explains the possibility of differences in expressions of femininity.

The tendency to nurture and care, which is the result of empathy, belongs to the ontological level and is thus applicable to all women, although it is manifest in different ways depending on their particular goal and the exercise of their freedom. This can be deduced from the exposition she makes regarding empathy. By identifying empathy as a cognitive act, a particular mode of knowing, she locates it in the process of knowledge. In the wider context of Aristotelian philosophy – on which, as we have seen, she founds her philosophy of the human person – the process of knowing is dependent on the essence of the being. Stein's notion of gender admits that human nature is stamped in a binate way, implying equality in capacity of knowledge but allowing for some distinction – in this case, in the mode of knowing. The distinction between the male and female mode of knowing is not comparable to the distinction between the act of knowing of animals and of human beings. This is because the latter is arising from a difference in essence, while the former is an act of two individuals with the same essence: that of the human person. As the essence of the human person exists in a double manifestation – male and female – this double manifestation allows for a difference in the mode of knowing and consequently in the mode of acting.

Stein recognized the tendency of women to empathy arising from the feminine ethos, and thus argues that they have a contribution to make to all professions and not only those that are more attuned to the feminine nature. She points out that it is precisely in professions that seem to be more naturally suited to men that a well-developed feminine nature could provide a healthy balance.[90] Whereas Stein did not explicitly develop an ethic of care, we argue that, by identifying empathy as the foundation of inter-subjective relations, she makes an important contribution to the ethic governing such relations. This ethic could be referred to as an ethic of care.

7.8 The Steinian ethic of care: a reconceptualization of the impact of women on the legal profession

As was suggested earlier in this chapter, Stein's thought provides a theoretical framework within which the ethic of care and the impact of women in the legal profession can be re-examined. The framework, it is argued in this chapter, provides a firmer foundation for an ethic of care and for the case of the impact that women have on the legal profession.

Stein's conception of gender and her wider philosophy of the human person help explain why there exists a possibility of distortion of care – one of the criticisms directed at Gilligan's theory by Bartky. An ethic of care founded on Stein is not oblivious to the negative aspects that may result from the excesses of the feminine natural tendencies. Stein observes that the tendency of the female to completeness and to the personal worth is not of itself a positive value. Indeed, she admits that the tendency can be harmful where it is exaggerated or not properly developed. This would be manifest, for instance, in a woman who had a bias towards securing her personal importance. This would lead her to focus all her energy and that of others on this pursuit. The possibility of underdevelopment or exaggeration of the tendency to care is thus acknowledged by Stein but, as explained in her methodology, the existence of the possibility of distortion does not mean that the tendency is inexistent or negative.

To counter these excesses, Stein urges moderation and direction of the tendencies through the intellect and the will.[91] She argues that the excesses of the feminine tendencies would be cured by an antidote of the masculine nature. For instance, she proposes the exposure to objective work as a means of balancing the excessive tendency to hyper-individuality among women.[92] This is based on her observation of objectivity as one of the predominant male tendencies that leads to their focusing less on the personal or the subjective. She does, however, caution that the solution to the excesses does not rest solely with the administration of an antidote of masculine nature. Early feminist movements, she argues, stopped at this point and this was ineffective.[93]

Stein observes that, aside from the use of antidotes, objectivity must be sought by individual women in the context of their search for their personal destiny. She explains that, just as with the innate tendencies in men, what determines whether the innate feminine tendencies develop into positive values is the mode in which they are managed to bring about the completeness of humanity. In the context of her philosophy of the human person, Stein recognizes a transcendental end or goal for all human persons.[94] She argues that all human beings are called to a personal goal, which constitutes the achievement of the total humanity of each individual. Each woman thus needs to develop these innate tendencies in the context of her individual goal.[95] The reference to the individual goal would ensure that the tendency to care does not result in the underdevelopment of self or the hyper-individuality referred to above.

The difficulties encountered in determining the effect of the entry of more women into the legal profession using empirical research prove Stein's observation in her discourse on the methodology that is appropriate in determining the differences between the genders. Stein observed a danger in empirical research caused by the demands and rigour of the scientific methodology.[96] She observed that empirical investigations on the differences between the genders tended to begin on the assumption that the difference between the sexes is a universal fact, as confirmed by experience of a majority of women. The objective of the investigation would then be to establish the details of the difference. The uniqueness of women would be determined on the basis of traits present on average or whose frequency or degree of occurrence could be quantified. Stein argues that with such an approach it is impossible to give an overall picture of the uniqueness of woman and even more difficult to determine whether the characteristics are the result of variable type or a fixed species.[97] Some contemporary feminists have concluded that, as empirical research is never based on the experience of the entire population but a sample, it always results in an exclusionist approach to gender issues. This is because there will always be a marginalized group of women who are not represented.[98] By contextualizing her thought in phenomenology, Stein avoids this criticism. As we explained earlier, her conclusions do not derive validity from the observation of experience of the entire population of women, but rather from the methodology of the investigation used, the direct investigation of essence of the reality of woman.

Stein anticipated the results of the empirical investigation on the effect that women have on the lawyering process. As Menkel-Meadow observed in concurrence with Epstein, following the re-examination of her earlier speculations, the results of empirical evidence vary depending on the frame of reference of the researcher. Epstein observes that those seeking differences will find them, just as those seeking to prove equality are likely to find greater overlap in the behaviour of men and women. Menkel-Meadow and Epstein seem to call into question the value of empirical research – as did Stein.

As previously pointed out by Stein, the contribution by women of characteristics proper to their gender is not automatic. It is dependent upon how they develop their feminine characteristics. As observed earlier, the danger of distortion will always exist – thus downplaying the capacity of women to bring feminine characteristics into the profession. This observation may explain why investigation of the mode of lawyering by women has not always demonstrated the expected results.

As pointed out by Menkel-Meadow, there is the possibility of women lawyers adapting male tendencies in a bid to survive in a male-dominated field. Menkel-Meadow uses the shrewd approach of Portia to demonstrate the capacity of women to adopt the same rules of the game as their male counterparts in a bid to beat a biased system. This would again undermine their capacity to contribute what is truly feminine to the profession. Stein warns against this danger when she speaks of the means of countering hyper-individuality among women through the fostering in such women of traits that are more predominant among men. She anticipated the danger of women adopting a male approach as a survival tactic and foresaw the ineffectiveness of such an approach.

Stein, as we have seen, advocated for the use of a philosophical method in determining the essence of a woman. This, she argues, would ensure that the objective reality, the essence of a woman, would not be blurred by experience. Stein is suggesting that experience may not always be reflective of objective reality, and thus implies that the results of empirical research do not nullify the objective reality – which is that women have characteristics which are proper to their gender, and that they retain the capacity to contribute this to all professions – including the legal profession.

Stein's philosophy of the human person – and thus her notion of gender – caution against one of the assumptions that Menkel-Meadow points out in her re-examination of the 'different voice'. The entry of women into the legal profession will not automatically result in an observation of the feminine characteristics, and more specifically to an ethic of care. As explained by Stein, the contribution of women would be dependent upon each individual woman's development of her innate tendency to care with regard to her personal destiny and that of others.

Even where women fully develop their feminine characteristic into positive values, the impact of this and the extent of their influence will also depend on a myriad of other factors, including the effectiveness with which they are allowed to practise once they are in the profession. Stein's philosophy appreciates the complexity of the human person. Accurate predications on how a human person – male or female – will act in future are a difficult exercise, as there are too many variables – as many as there are individuals – that may influence the behaviour of the person. An ethic of care founded on Stein's philosophy thus seems to provide a more flexible conceptual framework within which to study these complexities encountered in the attempt to determine the impact of women on the legal profession. It is hoped that this chapter has set the stage for further inquiry into this area.

Notes

1 U. Schultz and G. Shaw, *Women in the World's Legal Profession*, Oxford: Hart, 2003 have compiled contributions in this area from 15 countries over four continents. It is unfortunate that, due to the dearth in literature, contributions from Africa and other developing countries are missing.
2 Schultz and Shaw, *Women*, p. li.
3 C. Gilligan, *In a Different Voice: Psychological Theory and Women's Development*, Cambridge, MA: Harvard University Press, 1993.
4 L. Kohlberg, *The Philosophy of Moral Development: Moral Stages and the Idea of Justice*, New York: Harper & Row, 1981.
5 M. J. Larrabee, *An Ethic of Care: Feminist and Interdisciplinary Perspectives*, London: Routledge, 1993, p. 209.
6 This is implied from the observation of Amy and Jake's behaviour (her exemplification of the female and male respectively) when faced with a moral dilemma.
7 Gilligan, *In a Different Voice*, p. 16.
8 R. Tong and N. Williams, 'Feminist ethics', *The Stanford Encyclopaedia of Philosophy*, 2008. Available from: <http://plato.stanford.edu/archives/spr2008/entries/feminism-ethics> (accessed 19 May 2008).

9 Gilligan, *In a Different Voice*. In her introduction to this edition, Gilligan speaks of an 'attempt to turn the tide of moral discussion from questions of how to achieve objectivity and detachment to how to engage responsibly and with care'.

10 C. Gilligan, 'Response to Critics', *Signs*, 1986, vol. 11, 327.

11 Schultz and Shaw, *Women*, p. li. She questions whether it is possible to respond to the question what is the impact of women on the profession as it presupposes that there is such a thing as a 'woman jurist'.

12 C. J. Heyes, 'Anti-essentialism in practice: Caroline Gilligan and feminine philosophy', *Hypatia: A Journal of Feminist Philosophy*, 1997, vol. 12, 142–63.

13 T. Moi, *What is a Woman and Other Essays*, Oxford: Oxford University Press, 2001, p. 8.

14 D. Rhode, 'Gender and the profession: An American perspective', in Schultz and Shaw, *Women*, pp. 3–21.

15 S. L. Bartky (ed.), *Femininity and Domination*, New York: Routledge, 1990.

16 Ibid.

17 C. Menkel-Meadow, '*Portia* in a Different Voice: Speculations on a Women's Lawyering Process', *Berkeley Women's Law Journal*, 1985, vol. 1, 57.

18 Ibid., 58.

19 Ibid., 57.

20 Ibid., 58.

21 Ibid.

22 Ibid., 59.

23 Schultz and Shaw, *Women*, p. liv.

24 Ibid., xxxvii, xxxviii.

25 Ibid., lxi.

26 M. Thornton, *Dissonance and Distrust: Women in the Legal Profession*, Oxford: Oxford University Press, 1996.

27 Ibid., 72.

28 A. Boigeol, 'Male strategies in the face of the feminization of the profession', in Schultz and Shaw, *Women*, pp. 401–18.

29 V. Olgiati, 'Professional body and gender difference in court: The case of the first (failed) woman lawyer in modern Italy', in Schultz and Shaw, *Women*, pp. 419–36.

30 R. Hunter, 'Women barristers and gender difference in Australia', in Schultz and Shaw, *Women*, pp. 103–22.

31 Schultz and Shaw, *Women*.

32 Schultz and Shaw, *Women*, p. xlii.

33 L. E. de Groot Van Leuwen, 'Women in the Dutch legal profession (1950–2000)', in Schultz and Shaw, *Women*, pp. 341–52.

34 F. Bartlett, 'Professional Discipline Against Female Lawyers in Queensland: A Gendered Analysis', *Griffith Law Review*, 2008, vol. 17, 1.

35 Refer, for instance, to conclusions of studies conducted by H. Sommerlad, 'Can women lawyer differently: A perspective from the UK', in Schultz and Shaw, *Women*, in the United Kingdom; and Rhode, 'Gender and the profession', in the United States.

36 Boigeol, 'Male strategies'.

37 Boigeol, 'Male strategies', p. 415.

38 Shultz and Shaw, *Women*, p. lvii.

39 Rhode, 'Gender and the profession'.

40 J. Lipman-Blumen, 'Connective leadership: Female leadership styles in the 21st century workplace', *Social Perspectives*, 1992, vol. 35.

41 Rhode, 'Gender and the profession', p. 5.

42 C. Menkel-Meadow, 'Portia redux: Another look at gender, feminism, and legal ethics', in S. D. Carle (ed.), *Lawyers' Ethics and the Pursuit of Social Justice: A Critical Reader*, New York: New York University Press, pp. 274–81.

43 Ibid., p. 275.

44 Ibid., p. 279.

45 Schultz and Shaw, *Women*, p. lix.
46 Ibid.
47 B. S. Turner, *The Blackwell Companion to Social Theories*, Oxford: Blackwell, 2000, p. 270.
48 E. Stein, *Essays on Woman*, trans. F. M. Oben, Washington, DC: ICS Publications, 1987.
49 F. M. Oben, *The Life and Thought of Edith Stein*, Boston: Society of St Paul, 2001, pp. 24ff.
50 Turner, *The Blackwell Companion*, p. 273.
51 W. P. Montague, 'Concerning Husserl's phenomenology', *The Journal of Philosophy*, 1939, vol. 36, 232.
52 D. W. Smith, 'Phenomenology', in E. N. Zalta (ed.), *The Stanford Encyclopedia of Philosophy (Summer Edition)*, 2009. Available from: <http://plato.stanford.edu/archives/sum2009/entries/phenomenology> (accessed 5 November 2009).
53 Some of these include Scheler, Reinach, Hildebrand and Conrad Martius, as well as Edith Stein.
54 E. Stein, *On the Problem of Empathy*, trans. W. Stein, Washington, DC: ICS Publications, 1989, p. 1.
55 Oben, *The Life*, p. 87.
56 E. Stein, *Life in a Jewish Family, 1891–1916: An Autobiography*, trans. J. Koeppel, Washington, DC: ICS Publications, 1987, p. 219.
57 Stein, *On the Problem*, p. 3.
58 Ibid.
59 Ibid., p. 21.
60 Ibid., p. 22.
61 As observed in studies compiled in Schultz and Shaw, *Women*.
62 Oben, *The Life*, pp. 21–22.
63 H. Brown and L. A. Kennedy, *Images of the Human: The Philosophy of the Human Person in a Religious Context*, Chicago: Loyola Press, 1995, p. 420.
64 Ibid.
65 Oben, *The Life*, p. 88.
66 Stein, *Life*, p. 397.
67 Stein, *On the Problem*, p. 6.
68 Ibid., p. 7. She distinguishes between empathy and outer perception.
69 M. R. Michau, 'Edith Stein's contribution to a phenomenology of ethical (self-)revelation', 2004, p. 2. Available from: <http://www. web.ics.purdue.edu/~mmichau/mrm-roundtable2004.pdf> (accessed 18 May 2008).
70 F. J. Sancho, 'Filosofia y vida: El itinerario filosófico de Edith Stein', *Anuario Filosófico*, 1998, vol. 31, 674.
71 Oben, *The Life*, p. 104.
72 Stein seems to borrow from Thomistic philosophy of knowledge.
73 Oben, *The Life*, p. 104.
74 M. C. Baseheart, 'Edith Stein's philosophy of woman and of women's education', *Hypatia*, 1989, vol. 4, 123.
75 Ibid.
76 Stein, *Essays*, p. 176ff.
77 Baseheart, 'Edith Stein's', p. 124.
78 Although she did not regard herself as a feminist, her thoughts provide a basis for developing a type of feminism.
79 Baseheart, 'Edith Stein's', pp. 124–25.
80 Stein, *Essays*, p. 177.
81 Ibid., p. 162.
82 Ibid., p. 177.
83 Baseheart, 'Edith Stein's', p. 125.
84 Stein, *Essays*, p. 178.
85 Ibid., p. 177.

86 Ibid., pp. 177–78.
87 Ibid., pp. 44, 248.
88 Baseheart, 'Edith Stein's', p. 126.
89 Stein, *Essays*, p. 179.
90 Ibid., p. 48.
91 Ibid., pp. 96, 97.
92 Ibid., p. 251.
93 Ibid., p. 251. Stein here could be alluding to the efforts among early feminists to secure the entry of women into male dominated fields as a means of proving the equality of the sexes.
94 Ibid., p. 251.
95 Ibid., p. 252ff.
96 Ibid., pp. 165–67.
97 Ibid., p. 164.
98 Moi, *What is a Woman*.

8 Gender, ethics and the discretion not to prosecute in the 'interests of justice' under the Rome Statute for the International Criminal Court

Tina Dolgopol

8.1 Introduction

The International Criminal Court (ICC) was created by the international community to try the most serious cases of war crimes and crimes against humanity.[1] It is a reflection of the international community's belief that such crimes violate the 'rights and conscience . . . of particular victims and humanity as a whole'.[2] Within the structure of the ICC, it is the Office of the Prosecutor (OTP) that selects the situations to be investigated and the individuals to be prosecuted,[3] as well as determining the charges to be brought against those individuals. The confluence of the Rome Statute's admonition that only the most serious cases are to be brought before the ICC, the Statute's emphasis on complementarity[4] and the practicalities of holding international criminal trials[5] places substantial restrictions on the number of trials that can be held. These limitations make clear that a broad power of discretion must be exercised by the OTP in carrying out its work.

While such discretion is necessary and, as will be discussed later in this chapter, is an accepted part of prosecutorial practice in many parts of the world, discretion is not without its limits,[6] and should be exercised in a manner that allows scrutiny of the decision-making process.[7] Although the push to have published guidelines on the exercise of prosecutorial discretion is often discussed in terms of transparency,[8] it could also be understood as a method of publicly articulating the ethical dimensions of the work undertaken by prosecutors. Prosecutors, both domestic and international, play a role in the fulfilment of the public's expectations about justice[9] and crime prevention.[10] Their work is carried out with the knowledge that they are in some sense answerable to the community for their decisions.

Scholars in the field of ethics, such as Deborah Rhode, have suggested that ethical decision-making goes beyond the formal rules of conduct that typically govern the legal profession and that are used in disciplinary matters. Rhode argues that ethical decision-making takes account of the impact one's decisions will have on the broader community,[11] as well as the functioning of the institutions of the law:[12] 'lawyers, as officers of the justice system, have a special obligation to pursue justice. That obligation runs first and foremost not to particular clients, but to the rule of law and to the core values of honesty, fairness and social responsibility that sustain it'.[13] Further, the 'morally reflective' practice she espouses encompasses an obligation to understand the 'social context' in which decisions are made, in particular the uneven distribution of 'wealth, power and information'.[14]

This view of ethics is one that is particularly apt for those engaged in the commencement and conduct of trials involving war crimes and crimes against humanity. Such trials affect hundreds, if not thousands, of victims as well as the international community as a whole. Our knowledge of the past failures of international humanitarian law[15] with respect to the protection and promotion of the rights of women and other vulnerable minority groups,[16] as well as the ongoing discrimination that often exists in societies recovering from armed conflict,[17] makes it apparent that thought must be given to the implications of an international prosecutor's work on those living within these countries.

Pursuant to Article 53 of the Rome Statute, the OTP has the power to determine that it would not be in the 'interests of justice' either to continue an investigation or, once an investigation is complete, to prosecute a particular defendant. This power has been the subject of debate by a range of international actors.[18] The OTP issued a policy paper on Article 53 in September 2007.[19] In that paper, the OTP expresses its view that it will operate from the premise that investigations and prosecutions are generally in the interests of justice and that only extraordinary circumstances would warrant a determination that it would not be in the interests of justice to proceed.[20]

While that strong statement is to be applauded, the discussion about the factors that would militate against prosecution leaves many unanswered questions. Of concern is the failure of the OTP to articulate the specific issues it would consider if such a step were being considered. The Statute requires a balance to be achieved among factors such as the interests of justice, the interests of victims and the gravity of the crimes committed by the individual. Given the extent of crimes of sexual violence that have and are taking place in conflicts that would come within the jurisdiction of the court, it is surprising that the policy paper does not include a gender analysis, both with respect to the general issue of prosecutorial discretion and the specific issue of how the interests of victims will be handled in determining whether or not the interests of justice would support a decision either not to investigate or not to prosecute.

It is the thesis of this chapter that the OTP has an ethical obligation to give greater consideration to the gender dimensions of victims' concerns, and to articulate more fully its understanding of the discretion it has been given under Article 53. Before demonstrating the manner in which gender can influence our perceptions of justice, as well as the interests of victims, the chapter will commence with a brief overview of prosecutorial discretion and Article 53.

8.2 The Rome Statute and prosecutorial discretion

Many of the world's legal systems recognize the importance of prosecutorial discretion.[21] 'Its necessity springs from the practical need for a selective, rather than automatic, approach to the institution of criminal proceedings, thus avoiding the over-burdening and perhaps clogging of the machinery of justice.'[22] Although in specific instances the manner in which prosecutors exercise their discretion at the domestic level may be the subject of challenge or criticism, it is accepted in these systems that discretion is an inherent and necessary part of the functions of a prosecutor's office.[23] However, even in systems that accept the importance of prosecutorial discretion, there remains a general presumption that serious crimes will be brought to trial.[24] In recent years, prosecutors have commenced articulating and publicizing the guidelines that will influence the manner in which they exercise their discretion.[25]

In contrast to domestic systems, the ICC operates on the presumption that only the minority of potential cases will be investigated and prosecuted. This presumption arises from the principle of complementarity (Articles 1, 12 and 17) and the restriction of the ICC's jurisdiction to the most serious cases (Article 5). These limitations on the work of the ICC in conjunction with its yet unproven place in the international arena, its potential for assisting in the diminution of horrific crimes, the vast number of state and non-state actors that worked to bring the court into existence, the opposition to the court by the United States and the emerging nature of international criminal justice (in contrast to the more established rules of international humanitarian law) have all contributed to the burgeoning literature on the nature of and the limits to the exercise of discretion by the OTP.[26]

Article 53 has two prongs. Paragraph 1 deals with the investigatory stage, and would allow the prosecutor to determine that, even if there was 'a reasonable basis to believe that a crime within the jurisdiction of the Court has been or is being committed', it would not 'serve the interests of justice' to continue with an investigation despite 'the gravity of the crime and the interests of victims'.[27] A pre-trial chamber of the court[28] is to be advised of the prosecutor's decision not to proceed with the investigation. Paragraph 2 focuses on the bringing of a prosecution and calls on the prosecutor to inform the pre-trial chamber if a decision is reached not to prosecute, *inter alia*, because it would not be in the interests of justice, 'taking into account all the circumstances, including the gravity of the crime, the interests of victims and the age or infirmity of the alleged perpetrator, and his or her role in the alleged crime'.[29] The pre-trial chamber may review a decision of the prosecutor made in accordance with either paragraph on its own initiative.[30] A review of the decision may also take place if requested either by the Security Council for matters it has referred to the prosecutor or by a state that has referred a situation to the prosecutor.[31]

8.2.1 Discretion and the interpretation of paragraphs 1 and 2

One of the difficulties facing those wishing to interpret Article 53 of the Rome Statute is the paucity of information in the drafting history with respect to the meaning of the phrase 'interests of justice' and the intent of the drafters in inserting the language into the Article. The draft submitted to the Diplomatic Conference of Plenipotentiaries put a positive obligation on the prosecutor to make a determination that an investigation was in the 'interests of justice' prior to initiating an investigation; however, the phrase 'interests of justice' was in square brackets, as were the phrases 'taking into account the gravity of the offences' and 'the interests of victims'.[32] In contrast, the prosecutor, in determining not to file an indictment, was to conclude that 'a prosecution would not be in the interests of justice'.[33] This paragraph also referred to the 'interests of victims' in square brackets, but the placement of the phrase seems to suggest that it would be a factor in favour of prosecution; however, without more information it is not possible to draw a definitive conclusion. With respect to the phrase 'interests of justice', Human Rights Watch has observed that no consensus was reached by the drafters with respect to its meaning.[34] The OTP, having considered the drafting history and the language as adopted, has observed in its policy paper that the 'Interests of Justice test is a potential countervailing consideration' rather than a positive requirement, and that this is a crucial distinction. It means that the OTP has no obligation to 'establish that an investigation or prosecution *is* in the interests of justice' (emphasis added).[35]

Given the volume of information that comes before the OTP, as well as the limits on its resources – both human and material – it is obvious that a broad power of discretion must reside in its officers if the work of the office is to progress efficiently and expeditiously. There are a range of issues that one could envisage the office having to consider with regard to the myriad situations that have and will come to its attention.

For example, in the case of a state party referral where an initial assessment would have been made as to whether or not the situation is one in which crimes within the jurisdiction of the court are occurring and whether or not there is sufficient evidence to go forward with the matter, one could imagine that in a given set of circumstances an 'opt out' clause such as that in paragraph 1 might be useful. Although there might be evidence of crimes within the jurisdiction of the court, the conflict might be an interstate conflict, and the prosecutor might come to the conclusion that a state party is attempting to manipulate the jurisdiction of the court in order to win a tactical advantage in peace negotiations or in respect of its diplomacy in connection with the war.[36] Alternatively, in the context of an intrastate conflict, the state might wish to secure support for its bargaining position vis-à-vis armed resistance groups.[37] Another possibility is that the OTP's investigations in an ongoing conflict situation lead to a conclusion that the physical safety of victims and witnesses could not be guaranteed. In none of these circumstance would it be in the 'interests of justice' to proceed. At a later stage, when hostilities have ceased or peace negotiations have concluded, the

OTP might rely on Article 53 to reconsider its decision. This article allows the Prosecutor to reconsider a decision not to initiate an investigation or prosecution in light of new facts or information that has come to the OTP's attention.

At the prosecution stage, a situation might arise where the OTP, having reviewed the evidence, might come to the conclusion that the available evidence would only allow lesser charges to be brought and that, given the resources needed to go forward, it would not serve the larger interests of international criminal justice to bring this particular prosecution. Other considerations that might come into play are that a prosecution would not create a useful precedent or that this is the type of crime that is routinely prosecuted at the domestic level.

8.2.2 *Constraints on the OTP's exercise of discretion*

Aware of the breadth of the discretion being given to the OTP, the drafters of both the Statute and the Rules of Procedure included provisions for the oversight of this discretion. Although the Statute creates a difference in the obligations of the OTP to give reasons for its decision, depending on whether it is being made at the investigation stage (OTP to inform the Pre-Trial Chamber (PTC)) or the prosecution stage (OTP to inform either the Security Council or referring state as well as the PTC of their conclusions and is to give reasons for the conclusion), the Rules of Procedure[38] require reasons to be given in both circumstances. With respect to a decision not to proceed with an investigation, Rule 105(3) requires the notification to the state party or the Security Council to contain the conclusion of the OTP as well as its 'reasons for the conclusion', taking account of the need to protect victims and witnesses under Article 68. Rule 105(4) requires the notice to the PTC to include the conclusion and the reasons for the conclusion. Rule 106 mirrors the language in Article 53(2) with respect to the provision of conclusions and reasons at the prosecution stage.[39]

With respect to a Pre-Trial Chambers review of the OTP decisions, the outcomes will differ depending on who requested the review. If the Security Council or a referring state requests a review, the PTC may only ask the OTP to reconsider its decision. However, if the PTC undertakes a review on its own initiative, then the OTP's decision not to proceed is 'effective only if confirmed by' the Chamber.[40] Pursuant to Rule 110, if the PTC does not confirm the OTP's decision not to proceed with either investigation or prosecution, then the OTP is obligated to proceed.

8.2.3 *Are the constraints on the OTP's exercise of discretion sufficient to meet the expectation of ethical decision-making?*

There is a suggestion in the OTP policy paper with respect to the 'interests of justice' that the existence of judicial review of its decision-making functions should lessen the concern of organizations following the work of the court that a decision outside the bounds of reasonable discretion would or could be made by the OTP.[41] This view is put forward in order to support the OTP perspective that this type of decision-making is case or situation specific, and that it is not useful to enter into a more abstract discussion of what would or would not be a sufficient 'interests of justice' criteria warranting a decision not to investigate or prosecute.[42] However, this perspective ignores the fact that both paragraphs call on the OTP to give consideration to the interests of victims. Even though the Rome Statute gives greater status to victims than previous international tribunals, there are still profound limitations on their ability to access the court and to have their voices heard by the Pre-Trial Chamber. At the investigation stage, many victims will either not have been identified or will not be aware of their ability to apply to the ICC to have their status recognized. At the prosecution stage, there may be a narrowing of the class of persons able to participate as victims.[43] As women in many communities have limited access to information about their rights, these barriers may particularly affect them.

Further complicating this matter are the various interpretations that could be given to the phrase 'interests of victims'. Is Article 53 referring to victims of the situation being investigated by the prosecutor, victims associated with the crimes committed by a particular individual who may have an arrest warrant outstanding or, if either an arrest warrant has been issued or charges have been brought, those individuals who have been recognized by the court as being victims of the case? Despite the recognition that a broad interpretation should be given to the definition of victim in Article 68 of the Statute, which allows the 'views and concerns' of victims to be 'presented and considered' by the court in cases where their 'personal interests are affected', the number of persons who will receive recognition will always be far lower than the number of persons who have been victimized by a given conflict or even a given defendant.

If Article 53 is meant to encompass all possible victims, this has challenges for women in many societies as their concerns may not be on the public record or they may not have access to the public spaces in which the OTP consults affected communities.[44] There has been some criticism of the OTP's outreach efforts, including criticisms that it has not been gender sensitive.[45] As particular chambers can only rule on applications before them[46] the Statute presupposes that potential victims are aware that the ICC is investigating or considering matters relevant to them. If the ICC's outreach programmes are not ensuring the right to equality of access to justice, this is of particular concern, as this right has been considered a core obligation in the protection and promotion of human rights since the drafting of the Universal Declaration on Human Rights.[47]

In addition, a failure to provide mechanisms that ensure equality of access to victims can lead to what is often termed secondary victimization. Bassiouni, in his comprehensive overview of the development of a theory of victims' rights in international law, includes in his description of secondary victimization the process by which people are left feeling ostracized by their communities when the systems that are created to deal with violations of their rights are perceived to act unfairly.[48] It would be a failure of the OTP's ethical leadership in the field of international criminal justice if its approach to decision-making undermined victims' faith in the ICC and created a situation whereby those already traumatized by armed conflict were further victimized by the court's processes.

If, at the prosecution stage, the notion of victims' interest is limited to the interests of those who have been recognized by the court as victims of the case, then some consideration has to be given to the ratio of male and female victims recognized by the court and whether or not the interests of female victims are being put forward in a comprehensive manner. Further, some oversight of the nature of the cases brought by the OTP is necessary to ensure that a decision not to prosecute in the 'interests of justice' does not result in fewer resources being devoted to cases with gender implications. None of these matters is noted or addressed in the OTP policy paper.

As discussed above, if the matter of an interest of justice concern arises at the prosecution stage, victims of the case will have been identified and some may have received recognition by the court.[49] It is possible that there will be strongly divergent views among those recognized as to what is in their interests and how they perceive the balance should be struck between the interests of justice and the interests of victims.

For example, in some of the countries that have experienced conflict in recent years, women do not have a right to inherit land owned by their families; therefore, the loss of a father or husband during a conflict could mean that a woman is effectively rendered homeless.[50] Her situation may be exacerbated by the need to care for other family members, such as children, parents or siblings. This group of victims may not believe that prosecutions against those responsible for the death of family members should cease in the interests of justice as their ongoing harm leads them to believe they will be better served if the accused is tried. They may perceive a trial as one way of gaining better recognition for their plight within their own country. However, males in the community who have been able to inherit property from those killed in the conflict will have a diametrically opposed view of their interests. Although they too are indirect victims of the conflict, having watched family members die, their interests may be served by having the prosecution cease as this might bring to fruition a peace agreement that endorses the existing law with respect to inheritance.

It is important that the OTP begins to explore how the office will deal with these issues when they arise as they are part of the social context that forms the backdrop to the work of the OTP. The Statute states that the ICC is not to interpret the law in a manner that would create any adverse distinctions founded on matters such as gender.[51] Presumably the OTP will not wish to put forward an 'interests of justice' argument that could lead to such a result, as this would bring the law into disrepute (this itself is an 'interests of justice' concern).[52] This highlights the necessity of the OTP engaging in the 'morally reflective' practice described by Deborah Rhode.

The next two sections of this chapter deal with broader concerns about prosecutorial discretion and the gender dimensions of the concept of justice that could affect an assessment of whether or not the OTP is engaging in an ethical and 'morally reflective' decision-making process that takes due account of gender.

8.3 Gender and the exercise of prosecutorial discretion

Individuals and organizations working with women and girl children are aware of the past failures of international law with respect to the prosecution of gendered crimes. Traditionally, '[w]omen's interests fared notoriously poorly when accountability was sought for the behaviour of combatants'.[53] Despite some references to gendered crimes in the post-Second World War trials, it was not until the 1990s that the jurisprudence of the International Criminal Tribunal for the former Yugoslavia (ICTY) made it clear that rape and other forms of sexual violence 'were serious violations of international humanitarian law'.[54]

Due to these past shortcomings, those working in the area of women's rights have welcomed the inclusion of a more victim-centred approach in the Rome Statute. However, if the 'interests of justice' can either 'trump' the rights of victims or if the interests of victims can be considered a factor in a decision not to proceed in the 'interests of justice', then serious questions arise about the extent to which decision-making will be gender sensitive.

The OTP has acknowledged the need for a detailed policy framework on gender, 'addressing legal and operational issues relevant to the investigation and prosecution of crimes of gender and sexual violence'.[55] However, what appears to be missing is an understanding that gender bias can appear in all facets of its work. It is of concern that the gender dimensions of the OTP's decision-making powers pursuant to Article 53 were not addressed in its policy paper. In order for women survivors and those working with women who may have been subjected to or witnessed crimes within the jurisdiction of the court to have confidence in the operation of the OTP, it is crucial that issues related to gender be explicitly acknowledged by the OTP. This makes the public documents of the OTP about the operation of the office and the manner in which it will exercise its discretion vitally important. Ultimately, the ICC in general and the OTP in particular have to rely on international public opinion in order to continue to be effective. Increased levels of grievance against the court will undermine its effectiveness.

As noted earlier, the exercise of discretion is an integral part of the work of the OTP; however, there is little recognition in the published documents of that office of the possible negative consequences that can arise when discretion in not exercised in accordance with established guidelines and in a manner that is accessible to the community at large. 'Where law ends, discretion begins, and the exercise of discretion may mean either . . . justice or injustice . . .'.[56] The need for greater public articulation of the criteria by which decisions will be made is thoughtfully elucidated by Allison Marston Danner in her article 'Enhancing the legitimacy and accountability of prosecutorial discretion at the International Criminal Court'.[57] She highlights the significant effort that will have to be undertaken by the OTP to prioritize its workload due to both budgetary and statutory constraints on its work.[58] A potential problem in any situation where discretion is crucial to the functions of an organization is that it can be exercised arbitrarily or in a discriminatory fashion.[59]

Discretionary areas hold the biggest challenge to women. In exercising judgment, professionals often believe that they act without bias – but the day-to-day experience of women is to the contrary.[60] Gender bias can range from not taking seriously crimes against women to not thinking through the ways in which domestic hierarchical structures can silence women. Issues such as who categorizes individuals as victims of crime, who interviews potential victims and witnesses, who acts as an intermediary between the staff of the OTP and victims and witnesses, who translates the accounts of victims and witness, and whether or not barriers to women's participation have been identified by the OTP before it undertakes grassroots work are all important to the credibility of the process.

None of these comments should be read as insinuating that the OTP will inevitably make decisions that could be viewed as biased. Rather, without the formulation of guidelines that delineate in a clear and precise fashion[61] the manner in which gender can affect its work, it remains unclear whether the OTP has a sufficient understanding of the potential for bias in its work and whether it is taking adequate steps to ensure that any bias will be identified and overcome. As noted by Allison Marston Danner, it is the cumulative effect of a series of discretionary decisions that leads to the formation of policy.[62] It is incumbent on the office to acknowledge that its decisions about what will and will not be considered to be a factor in its decision-making pursuant to the 'interests of justice' clause will result in a series of precedents for future prosecutors, and that each of its decisions will have an impact on the future administration of international criminal justice.

A specific area of concern in this regard, and one that is related to an example utilized in the OTP policy paper, is a decision not to prosecute because adequate protection cannot be provided to witnesses and victims.[63] The manner in which this assessment is made can have consequences for women. If the decision is made in part on the basis of information supplied by local leaders, as suggested by the OTP, then questions need to be asked about the extent to which they speak on behalf of the entire population. It has been the case that some members of society do not wish to discuss in public the crimes that have been committed against women. This may have many underlying reasons, from a sense of shame for their inability to protect women as a group to a belief that such crimes are not as important as other crimes such as murder or torture. There are also issues related to the domestic treatment of such crimes. If few resources are given to the prosecution of crimes of sexual violence and if women face a criminal justice system that is unsympathetic to their concerns, then it is likely that such attitudes will carry forward when discussions are held about the possibility of bringing prosecutions before the ICC. Again, the author is not suggesting that the OTP itself is unsympathetic to women's concerns. The issue is the articulation of gender as a matter for reflection and the public's need to feel that the prosecutor has thought through the gender implications of its work and the manner in which it will deal with specific problems when they arise.

Although focused on deaths in custody, the observations of His Honour Gerald Butler QC during the 1999 Inquiry into the Crown Prosecution Service is apt:

What, however, is clear is this. Any decision as to whether or not there should
be a prosecution in a case where there has been a death in custody is always
a decision of great importance … If a prosecution is not brought when
it should be, then the family and friends of the deceased will suffer a deep
sense of grievance, accompanied by a loss of confidence in the criminal
justice system.[64]

The past failure of international law to take seriously issues of importance to
women has meant that women do not yet have confidence that the system will
operate with their concerns in mind. There is a potential for both victims
of gender-based crimes and observers of the court to lose confidence in its
operations unless the decision-making process is explained fully. The type of
ethical approach to the OTP's work being suggested in this chapter would assist
in strengthening victims' and the international community's respect for the
institutions of international criminal justice, as it would ensure that the OTP had
publicly explained its understanding of the consequences of its work on affected
societies.

8.4 Gender and the concept of justice

Giving meaning to the phrase 'interests of justice' is problematic, as it is open to a
range of interpretations because the word 'justice' itself is so amorphous.[65] As a
concept, justice has legal, moral and philosophical overtones.[66] The literature on
transitional justice contains material that is both about traditional criminal justice
as well as restorative justice and nation-building – issues which are outside the
scope of traditional criminal justice concerns. Although indicating its awareness
of the debates surrounding the term 'justice', the OTP appears to have taken the
position that its role is to fulfil traditional criminal justice objectives – that is,
accountability requires a trial and that retribution and deterrence are the two
main purposes of the criminal justice system.[67]

Following on from this interpretation, the phrase 'interests of justice' is more
likely to be perceived as being akin to some of the concerns in common law legal
systems that come under the rubric 'administration of justice'.[68] Among the issues
that a prosecutor would have to consider would be whether or not a particular
investigation or prosecution would serve the purposes of the Rome Statute, the
operation of the ICC and the furtherance of international criminal law. Examples
of such a consideration are: the ability of the OTP to obtain the support of the
international community in carrying out investigations or in arresting a suspect,[69]
as it would significantly undermine public confidence in the court if an arrest
warrant were issued in circumstances where a state had and would continue to
refuse all cooperation with the court and the court was viewed as impotent;
continuing an investigation or prosecution where the evidence had been obtained
through the use of torture;[70] and the pursuit of an investigation or the bringing of
a prosecution that was viewed as discriminatory.[71]

The OTP has expressed its view that the concept of 'interests of justice' is tied to the importance of ending impunity for mass atrocities. Effectively, this position puts a premium on the idea that the prosecution acts as a deterrent to the commission of crimes in the future.[72] But the focus on deterrence can result in a failure to address the complexities of mass violence and the relationship between societal breakdown and the occurrence of violence. By not articulating its understanding of the connection between impunity and justice, the OTP leaves itself open to a critique that it does not fully appreciate the connection between state-building and justice or the need for communities to re-establish moral order in their societies. The complex nature of mass atrocities, as well as the fact that they 'would not [have] reach[ed] truly epidemic levels but for the vigorous participation of the masses',[73] makes it crucial that thought be given to how prosecutorial strategies fit in with the need to acknowledge the complicity of many ordinary people.[74]

8.4.1 Mass atrocities and 'philosophical justice'

Reading the policy paper, it appears that the OTP has not sufficiently addressed what Tom Campbell terms 'philosophical justice'.[75] This is also a component of ending impunity as it relates to societal transformation. The process of handling investigations and potential prosecutions should acknowledge that mass atrocities occur because of the suspension of moral values, and should encourage the community to reassert them. When the OTP refers to discussions with local leaders, one has to ask how they will be selected, what assurances the OTP will seek to demonstrate that they are not tainted with complicity in the events under consideration, and how the OTP will ensure they are in fact speaking for a larger group.

Another facet of this problem is that in any situation the OTP is likely to consider for investigation, multiple actors will have contributed to the breakdown in societal cohesion and the local population may perceive all of them as having a role in the harms that have occurred. The population may perceive themselves as pawns in a game being played by the government and other groups. On the other hand, significant numbers of the local population may have played a role in the conflict and their views about security and about the need for retribution may be skewed by their own allegiances:

> For the victims and survivors of acts of mass atrocities justice has a range of connotations. For them justice is about the restoration of their dignity, receiving a reaffirmation of their value as human beings, obtaining assurances that the larger community understands the impact mass atrocities have had on their lives, and knowing that the perpetrators either have been punished or been made to acknowledge their crimes. It is also about being part of a process that empowers rather than dehumanises them.[76]

Research undertaken in Northern Uganda by the Gulu District NGO Forum/Liu Institute for Global Issues[77] supports this characterization of a victim's/survivor's perspective of justice. Consultations were organized with survivors and the families of victims of past atrocities. During this process, participants expressed their desire to learn about the fate of relatives, to hear admissions from those responsible about their activities and to receive an acknowledgement from the perpetrators that their acts were crimes. They also recognized the necessity of discussing the underlying tensions and societal fault lines in order to avoid future conflicts. Further, community members emphasized the importance of a partnership between the Acholi people, the Government of Uganda and the ICC and their desire to have the ICC recognize their knowledge and their right to influence decisions about what would constitute justice.[78]

8.4.2 Empowering victims

When balancing the 'interests of justice' and the interests of victims, it is important that the OTP thinks carefully about how an assessment will be made in light of the possibility that victims of sexual assault in particular may be continuing to experience severe ongoing trauma. Former Gender Adviser to the International Tribunal for Yugoslavia, Patricia Viseur Sellers, observed that in her conversations with interpreters and investigators about their interactions with victims, they opined that sexual assault witnesses 'tended to be more severely affected by the overall ordeal, placing them into a different category of witness altogether . . . It tended to detrimentally affect the personal relations of the victims/witnesses for years – especially with men'.[79] Further: 'The emotionally and physically devastating experience of sexual assault victims/witnesses seemed to be the issue that tested the professional skills of a number of investigations/interpreters interviewed'.[80]

This is not to suggest that such victims would not want the criminal process to proceed. Despite the emotional hardship of discussing events, it is also true that many victims and witnesses find that the telling of their stories assists them to recover from their trauma. They can develop a sense of empowerment and a feeling of control over their lives.[81] Many women want to tell their stories in the hope that it will prevent atrocities from occurring in the future. In undertaking consultations with 'local leaders',[82] the OTP should ensure that its consultations do not undermine the rights of women.[83] The utilization of leaders or other proxies may undermine the ability of victims to speak for themselves and to work for societal change. Even where there are sound reasons for not commencing or continuing an investigation or prosecution, the manner in which the decision-making process is undertaken and explained can be crucial in either fostering or diminishing a sense of empowerment.

The observations of André Laperrière, the Executive Director of the Victims' Trust Fund are pertinent:

> Our first challenge is to change the perception of the Western World from seeing victims as hopeless dependents, into their true nature as fully fledged citizens wanting to contribute to their community and country. Victims are and deserve to be considered as partners, which [sic] deserve our respect and support . . . We have to show them that they are not alone, and that they have

nothing to be ashamed of; on the contrary, they have to be proud to have been able to manage despite the atrocities they had to face.[84]

Another issue that can arise from the focus on consultations with local leaders and non-government organizations is the possibility that local hierarchal structures exclude the participation of women.[85] The Victims' Rights Working Group[86] has observed that:

> obtaining a real understanding of the views and concerns of victims is a complex process, owing to the fact that often the most marginalized victims have the least access to debates about such issues . . . This is because 'victims' as such are not a homogenous group and will generally have a variety of views and perspectives.[87]

Working through the range of issues that have to be considered when interacting with victims is not a simple task. As the discussion in this chapter demonstrates, there is an ever-present concern that the marginalization of women could be exacerbated if the process is not handled carefully. Adding to the complexity is the fact that, in some cases, women who have been forced into being a victim/survivor by the crimes perpetrated against them have emerged as actors for political change. They may have become involved in politics within their own countries or become active participants in regional and international movements.[88] The OTP must ensure that, when thinking about the necessity of balancing the protection of victims with the 'interests of justice', it does not undermine the steps women have taken towards their own empowerment. Decisions should not be made that assume women are passive and require protection. Some women may be willing to take the risk of telling their stories in order to influence the international community's understanding of events in their country or to further the rights of women more generally.

8.4.3 Unrecognized bias and its implications for women

One of the most difficult steps for lawyers (and judges) to take is to acknowledge that there can be biases in the system within which they operate. The professionalism of those working within the system provides them with a sense that they are operating impartially and with objectivity. Yet when a systematic examination is undertaken of the interactions that occur within the legal system, biases become evident. The findings of the review of the Ninth Circuit in the United States included the following observation: 'Thus we know that is not only having a different experience but also that, when witnessing or engaging in the very same behaviours, women and men experience, describe, and report different events'.[89] The recognition of the potential for bias – and the differing ways in which women, particularly women who have experienced gendered violence – should be the starting point for the outreach work of the OTP and those who will engage in the investigation and prosecution of possible crimes.

A further area requiring exploration by the OTP is the effect of its work on the levels of violence, including domestic violence, experienced by women in the post-conflict period. The chaos brought about by a conflict may have lead to a generalized increase in crimes of violence against women. Members of the population can take advantage of the breakdown in law and order to commit crimes.[90] This violence often does not cease when the conflict ends; the general level of societal disarray and the proliferation of small arms in conflict-ridden states can lead to a sustained level of crimes of violence against women during the transitional period.[91] The failure of the OTP to acknowledge the effect its work can have on the continued vulnerability of women can be a cause of dissatisfaction and as with other issues addressed in this paper could lead to a loss of confidence in its work.[92] Once again, it is important to stress that it is not being suggested that the OTP must investigate or prosecute every crime; rather, a thoughtful analysis of how its efforts affect the lives of ordinary women is necessary. The desire of the OTP to be viewed as effective (in the sense of bringing targeted and resource-limited prosecutions)[93] should not outweigh its obligation to set standards and to work closely with national governments to ensure that an unintended consequence of its activities is to contribute to the marginalization of women.[94]

The OTP has indicated that it will pay regard to alternative justice mechanisms when working with countries to address what has been termed the 'impunity gap' – that is, the limited ability of courts, whether national or international, to deal with all perpetrators of mass atrocities.[95] However, traditional justice mechanisms are not always sympathetic to the rights of women. Those working with women who have lived through conflict are aware that the utilization of such mechanisms should be reformed so that they reflect a commitment to women's equality including their right to be treated as both decision-makers and active participants.[96] As Mark Drumbl has observed, it is necessary to be careful when dealing with local structures because they may 'institutionalize the power of unaccountable local elites'.[97]

A further consideration that should be addressed by the OTP is the impact a decision not to proceed will have on the ability of victims and witnesses to recover from what they might consider to be a breach of trust. It is beyond the scope of this chapter to consider the manner in which the OTP initiates contact with affected populations and the nature of its outreach work in explaining the processes of the ICC, as well as the possibility that there may not be a tangible outcome from their cooperation. What is clear, however, is that the lack of comprehensible and sensitive case management can lead to a further loss of self-esteem and a diminution in a victim's or witness's ability to trust authority figures.

A victim undertakes a difficult emotional journey to come to the point where they are willing to recount the traumatic story of sexual violence. The sensitivity and respect displayed by interpreters and investigators instils a sense of trust in the victims and witnesses.[98] To find out that their effort to give an accurate narrative of the acts of extreme horror inflicted on them will not result in a prosecution can be emotionally damaging for a victim. For some, it was the belief that what happened to them would be placed before a court, and that this would help them to find closure,[99] that allowed them to find the strength to divulge their secrets.

Flowing on from the above is the necessity of giving effect to one of the basic rights of victims: the right to be informed about the progress of the proceedings.[100] The right is not only about being given adequate information and a reasoned explanation, but also about receiving the information in a manner that respects the dignity of the individual. If not handled sensitively, communications may contribute to the ongoing isolation of the victim.

The reasons for a decision not to proceed must be made clear to the local population and materials should be distributed in local languages.[101] Witnesses and victims can feel that their testimony is being appropriated for a purpose outside of their control. Their experiences form the basis of the work of the OTP, yet they are not in control of their own stories or the impact that the telling of their stories will have.[102] For women, the decision to come forward may be extremely difficult due to the fear of the community's reaction. A decision not to proceed may leave women feeling and being even more marginalized and subject to community control and approbation. Without an adequate explanation of the OTP's decision, it might be possible for either the women themselves or members of their communities to come to the conclusion that they were not believed. The consequences for women if such a view did develop could be devastating to their future relationship with family members and their communities.

8.5 Conclusion

In order for the work of the OTP to be described as 'morally reflective', it must demonstrate that is attempting to come to grips with the mismatch of perceptions between institutional actors and those working with women. The former assume that they act in the common good, with impartiality and objectivity. The latter are aware of the historical failure of international law and its institutions to deal with crimes against women. When decisions are made not to investigate or prosecute crimes of sexual violence or to terminate prosecutions without ensuring adequate consultations with the full panoply of victims, many women and organizations will question whether or not those decisions are compromised due to a lack of appreciation of the seriousness of the crimes or through the operation of subtle biases about women's ability to speak for themselves. In order for the work of the OTP to further the interests of justice, it is essential that it publicize its understanding of the factors that will guide the exercise of its discretion and that its policy papers contain an explicit and transparent gender analysis. Unless the OTP adopts such an approach, there will be an ongoing fear that the past failures of the international legal system will be replicated in its work. This fear has the potential to erode public confidence in the ICC, an outcome that would undermine rather than garner support for the institutions of international criminal law.

Acknowledgement

The content of this chapter was inspired by the work the author has undertaken as a member of the Advisory Council for the Women's Initiatives for Gender Justice. The author would like to thank Professor Roger Clark of Rutgers University, Camden, Professor Christine Chinkin of the London School of Economics and Lesley Petrie of Flinders University for their useful feedback on this chapter. The views contained in the text are those of the author and any mistakes or misunderstandings are solely attributable to the author.

Notes

1 Article 5, Rome Statute of the International Criminal Court, UN Doc. A/CONF.183/9. Available from: <www.un.org/law/icc/statute/romefra.htm> (accessed 10 July 2008).

2 S. Economides, 'The International Criminal Court: Reforming the politics of international justice', *Government and Opposition: An International Journal of Comparative Politics*, 2003, vol. 38, 29–30.

3 Pursuant to Article 13, the ICC has jurisdiction over the nominated crimes resulting from investigations conducted by the prosecutor as a result of a referral of situations by either the Security Council or a state party. The prosecutor may initiate their own investigations in accordance with Article 15 of the Statute. The powers of the prosecutor with respect to investigations and prosecutions are set out in Articles 53–61, Rome Statute of the International Criminal Court.

4 Articles 1, 12 and 17, Rome Statute of the International Criminal Court.

5 The recent submission by the ICC to the Assembly of States Parties encompasses an overview of the OTP's expenditures since 2006. The following information is taken from Table 14: Changes in OTP budget and staff allocation per situation which sets out the budgetary figures from 2006 onward that have been allocated to the cases being investigated by the OTP. For 2009 the approved budget included the following costs (set out in euros) with figures in parentheses setting out the number of staff working in a particular area and the number of cases being pursued: Operational Support, 5,012,700 (59) (9 cases); Uganda, 898,900 (3) (one case); Democratic Republic of Congo 6,124,300 (53) (four cases); Darfur 4,590,500 (32) (three cases); Central African Republic 4,206,300 (24) (one case). See ICC-ASP/8/10, Assembly of States Parties, Proposed Programme Budget for 2010 of the International Criminal Court, 30 July 2009 <www.icc-cpi.int/NR/rdonlyres/F945056A-F020–24F6A-A626-B8015D20D925/0/ICCASP810ENG.pdf> (accessed 31 October 2009).

6 *R (on the application of Purdy v Director of Public Prosecutions)* [2009] UKHL 45.

7 Ibid.; see also B. A. Grosman, *The Prosecutor*, Toronto: University of Toronto Press, 1969, pp. 100–105, although – unlike the House of Lords in *R (on the application of Purdy v Director of Public Prosecutions)* [2009] UKHL 45, which found the Director of Public Prosecutions was obliged to issue publicly available guidelines – Grosman suggests that guidelines may be too restrictive. It should be noted that the House of Lords' judgment relies, in part, on the judgment of the European Court of Human Rights in *Pretty v United Kingdom* (2002) 35 EHRR 1, and therefore is both more recent and more in tune with the development of human rights law.

8 Ibid.

9 R. K. Flowers, 'Foreword to the Prosecution Law Symposium', *Stetson Law Review*, 1999–2000, vol. 29, 2.

10 M. Wade, B. Aubusson de Cavarlay and J. Zila, 'Tinker, tailor, policy-maker: The wider context of prosecution service work', *European Journal on Criminal Policy and Research*, 2008, vol. 13, 181–90.

11 D. L. Rhode, 'Law, lawyers, and the pursuit of justice', *Fordham Law Review*, 2001–2, vol. 70, 1543: 'Lawyers, individually and collectively, need to assume greater responsibility for the consequences of their professional actions [and] for the performance of the legal system . . .' (p. 1545).

12 D. L. Rhode, 'Personal integrity and professional ethics', Keynote Address to Third Legal Ethics Conference, Gold Coast, Australia, 14 July 2008, p. 2; a copy of the paper is in the personal possession of the author.

13 Rhode, 'Law, lawyers, and the pursuit of justice', 1546.

14 Rhode, 'Personal integrity', 4.

15 Commonly referred to as the laws of war or the law and customs of armed conflict.

16 F. Ní Aoláin, 'Political violence and gender during times of transitional justice', *Columbia Journal of Gender and Law*, 2005, vol. 15, 838; J. Campanaro, 'Women, war, and international law: The historical treatment of gender-based war crimes', *Georgetown Law Journal*, vol. 81, 2557–92. P. V. Sellers, 'Individual(s)' liability for collective sexual violence', in K. Knop (ed.), *Gender and Human Rights*, Oxford: Oxford University Press, 2004.

17 H. Charlesworth, 'Not waving but drowning: Gender mainstreaming and human rights in the United Nations', *Harvard Human Rights Journal*, 2005, vol. 18, 1–17; International Committee of the Red Cross, *Addressing the Needs of Women Affected by Armed Conflict*, Geneva: International Committee of the Red Cross, 2004; C. Chinkin, *Peace Agreements as a Means for Promoting Gender Equality and Ensuring the Participation of Women*, United Nations Division for the Advancement of Women, EGM/PEACE/2003/BP.1, 31 October 2003; UNHCR, *Respect our Rights, Partnerships for Equality – Report on the Dialogue with Refugee Women*, Geneva: 2001. Available from: <www.unhcr.org/refworld/docid/4649d5d72.html> (accessed 31 October 2009); UNDAW, International Peace Research Institute Oslo, Expert Group Meeting on Political Decision-Making and Conflict Resolution: The Impact of Gender Difference (October 1996). EGM/PRDC/1996/REP.1, 7 November 1996.

18 Most of the discussion has centred on whether or not the wording of this paragraph would allow the OTP to decide not to go forward with an investigation or prosecution if proceeding would jeopardize peace negotiations, the argument being that victims are part of the general population and it is in everyone's interest for a peace agreement to be reached. See, for example, H. Kaul, 'Developments at the International Criminal Court. Construction site for more justice: The International Criminal Court after two years', *American Journal of International Law*, 2005, vol. 99, 375; H. M. Lovat, 'Delineating the interests of justice: Prosecutorial discretion and the Rome Statue of the International Criminal Court', 2006. Available from: <http://law.bepress.com/expresso/eps/1435> (accessed 20 October 2009). Others have argued that it gives the prosecutor discretion to accept the granting of amnesties to some perpetrators in order to assist the transition to peace (particularly in situations where other mechanisms are used to identify perpetrators such as truth and reconciliation procedures). See, for example, R. J. Goldstone and N. Fritz, '"In the interests of justice" and independent referral: The ICC prosecutor's unprecedented powers', *Leiden Journal of International Law*, 2000, vol. 13, 655–57 and E. Blumenson, 'The challenge of a global standard of justice: Peace, pluralism and punishment at the International Criminal Court', *Columbia Journal of Transnational Law*, 2006, vol. 44, 801–74. A more cautious approach is taken by R. Wedgwood, 'The International Criminal Court: An American view', *European Journal of International Law*, 1999, vol. 10, 93–107, J. Gavron, 'Amnesties in the light of developments in international law and the establishment of the International Criminal Court', *International and Comparative Law Quarterly*, 2002, vol. 51, 91–118. See C. Gallavin, 'Article 53 of the Rome Statute of the International Criminal Court: In the interests of justice?', *Kings Law Journal*, vol. 14, 185–86; D. Robinson, 'Serving the interests of justice: Amnesties, Truth Commissions and the International Criminal Court', *European Journal of International Law*, 2003, vol. 14, 488. The counter-argument

is that amnesties allow those who perpetrated crimes to continue to wield influence and act as a corrupting force on the rule of law, and ultimately may lead to renewed violence. See discussion of *Vélásquez-Rodríguez* in C. Bassiouni, 'International recognition of victims' rights', *Human Rights Law Review*, 2006, vol. 6, 226–28 and the work of D. Orentlicher, appointed by the United Nations Secretary-General as the independent expert to update the Set of Principles to combat impunity, cited in Office of the Prosecutor (OTP), 'Policy paper on the interests of justice', ICC-OTP-2007. Available from: <www.icc-cpi.int/NR/rdonlyres/772C95C9-F54D-4321-BF09–73422BB23528 / 143640/ICCOTPInterestsOfJustice.pdf> (accessed 11 October 2009). See also D. G. Newman, 'The Rome Statute, some reservations concerning amnesties, and a distributive problem', *American University International Law Review*, 2005, vol. 20, 93: 343, who argues that the analysis of amnesties in context of international criminal law is 'analytically underdeveloped'. He focuses on the hardships that may be experienced by states that do prosecute or refer in accordance with international expectations, and argues that the global community, having demanded adherence to its standards, has an obligation to offer real support for 'democratic transition in conflict ridden states' (p. 357). The OTP has stated that in its view 'there is a difference between the concepts of the interests of justice and the interests of peace and that the latter falls within the mandate of institutions other than the Office of the Prosecutor'. OTP, 'The interests of justice', 1.

19 OTP, 'The interests of justice'.

20 Ibid., 1 and 3.

21 P. J. P. Tak describes the two main underpinnings of prosecutorial work as the legality principle and the opportunity (expediency) principle. (See P. J. P. Tak, 'Prosecutorial discretion: The filter function of the prosecution service', Keynote Address, 11th IAP annual conference, Paris, 2006.) The legality principle operates on the premise 'prosecutions[s] must take place in all cases in which sufficient evidence exists of the guilt of a suspect and in which no legal hindrances prohibit prosecution' (p. 2). In contrast, the opportunity principle 'does not demand compulsory prosecution [but rather] allows the prosecution service discretion over the prosecutorial decision' (p. 2). Tak notes that the following European countries have adopted the opportunity principle: Belgium, Cyprus, Denmark, England and Wales, France, Ireland, Luxembourg, Malta and the Netherlands (p. 2). The principle also operates in Australia, Canada, New Zealand and the United States. Hassan Jallow, the chief prosecutor at the International Criminal Tribunal for Rwanda, has noted that 'certain factors came to be accepted as relevant to the exercise of the discretion of whether to prosecute or not to prosecute. Among such factors, apart from the obvious technical one of *evidential sufficiency*, were such public-interest issues relating to the *gravity of the offence*, the *staleness* of the offence, the *likely penalty*, the *potential impact* on community stability of a decision either way, the *age* of the offender – and of the victim too'. H. B. Jallow, 'Prosecutorial discretion and international criminal justice', *Journal of International Criminal Justice*, 2005, vol. 3, 145–61, n. 1. See also P. Webb, 'The ICC prosecutor's discretion not to proceed in the "interests of justice"', *Criminal Law Quarterly*, 2005, vol. 50, 305–48 for a discussion of how discretion is slowly entering legal systems that traditionally employed the legality principle.

22 Jallow, 'Prosecutorial discretion', 145.

23 See *R (on the application of Purdy v Director of Public Prosecutions)* [2009] UKHL 45.

24 Tak, 'Prosecutorial discretion: The filter function', p. 5. See, for example, Commonwealth Director of Public Prosecutions (Australia), 'Prosecution policy of the Commonwealth'. Available from: <www.cdpp.gov.au/Publications/ProsecutionPolicy/ProsecutionPolicy.pdf> (accessed 30 January 2007).

25 Tak, 'Prosecutorial discretion: The filter function'; Jallow, 'Prosecutorial discretion'; Webb, 'The ICC'. A comparative study of 13 European countries revealed that in all but three guidelines were issued regulating the manner in which discretion could be

exercised in order 'to ensure uniform application in line with defined public interest and or policy considerations'; J. Jehle, P. Smit and J. Zila, 'The public prosecutor as key-player: Prosecutorial case-ending decisions', *European Journal on Criminal Policy and Research*, 2008, vol. 14, 173. Examples of such codes are contained in Gallavin, 'Article 53', 188–90; see also Commonwealth Director of Public Prosecutions (Australia), 'Prosecution policy'.

26 See material cited in notes 18, 21, 24, 25 and 26 above.

27 Article 53(1)(c), Rome Statute of the International Criminal Court.

28 The judicial functions of the court are carried out by three divisions known as Chambers: Pre-Trial Chamber, Trial Chamber and Appeals Chamber. For a description of each of the divisions, see the official website of the ICC at <www.icc-cpi.int/organs/chambers.html>.

29 Article 53(2)(c), Rome Statute of the International Criminal Court. There is a divergence in language between paragraphs in Article 53(1) and (2). Paragraph 1 seems to create a dichotomy between the gravity of the crime and the 'interests of victims' on one side with the 'interests of justice' on the other, suggesting that the interests of justice could outweigh the other factors. See Gallavin, 'Article 53', 185–86; Robinson, 'Serving the interests', 488. See also Human Rights Watch, 'Policy paper: the meaning of the interests of justice in Article 53 of the Rome Statute', June 2005. Available from: <www.iccnow.org/?mod=interestofjustice> (accessed 11 October 2009). Human Rights Watch, while not exploring this point fully, observed that the difference 'between the two provisions was most probably not accidental': p. 19. The OTP paper does not comment on the difference in the wording of the two sub-sections. It merely notes that they 'create an obligation to consider various factors'. OTP, 'The interests of justice', 2. Paragraph 2, in contrast, lends itself to an interpretation that the interests of victims, the gravity of the crimes and the other nominated factors are all possible circumstances to be taken into account in determining that there is 'not a sufficient basis for a prosecution' because 'a prosecution [would] not [be] in the interests of justice'.

30 Article 53(3)(b), Rome Statute of the International Criminal Court.

31 Article 53(3)(a), Rome Statute of the International Criminal Court.

32 Report of the Preparatory Committee on the Establishment of an International Criminal Court, Addendum, A/Conf 183/2/Add 1, paragraph 54(2)[ii].

33 Ibid., para. 54(6).

34 Human Rights Watch, 'Policy paper'. See also Webb, 'The ICC', 325.

35 OTP, 'The interests of justice', 2–3.

36 The potential for such a problem is alluded to in J. D. van der Vyver, 'Book review: *International Justice and the International Criminal Court: Between Sovereignty and the Rule of Law*', *Emory International Law Review* 2004, vol. 18, 139: van der Vyver then explains how the utilization of traditional international law principles could overcome the problem.

37 A suggestion that the Government of Uganda had political motivations for referring the situation in Northern Uganda to the International Criminal Court is contained in M. H. Arsanjani and W. M. Reisman, 'Developments at the International Criminal Court: The law-in-action of the International Criminal Court', *American Journal of International Law*, 2005, vol. 99, 385–403. In contrast, Akhavan Payam argues that the referral was a positive step toward the restoration of peace: see A. Payam, 'Developments at the International Criminal Court: The *Lords Resistance Army Case*: Uganda's submission of the first state referral to the International Criminal Court', *American Journal of International Law*, 2005, vol. 99, 403–21.

38 International Criminal Court, 'Rules of procedure and evidence': UN Doc. PCNICC/2000/1/Add.1, 2000. Available from <www.icc-cpi.int/NR/rdonlyres/F1E0AC1C-A3F3–4A3C-B9A7-B3E8B115E886/140164/Rules_of_procedure_and_Evidence_English.pdf> (accessed 31 October 2009).

39 In contrast, Article 15, Rome Statute of the International Criminal Court merely

requires the OTP to inform those who provided information of its decision not to proceed with an investigation; no explanation for this course of action is required.

40 Article 53(3)(b), Rome Statute of the International Criminal Court.

41 OTP, 'The interests of justice', 1, 9.

42 Ibid.

43 For a discussion of the complex nature of the case law surrounding the recognition of victims, see E. Baumgartner, 'Aspects of victim participation in the proceedings of the International Criminal Court', *International Review of the Red Cross*, 2008, vol. 409 and Human Rights Watch, 'Courting history: the landmark International Criminal Court's first years', 10 July 2008, Section VII. Available from: <www.hrw.org/en/reports/2008/07/10/courting-history> (accessed 29 August 2009).

44 For an overview of the efforts made at outreach, see Human Rights Watch, 'Courting history', Sections V and VI.

45 Ibid.

46 For a description of some of the recent cases concerning victim participation, see Women's Initiatives for Gender Justice, *2008 Gender Report Card on the International Criminal Court*, 2008, pp. 52–63. Available from: <www.iccwomen.org/publications/index.php> (accessed 11 October 2009).

47 Pursuant to Article 21(3), Universal Declaration of Human Rights, GA res. 217A (III), UN Doc A/810 at 71 (1948): 'The application and interpretation of law . . . must be consistent with internationally recognized human rights'. Article 7 states: 'All are equal before the law and are entitled without any discrimination to equal protection of the law'. Article 10 states: 'Everyone is entitled in full equality to a fair and public hearing by an independent and impartial tribunal'. Universal Declaration of Human Rights, GA res. 217A (III), UN Doc A/810 at 71 (1948). Available from: <www.unhchr.ch/udhr/lang/eng.htm> (accessed 26 February 2008). For an elucidation of the nature of the right to equality before the courts contained in Article 14 of the International Covenant on Civil and Political Rights, UN Doc. A/6316 (1966) (ICCPR), see General Comment 32. The Human Rights Committee observed that the right to equality before the courts included equal access to the courts. Human Rights Committee, General Comment No 32, CCPR/C/GC/32, 23 August 2007. Although the ICCPR applies only to state parties, the commentary of the Human Rights Committee on the rights protected by the Covenant is persuasive authority on the meaning and interpretation of those rights. The Committee has also highlighted the importance of ensuring equal access to justice for women in its General Comment on Article 3 of the ICCPR (equality of rights between men and women). See Human Rights Committee, General Comment 28, CCPR/C/2/Rev.1/Add.10.

48 L. Montada, 'Injustice in harm and loss', *Social Justice Research*, 1994, vol. 7, 1573–6725.

49 In determining whether or not to allow the participation of victims, the court must make an assessment that their participation is appropriate to the stage of the proceedings and ensure that their participation would not jeopardize the rights of the accused. For a discussion of the various interpretations that have been given to this Article by the Pre-Trial and Trial Chambers, see Baumgartner, 'Aspects of victim participation' and Human Rights Watch, 'Courting history'.

50 Burundi is a case in point. With respect to the problems faced by women in the post-conflict period due to their inability to own or inherit land, see U. Dolgopol, 'Women and peace building: What we can learn from the Arusha Peace Agreement', *Australian Feminist Studies*, 2006, vol. 21, 257–73 and UNDP, *Rapport d'Avancement, Objectifs du Millénaire pour le Développement* (2004), 17–18 (copy with author and editors). Problems facing women in the pursuit of economic rights, and the situation of women with respect to land and their participation in the informal economy, are cogently outlined in R. Rebouché, 'Labor, land, and women's rights in Africa: Challenges of the new Protocol on the Rights of Women', *Harvard Human Rights Journal*, 2006, vol. 19, 235–56.

51 Article 21(3), Rome Statute of the International Criminal Court.
52 Several authors have argued that the phrase 'interests of justice' is analogous to the responsibility of domestic prosecutors to make decisions in the 'public interest'. See, for example, Gallavin, 'Article 53'; Webb, 'The ICC'; D. D. Ntanda Nsereko, 'Prosecutorial discretion before national courts and international tribunals', *Journal of International Criminal Justice*, 2005, vol. 5, 124–44.
53 Ní Aoláin, 'Political violence', 838; Campanaro, 'Women, war, and international law', 2557.
54 P. V. Sellers, 'Individual(s)' liability for collective sexual violence', in K. Knop (ed.), *Gender and Human Rights*, Oxford: Oxford University Press, 2004. See also, U. Dolgopol and S. Paranjape, *Comfort Women: The Unfinished Ordeal*, Geneva: International Commission of Jurists, 1993; and Jallow, 'Prosecutorial discretion'.
55 Summary of recommendations received during the first public hearing of the Office of the Prosecutor, convened from 17–18 June 2003 at The Hague, Comments and Conclusions of the Office of the Prosecutor, ICC-OTP 2003, p. 6.
56 K. Davis, *Discretionary Justice: A Preliminary Inquiry*, 1969, 3, cited in A. M. Danner, 'Prosecutorial discretion and legitimacy', 13 June 2005, Guest Lecture Series of the Office of the Prosecutor, n. 65, originally published as 'Enhancing the legitimacy and accountability of prosecutorial discretion at the International Criminal Court', *American Journal of International Law*, 2003, vol. 97, 510–52.
57 Ibid.
58 Ibid., 520.
59 Ibid., 521.
60 The final report of the Ninth Circuit Gender Bias Task Force, 'The effects of gender in the federal courts', *Californian Law Review*, 1994, vol. 67, 1106.
61 The decision of the House of Lords in *R* (*on the application of Purdy v Director of Public Prosecutions*) [2009] UKHL 45, emphasizes the importance of precision in a prosecutor's analysis of what will be taken into account when a decision is being made about whether or not to go forward with a criminal prosecution. Although the decision concerns the importance of potential defendants and their relatives being able to determine the likelihood of a criminal prosecution in the case of assisted suicides in foreign jurisdictions, the reasoning is applicable to the situation of victims of mass conflicts.
62 'Discretion also forces prosecutors to make decisions that cumulatively affect the criminal justice system as a whole. It requires them to make judgments about the purpose and priorities of their particular system. Of all the by-products of discretion, this policy-making role has perhaps the greatest systemic consequences for criminal justice.' Danner, 'Prosecutorial discretion and legitimacy', 518.
63 OTP, 'The interests of justice', 5–6.
64 See Inquiry into Crown Prosecution Service, Decision-Making in Relation to Deaths in Custody and Related Matters, His Honour Gerald Butler QC, August 1999, section 9, para. 4. Available from: <www.archive.official-documents.co.uk/document/cps/custody/sec9.htm> (accessed 30 January 2007).
65 Wedgwood, 'The International Criminal Court', 662: '[Justice] conveys a concept which is tremendously contested – meaning different things to different people'. The OTP, although recognizing the difficulty created by the lack of any definition of the phrase in the statute, does not explain fully its understanding of the term but rather leaves the reader with the impression that it prefers a narrow criminal justice approach. OTP, 'The interests of justice'.
66 T. Campbell, 'Justice', in P. Jones and A. Weale (eds), *Issues in Political Theory*, 2nd edn, Basingstoke: Macmillan, 2001; and Ní Aoláin, 'Political violence', 814.
67 OTP, 'The interests of justice'. See M. Minow, *Between Vengeance and Forgiveness: Facing History after Genocide and Mass Violence*, Boston: Beacon Press, 1998, who contrasts traditional criminal law understandings of justice with a moral approach to justice in her exploration of the role of truth commissions.

68 This phrase itself does not have a precise meaning and some authors consider it analogous to the responsibility of prosecutors to make decisions in the 'public interest'. See, for example, Webb, 'The ICC'; Gallavin, 'Article 53'; Nsereko, 'Prosecutorial discretion'. The phrase is often used in statements suggesting that taking (or failing to take) a particular course of action would undermine public confidence in the administration of justice. Not all the factors falling within either the notions of administration of justice or the public interest can be transposed to the phrase interests of justice in Article 53 as many of them relate to factors that are dealt with either in other paragraphs of Article 53 or in other articles of the Rome Statute such as the severity of the crime, the strength of the evidence available to the OTP and the health of the accused. A traditional factor in determining whether or not to proceed with a criminal prosecution is the effect such a course of action would have on the physical and mental health of the victim. Gallavin, 'Article 53', 190 and OTP, 'The interests of justice', 5–6. Pursuant to Article 21 of the Rome Statute of the International Criminal Court, the ICC has the ability to take account of general principles of law from national legal systems.

69 Office of the Prosecutor, 'Paper on some policy issues before the Office of the Prosecutor', ICC-OTP 2003, September 2003. Available from: <www.amicc.org/docs/OcampoPolicyPaper9_03.pdf> (accessed 11 October 2009).

70 International Association of Prosecutors, 'Draft code of professional conduct for prosecutors for the International Criminal Court', 2002, Article 8 (a copy is in the personal possession of the author), and OTP, 'The interests of justice', 7.

71 International Association of Prosecutors, 'Draft code', Article 1.

72 OTP, 'The interests of justice', 3–4.

73 M. A. Drumbl, 'Collective violence and individual punishment: The criminality of mass atrocity', *Northwester University Law Review*, 2005, vol. 99, 569.

74 Ibid.

75 Campbell, 'Justice'.

76 U. Dolgopol, 'Redressing partial justice: A possible role for civil society', in U. Dolgopol and J. Gardam (eds), *The Challenge of Conflict, International Law Responds*, The Hague: Martinus Nijhoff, 2006.

77 Notes from Hannah Gaertner and Stephen Arthur Lamony on the July 2007 launch of research reports entitled: *The Cooling of the Hearts: Community Truth Telling in Acholi-land* and *Remembering the Atiak Massacre: April 20, 1995*, distributed by the Coalition for the International Criminal Court on 22 August 2007.

78 This particular report focused on the Acholi. Work undertaken by the Women's Initiatives has encompassed the Greater North of Uganda which includes the Acholi, Lango, Teso and West Nile. See reference to *Position Paper: Views of women from North and North Eastern Uganda on the Peace Talks, Mechanisms for Accountability and Reconciliation*, August 2007. Available from:<www.iccwomen.org/news/docs/Views_of_ women_from_ North_and_North_Eastern_Uganda_on_the_Peace_Talks2.pdf> (accessed 11 October 2009).

79 P. V. Sellers, 'The other voices: Interpreters and investigators of sexual violence in international criminal prosecutions', in H. Durham and T. Gurd (eds), *Listening to the Silences: Women and War*, Leiden: Brill, 2005, p. 162.

80 Ibid.

81 U. Dolgopol and S. Paranjape, *Comfort Women: An Unfinished Ordeal*, Geneva: International Commission of Jurists, 1994; and Minow, *Between Vengeance*.

82 OTP, 'The interests of justice', 5–6.

83 Women in conflict situations have made clear pronouncements about the importance of including them in both the peace process and the design of accountability mechanisms. See, for example, Greater North Women's Voices for Peace Network and the description of the Burundi All-Party Women's Conference in Dolgopol, 'Women and peace building'.

84 Access, 'Interview with André Laperrière, the new Executive Director of the Victims' Trust Fund', *Victims' Rights Working Group Bulletin*, summer/autumn 2007, 4.
85 Initial Reports of State Parties – Burundi, CEDAW/C/BDI/1, 3 July 2000; special report of the Secretary-General on the United Nations Operation in Burundi, S/2005/586, 14 September 2005; and fifth report of the Secretary-General on the United Nations Operation in Burundi, S/2005/728, 21 November 2005.
86 Victims' Rights Working Group website. Available at <www.vrwg.org> (accessed 20 October 2009).
87 'Interests of victims', statement on web page of Victims' Rights Working Group. Available from: <www.vrwg.org/Interests_of_Victims.html> (accessed 20 August 2007).
88 V. Nesiah, 'Discussion lines on gender and transitional justice: An introductory essay reflecting on the ICTJ Bellagio Workshop on Gender and Transitional Justice', *Columbia Journal of Gender and Law*, 2006, vol. 15, 808.
89 The final report of the Ninth Circuit Gender Bias Task Force, 'The effects of gender', p. 193.
90 Special report of the Secretary-General on the United Nations Operation in Burundi; and fifth Report of the Secretary-General on the United Nations Operation in Burundi; and Greater North Women's Voices for Peace Network et al.
91 See Report of the Secretary-General on Burundi, S/2004/210, 16 March 2004 and UNIFEM, Burundi. Available from: <www.womenwarpeace.org/burundi/burundi/htm> (accessed 27 May 2005). See also Ní Aoláin, 'Political violence', 848.
92 This point has similarities to the issue of 'pragmatic accountability', discussed in Danner, 'Prosecutorial discretion and legitimacy', 525.
93 The Office of the Prosecutor, 'Report on prosecutorial strategy', 14 September 2006.
94 H. Charlesworth, 'Building democracy and justice after conflict', Academy of the Social Sciences Australia, Cunningham Lecture, Canberra, 21 November 2006.
95 OTP, 'The interests of justice', 7–8; OTP, 'Paper on some policy issues'.
96 'Voices of women from north and north eastern Uganda on the peace talks: Mechanisms and accountability and reconciliation, August, 2007'.
97 Drumbl, 'Collective violence and individual punishment', 549.
98 Sellers, 'The other voices'.
99 Ibid., 162.
100 This issue is connected to the general right of equality of access to justice discussed in Section II B above. Article 6 of the Declaration of Basic Principles of Justice for Victims of Crime and Abuse of Power, General Assembly Resolution 40/34, 29 November 1985 states that that: 'The responsiveness of judicial and administrative processes to the needs of victims should be facilitated by: (a) Informing victims of their role and the scope, timing and progress of the proceedings and of the disposition of their cases, especially where serious crimes are involved and where they have requested such information'. Although at the time of its adoption the Declaration's focus was the domestic legal systems of member states of the United Nations, the focus on the rights of victims in the Rome Statute and the ability of the court to give effect to human rights norms pursuant to Article 21 of the Statute makes the Declaration relevant to the activities of the OTP. See the discussion of this issue in *The Prosecutor v Thomas Lubanga Dyilo*, ICC-01/04–01/06, 18 January 2008. Further, Article 21 would allow the OTP to incorporate practices that are common in many of the legal systems of UN member states (see International Federation for Human Rights, 'Chapter 1: The Evolution of Victims' Access to Justice' in *Victims' Rights Before the International Criminal Court: A Guide for Victims, their Legal Representatives and NGOs*, 2007, vol. 36. Available from: <www.fidh.org/IMG/pdf/4-CH-I_Background.pdf> (accessed 11 October 2009)). Although the Basic Principles and Guidelines on the Right to a Remedy and Reparation for Victims of Gross Violations of International Human Rights Law and Serious Violations of International Humanitarian Law,

A/RES/60/147, 21 March 2006, does not contain similar precise wording, the importance of informing the public as well as victims of their rights and remedies is contained in Article 24, and many of the other articles assume communication between the victim and those responsible for assisting them to access justice.

101 The necessity of establishing community outreach programmes for groups affected by indictments has been acknowledged by the OTP. See Summary of Recommendations received during the first public hearing of the Office of the Prosecutor, convened from 17–18 June 2003 at The Hague, 'Comments and conclusions of the Office of the Prosecutor', ICC-OTP 2003, p. 5.

102 Nesiah, 'Discussion lines on gender and transitional justice'; K. M. Franke, 'Gendered subjects of transitional justice', *Columbia Journal of Gender and Law*, 2006, vol. 15, 821.

9 Exploring the potential of contextual ethics in mediation

Rachael Field

9.1 Introduction

The Australian National Mediator Standards state that 'the purpose of a mediation process is to maximise participants' decision making'.[1] To achieve this, the dominant model of mediation practised in Australia – the facilitative model[2] – ethically requires the mediator to be in an 'outsider-impartial' role,[3] as opposed to an 'insider-partial' role.[4] That is, mediation ethics require mediators to be impartial facilitators of the *process* in order to ensure that the *content and outcome* of the dispute are self-determined by the parties.[5] In managing the process impartially, a mediator is expected to be fair, even-handed, unbiased and free of prejudice.[6] A mediator who is coercive, who favours one party over another or who makes a decision for the parties is not impartial and thereby is said to violate the possibility of party self-determination.[7]

However, as the discussion below will demonstrate, the theoretical ethical imperative of mediator impartiality as the basis for achieving party self-determination has been challenged by practitioners and commentators alike as being practically unattainable, unreal and unworkable. Realistically, mediators in practice are unable to be completely even-handed and at arm's length from the parties. And if they were, then the process would simply support the more powerful party in imposing their interests on the weaker party. In that case, the decision-making of only one of the parties would be maximized.

For mediators, the dissonance that exists between the ethical theory of mediation and the reality of its practice is a significant professional stressor, and could even be said to raise questions about the legitimacy and credibility of the mediation process itself. This work therefore argues that a reformed approach to mediation ethics is necessary – one that supports party self-determination, but that also acknowledges the reality of the relational, interactive and engaged nature of mediation practice. The need for reform has been articulated by esteemed authors in the mediation field such as Mulcahy, Taylor, Astor and Bagshaw,[8] who call for greater recognition in mediation theory of the complex, nuanced and contexualized nature of mediation practice. Contextual ethics, the ethical approach considered here as a contender for a reformed ethical approach in mediation, acknowledges that abstract, universal, generic 'rules' about mediator behaviour and conduct, such as those relating to mediator impartiality, are not able adequately to address the diverse and complex requirements of ethical decision-making in the process. This work suggests that contextual ethics have the potential to guide ethical decision-making in mediation where rule-like standards of mediator impartiality have missed the mark.

The analysis of this chapter places the normative good of relational party self-determination at the centre of a contextual ethical approach, such that only support for, and fulfilment of, relational party self-determination is considered ethically categorical. In other words, ethical decision-making in mediation – what ought to be done in following this ethical method – is suggested here as being contingent only on that which upholds relational party self-determination. Supporting the parties in achieving relational self-determination is argued to be a mediator's primary ethical responsibility and their overriding professional ethical concern.

The chapter begins with a discussion of the ethical dilemma in mediation created by the disconnect between impartiality and party self-determination. Second, relational party self-determination in the context of mediation is discussed. Contextual ethical approaches are then introduced and some possible benefits and disadvantages of contextual ethics in the mediation context are considered. Finally, some preliminary principles for the possible practice of such an ethic are sketched out. The chapter concludes that contextual ethics have the potential to provide a more process-relevant ethical approach to mediation than the one that currently exists.

9.2 The current ethical dilemma in mediation

The current ethical imperative for mediators to be impartial in order to uphold party self-determination is found in mediation theory,[9] as well as in current standards and guidelines for ethical practice.[10] Many such codes make an explicit statement of the primacy of party self-determination. For example, the 2005 US Model Standards of Conduct for Mediators expresses self-determination as the *first* standard as follows:

> A. A mediator shall conduct a mediation based on the principle of party self-determination. Self-determination is the act of coming to a voluntary, uncoerced decision in which each party makes free and informed choices as to process and outcome.[11]

In Australia, the Law Council of Australia's Ethical Guidelines for Mediators, while not replicating such a provision, define the process in a way that highlights party self-determination by referring to an impartial mediator as one who facilitates 'the resolution of a dispute by promoting *uncoerced* agreement by the parties to the dispute', enabling 'the parties to reach their *own* agreement'.[12]

Approaches to the ethic of impartiality are also relatively similar in both the United States and Australia. The 2005 US Model Standards, for example, state the ethic of impartiality as follows:

a   A mediator shall decline a mediation if the mediator cannot conduct it in an impartial manner. Impartiality means freedom from favoritism, bias or prejudice.
b   A mediator shall conduct a mediation in an impartial manner and avoid conduct that gives the appearance of partiality . . .
c   If at any time a mediator is unable to conduct a mediation in an impartial manner, the mediator shall withdraw.[13]

The apparent simplicity of the ethical relationship between mediator impartiality and party self-determination is appealing: a mediator who is free of favouritism, prejudice or bias makes it possible for the parties to reach their own, uncoerced agreement; a mediator who favours one party over another, or who is prejudiced or biased towards a particular party, does not. A mediator is ethically required to uphold party self-determination; a mediator is therefore ethically required to be impartial.

Yet this ethical premise is relatively easily exposed as superficial and unsatisfactory. First, if a mediator were completely even-handed and at arm's length from the parties, the process would simply result in an outcome to the dispute that satisfies the needs and interests of the more powerful party.[14] That is, if a mediator were to act in a strictly impartial fashion, they would allow the power dynamics between the parties to play out, and this would result in an outcome dominated by the party who was, on balance, more powerful. In such a case, only one party would experience self-determination – the more powerful party. In the mutual, relational and consensual environment of mediation, such an outcome is difficult to justify ethically.

Second, the extent of the ethical support for party self-determination provided by mediator impartiality can be questioned from the perspective that realistically any claim to impartiality by mediators is imperfect.[15] As human beings, mediators cannot fulfil an expectation of strict impartiality in practice. They inevitably bring their individual and personal values and beliefs to their facilitation of the process, and are inevitably affected by their own 'set of cognitive and motivational biases'.[16] There is also evidence that mediators influence the content and outcomes of the disputes they mediate through a process identified by Greatbatch and Dingwall as 'selective facilitation'.[17]

Selective facilitation involves a mediator using the mediation process, and particular skills in its practice (albeit perhaps unconsciously), to direct the parties towards their own preferred outcome. Clearly, in such a situation, party self-determination is potentially compromised as such an outcome is, at least to some extent, imposed or coerced. Even where selective facilitation does not occur, the practicalities of dealing effectively with common process issues in mediation, such as difficult parties, impasses, power imbalances and ensuring informed consent to outcomes, often require mediator activism and intervention at a level that can be said to contravene 'impartiality'.[18] Realistically, with some parties and in some situations, a mediator might need to favour one party over another. Such action could well be necessary to assist the parties to reach a mutual, self-determined decision, despite the fact that it may appear (or might in fact even *be*) biased.[19]

In my experience, many mediators – particularly those with significant experience and expertise – are in fact prepared to acknowledge these realities of practice, and the difficulties that arise from the ethical aspiration of impartiality. Their aim is often simply to try to uphold party self-determination by being as even-handed and fair as possible in the circumstances. The aspiration of fulfilling the ethical requirement of impartiality does, however, place mediators in a difficult and stressful professional position. Indeed, as Marshall's recent Australian study has revealed, one of the key stressors mediators face in practice relates to trying to uphold both an ethic of party self-determination and an ethic of mediator impartiality.[20] The enduring nature of this ethical problem is evidenced by the fact that it was first articulated in Bush's US study of ethical dilemmas experienced by mediators in practice in 1994. In that study, the conflict between mediator impartiality and the practical need to support party self-determination 'was more reported than any other' type of dilemma.[21]

Despite these difficulties, party self-determination and mediator impartiality continue to be articulated as the core ethical imperatives of mediation practice – they are, for example, in the new Australian National Standards for Mediators.[22] A level of dissonance therefore exists between the theory of mediation and its ethics, and the reality of mediation practice. This is not only destabilizing for the mediation community,[23] but undoubtedly compromises the legitimacy of current mediation ethics, at least to some extent, and therefore compromises the credibility of the mediation process itself.[24] The remaining sections of this chapter therefore explore the potential of the alternative contextual ethical approach in addressing this dilemma. The next section begins this process by explaining the notion of relational party self-determination in the mediation context in more detail, in order to demonstrate why it is that rule-based ethics are not appropriate in achieving it.

9.3 The fundamental ethical duty of mediators: to uphold relational party self-determination

Jay Folberg, a founder of modern mediation practice in the United States, highlighted the significance of party self-determination as a core value of mediation in 1983 when he described the process as providing the parties with the ultimate authority to 'fashion a unique solution that will work for them without a concern for existing precedent or for the precedent they may set for others'.[25] The subsequent literature on mediation, along with the ethical codes and standards mentioned above, have affirmed that self-determination is a major (even *the* major) principle and goal of the process,[26] and that it is a 'hallmark and central value for mediators'.[27]

At the centre of the notion of party self-determination is the fact that, in mediation, 'a mediator is someone who tries to help parties to a dispute settle their quarrel, without having the power to impose a settlement upon them'.[28] As Taylor has said, in mediation 'no one should be telling others what to do'.[29] It is the mediator's role, in upholding party self-determination, to support the active and direct participation of the parties in communicating and negotiating; to facilitate party choice and control over the substantive norms that guide their decision-making; to involve the parties in the creation of options for settlement; and to support the parties in taking control of whether they will come to an agreement, and the terms of that agreement.[30]

Mediation therefore represents 'a move *away* from third-party decision-making toward a solution which the parties themselves have constructed'.[31] In this way, the process is grounded in a belief that the parties themselves have the best knowledge, and the greatest ability, 'to reach an agreement that maximizes their individual preferences'.[32] For this reason, party self-determination and party empowerment are often used simultaneously;[33] party self-determination cannot occur without party empowerment. In empowering the parties, the mediator encourages them 'to exercise their autonomy and independent choice in deciding whether and how to resolve their dispute'.[34] Empowered parties are enabled 'to determine their own fates',[35] they experience fairness and dignity through the process,[36] and they are given power and control over their dispute – something the formal legal system, for example, can be criticized as failing to do.[37]

Clearly, giving the parties the capacity to exercise their own autonomy is important to party empowerment, and therefore to party self-determination. As Greatbatch and Dingwall acknowledge in relation to the mediation process, 'client control must surely rank among the great unquestioned goods of our time'[38] – not least because it is 'both more efficient and morally superior to determination by some public authority'.[39] Indeed, it is perhaps the connection between party self-determination and the long-standing Kantian, liberal, universalist notions of individual autonomy in ethics that have given rise to the ethical primacy of party self-determination in mediation, and of an impartial mediator as a necessary requirement in achieving it.[40]

And yet, while respectful of party autonomy, party self-determination in mediation is not individualist. Party self-determination in mediation is special – even unique – because it is *relational* in nature. It is relational because it is rooted in party connection, cooperation, collaboration and consensus. In mediation, there is no emphasis on the rights and entitlements of the private self, as might be found in the competitive, adversarial process of litigation. Rather, a mediator makes relational party self-determination possible in the mediation context because they help the parties to develop a relationship of mutual 'understanding that will enable them to meet shared contingencies'.[41]

Relational party self-determination is achieved, then, where both parties are supported in reaching an integrated solution to their dispute, and where the outcome can be said to respond to *each* party's concerns, needs and interests – not just those of one party.[42] Relational party self-determination cannot exist on an individual level; it exists at a level that enables the mediation process to be just to all the parties. If only one party achieves self-determination, the mediation process has failed. For example, in Bush's work on taxonomies of standards of quality in dispute resolution, the standards relating to 'individual satisfaction' and 'individual autonomy' are consistently expressed as relating to both parties in the process, not to one party alone.[43]

Realistically, in order for a mediator to be able to promote the mutual understanding between the parties that is necessary for relational party self-determination, and in order for mediators to support the parties in being creative about generating a range of options that can respond to their shared contingencies, they must engage deeply with the parties – with their personalities, their issues and their dispute. This means that if relational party self-determination is to be achieved, the mediator must be free to make active, responsive and engaged decisions about balancing the power dynamics between the parties. It might be necessary, then, to work in ways that more strongly support a vulnerable party, or in ways that keep in check the controlling directiveness of another.

It is important to recognize that mediator impartiality is an imperfect ethic for upholding the relational form of self-determination that is found in the mediation environment. This does not have to mean that mediation theory at large is wholly compromised, or that the value of the process itself and the history of its practice is undermined. It simply means that a more appropriate ethical framework must be found. It also means that a more appropriate definition of mediation must be adopted – one that that does not make mediator impartiality a central requirement. Fortunately, Boulle has already developed such a definition:

> Mediation is a decision making process; in which the parties are assisted by an outside intervenor, the mediator; who attempts to assist the parties in their process of decision-making; and reach an outcome to which each of them can assent; without the mediator having a binding decision-making capability.[44]

Further, it must be acknowledged that engaging with the parties to assist them, and working collaboratively with them to achieve a consensual outcome, does not mean that a mediator is thereby inevitably directive, controlling or coercive. Nor does it mean that the mediator cannot be even-handed, fair and professionally ethical in the way they practise that engagement. The pursuit of relational party self-determination through ethical active intervention and use of mediator power *is* possible if it is guided by an adequate ethical framework.

To summarize: relational party self-determination can be said to be the characteristic of mediation that makes the process unique and special. It is a mediator's capacity to support relational party self-determination that separates them 'from all other dispute resolution practitioners'.[45] Upholding relational party self-determination is something 'mediation *can* do that other processes cannot'.[46] However, the ethic of mediator impartiality – a rule-like, imperative ethic – does not 'fit' with what is required of mediators in practice to uphold relational party self-determination. What *is* required is alternative ethical guidance as to how mediators can be ethically active, as well as engaged with and responsive to the parties in ensuring that relational party self-determination is made possible.

The next section of this chapter begins the exploration of ethical reform for mediation practice through a contextual ethical framework.

9.4 Contextual ethics

Contextual ethics are ethical approaches – sometimes referred to as contextualism, occasionalism, circumstantialism and actualism[47] – that are not rule based, but that require the ethical agent to engage with, assess and take account of the context of the situation in which a decision must be made in order to come to an ethically justifiable position. Contextual ethics are not concerned with specifically articulating what is good or what is right. Instead, contextual ethics are about determining what is ethically appropriate and justifiable for the context of a given situation.[48]

As contextual ethical approaches do not prescribe a particular path to resolving a particular dilemma, they require complex discretionary judgments to be made that take account of the particular circumstances of individual cases and respond to them reflectively and relationally.[49] Preston notes that contextual approaches do not provide neat formulae for resolving ethical dilemmas; they do not point to only one right answer to an ethical problem.[50] In this way, contextual ethics stand against universalist, individualist rules-based ethical methods, such as those posited in the work of, for example, Kant and Rawls.[51] Instead, they 'offer a method for arriving at an ethical decision for which sound moral reasons can be given, and which can be defended as a fitting ethical response'.[52]

For example, there can be no simple rule in a contextual ethic that lying is always wrong. Coming to an ethically justifiable decision about whether a lie can be morally justified, according to a contextual ethical method, requires a full assessment of the demands of the particular situation. Such assessments are inevitably difficult. However, as Fletcher has written, it is because of their nuanced and complex nature that such ethics are 'the only ethics for a mature human race'.[53]

A number of contextual ethical approaches have been articulated. For example, Charles Morris wrote in the *International Journal of Ethics* in 1927 of a 'total-situation theory of ethics'.[54] In the 1960s, H. Richard Niebuhr developed an ethic of response and responsibility in his work *The Responsible Self*,[55] echoed in the writing of Seyla Benhabib;[56] this requires choosing 'the fitting action'.[57] Joseph Fletcher has written of situation ethics[58] and Carol Gilligan identified an ethic of care in her work in the early 1980s.[59] These approaches all inform the contextual ethical framework explored here for mediation.

Before that exploration begins, it is useful to consider other professional environments in which such approaches have been analysed or proposed. One such professional environment is family therapy.[60] In the family therapy context, a relational ethical approach allows 'the dynamics of the family as a whole to trump the individuality of its members', and relationship factors such as 'care, love, friendship and mutuality' are the focus.[61] Although much of the literature on family therapy ethics in fact highlights the Kantian notion of 'respect for the dignity, rights and needs of individual family members',[62] Wall et al.'s study of the ethical values and preferences of family therapists overwhelmingly rejected an ethic of individualism. The results of that study indicated a strong preference across both genders of therapists for an ethic of relationality.[63] In such an ethic, it is the quality of relationships within families that is prioritized, with equality and fairness being served through a focus on loving and caring approaches that prevent family relationships from degenerating into manipulative or unfair interactions.[64] There are clearly strong synergies here with a possible contextual ethic in mediation that works to support relational party self-determination.

Contextual ethics have also been explored for application in the legal profession by Professor William Simon. Simon argues that legal professionalism is better satisfied by lawyers engaging in an ethical approach that is based on contextual judgment making in which abstract norms are applied 'to a broad range of the particulars of the case at hand'.[65] For Simon, 'lawyers should take those actions that, considering the relevant circumstances of the particular case, seem likely to promote justice'.[66] The goal of Simon's work is to 'show how the dominance of an ethical regime that repudiates contextual judgment is both an anomaly and an obstacle to the deepest ambitions that animate legal professionalism'.[67] His position is that a contextual approach to legal ethics provides modern legal professionals with a stronger sense of 'meaningful work' that is 'both a form of self-assertion and a point of connection and solidarity with the larger society'[68] that in turn is important to professional self-conception.[69]

Another contextual ethic, the ethic of care, has also been suggested as an appropriate ethic for the legal profession in terms of allowing lawyers to engage in relational lawyering.[70] The articulation of an ethic of care is attributed to the work of Carol Gilligan.[71] Gilligan's empirical work with women and men on moral imperatives found that women repeatedly evidenced 'an injunction to care',[72] whereas for men 'the moral imperative appeared rather as an injunction to respect the rights of others and thus to protect from interference the right to life and self-fulfillment'.[73] Susan Mendus comments that, since Gilligan's work: 'Moral theories couched in terms of rights, justice and abstract rationality have given way to moral theories which emphasize care, compassion and contextualization'.[74]

The next section suggests that a contextual ethical approach to decision-making in mediation practice could address the ethical dissonance created by the current inconsistencies between the theory of mediator impartiality and the primacy of the principle of party self-determination. A contextual ethical approach is proposed as possibly better supporting mediators in taking those actions that, considering the relevant circumstances of the particular case, are most likely to uphold relational party self-determination – even where this might, for example, involve practising in a way that is not completely 'even-handed', or that involves a level of partial treatment of a party.

9.5 A contextual ethic for upholding relational party self-determination in mediation

The conceptualization of contextual ethics for mediation explored here is informed by the range of approaches identified above, integrating aspects of contextualism, situation ethics, an ethic of responsibility and an ethic of care. The analysis of this chapter places the normative good of relational party self-determination at the centre of this ethical approach, such that only support for and fulfilment of party self-determination are considered ethically categorical.[75] It should be noted from the outset, however, that the method is not seen as extending to ethical considerations involving matters, such as confidentiality, that are otherwise dealt with by law.

9.5.1 The possible benefits of a contextual ethical method in mediation

One of the possible key benefits of a contextual ethical method for mediation is that it is not based on rules. We have seen how the 'rule' that a mediator must be impartial fails in the mediation context. Rules-based or codified approaches to ethics in mediation, particularly around the issue of upholding relational party self-determination, are inappropriate because they do not respond adequately to the special and unique character of the mediation process itself – its contextual and relational quality, and the intuitive, responsive, reactive and integrated nature of its practice.

Fletcher comments that moving away from laws, rules and specific 'blueprint' systems towards accepting responsibility for the challenge, rigour and 'adventure' of making complex decisions in the moment can be professionally threatening.[76] Yet the mediation community may well have to accept such a challenge if their professionalism is to be reflected in a system of ethics for mediation practice that is real and relevant, as opposed to the current falsely aspirational system.

Two critical arguments support a non-rules-based approach to ethical decision-making in mediation that aims to uphold relational party self-determination. First, a contextual, discretionary approach frees mediators to respond to the individual imperatives, requirements and characteristics of each particular mediation, and the relational needs and interests of the parties. The freedom to take an 'open-ended approach to situations' is, for Fletcher, that which makes *real* ethical decision-making possible.[77] Mediators work in a complex environment. A closed ethic of impartiality does not adequately assist them to manage the ambiguities and fluidities of everyday practice as they make real decisions about how to enable the parties to reach a mutual decision. Rather, professional decision-making in mediation is better supported by an open contextual ethic that provides the freedom necessary to respond to the exigencies of practice, as well as providing a level of guidance about how to appropriately exercise that freedom.

Second, a contextual ethical method in mediation would avoid the inevitable problems that arise with the application of rules in ambiguous, difficult or complex scenarios. As Fletcher comments, it can be 'difficult and hazardous to stick to rules' because 'rules can be hard to understand or apply in a given situation'; they can be problematic to follow.[78] Further, rules often contradict each other, making choices as to their prioritization an additional burden in complex practice. Such a contradiction is evident in the struggle in which mediators engage to uphold relational party self-determination *and* remain impartial. A contextual ethical method focused on upholding party self-determination would ameliorate such dilemmas, while also providing mediators with a way of coping adequately with the real requirements of the mediation room.

A third benefit of contextual ethics is that such ethics are able to accommodate the fact that human behaviour necessarily changes and varies depending on the situation. A contextual ethical method would not require mediators to be 'super-human' in terms of always being completely consistent, stable and evaluatively integrated in their decision-making. Rather, such a method would recognize that ethical decision-making is sensitive to, and contingent upon, variation in circumstance,[79] and that it requires mediators to adjust their behaviour in response to the individual, relational issues and imperatives that emerge in each mediation. It is positive, then, that contextual ethics are able to accommodate an infinite variety of mediator styles, characteristics and behaviours.

9.5.2 *Some concerns regarding a contextual ethical method for mediation*

There is no doubt that along with the benefits of a contextual method in mediation come criticisms and concerns. The foremost concern is that, without clear, rule-like ethical guidelines, contextual ethics 'can descend into moral relativism'.[80] Further, the idea of a professional ethics regime that relies on contextual judgment may well be considered 'almost inconceivably utopian'.[81] In addition, the complexity of the decision-making that a contextual ethical approach would require means that its implementation necessitates not only a significant investment in professional training, but also far more time, effort and practical competence than would be the case for a formulaic ethical method.[82] Finally, contextual approaches can be criticized on the basis that the judgments such methods promote can themselves be controversial,[83] particularly when determined against judgments reached via rule-based approaches.

These are legitimate concerns, and a full explication of a contextual ethic for mediation would need to address them thoroughly. The exploratory scope of this chapter, however, limits consideration of these concerns to the most significant criticism – namely that contextual ethics are 'anything goes' ethics, too easily 'manipulated into relativism or subjectivism',[84] lacking probity, integrity and principle.[85] The following paragraphs outline some possible responses to this criticism in the context of the mediation environment.

First, a shift to practising a contextual ethical approach for decision-making focused on upholding party self-determination would not require mediators altogether to abandon the established ethical culture of mediation practice. It is possible that any new contextual approach to mediation could be informed by the content of existing ethical guidelines, or by aspects of current standards documents. Contextual ethics in mediation could therefore be argued to be principled in terms of accepting and working with the values and principles that have been developed to date for ethical mediation practice.[86]

For example, the ethic of impartiality would not necessarily be abandoned entirely, but could be accepted in a contextual approach, along with others, as a guiding maxim that informs practice. The impartiality maxim might state that where possible a mediator should act, and make decisions about the implementation of the process, even-handedly and without favour, bias or prejudice. Such a maxim, however, would not be treated as a rule, and would have no categorical claim upon mediators in such a method. The extent to which it could inform decisions would depend 'extrinsically upon variable circumstances'.[87] Envisage, for example, a situation where in order to uphold relational self-determination, it is necessary for a mediator to give one party more speaking time, or to treat them differently during a private caucus, or to work longer or harder at helping them to adequately express their needs and interests. On the face of it, a decision to work with a party in these ways is not even-handed, but it could be ethically justifiable in terms of practically supporting relational party self-determination. Therefore, current maxims could work in a new contextual system as 'advisers without veto power',[88] being considered relevant and informative but 'only relatively obliging and valid'.[89]

Second, contextual ethics in mediation could be argued to be *not unprincipled* because they remain true to one primary norm, the fundamental good of mediation: relational party self-determination. As the core normative principle guiding and justifying the ethical nature of mediators' decisions and choices in the process, relational party self-determination would act as the key to a mediator's evaluation of a dispute, its parties and its issues. A requirement that mediators consistently professionally evaluate the developing requirements of the parties during the process, and then respond to those needs with appropriate choices and decisions, would evidence that mediators are working in a principled way. Relational party self-determination is therefore the ordering principle that ensures that mediation, under a contextual ethical approach, cannot be said to be 'absolutely relative',[90] or 'inchoate, random, unpredictable, unjudgeable, meaningless, or amoral'.[91] Rather, a contextual ethic in mediation can be thought of as 'principled relativism'.[92]

This is an important point. As Simon has said, 'a contextual ethic doesn't necessarily require less specification than a categorical one, just a different kind of specification'.[93] Therefore, if a contextual ethic for mediation were to be adopted, rebuttable presumptions and exemplary cases would be required to support its operation. And professionals using this method would be encouraged (or required) to, in Simon's words, 'develop a set of practices that tend, in the settings in which they work, to contribute to just resolutions'.[94]

Third, contextual ethics can be said to be far from an 'anything goes' approach because, as a higher order ethics than one based on abstract, aspirational, generic rules, the practice of such ethics requires a higher level of professional competence and artistry.[95] Rules-ethics could be said to be 'easy ethics'[96] because 'rules leave little room for decision-making'.[97] Rules-based ethical systems provide decision-makers with prefabricated reasons for their decisions, but not always an ethically justifiable outcome. For example, a mediator in the current ethical system for mediation could say: 'I can't work to help this particularly needy party to achieve relational self-determination because if I did I would not be acting impartially.' The ethical rule of impartiality makes it an easy decision, and provides a very tidy route to morally excusing a mediator in such a situation for failing to work to uphold relational party self-determination for that party. Yet it is precisely because such a decision fails in such a way that it could be considered ethically unjustifiable.

It is pertinent at this point to consider that the creativity required of ethical mediators in a contextual ethical system, to ensure that they are satisfying its requirements, is significant. The imperative for professional creativity is positive because it opens up opportunities to increase the depth of mediation practice through the development of more effective, innovative and useful approaches to the challenging and difficult aspects of practice.

Fourth, and relatedly, a contextual ethical method would not only require mediators to make principled and professional evaluations to inform the making of intelligent, creative choices around difficult practice issues; it could also be regulated in order to require them to be ethically accountable for the exercise of their discretion in making those choices.[98] This is not necessarily something that has been required of mediators to date. Mediators have largely been able, in the unregulated, private and confidential environment of mediation practice, to avoid the professional scrutiny that should rightly accompany their moral agency, authority and power in the process. The potential in a new system of contextual ethics for mediators to take greater responsibility for their ethical decision-making is important. As Simon asserts, 'an ethical program that resists institutionalisation is handicapped'[99] because 'the credibility of ethical commitments depends substantially (though not exclusively) on the availability of effective sanction for breach'.[100] A professional regulatory system for mediators would work to ensure that ethical relativism is harnessed for the benefit of the parties and for the integrity of the process.

It is beyond the exploratory scope of this chapter to articulate the detail of how such a regulatory system might be structured or operate. A full explication of a contextual ethical approach for mediation would, however, need to consider this issue further. There is a significant body of work, including that of Simon, that could inform the development of such a regime. Further, current work being conducted in Australia by the National Alternative Dispute Resolution Advisory Council on the issue of mediation ethics and a regulatory system for the recently introduced accreditation system for mediation could also inform the articulation of how a contextual ethic might be regulated.[101]

9.6 Possible ethical guidelines for a contextual ethic in mediation centred on upholding party self-determination

If contextual ethics were adopted for mediation, how would they work? Although there is the necessary freedom in a contextual ethic to respond creatively to the exigencies of practice, there is still a need for a level of guidance about how mediators can and should make appropriate decisions in working to uphold relational party self-determination. This section turns, therefore, to sketching out six possible guiding principles that would underscore the implementation of a contextual ethic for mediation.

The following principles are suggested as a preliminary way of thinking about the fundamental truths of the ethical approach, to exemplify the sort of base from which mediators would start their ethical reasoning. Foundation principles are necessary because, if a contextual ethic in mediation is to be successful, it needs to assist mediators in making decisions and choices in pursuing relational party self-determination that *work*.[102] That is, it must lead mediators to adequate and concrete courses of action.[103] The foundation principles suggested here therefore aim to help mediators to be pragmatic and results oriented in their ethical method.[104]

Manning describes an ethical method as 'the process which a chooser, according to a certain ethical system, has to carry out in order to come to a decision regarding what they ought to do in a certain choice-situation'.[105] The focus of the method provided by a contextual approach to decision-making in mediation, given that the mediation room is an environment where instinct, context and relativities are significant, is to cope with the multiple variables of discretionary and intuitive practice, in order to *make decisions*.

9.6.1 Principle 1: relational self-determination is the intrinsic good of mediation and its ruling norm

The first suggested guiding principle is that in mediation relational party self-determination is accepted as *the* intrinsic good of mediation and its ruling norm. Facilitating relational party self-determination under such an ethic would therefore be the central *justification for the role* of the mediator, and the *core service* that mediators offer the parties. This makes upholding relational party self-determination a mediator's key ethical obligation, above and before all others. Mediators would therefore be 'good faith stewards' of relational self-determination.

Mediators would know that they are exercising their role ethically, and that their actions and decisions in practice are ethically justified, if they lead to relational party self-determination. In other words, conduct that contributes to relational party self-determination would be ethically justifiable, conduct detracting from that possibility would not. No mediator conduct or intervention in a contextual ethic could be said to be inherently or intrinsically valuable or good or bad. The ethical value of any mediator conduct in the process would be judged by whether it upholds relational party self-determination, by whether it is fitting, because 'anything and everything' can be 'right or wrong depending on the situation'.[106]

As the univalent norm of a contextual ethic for mediation, upholding relational party self-determination becomes the axiomatic, categorical, logical driver of all ethical decisions and choices in the mediation process. While other maxims – for example, impartiality – may be influential or important to the process at various times, such maxims would be informative rather than normative. Where conflict arises between pursuing relational party self-determination and the practice of those principles, the pursuit of party self-determination takes precedence and priority.

For example, mediators report that in practice they often face a situation where the parties have reached a block in their capacity to generate options and are starting to tire. In such situations, it is tempting for the mediator to step in, *do* the process of option generation *for* the parties and offer proposals for agreement. The potential in such activity to breach the current ethic of impartiality is significant. Practising a contextual ethic that upholds relational party self-determination as the ruling norm, however, places mediators in a position to analyse the context and the circumstances of the parties and the dispute, and gives them permission to act in those ways that best support the achievement of relational party self-determination. If putting suggestions to the parties would break an impasse by opening a pathway for further discussion, thus enabling the parties to engage in their own option generation, then the mediator would know that their decision to act in this way is ethically justifiable. If, however, the context suggests that one party will use the authority behind the mediator's suggestion to press the other party into a particular outcome, then other interventions or strategies (such as taking a break, persisting with questioning, summarizing and reframing, or moving on to an alternative agenda item for a time) would be the ethically appropriate approach.

Making ethical decisions in mediation that have relational party self-determination as their normative predicate requires mediators to draw on a high level of process knowledge and competence, as well as a high level of analytical capability. Such an ethic therefore respects the professional capacity of mediators, and the 'depth, competence and responsibility of free decision' that they carry.[107] It also requires, however, that a significant emphasis is placed on quality training for mediators, and on ongoing professional development, in order to support the operation of the ethic.[108]

Importantly, in a contextual ethical approach, decisions that uphold relational party self-determination are not excused or explained, but rather are *positively justified* as ethically right. Fletcher refers to the principle of justification as 'the basis of situation ethics'.[109] In mediation, pursuing the intrinsic good and univalent norm of relational self-determination, justifies decisions as right and ethical for a *given situation*.[110] To return to the example of a mediator struggling with whether to option generate or make settlement suggestions for parties who have reached an impasse in their negotiations, if making those suggestions supports party self-determination, then the decision to proceed is ethically justified as the right thing to do. The fact that the making of the suggestions in the given circumstances is the path to fulfilling the normative good of the process makes it so.

9.6.2 Principle 2: ethical decision-making to uphold relational party self-determination is relative and relational

Fletcher sees relativism as a critical working principle of a contextual ethic[111] because it takes the ethical agent 'away from code ethics, away from stern iron-bound dos and don'ts, away from prescribed conduct and legalistic moral-ity'.[112] Relativism recognizes and values 'either–ors' rather than polarities.[113] A second principle for the operation of a contextual ethic in mediation therefore *requires* mediators to move beyond ideals of strict impartiality in their moral reasoning and embrace otherness and difference.[114] *How* party self-determination is supported in any given mediation will depend on the mediator's own respon-sible estimate and evaluation of the situation,[115] and their relationship with the parties. That estimate, as a *relative* one, will rightly be 'contingent'.[116]

A contextual ethic is also *relational* because it puts people at the centre of the ethical obligation. The value of the mediation process could be said, for example, to be real only in terms of the parties who engage in it.[117] For this reason, an ethic of care can contribute to the operation of a contextual ethic in mediation that upholds relational party self-determination. A number of writers have observed the synergies between an ethic of care and the relational requirements of ethical practice in mediation.[118] When considering the imperative to uphold relational party self-determination, such synergies include the ethic's emphasis on recogniz-ing difference and the reality of inequities in relationships and in human life;[119] the importance the ethic places on 'small-scale, face-to-face relationships';[120] and the recognition of the integrated nature of moral problems with their social contingencies.[121] An ethic-of-care approach supports mediators in seeing the parties 'thickly, as constituted by their particular human face, their particular psychological and social self',[122] and it releases mediators from the abstract requirements of impartiality, allowing them to acknowledge in the process the valid, but complex nature of their moral interdependency and interrelatedness with the parties.[123]

9.6.3 Principle 3: ethically upholding relational party self-determination leads to just outcomes

Centring relational party self-determination as the intrinsic good, and core norm, of a contextual ethical approach in mediation also requires a foundational prin-ciple that confirms for mediators and parties alike that upholding party self-determination serves justice. Justice here refers to substantive justice in the parties' terms – resulting from informed consent, recognition of each party's needs and interests, and mutual option generation.

This principle is required because, although on one level it is difficult to contra-dict the inherent good of party self-determination that results from its association with party autonomy, party control and party empowerment, there is nevertheless a substantial body of literature on the potential dangers and pitfalls of informal dispute resolution and private settlement. Much of this literature argues against agreements reached outside of the public, formal, legal environment of the court on the basis that such agreements are flawed, even though they might reflect party autonomy, because they fail to comply adequately with nominal (namely legal) notions of justice.[124]

In mediation, pursuit of relational party self-determination as justice distributed acknowledges the possibility of justice without law: a notion that, according to Auerbach, many find 'preposterous, if not terrifying'.[125] For Benjamin, however, 'the myth of justice is dysfunctional in mediation practice', needing to be replaced by concepts of situational or relational fairness that are reached in the context of an awareness of external standards of fairness.[126] Therefore, this principle maintains that notions of individual or self-determined justice – that is, justice in the eyes of the individual parties – *are* compatible with a principled notion of just and fair outcomes, even if those outcomes do not mirror what is legally normative.[127]

The first argument in support of this position is that relational party self-determination leads to just outcomes because it reflects important values that are 'consistent with the fundamental values of our legal and political systems'.[128] These values include 'consent, participation, empowerment, dignity, respect, empathy and emotional catharsis, privacy, efficiency, quality solutions, equity, and access'.[129] In mediation, parties reach a just and fair agreement because they are deeply and thoroughly involved in working through the issues, in discussing their individual and mutual perspectives, and in developing the terms of the final resolution.[130]

Second, relationally self-determination outcomes in mediation are just because they are a democratic and real form of justice, not a form of 'unprincipled compromise'.[131] This is because 'parties who identify their complementary, not necessarily competitive, needs and interests, can achieve more of what they want by trading for what they value more but what the other party values less'.[132] As Menkel-Meadow argues, negotiated compromises should therefore not be conceived of as 'lawless, rightless "giveaways"'.[133]

Third, it could be said that relational self-determinant outcomes 'often provide greater, not lesser, possibilities for just results'.[134] This is because formal legal justice may not acknowledge, for example, that 'the feelings of the parties are an important consideration in evaluating fairness',[135] and that the opportunity to have their voice heard and their story told in mediation is a vital contributing factor when it comes to reaching a just outcome. The assumption that only formally adjudicated results are just ignores the value to disputants of non-legal principles, such as 'social, psychological, economic, political, moral or religious principles'.[136] Issues that the law, or dispute resolution processes other than mediation, may deem irrelevant to the determination of a dispute – such as emotional catharsis or empathy, efficiency or privacy – may well be the critical aspect of a dispute that mediation deals well with, thus resulting in a just outcome.[137]

Further, pursuit of relational party self-determination in mediation creates opportunities for the parties to generate a range of (what the parties consider to be) just remedial options – options for the resolution of a dispute that litigation and other processes may well be unable to offer. Menkel-Meadow has coined the phrase 'remedial imagination'[138] to refer to 'the opportunity to craft solutions that do not compromise, but offer greater expression of the variety of remedial possibilities in a post-modern world'.[139] The vastly increased range of remedial options created through pursuit of relational party self-determination can be, and often is, informed by the law (and therefore may be principled in that respect also); however, that range is positively informed by the law, not negatively limited by it.[140]

9.6.4 Principle 4: mediators must be professionally accountable for upholding relational party self-determination

Mediators' accountability for their moral agency in decision-making in mediation is critical to the efficacy of the relational and contextual nature of the process itself, and of the ethical decisions mediators make.[141] The final principle for the operation of a contextual ethic in mediation is therefore that mediators must be *responsible* for their ethical choices.

Niebuhr has identified four elements to guide the application of responsibility for moral agents: response, interpretation, accountability and social solidarity.[142] Preston offers an articulation of how this method of responsibility might work for an ethicist working in contextually responsive ways. First, it requires evaluating and responding to the facts of the situation, the people, the alternative actions available, the possible consequences of those actions and also the consequences of those consequences.[143] Second, it requires interpretation of these matters, both within a framework of social solidarity that acknowledges and respects the interconnectedness of life[144] and also within the framework of the values and principles of the moral agent (which in mediation would relate to the normative primacy of upholding relational party self-determination). Finally, it requires a fitting decision to be made 'for which the responsible self remains accountable'.[145] Responsiveness to others, then, creates a 'metaphysical platform' on which responsibility for one's professional actions can rest.[146]

A mediator's responsibility for their ethical decision-making under a contextual ethic would be both privately personal (in terms of being supported through collegial supervision and a mediator's own commitment to the ongoing development of their professional artistry) and professionally public (in that, as suggested above, some form of regulatory system would be necessary to support the operation of a contextual ethical approach). Asking mediators to take greater responsibility for the ethical nature of their decisions in mediation heightens the importance of the professional evaluation task that precedes the making of those choices and decisions. It potentially exposes the depth and thoroughness of the ethical assessment of the myriad of variables at issue: 'the people involved, their relationships, the objective circumstances, past as well as future factors, and remote as well as immediate consequences'.[147]

Certainly, the complexities of the mediation room, and the high number of variables to be considered, mean that there is potential for mediators who are not trained well, or who are not consistently developing their professional artistry, to err in the evaluations they make. However, in requiring mediators to take greater professional responsibility for the ethics of their practice, there must also be some recognition that 'risk of error and risk of harm must be taken as given inescapable features of our finite human condition'.[148] This principle would not place an expectation on mediators of perfect practice. Rather, it would call on mediators to engage with the evaluation of each ethical situation comprehensively and responsively,[149] with the expectation that they will work diligently as they seek to uphold relational party self-determination, and make decisions that are ethically justifiable.

9.7 Conclusion

The legitimacy and credibility of the mediation process has been brought into question as a result of the ethical dissonance that exists between mediator impartiality and relational party self-determination. Professional ethical mediation practice requires mediators to make difficult decisions about appropriate uses of their power in order to uphold relational party self-determination, in what is a highly individual, contextualized environment, and also one that is private and confidential. A contextual ethical method in mediation, with the pursuit of relational party self-determination as its foundational tenet and norm, would free mediators to use their professional judgement, and their moral agency, to make ethical decisions to ensure that the promise of relational party self-determination is made possible and real. A contextual ethical approach would not involve a system of 'anything goes' decision-making, but rather would offer a new, higher order, principled, accountable ethical method that enables the parties to reach just outcomes.

Notes

1 *Australian National Mediator Standards: Practice Standards for Mediators Operating Under the National Mediator Accreditation System* (2007), p. 5.
2 L. Boulle, *Mediation: Principles, Process Practice*, 2nd edn, Sydney: LexisNexis Butterworths, 2005. See also L. Fuller, 'Mediation – Its forms and functions', *South California Law Review*, 1971, vol. 44, 305; K. K. Kovach and L. Love, ' "Evaluative" mediation is an oxymoron', *Alternatives to High Cost Litigation*, 1996, vol. 14, 31; L. Love, 'The top ten reasons why mediators should not evaluate', *Florida State University Law Review*, 1997, vol. 24, 937.
3 D. Dyck, 'The mediator as nonviolent advocate: Revisiting the question of mediator impartiality', *Mediation Quarterly*, 2000, vol. 18(2), 130.
4 Ibid., 131.
5 The words 'impartiality' and 'neutrality' are sometimes used interchangeably in the mediation context, but are also distinguished. For example, the National Alternative Dispute Resolution Council, in its work *A Framework for ADR Standards*, explains that neutrality refers to questions of interest while impartiality refers to behaviour. NADRAC comments that neutrality suggests 'particular responsibilities on the part of an ADR practitioner. These responsibilities are to identify and disclose any existing or prior relationship between the practitioner and the parties, any interest in the outcome of the dispute, any present or future conflicts of interest and any values, experience or knowledge that may prevent a practitioner from acting impartially'. Impartiality, then, is said to be demonstrated by, amongst other things, 'an even-handed conduct of the process' and 'avoiding any appearance of partiality or bias through word or conduct': National Alternative Dispute Resolution Advisory Council, *Report to the Commonwealth Attorney-General: A Framework for ADR Standards*, April 2001, pp. 114, 108. Available from: <www.nadrac.gov.au/www/nadrac/nadrac.nsf/Page/Publications_PublicationsbyDate_FrameworkforADRStandards> (accessed 16

October 2009). The literature on neutrality in mediation is extensive. A sample includes: L. L. Riskin, 'Understanding mediators' orientations, strategies, and techniques: A grid for the perplexed', *Harvard Negotiation Law Review*, 1996, vol. 1, 7; S. E. Bernard et al., 'The neutral mediator: value dilemmas in divorce mediation', *Mediation Quarterly*, 1984, vol. 4, 61; S. Cobb and J. Rifkin, 'Neutrality as a discursive practice: The construction and transformation of narratives in community mediation', *Studies in Law, Politics and Society*, 1991, vol. 11, 69; S. Cobb and J. Rifkin, 'Practice and paradox: deconstructing neutrality in mediation', *Law and Social Inquiry*, 1991, vol. 16, 35; J. Forester and D. Stitzel, 'Beyond neutrality: The possibilities of activist mediation in public sector conflicts', *Negotiation Journal*, 1989, vol. 5, 251; C. Honeyman, 'Patterns of bias in mediation', *Journal of Dispute Resolution*, 1985, 141; J. Rifkin, J. Millen and S. Cobb, 'Toward a new discourse for mediation: A critique of neutrality', *Mediation Quarterly*, 1991, vol. 9(2), 151; L. Mulcahy, 'The possibilities and desirability of mediator neutrality – Towards an ethic of partiality?', *Social and Legal Studies*, 2001, vol. 10, 505. The Australian literature includes, H. Astor, 'Rethinking neutrality: A theory to inform practice – Part I', *Australian Dispute Resolution Journal*, 2000, vol. 11, 73; H. Astor, 'Rethinking neutrality: A theory to inform practice – Part II', *Australasian Dispute Resolution Journal*, 2000, vol. 11, 145; H. Astor, 'Mediator neutrality: Making sense of theory and practice', *Social and Legal Studies*, 2007, vol. 16, 221; R. Field, 'Mediation and the art of power (im)balancing', *QUT Law and Justice Journal*, 1996, vol. 12, 264; R. Field, 'Impartiality and power: myths and reality', *ADR Bulletin*, 2000, vol. 3(1), 16; R. Field, 'The theory and practice of impartiality in mediation', *Arbitrator and Mediator*, 2003, vol. 22(1), 79; K. Douglas and R. Field, 'Looking for answers to mediation's neutrality dilemma in therapeutic jurisprudence', *Murdoch E-Law Journal*, 2006, vol. 13(2), 177; D. Cooper and R. Field, 'The family dispute resolution of parenting matters in Australia: An analysis of the notion of an "independent" practitioner', *QUT Law and Justice Journal*, 2008, vol. 8(1), 158; S. Douglas, 'Neutrality in mediation: A study of mediator perceptions', *QUT Law and Justice Journal*, 2008, vol. 8(1), 139.

6 See, for example, M. Stone, *Representing Clients in Mediation – A New Professional Skill*, London: Butterworths, 1998; J. Folger, *The Promise of Mediation – Responding to Conflict Through Empowerment and Recognition*, San Francisco: Jossey-Bass, 1994.

7 See, for example, American Bar Association, American Arbitration Association, Association for Conflict Resolution, *Model Standards of Conduct for Mediators*, August 2005, available from: <www.mediate.com/pdf/ModelStandardsofConductfor Media torsfinal05.pdf> (accessed 16 October 2009).

8 A. Taylor, 'Concepts of neutrality in family mediation: Contexts, ethics, influence and transformative process', *Mediation Quarterly*, 1997, vol. 14, 215; Mulcahy, 'The possibilities and desirability of mediator neutrality'; H. Astor, 'Some contemporary theories of power in mediation: A primer for the puzzled practitioner', *Australasian Dispute Resolution Journal*, 2005, vol. 16; D. Bagshaw, 'Challenges facing today's practitioners', *Balance*, August 1997, 14.

9 See, for example, J. Folberg and A. Taylor, *Mediation: A Comprehensive Guide to Resolving Conflict Without Litigation*, San Francisco: Jossey-Bass, 1984; C. W. Moore, *The Mediation Process: Practical Strategies for Resolving Conflict*, 2nd edn, San Francisco: Jossey-Bass, 2003; H. Astor and C. Chinkin, *Dispute Resolution in Australia*, 2nd edn, Sydney: Butterworths, 2002; T. Sourdin, *Alternative Dispute Resolution*, 3rd edn, Sydney: Law Book Company, 2008.

10 *Model Standards of Conduct for Mediators*; Law Council of Australia, *Ethical Guidelines for Mediators*, February 2006, available from: <www.lawcouncil.asn.au/library/policies-&-guidelines/adr-guidelines.cfm> (accessed 16 October 2009).

11 *Model Standards of Conduct for Mediators*, p. 3.

12 *Ethical Guidelines for Mediators*, p. 3, italics added.

13 *Model Standards of Conduct for Mediators*, p. 4.

14 On the complex issue of power in mediation, see B. Mayer, 'The dynamics of power

in mediation and negotiation', *Mediation Quarterly*, 1987, vol. 16, 75; Astor, 'Some contemporary theories of power in mediation', 30; T. F. Marshall, 'The power of mediation', *Mediation Quarterly*, 1990, vol. 8(2), 115; Bagshaw, 'Challenges facing today's practitioners', 14; D. Bagshaw, 'Language, power and mediation', *Australasian Dispute Resolution Journal*, 2003, vol. 14, 130.

15 See the literature regarding neutrality in mediation, note 5 above. See also G. Tillet, *The Myths of Mediation*, Sydney: Centre for Conflict Resolution, Macquarie University, 1991; G. Kurien, 'Critique of myths of mediation', *Australian Dispute Resolution Journal*, 1995, vol. 6, 43.

16 K. Gibson, L. Thompson and M. H. Bazerman, 'Shortcomings of neutrality in mediation: Solutions based on rationality', *Negotiation Journal*, 1996, vol. 12, 76.

17 See R. Dingwall and D. Greatbatch, 'Who is in charge? Rhetoric and evidence in the study of mediation', *Journal of Social Welfare and Family Law*, 1993, 365; D. Greatbatch and R. Dingwall, 'Selective facilitation: Some observations on a strategy use by divorce mediators', *Law and Society Review*, 1989, vol. 23, 613. See also S. S. Silbey, 'Mediation mythology', *Negotiation Journal*, 1993, vol. 9, 349.

18 For an early but still relevant articulation of the key dilemmas mediators face in practice, see R. A. B. Bush, 'The dilemmas of mediation practice: A study of ethical dilemmas and policy implications', *Journal of Dispute Resolution*, 1994, vol. 1, 1.

19 Cobb and Rifkin coined the phrase 'equidistance' to refer to a form of a nuanced neutrality in which the mediator assists 'the disputants in expressing their "side" of the case' by using a technique of temporary alignment with each of the parties as they elaborate their positions: Rifkin, Millen and Cobb, 'Toward a new discourse for mediation', 152–53. See also Mulcahy, 'The possibilities and desirability of mediator neutrality', discussing an 'ethic of partiality'; and Astor, 'Mediator neutrality', where a way of 'doing neutrality' is offered that can cope with power imbalances in the process and maximize party control.

20 P. Marshall, 'Political competence and the mediator: A new strategy for managing complexity and stress', *QUT Law and Justice Journal*, 2008, vol. 8(1), 177.

21 Bush, 'The dilemmas of mediation practice', 22.

22 *Australian National Mediator Standards: Practice Standards for Mediators Operating Under the National Mediator Accreditation System* (2007), pp. 5 and 8. Available from: <www.leadr.com.au/accreditation.htm> (accessed 16 October 2009).

23 Astor, 'Rethinking neutrality – Part I', 77–78.

24 Astor, 'Mediator impartiality: Making sense', 221.

25 J. Folberg, 'A mediation overview: History and dimensions of practice', *Mediation Quarterly*, 1983, vol. 1, 3.

26 See J. Feerick, C. Izumi, K. Kovach, L. Love, R. Moberly, L. Riskin and E. Sherman, 'Symposium: Standards of professional conduct in alternative dispute resolution', *Journal of Dispute Resolution*, 1995, vol. 1, 117. Bush, for example, describes party self-determination as 'one of the central bases and values of the mediation process': Bush, 'The dilemmas of mediation practice', 22.

27 Taylor, 'Concepts of neutrality in family mediation', 230. 'It is in self-determination that mediation is distinguished from virtually all other third-party approaches to conflict resolution.' L. M. Cooks and C. L. Hale, 'The construction of ethics in mediation', *Mediation Quarterly*, 1994, vol. 12(1), 61.

28 G. Davis, *Partisans and Mediators: The Resolution of Divorce Disputes*, Oxford: Clarendon Press, 1988, p. 51.

29 Taylor, 'Concepts of neutrality in family mediation', 230.

30 N. A. Walsh, 'The thinning vision of self-determination in court connected mediation: The inevitable price of institutionalisation?', *Harvard Negotiation Law Review*, 2001, vol. 6, 4.

31 S. Roberts, 'Mediation in family law disputes', *Modern Law Review*, 1983, vol. 46, 540.

32 J. L. Maute, 'Mediator accountability: Responding to fairness concerns', *Journal*

of Dispute Resolution, 1990, 350; J. Nolan-Haley, 'Self-determination in international mediation: some preliminary reflections', *Cardozo Journal of Conflict Resolution*, 2005, vol. 7, 277. See also Folberg and Taylor, *Mediation: A Comprehensive Guide*, 10–14.

33 For example: Feerick et al., 'Symposium: Standards of professional conduct', per Moberly, 117. Astor has devised the notion of 'maximizing party control' as another way of looking at party self-determination, putting it at the centre of good mediation practice: Astor, 'Rethinking neutrality – Part I'.

34 R. A. B. Bush, 'Efficiency and Protection, or Empowerment and Recognition', *Florida Law Review*, 1989, vol. 41, 253.

35 J. G. Shailor, *Empowerment in Dispute Mediation: A Critical Analysis of Communication*, Westport, CN: Praeger, 1994, p. 6.

36 Nolan-Haley, 'Self-Determination in International Mediation', 278–79: 'Parties' perceptions of procedural justice are enhanced when they actively participate in the mediation process and voluntarily consent to an outcome that is free of any coercive influences.'

37 Shailor, *Empowerment in Dispute Mediation*, p. 6; Davis, *Partisans and Mediators*, p. 52.

38 Greatbatch and Dingwall, 'Selective Facilitation', 639.

39 Ibid., 614.

40 I. Kant, *Foundations of the Metaphysics of Morals*, 2nd edn, L. W. Beck trans., Englewood Cliffs, NJ: Prentice Hall. See also Rawls, who represents a liberal rights-based liberal ideology. He writes that 'each person possesses an inviolability that even the welfare of society as a whole cannot over-ride': J. Rawls, *A Theory of Justice*, Cambridge, MA: Harvard University Press, 1971, p. 3. See also R. Nozick, *Anarchy, State and Utopia*, New York: Basic Books, 1974; A. C. Hutchinson, 'Beyond no-fault', *California Law Review*, 1985, vol. 73, 755; C. F. Murphy, 'Liberalism and political community', *American Journal of Jurisprudence*, 1981, vol. 26, 125.

41 L. Fuller, 'Mediation – its forms and functions', *South California Law Review*, 1971, vol. 44, 326.

42 J. M. Nolan-Haley, 'Informed consent in mediation: A guiding principle for truly educated decision-making', *Notre Dame Law Review*, 1988–99, vol. 74, 790, referring to A. Etzioni, *The Spirit of Community: The Reinvention of American Society*, New York: Touchstone, 1993, p. 261; and J. Nedelsky, 'Reconceiving autonomy: Sources, thoughts and possibilities', *Yale Journal of Law and Feminism*, 1989, Vol. 1, 8 and 26.

43 R. A. B. Bush, 'Defining quality in dispute resolution: Taxonomies and anti-taxonomies of quality arguments', *Denver University Law Review*, 1988–89, vol. 66, 349–50.

44 Boulle, *Mediation: Principles, Process Practice*, p. 13.

45 Taylor, 'Concepts of neutrality in family mediation', 230. 'It is in self-determination that mediation is distinguished from virtually all other third-party approaches to conflict resolution.' See Cooks and Hale, 'The construction of ethics in mediation', 61. 'Undue influence is coercive, and mediation done in this way, regardless of the model or theory employed, is unacceptable if it takes away client self-determination.' See Taylor, 'Concepts of neutrality in family mediation', 229.

46 Bush, 'Efficiency and protection', 266; see also Nolan-Haley, 'Informed Consent in Mediation', 790.

47 J. Fletcher, *Situation Ethics*, London: SCM Press, 1966, p. 29.

48 Ibid., pp. 27–28.

49 W. Simon, *The Practice of Justice: A Theory of Lawyers' Ethics*, Cambridge, MA: Harvard University Press, 1998, p. 141.

50 N. Preston, *Understanding Ethics*, Sydney: The Federation Press, 2001, p. 71.

51 Greatbatch and Dingwall, 'Selective Facilitation'.

52 Preston, *Understanding Ethics*, p. 77.

53 Fletcher, *Situation Ethics*.

54 C. W. Morris, 'The Total-Situation Theory of Ethics', *International Journal of Ethics*, 1927, vol. 37(3), 258.

55 H. R. Niebuhr, *The Responsible Self: An Essay in Christian Moral Philosophy*, San Francisco: Harper & Row, 1963.

56 Preston, *Understanding Ethics*, p. 87.

57 Ibid., p. 72: Preston comments that: 'If teleology is a theory of "the good", and deontology a theory of "the right", then the ethics of response is one of "the fitting" '. Preston (p. 76) maintains that the ethic of response is 'a process enabling and justifying normative ethical decisions including the following: (i) it is organized around the idea of responsibility and the quest for a fitting response, (ii) it supports the employment of a synthesis incorporating other normative approaches, (iii) it is amenable to practical, responsive and comprehensive ethical decision-making, and (iv) it facilitates justificatory discourse which enables others to evaluate ethical decisions, without being obstructed by the conflict between normative perspectives, although it must still confront the difficulties raised by them'.

58 Fletcher, *Situation Ethics*; J. Fletcher, 'Situation ethics, law and Watergate', *Cumberland Law Review*, 1975, vol. 6, 35.

59 See C. Gilligan, 'In a different voice: women's conceptions of self and morality', *Harvard Educational Review*, 1977, vol. 47, 481; C. Gilligan, *In a Different Voice*, Cambridge, MA: Harvard University Press, 1982.

60 See, for example, J. Wall, T. Needham, D. S. Browning and S. James, 'The ethics of relationality: the moral views of therapists engaged in marital and family therapy', *Family Relations*, 1999, vol. 48(2), 139 and the references listed there.

61 Ibid., 139.

62 Ibid., referring also to the *Ethical Principles and Codes of Ethics of the American Psychological Association and the American Association for Marriage and Family Therapy*. See also K. S. Pope, B. G. Tabachnick and K. Spiegel, 'Ethics of practice: The beliefs and behaviours of psychologists as therapists', *American Psychologist*, 1987, vol. 42, 993; J. Haley, *Problem-Solving Therapy*, San Francisco: Jossey-Bass, 1987; K. S. Pope and M. J. T. Vasquez, *Ethics in Psychotherapy and Counseling: A Practical Guide for Psychologists*, San Francisco: Jossey-Bass, 1991; J. Haley, *Learning and Teaching Therapy*, New York: Guilford, 1996.

63 Wall et al., 'The ethics of relationality', 141.

64 Ibid., p. 144.

65 Simon, *The Practice of Justice*, pp. 10–11.

66 Ibid., p. 138.

67 Ibid., p. 110.

68 Ibid., p. 112.

69 Ibid., p. 110.

70 C. Parker and A. Evans, *Inside Lawyers' Ethics*, Melbourne: Cambridge University Press, 2007, pp. 31–37. Bartlett and Aitken refer to a range of literature in which the theory is applied to the legal profession, such as: C. Menkel-Meadow, 'The comparative sociology of women lawyers: The "feminisation" of the legal profession', *Osgoode Hall Law Journal*, 1986, vol. 24, 897; C. Menkel-Meadow, 'Portia redux: Another look at gender, feminism and legal ethics', *Virginia Journal of Social Policy and the Law*, 1994–95, vol. 2, 75; C. Parker, 'A critical morality for lawyers: four approaches to lawyers' Ethics', *Monash University Law Review*, 2004, vol. 30, 49; S. Ellmann, 'The ethic of care as an ethic for lawyers', *Georgetown Law Journal*, 1992–93, vol. 81, 2665; S. Ellmann, 'Empathy and approval', *Hastings Law Journal*, 1991–92, vol. 43, 991; B. Bogoch, 'Gendered lawyering: Difference and dominance in lawyer–client interaction', *Law and Society Review*, 1997, vol. 31, 677. See F. Bartlett and L. Aitkin, 'Competence in caring in legal practice', *International Journal of the Legal Profession*, 2009, vol. 16, 319.

71 Gilligan, 'In a different voice'.

72 Ibid., 511.

73 Ibid.

74 S. Mendus, 'Different voices, still lives: Problems in the ethics of care', *Journal of Applied Philosophy*, 1993, vol. 10(1), 17.
75 Fletcher, *Situation Ethics*, p. 26.
76 Ibid., p. 135.
77 Ibid., p. 138.
78 Ibid., p. 38.
79 J. Doris, *Lack of Character*, Cambridge: Cambridge University Press, 2002, p. 2. See also L. Ross and R. Nisbitt, *The Person and the Situation*, Philadelphia: Temple University Press, 1991.
80 Bartlett and Aitkin, 'Gender, care and complaints', 17.
81 Simon, *The Practice of Justice*, p. 11.
82 Compare ibid., p. 157.
83 Ibid., p. 201.
84 Preston, *Understanding Ethics*, p. 74.
85 Fletcher, *Situation Ethics*, p. 34.
86 Ibid., p. 44.
87 Ibid., p. 36.
88 Ibid., p. 55. Fletcher's view is that: 'For the situationist there are no rules – None at all'.
89 Ibid., p. 36.
90 Ibid., p. 45.
91 Ibid., p. 44.
92 Ibid., p. 31.
93 Simon, *The Practice of Justice*, p. 207.
94 Ibid., p. 140.
95 See, for example, M. D. Lang and A. Taylor, *The Making of a Mediator: Developing Artistry in Practice*, San Francisco: Jossey-Bass, 2000.
96 Fletcher, *Situation Ethics*, p. 38.
97 Ibid.
98 Ibid.
99 Simon, *The Practice of Justice*, p. 195.
100 Ibid., p. 208.
101 See National Alternative Dispute Resolution Advisory Council, Ethical Guidelines for Mediators Project, available from: <www.nadrac.gov.au/www/nadrac/nadrac. nsf/Page/AboutNADRAC_NADRACProjects_EthicalGuidelinesforMediators> (accessed 16 October 2009).
102 Fletcher, *Situation Ethics*, p. 42.
103 Ibid., p. 43.
104 Ibid., p. 40.
105 K. Manning, 'A socio-ethical foundation for meeting the obligations of the legal profession', *Cumberland Law Review*, 1974, vol. 5, 243.
106 Fletcher, *Situation Ethics*, pp. 122, 124.
107 Ibid., p. 83.
108 Hilary Astor has also consistently called for an emphasis on quality mediation training in the context of, for example, coping with the theoretical requirements of neutrality in the practice of mediation: H. Astor and C. Chinkin, 'Mediator training and ethics', *Australian Dispute Resolution Journal*, 1991, vol. 2(4), 205–23; Astor, 'Mediator neutrality', 229.
109 Fletcher, *Situation Ethics*, p. 41.
110 Ibid., p. 51. 'The rightness of an act, then, nearly always and perhaps always, depends on the way in which the act is related to circumstances; this is what is meant by calling it relatively right; but this does not in the least imply that it is only doubtfully right. It may be, in those circumstances, certainly and absolutely right' (quoting Temple, *Religious Experience*, London: James Clarke, 1958, pp. 173–74).
111 Fletcher, *Situation Ethics*, p. 43.

112 Ibid., p. 45.
113 Ibid.
114 See S. M. Okin, 'Reason and feeling in thinking about justice', *Ethics*, 1989, vol. 99, 247; I. M. Young, 'Impartiality and the civic public: Some implications of feminist critiques of moral and political theory', in S. Benhabib and D. Cornell (eds), *Feminism as Critique*, Minneapolis: University of Minneapolis Press, 1987, p. 57.
115 Fletcher, *Situation Ethics*, p. 45.
116 Ibid., p. 43.
117 Fletcher, *Situation Ethics*, p. 50 refers to Brunner's comment that the notion of value as separate from people is a 'phantasmagoria', with reference to Brunner, *The Divine Imperative*, p. 194.
118 See, for example, M. Lichtenstein 'Mediation and feminism: Common values and challenges', *Mediation Quarterly*, 2000, vol. 18(1), 19. See also Parker and Evans, *Inside Lawyers' Ethics*, and the work of Carrie Menkel-Meadow: 'The comparative sociology of women lawyers' and 'Portia redux'.
119 Gilligan, 'In a different voice', 511.
120 Mendus, 'Different voices, still lives', 18.
121 Gilligan, 'In a different voice', 511.
122 Mendus, 'Different voices, still lives', 19: 'Unlike an ethic of justice, an ethic of care emphasizes the extent to which people are at least partly constituted by their relationships with those around them'.
123 C. Calhoun, 'Justice, care, gender bias', *Journal of Philosophy*, 1988, vol. 85, 458; E. F. Kittay and D. T. Meyers (eds), *Women and Moral Theory*, Totowa, NJ: Rowman & Littlefield, 1987, p. 10.
124 For a sample of the debate, see R. Abel (ed.), *1 The Politics of Informal Justice: The American Experience*, New York: Academic Press, 1982; R. Abel (ed.), *2 The Politics of Informal Justice: Comparative Studies*, New York: Academic Press, 1982; O. Fiss, 'Against settlement', *Yale Law Journal*, 1984, vol. 93, 1073; C. Harrington, *Shadow Justice: The Ideology and Institutionalisation of Alternatives to Court*, New York: Oxford University Press, 1985; R. Delgado, C. Dunn, P. Brown, H. Lee and D. Hubbert, 'Fairness and formality: minimising the risk of prejudice in alternative dispute resolution', *Wisconsin Law Review*, 1985, 1359; M. Galanter, 'The quality of settlements', *Journal of Dispute Resolution*, 1988, 55; Coleman and Silver, 'Justice in settlements', *Sociology, Philosophy and Policy*, 1986, vol. 4, 102; H. T. Edwards, 'Alternative dispute resolution: Panacea or anathema?', *Harvard Law Review*, 1986, vol. 99, 668; J. Resnik, 'Failing faith: Adjudicatory procedure in decline', *University of Chicago Law Review*, 1986, vol. 53, 494; E. Brunet, 'Questioning the quality of alternative dispute resolution', *Tulane Law Review*, 1987, vol. 62, 1; J. L. Maute, 'Public values and private justice: A case for mediator accountability', *Georgetown Journal of Legal Ethics*, 1990–91, vol. 4, 503.
125 J. S. Auerbach, *Justice Without Law?* New York: Oxford University Press, 1983, p. 3.
126 R. D. Benjamin, 'The physics of mediation: reflections of scientific theory in professional mediation practice', *Mediation Quarterly*, 1990, 8(2), 106.
127 Maute, 'Mediator Accountability', 350. Folberg and Taylor, *Mediation: A Comprehensive Guide*, p. 246; Auerbach, *Justice Without Law?* p. 4.
128 C. Menkel-Meadow, 'Whose dispute is it anyway? A philosophical and democratic defence of settlement (in some cases)', *Georgetown Law Journal*, 1994–95, vol. 83, 2669.
129 Ibid., 2669–70.
130 Maute, 'Mediator Accountability: Responding to Fairness Concerns', p. 350; Folberg and Taylor, *Mediation: A Comprehensive Guide*, 248.
131 Menkel-Meadow, 'Whose dispute is it anyway?' 2672. On the issue of negotiation requiring the compromise of principles, see D. Luban, 'Bargaining and compromise: Recent work on negotiation and informal justice', *Philosophy and Public Affairs*, 1985, vol. 14, 397. See also A. Kuflik, 'Morality and compromise', in J. R. Pennock and J. W. Chapman (eds), *Compromise in Ethics, Law and Politics*, New York: New York

University Press, 1979, p. 63; M. P. Golding, 'The nature of compromise', in Pennock and Chapman, *Compromise in Ethics, Law and Politics*, p. 5.

132 Menkel-Meadow, 'Whose dispute is it anyway?', 2673, referring to G. C. Homans, *Social Behaviour*, 1961; I. W. Zartman and M. R. Berman, *The Practical Negotiator*, 1982. See also R. Fisher and W. Ury, *Getting to Yes*, London: Business Books, 1981. In 'Whose dispute is it anyway?' 2673, Menkel-Meadow says: 'If we don't actually value the same things equally, then negotiated settlement is more democratic'.

133 Ibid., 2673.

134 Ibid., 2687.

135 J. Dworkin and W. London, 'What is a fair agreement?' *Mediation Quarterly*, 1989, vol. 7(1), 8.

136 Menkel-Meadow, 'Whose dispute is it anyway?' 2677.

137 Ibid., 2666.

138 C. Menkel-Meadow, 'Toward another view of legal negotiation: the structure of problem-solving', *UCLA Law Review*, 1984, vol. 31, 791.

139 Menkel-Meadow, 'Whose dispute is it anyway?', 2675. Compare Fiss's view that 'the dispute-resolution story trivializes the remedial dimensions of law-suits and mistakenly assumes judgment to be the end of the process': Fiss, 'Against settlement', 1082.

140 See R. H. Mnookin and L. Kornhauser, 'Bargaining in the shadow of the law: the case of divorce', *Yale Law Journal*, 1979, vol. 88, 950 – although note that that article in fact argues that legal rules and principles limit and constrain remedial option generation. See also M. A. Eisenberg, 'Private ordering through negotiation: Dispute-settlement and rulemaking', *Harvard Law Review*, 1976, vol. 89, 637.

141 Niebuhr, *The Responsible Self*.

142 Preston, *Understanding Ethics*, p. 73.

143 Ibid.

144 Ibid.

145 Ibid.

146 Ibid., p. 71.

147 Fletcher, 'Situation ethics, law and Watergate', 38.

148 J. Fletcher, 'Ethics and recombinant DNA research', *Southern California Law Review*, 1977–78, vol. 51, 1139.

149 Preston, *Understanding Ethics*, p. 77.

10 Nefarious conduct and the 'fit and proper person' test

Duncan Webb

10.1 Introduction

Maurice Sychuk,[1] a prominent Canadian lawyer, murdered his wife in a fit of rage, stabbing her 22 times. He served 10 years in prison for his crime. This chapter poses the question of why his name was struck from the roll (and further, why he was refused readmission 10 years later). Some would say that this was inevitable given the heinous nature of his crime. However, the debate around Maurice Sychuk's application for readmission to the profession on having served his term of imprisonment touched on central issues regarding the nature and purpose of professional discipline. It showed that the reasons for striking from the roll in such cases are based on values other than the usual disciplinary justifications regarding the protection of clients from dodgy lawyers. Sychuk had rehabilitated himself and was a gifted oil and gas lawyer; there was no suggestion from any quarter of a risk of reoffending, let alone that he would misconduct himself in the course of legal practice. The striking off and refusal of readmission was based squarely on reputation, and in particular whether Sychuk's conduct was so egregious that the only way to restore the tarnish he had brought to the profession was to continue to exclude him from it and to deny readmission.[2]

The problem with such an analysis is that, while its rhetoric pervades this and other cases, there is little evidence either that such lawyers harm the reputation of the wider profession, or that the profession needs such reputational protection to discharge its duties. This, of course, flies in the face of orthodoxy, which is premised on the oft-repeated assertion that the most fundamental purpose of discipline is to maintain the profession's reputation 'to the ends of the earth' to ensure the public can repose both their confidences, their affairs and their money in lawyers.[3]

This rhetoric of character pervades discussion about the legal profession. The assertion that a person in a position of trust such as a lawyer should be of good character is difficult to argue against.[4] However, the assertion is a broad one. The question that this chapter asks is whether conduct which is egregious ought necessarily to preclude the practice of law, especially when the failings of the lawyer bear no direct relationship to the effective discharge of the duties of the lawyer.

This chapter argues that the character element of the fit and proper person test as it is currently applied is outdated and does not withstand scrutiny. There is a pervasive and underlying thread throughout the discussions of the profession that lawyers ought to be 'of the right sort'. While there is no longer the suggestion that people of the wrong class, gender or ethnicity be precluded from the profession, arguably the current articulation of the good character test is the last vestige of an approach to entry and exit of the profession based on social acceptability to peers.

The chapter embarks on an analysis of the current approach to regulation of lawyers' personal conduct, focusing on Australia, Canada and New Zealand. It considers the history, legislative framework and current application of this regulatory doctrine, critiquing in particular the normative justifications offered by disciplinary authorities[5] and courts for exercising regulatory authority over a lawyer's personal conduct.

10.2 Regulation of lawyers' personal conduct

10.2.1 Professional and personal misconduct

It is uncontentious that a power exists to strike a lawyer from the roll for misconduct in the course of practice. In general, this will occur when the conduct is such as to demonstrate either that they are incapable (by dint of incompetence or impairment) of practising law to the required standard, or unable to be entrusted with the affairs of third parties due to a serious flaw of character. There has also long been a strand of cases in which conduct outside the professional life of the lawyer has been considered relevant.

When considering the question of the relevance of conduct outside of legal practice, the disciplinary authorities (whether the court or a professional tribunal) find it necessary to expand on the relatively simple protection of the public rhetoric which serves when disciplining lawyers who have breached the duties owed to their clients. To justify sanctioning a lawyer for conduct in their private life, the tribunal needs to show that some meaningful risk exists, or some important value needs preserving. Thus, for example, it has been said in a case concerning a failure by a lawyer to file tax returns over many years:[6]

> There are four interrelated interests involved. Clients must feel secure in confiding their secrets and entrusting their most personal affairs to lawyers. Fellow practitioners must be able to depend implicitly on the word and the behaviour of their colleagues. The judiciary must have confidence in those who appear before the courts. The public must have confidence in the legal profession by reason of the central role the profession plays in the administration of justice. Many aspects of the administration of justice depend on the trust by the judiciary and/or the public in the performance of professional obligations by professional people.

It also appears that the courts and professional tribunals – perhaps understandably – will be more reluctant to discipline a lawyer in respect of conduct undertaken in a personal capacity than similar conduct undertaken professionally. The reasons for this may be manifold. On the one hand, there is the dominant liberal view that suggests there should be a clear divide between public functions and private life, which should not be crossed lightly. It may also be that a court is less ready to draw the inference that behaviour in a private capacity has predictive value for behaviour in a professional/public capacity. Thus, in *Ziems* (concerning a lawyer convicted of manslaughter by driving), Fullagar J said:[7]

> But the whole approach of a court to a case of personal misconduct must surely be very different from its approach to a case of professional misconduct. Generally speaking, the latter must have a much more direct bearing on the question of a man's fitness to practise than the former.

In *A Solicitor v The Council of the Law Society of New South Wales*, the High Court of Australia drew a sharp dividing line between the professional and the personal in reaching the conclusion that sexual offending against minors was not 'professional misconduct' and, given the circumstances, effluxion of time and rehabilitation of the lawyer, the lawyer remained a fit and proper person to practise.[8] The High Court was of the view that the Court of Appeal was wrong to reason that, because 'the conduct constituted a most serious breach of trust on the [appellant's] part given the paternal like role he had with the victims', it showed him to be unfit. Rather, the court reasoned that 'the nature of the trust, and the circumstances of the breach, were so remote from anything to do with professional practice that the characterisation of the appellant's personal misconduct as professional mis-conduct was erroneous'.[9]

10.2.2 History

The rule that a lawyer may be struck from the roll if guilty of misconduct which shows that they are not a fit and proper person to practise law is of considerable antiquity.[10] As long ago as 1275, the law provided that if any sergeant or pleader engaged in any deceit or collusion to beguile the court or the party, they would suffer imprisonment for a year and a day.[11] For nearly 500 years, the regulation of the profession fell to the serjeants-at-law and barristers whose Inns of Court undertook the role of disbarring offending barristers beyond the scrutiny of the courts.

With the rise of attorneys, and later solicitors, who were unregulated by the Inns, a need arose for legislative intervention. In 1725, the Parliament of Great Britain imposed the truly cruel punishment of transportation for seven years to 'His Majesty's colonies or plantations in America' for attorneys found guilty of certain felonies. The stated purpose of that legislation was to avoid the 'michiefs and abuses which arise from infamous and wicked persons already convicted of wilful perjury or forgery, practising as attorneys or solicitors in courts of law and equity'.[12] This was an early recognition of the perceived need for lawyers to conduct themselves appropriately in both private and professional capacities.

The courts have also long assumed an inherent jurisdiction to determine who is entitled to appear before them and to impose disciplinary sanctions in respect of those conferred with the privilege of audience.[13] An early example of the exercise of this jurisdiction and of discipline for an offence not directly related to the practice of law is to be found in *Ex parte Brounsall*,[14] which also stands as an authority for the principle that striking from the roll is not considered double jeopardy. In that case, an attorney had been found guilty of the theft of a guinea. Lord Mansfield, in that case, made it clear that the decision to strike the attorney from the roll was on the basis that he was an 'unfit person to practise as an attorney' and because he was a member of a profession 'which should stand free from all suspicion'.

The inherent jurisdiction of the courts was recognized by the US Supreme Court in *Ex parte Burr*,[15] where Marshall CJ justified the continuance of an order for suspension on the basis that 'it is extremely desirable that the respectability of the bar should be maintained, and that its harmony with the bench should be preserved' and that the existence of the discretion to suspend was 'necessary for the preservation of decorum, and for the respectability of the profession'.[16]

In the United States, it has generally been considered that a court ought not to regulate attorney misconduct unconnected with the profession unless it was 'very aggravated';[17] however, the courts also seem to have reached a consensus that private conduct can be capable of reflecting a lack of character, justifying disbarment. Thus the Supreme Court of Ohio held that 'official delinquency and base immorality' will constitute a good ground for revoking an attorney's licence.[18] And in *Re Mills*[19] it was held that an attorney could be struck from the roll if it could be proved that 'the reputation of said Mills for truth and veracity is so notoriously bad, that he is not to be believed under oath'. In so finding, Chief Justice Whipple justified the need for a good character in all aspects of the attorney's behaviour:[20]

> That no person can faithfully and honorably discharge the delicate and responsible duties of an attorney, unless fortified by strong moral principle, is too clear for argument. The nature of those duties necessarily implies the possession of high moral character, in order to their conscientious performance.

This is consistent with the approach taken in England, where it was sufficient to show that the conduct of the attorney demonstrated them to be 'a very improper person to remain as an attorney', even though the conduct was not criminal nor connected with the attorney's professional practice.[21]

10.2.3 The legislative frameworks

A considerable statutory gloss has been laid over the inherent jurisdiction of the courts to discipline and strike off lawyers (or disbar them, to use North American terminology). In most cases, legislation will identify the fact that conduct outside of professional practice may be a trigger for discipline. It should be noted at the outset that the language adopted across jurisdictions is not consistent. Some jurisdictions use the global concept of misconduct to cover conduct both within and outside of practice. Other jurisdictions adopt the term 'conduct unbecoming' for conduct outside of practice, and reserve the term 'professional misconduct' for actions taken in the course of legal practice.

Most uncontroversial are those articulations stating that action may be taken where the conduct of the lawyer, although unconnected with the provision of legal services, would justify a finding that the lawyer or incorporated law firm is 'not a fit and proper person' to engage in practice as a lawyer. Many legislative formulations expressly include such a 'fit and proper' test when referring to conduct engaged in other than in the course of providing legal services. Most recently, Australasian reforms have jettisoned any other grounds (such a reputational damage to the profession), leaving conduct showing that the lawyer is not a fit and proper person to practise law as the only basis upon which discipline may be imposed for conduct outside of the practice of law.[22]

The law also tends to recognize that criminal offences are a matter in respect of which a disciplinary response may be appropriate. It is, however, generally recognized that not all crimes reflect on fitness to practise. Thus the New Zealand provisions reinforce the 'fit and proper' approach and permit disciplinary orders to be made in response to criminal convictions that are 'punishable by imprisonment and the conviction reflects on his or her fitness to practise, or tends to bring his or her profession into disrepute'.[23] Other legislative frameworks look primarily to the moral taint of offence. Thus the South Australian Act includes in its definition of unprofessional conduct 'an offence of a dishonest or infamous nature'.[24]

Strangely, it appears that in South Australia there is no legislative authority for a disciplinary finding against a practitioner for conduct outside of practice that is not criminal.[25] In practice, this gap may be filled by the inherent jurisdiction of the court.[26] More modern Australasian articulations look simply to the fact that an offence concerns dishonesty or is 'serious'.[27] Interestingly, some of those statutes expressly include tax offences as capable of triggering discipline.[28]

In contradistinction, the applicable legislation in the Canadian jurisdictions takes a much broader approach. Some jurisdictions simply use the terms 'misconduct' and 'conduct unbecoming' as triggers for sanction, leaving it to the law societies to give content to the concepts.[29] However, in many provinces the basis for discipline in respect of conduct outside of practice is that the offending conduct is 'contrary to the best interest of the public or of the legal profession, or harms the standing of the legal profession'.[30] While the recognition of the interests of the public resonates with the fit and proper person approach taken in Australasia, the inclusion as a stand-alone consideration of the interests and standing of the legal profession is of considerable note.

10.2.4 Justifications

As is to be expected in the common law tradition, the courts and tribunals have looked to precedent when articulating the relevant justifications for disciplining a lawyer for conduct outside of practice. Separating out the different justifications is a somewhat artificial exercise, given the factual complexity of some of the cases – including the fact that in many cases the lawyers have engaged in multiple courses of conduct, some professional and some personal. It is not always easy to discern the weight given to the respective justifications. It is also the case that courts and regulators frequently give formulaic reasons, with little or no actual analysis of the connection between the reasons they give and the orders made.[31] With that caveat, we now turn to consider some of the reasons used to justify disciplining lawyers for personal misconduct.

10.2.5 *Trust*

Trustworthiness is frequently stated to be the most fundamental quality of a lawyer, and justifying regulation on the grounds that it ensures lawyer trustworthiness is facially uncontentious. 'Trust' is sometimes taken further, however, and it is stated that not only should the lawyer be trustworthy, but clients should also be able to feel confident that this is the case. This moves the question from a simply objective fact about whether there is a risk of future dishonesty to a far more subjective question about what the perceptions of clients actually may be. This is of particular relevance when considering conduct outside of the confines of professional practice. While it is not suggested in any of the cases that the apprehensions of a particularly tremulous member of the public should be taken into account, the possibility exists that reasonable citizens make errors in assessing the probative value of certain kinds of conduct as predictors of subsequent lawyer dishonesty.

In some cases, the leap from conduct outside of practice to the finding of professional untrustworthiness will readily be made. Thus, where the conduct has involved a deliberate fraudulent course of conduct intended to deprive others, the courts are quick to assume that the lawyer is broadly dishonest and not a fit and proper person to be a lawyer.[32] In the early case of *In re Blake*,[33] an attorney was suspended for two years for loaning money from a third party and dishonestly depriving the creditor of the security for the loan. The suspension was ordered to 'hold his case out as a warning and to show our vigilance in protecting persons who may have similar dealings with other attorneys'.[34] Of particular relevance to the court was the fact that, even though the conduct undertaken was not strictly undertaken as an attorney, it was closely connected with Blake's work as an attorney and his status as such was used to gain the fraudulent advantages.

In other cases, the link between conduct in private affairs and professional practice is not nearly so easy to make. In *New South Wales Bar Association v Hamman*,[35] the New South Wales Court of Appeal was of the view that deliberate evasion of personal tax obligations was indicative of a dishonest disposition that was transferable into professional practice. It equated defrauding the revenue with defrauding a client, a member of the public or a corporation.[36]

The rationale of the professional disciplinary response to sexual offending is sometimes particularly difficult to unravel. While few would disagree that the crimes are repugnant and serious, there is no clear nexus between the wrongdoing and any risk to current or prospective clients. However, the courts tend to adopt an – arguably stretched – analogical process in finding that the offending indicated that the lawyer is not trustworthy. Thus, in a case concerning offending against children who were under the domestic care of a lawyer, the court noted that a central aspect of the wrongdoing was a breach of trust.[37] In that case, the court did not stop at observing that the wrongdoing showed a serious flaw of character, but went further and found that it reflected upon his ability to discharge the professional duty of a solicitor. The argument was that the wrongdoing showed the solicitor was less likely to be faithful to his professional obligations.[38]

Other decisions have, however, recognized that the link between professional practice and personal offending may be weak at best. In considering whether sexual offending against minors was 'professional' misconduct, the High Court of Australia observed that:[39]

> It is true that the conduct involved a form of breach of trust, being the trust reposed in the appellant by the mother of the children (who later forgave, and married, him) and the children themselves. However, the nature of the trust, and the circumstances of the breach, were so remote from anything to do with professional practice that the characterisation of the appellant's personal misconduct as professional misconduct was erroneous.

In that case, the court did recognize that the conduct could reflect on fitness to practise. Ultimately, no further sanction was imposed on the solicitor who, by virtue of orders of the Court of Appeal, had in substance been suspended for five years; however, the court seems to have concluded that the offending did not create any risk to clients of the solicitor and did not warrant further sanction.

We are all vulnerable to a greater or lesser degree to breaches of trust. Such vulnerability arguably makes us particularly sensitive to suggestions, which also appeal to our intuition, that dishonesty in one sphere of activity will infect the reliability and trustworthiness of the wrongdoer in other spheres.[40] Moreover, the prophylactic nature of the disciplinary jurisdiction leans in favour of a precautionary approach in cases of trust in particular. This fact, when combined with our (largely fallacious) intuitions about the existence of predictive character traits, results in a conservative regulatory approach to personal misconduct by lawyers, and to the use of trustworthiness as a justification for imposing disciplinary sanctions at the expense of the lawyer.

10.2.6 Respect for the law

Lawyers, on a traditional view, are expected to be upholders of the system of justice on the basis that they serve and are part of that system. Most articulations of professional rules contain more or less explicit statements of this duty,[41] and the courts and tribunals, in imposing discipline, suggest that 'it may be thought to be unseemly to permit someone to practise law who has been found guilty of a serious violation of the law which he is bound to uphold'.[42]

This vision of a lawyer as a pillar of the system within which he or she works has considerable elegance, as well as perhaps romanticism. In contrast, there is a degree of tension in the converse view which accepts that lawyers may be dissenters, radicals and subverters of the system within which they work. It is perhaps to bolster the traditional view of lawyers as upholders of the system of justice that a flagrant disregard for the law has, of itself, been seen as a relevant consideration in a number of disciplinary cases. This is often expressed as a finding that the lawyer has no respect for the law.[43]

As a basis for discipline, this reason presumably proceeds on the basis that a person with no respect for the law should not be trusted with the lawyer's role in the administration of justice. It also, however, appears to contain an aspect of concern for the public perception of lawyers' ability to fulfil that role – that a lawyer who does not respect the law should not be represented by the admission body as fit to practise.

In a number of cases concerning sexual offending – especially where children have been involved – the courts have articulated the reason for discipline in terms of respect for the law. This was the case in *Barristers' Board v Pratt*,[44] where the court, in a terse judgment, stated: 'It is intolerable to think that the Court would hold out as fit to practise as a barrister a person who has shown such blatant disrespect for the law he is ethically and otherwise obliged to uphold', and ordered that the name of the barrister be struck from the roll. While there might be a suggestion in such a statement that the sanction has a protective element, the core condemnation seems to be of the lawyer's palpable lack of respect for the law.

Where the lawyer has engaged in conduct that undermines legal or judicial processes, the courts and tribunals have articulated their concerns using, at least in part, the language of respect for the law. Thus where a barrister was found to have engaged in electoral fraud and having given false evidence, the Queensland Court of Appeal was of the view that this was 'utterly repugnant to the essence of what goes to make up a barrister's fitness to practise: such as to erode, if not destroy, the complete confidence which a client, a fellow practitioner, the courts and the public should be able, without hesitation, to assume'.[45] Similarly, where a lawyer smuggled narcotics into a prison, the court saw this as a breach of the trust reposed in the profession by such secure institutions.[46]

On the other hand, not every breach will be viewed as serious, or even in breach of professional standards. A key element will be the underlying intent of the lawyer involved, as well as the seriousness of the conduct. In *Law Society of British Columbia v MacAdam*,[47] the lawyer had misled conservation officers with regard to the killing of a grizzly bear without a licence by getting his companion (who had the requisite permit) to say that he (the companion) had shot it. While the tribunal was concerned at what was a concerted course of deception, it considered a fine the appropriate penalty, given the regulatory nature of the underlying offence.

An indication of a lack of respect for the law may also explain the response of the courts to lawyers who have failed to comply with requirements to file tax returns (as opposed to other cases where lawyers have positively defrauded the revenue). Thus, in *New South Wales Bar Association v Cummins*,[48] the extraordinary fact that a senior barrister had failed to file tax returns for 38 years led to the conclusion that he had flouted the law and did not consider himself bound to adhere to his obligations to pay tax. In that case, the magnitude of the failure was suggestive of outright fraud.[49] Similarly, in *New South Wales Bar Association v Hamman*,[50] the court overtly linked the discipline to the need publicly to sanction conduct that showed a disrespect for the law when it stated that 'in its own interest, the organised Bar simply cannot permit the public to gain the impression that its members flout the revenue laws or that it condones or tolerates or belittles the seriousness of crimes against the revenue'.[51]

These decisions clearly rely on the existence of an causative relationship between the effective and scrupulous delivery of the legal service to the client and the identification by the court or regulator of the lawyer's lack of respect for the law. As discussed further below, the statement that a lawyer who showed a disdain for the very system within which he worked was not a 'fit and proper' person to hold the position has considerable difficulties. If it goes no further, such a statement has rhetorical force only. It amounts to little more than an emotive exclamation that lawyers whose conduct shows no allegiance to the legal system are bad.

In addition, the regulatory concern with trustworthiness in some of these cases – most notably *Hamman* – appears to arise less from the relationship between respect for the law and the lawyer's conduct in practice, than with ensuring that the public sees the regulator or court as properly concerned with the lawyer's actions. That is, the court may apparently be concerned with the lawyer's future conduct, but it is also indirectly, and importantly, concerned with the profession's reputation.

10.2.7 Need for courts' confidence

Competent lawyers who are able to present facts and legal arguments to the court are essential to the effective discharge of the courts' functions. To a lesser extent, the courts rely on counsel who appear before them to honour certain obligations of honesty and frankness. This is particularly so in respect of matters such as the presentation of all relevant law, avoiding the presentation of evidence that is known to be false, and ensuring clients are aware of obligations of discovery. It has been stated that judicial officers must be able to be confident that lawyers appearing before them and managing litigation will assist the court and act properly, even when the eye of the court is not upon them.[52] While such obligations touch only on lawyers who act in litigation, the courts have on numerous occasions identified the fact that if a court cannot have confidence that a lawyer will discharge these obligations, this reflects on their fitness to practise.

There are a number of cases concerning barristers in particular where special emphasis has been placed on the need for the court before which a lawyer appears to have confidence in the lawyer's trustworthiness. The seminal Australian case of *Ziems* concerned a barrister who had been found guilty of manslaughter when he struck a motorcyclist while driving his car. This case is, at least in Australasia, a starting place of any judicial consideration of the relevance of conduct outside of the course of legal practice to a lawyer's fitness to practise. In considering the 'fit and proper' test, Kitto J opined that:[53]

> A barrister is more than his client's confidant, adviser and advocate, and must therefore possess more than honesty, learning and forensic ability. He is, by virtue of a long tradition, in a relationship of intimate collaboration with the judges, as well as with his fellow-members of the Bar, in the high task of endeavouring to make successful the service of the law to the community.

There are now few, if any, jurisdictions remaining in which the right to appear before the court is reserved exclusively for a formal Bar. Accordingly, the argument that a court must have confidence in a barrister can be extended to any lawyer who has a right of audience.

One area in which the courts have been particularly quick to infer that the behaviour of a lawyer is suggestive of a predisposition to deceive the courts is where the lawyer has been before the court in a personal capacity and has acted improperly in those proceedings. Thus in *In re Thom; ex parte The Prothonotary*,[54] a lawyer failed to admit his adultery in matrimonial proceedings (as required by the applicable procedural rules) and effectively deceived the court. The court held that such conduct showed that the lawyer was also not to be trusted in his dealings with the court in a professional capacity.

In *Chamberlain v The Law Society of the Australian Capital Territory*,[55] a lawyer had taken advantage of a typographical error to settle a piece of litigation in respect of his personal tax for one-tenth of the actual amount due. The shortfall was unable to be recovered. The conduct of the lawyer was considered to be 'unconscionable', comprising 'a combination of silence and half-truths amounting to a misrepresentation'.[56] It was relevant that the lawyer did not merely passively accept the benefit of the mistake, but sought to cement the advantage by drafting (and securing) a consent order based upon it. In finding that this was professional misconduct, the court was of the view that the lawyer's behaviour was 'indicative of a failure on his part to understand or practise the precepts of fair dealing in relation to his opponent and to the court'.[57]

Chamberlain is interesting because the Federal Court affirmed the finding of misconduct (by a majority) but reduced the sanction to a mere reprimand. It appears that the court was uneasy with the fact that conduct through which the lawyer obtained a personal advantage which was permissible at law and which he was able to defend against a legal challenge led to professional discipline.

10.2.8 The public reputation of the profession

The legislation in a number of (especially Canadian) jurisdictions recognizes that where conduct damages the reputation of the profession, disciplinary action may follow.[58] The argument that the reputation of the profession is deserving of protection is of high pedigree. Its clearest and most defensible articulation is probably found in *Bolton v The Law Society*,[59] where Lord Bingham in the Court of Appeal considered:

> The second purpose [of the Tribunal's orders] is the most fundamental of all: to maintain the reputation of the solicitors' profession as one in which every member, of whatever standing, may be trusted to the ends of the earth. To maintain this reputation and sustain public confidence in the integrity of the profession it is often necessary that those guilty of serious lapses are not only expelled but denied re-admission . . . A profession's most valuable asset is its collective reputation and the confidence which it inspires.

Those words tie the reputation of the profession to public confidence, and in turn the wider discussion in the case ties that confidence to the ability of lawyers to fulfil their functions effectively. The argument is that unless lawyers 'may be trusted to the ends of the earth', they will not be able to act effectively as transactional intermediaries (in *Bolton*, the lawyer misapplied funds advanced on a mortgage in breach of an undertaking) or advocates.

Where the reputational harm relates directly to the honesty of the members of the profession, there may be a ghost of an argument that the dishonesty of one practitioner reflects on the trustworthiness of all members of the profession. However, this is not the basis upon which many cases dealing with such reputational harm proceed. Rather, where a lawyer has engaged in some distasteful activity that has little bearing on trustworthiness in legal practice, the courts have nonetheless suggested that discipline should follow.

Thus, in *The Law Society of South Australia v Rodda*,[60] Doyle CJ noted that the issue in respect of a practitioner who had been convicted of sexual offences against a young woman aged under 16 was not only his capacity to act as a practitioner, but also 'how that conduct and those convictions would reflect on the legal profession were Mr Rodda permitted to remain a member of it'. In the view of the Chief Justice, 'the public would rightly doubt the standards of a profession which permitted a person who has recently committed such serious offences to remain one of its members'. While it is undoubtedly true that there is a visceral reaction to the offences that the lawyer committed in *Rodda*, the assertion that to allow Rodda to continue to practise would taint the reputation of other lawyers was tenuous at best.

Similarly, the Law Society of British Columbia relied upon concern with the profession's reputation in reprimanding a practitioner who had been convicted of various regulatory offences under the provincial Prevention of Cruelty to Animals Act arising from her and her husband's neglect of cattle at their farm. The Law Society stated that:[61]

> The reputation of each member of the Law Society in the eyes of the public is of utmost importance to the standing of the profession generally. A member must conduct herself or himself in such a manner that the reputation of the profession as a whole is not damaged or diminished by her or his conduct.

Given Ms Stevens' negligence relative to the health of the cattle, and given the attention paid by the community to the case, her conduct could 'properly be said to harm the standing of the legal profession in the eyes of right-thinking members of the public'.[62]

10.2.9 Peer esteem

A number of cases extend the reputation factor further and suggest that a relevant consideration will be that the conduct complained of lowers the esteem of the practitioner in the eyes of professional colleagues to such an extent that they will be unable to form workable professional relationships. Thus, in *Rodda*, not only did the offending lower the esteem of the profession as a whole, but it was also such as to 'damage the ability of Mr Rodda to maintain the relationship with other members of the profession that is an essential aspect of being a practitioner ... other practitioners would not readily place trust and confidence in a practitioner who has committed such a serious offence. Another practitioner could not assume that Mr Rodda accepts the high standard of conduct which membership of the legal profession requires'.[63]

Emphasis on esteem from peers may perhaps be another way of articulating the view that some offences are so repugnant that lawyers do not want to be associated with those who are guilty of them. This was openly stated in *Ziems* by Kitto J, when he bluntly opined:[64]

> A conviction may of its own force carry such a stigma that judges and members of the profession may be expected to find it too much for their self-respect to share with the person convicted the kind and degree of association which membership of the Bar entails.

A similar approach was taken in the older case of *In re Weare; re the Solicitors Act 1888*,[65] where Lord Esher put the question of character 'another way' in asking 'ought any respectable solicitor to be called upon to enter into that intimate intercourse with him which is necessary between two solicitors even though they are acting for different parties?'.[66]

The relevance of the esteem of peers can only be understood if the profession is viewed as a kind of private guild or club. Any queasiness on the part of one lawyer in having to engage with another is wholly irrelevant to the wider question of whether the interests of the public are protected. Nonetheless, the esteem from peers reason may well be the unstated root of many professional discipline decisions. It represents the intuitive response that people guilty of some wrongs simply ought not be allowed to belong to the profession. Such a conclusion might be explained as obvious, intuitive or self-evident. However, those epithets simply indicate that the reason is in fact not susceptible to further explanation, analysis or justification.

10.2.10 Infamy

Many legislative articulations of professional disciplinary standards state that conduct showing that the lawyer is not of 'good fame and character' will trigger sanction. The 'fame' aspect of this test is entirely reputational, and is conceptually distinct.[67] Thus, while a disciplinary body might be sure that the wrongdoer is of good character and there is no risk of further wrongdoing, the mere fact that his or her conduct has rendered him or her infamous is of itself a relevant consideration. While the concept of infamy is closely related to the reputational and esteem from peers reasons, it arguably stands alone. Certainly infamy is considered a distinct ground of discipline in some legislative frameworks.[68]

The approach of the courts in this regard is often traced to the decision of *In re Weare; re the Solicitors Act 1888*,[69] where a solicitor was struck off on having been convicted of allowing houses of which he was the landlord to be used as a brothel. In that case, Lord Esher MR was of the view that:[70]

> This solicitor has been convicted of a criminal offence of such a disgraceful kind that he ought to be struck off the roll. The Court is not bound to strike him off the rolls unless it considers that the criminal offence of which he has been convicted is of such a personally disgraceful character that he ought not to remain a member of that strictly honourable profession.

What may amount to infamous or dishonourable conduct necessarily changes with the mores of the time. In *Re Shortland*,[71] in which the infamy of the lawyer was at issue, a lawyer had been convicted of the offence of criminal libel. The libel related to a woman who had broken off an engagement to marry him. He had then written to acquaintances of the woman stating that he had 'seduced' her, implying that the intended marriage was due to pregnancy[72] and that she had 'misconducted herself' with other men. For this libel, the lawyer was convicted and sentenced to imprisonment. In striking him off on the basis that he was not a fit and proper person, the court considered his conduct to show that he had 'a perverted intellect and a wicked mind'.[73]

In cases where the personal misconduct relates to conviction for sexual offences, infamy is easier to identify than any direct link with a lack of character that affects the trustworthiness or ability to practise law. In this respect, it can be observed that the degree of seriousness of certain offences has changed over time. In one 1950s case, a court of the Queen's Bench reversed a decision of a disciplinary committee striking off a lawyer for the offence of indecent assault on a male person by another male person, imposing a two-year suspension.[74] In contrast, in *In re H (a Barrister)*,[75] the judges (sitting as visitors to the Inn of Court) were of the view that values had changed significantly and substituted a reprimand for the suspension that had been imposed by the disciplinary tribunal in a case where the barrister had been convicted of repeatedly 'importuning in a public place for immoral purposes'.[76]

Many would agree that times have changed and a serious professional response to many offences that may be loosely described as 'vice' is inappropriate.[77] There remain, however, a number of offences that are regarded as very serious indeed, and the intuitive response is that a conviction is prima facie inconsistent with the continued practice of law.

The courts have been troubled on a number of occasions where lawyers have been convicted of the comparatively recently created offence of stalking (sometimes referred to as harassment). Where the conduct is serious and sustained, striking-off orders have been made. Thus, in *Legal Practitioners Complaints Committee v Tomlinson*,[78] the practitioner was struck off for stalking behaviour that included repeatedly damaging the victim's car, and sending videotapes showing sexual activity between the perpetrator and victim to the victim's workplace. There also appeared in that case to be an absence of remorse and no steps taken to rehabilitate. While such conduct is, as the court observed, 'utterly deplorable', it is difficult to see that a striking off order is necessary to protect any identifiable interest. In one such case, the nearest the court got to giving a clear reason for striking off was that he had engaged in 'conduct inimical to his capacity to practise as a legal practitioner'.[79]

10.2.11 Turpitude and denunciation

As noted earlier, some legislatures explicitly recognize that conduct involving moral turpitude will be a ground for the imposition of disciplinary orders.[80] However, the element of turpitude also occasionally underpins the decisions of courts and tribunals when seeking to justify why conduct that has no apparent bearing on the ability to practise law ought to be the subject of sanction.[81] Thus, in *Law Society of Upper Canada v Johnstone*,[82] the tribunal disbarred a lawyer for having sex with under-age prostitutes. The tribunal adopted the reasoning of the criminal court in condemning the conduct and viewed it as 'more egregious, to the public than stealing money'.[83]

The courts and tribunals have repeatedly stressed that there is no punitive element in the role of disciplining lawyers.[84] Rather, the role of discipline is to protect clients, the profession and the legal system (and, on occasion, other identified values). Nonetheless, some cases seem to be explicable only as an expression of extreme disapprobation by the professional body. Indeed, it is hard to escape the conclusion that an underlying punitive or professional retributive element exists. This has been cast by some as a denunciation rather than a punishment. Thus, in *Law Society of Alberta v Sychuk*,[85] the tribunal adopted the dicta from a criminal sentencing case, *R v CAM*,[86] in stating that:

> The objective of denunciation mandates that a sentence should also communicate society's condemnation of that particular offender's conduct. In short, a sentence with a denunciatory element represents a symbolic, collective statement that the offender's conduct should be punished for encroaching on our society's basic code of values as enshrined within our substantive criminal law.

While – as indicated by the quotation at the beginning of this chapter – the law society did not itself seek to denounce Sychuk, it took the position that reinstating him would undermine the denunciatory effect of the life sentence to which he was still subject as a result of his second-degree murder conviction.

The denunciation of the conduct of the lawyer may extend beyond merely the conduct complained of and include their subsequent behaviour. Thus, in *Legal Practitioners Complaints Committee v McKerlie*,[87] the practitioner had been convicted of rape and had defended the charge in a way that caused considerable distress to the victim and was in the view of the court a 'farrago of lies'. While the court suggested that the conduct was indicative of a lack of probity, arguably more important in reaching the decision to disbar was the 'extent of premeditation' and the fact that the crime indicated 'a tendency to vice'.[88]

Conversely, where the offences are of a nature that does not attract a high degree of disapprobation, the courts tend to be far more forgiving. This can particularly be seen in respect of drug offences. While the courts and tribunals take pains to emphasize that each case is considered on its own facts, it appears well established that conviction for a drug-related offence – even a serious offence – will not lead automatically to disbarment.[89] Thus, for example, in *Prothonotary of the Supreme Court of New South Wales v P*,[90] a lawyer was not struck off in the face of a conviction for trafficking in cocaine.[91]

10.2.12 Contextual factors

Once a disciplinary body has found that a lawyer has engaged in personal misconduct warranting professional discipline, other factors become relevant in determining the appropriate sanction. These factors are themselves indicative of the concerns that motivate the exercise of this disciplinary authority in the first place – that is, concern with the protection of the public (secondarily) and protection of the reputation of the profession (primarily).

10.2.13 Remorse and rehabilitation

A recurring theme throughout cases in which the courts have had occasion to discipline lawyers is the attitude of the wrongdoer to his or her own conduct. It is, of course, routine for the wrongdoer to express remorse, and it does appear that in many cases the degree to which they persuade the court or tribunal of its genuineness may have a considerable bearing on the orders made.[92]

Thus, in *Prothonotary of the Supreme Court of New South Wales v P*,[93] the lawyer was guilty of serious drug-trafficking offences; however, no order to strike off was made. The factors that led to this included the lawyer acknowledging the addiction that led to the offending; that in an intervening period of four years (having voluntarily suspended herself in the interim) she had made tangible efforts and progress towards rehabilitation; and that she was prepared to subject herself to ongoing medical analysis to determine her drug-free status. While this and other cases of remorse and rehabilitation can be analysed in terms of the degree of risk that the lawyer would present to the public, there may be more to it.

The effect of an indication of genuine remorse may be seen as more subtle, and reflects a submission to the values of the profession and an agreement to work within them in a cooperative way. In a sense, the stance of the wrongdoer is more than just remorseful in such cases in that it exceeds a mere acknowledgement of regret and associated shame. Rather, it approaches the religious idea of repentance in that it signals recognition of the wrongness of the conduct engaged in, and a commitment to amend behaviour in order to comply with the proper framework of professional values. In a sense, this repentance restores the disruption to the moral community that the transgression has caused.[94] One US court used truly religious overtones suggesting that a striking off would 'cleanse the stain' on the legal profession.[95] Where remorse of this kind exists, professional bodies are more likely to allow the lawyer to remain within the fold. On such an approach, the professional body has no motive to remove the wrongdoer as they (now) conform to the social and cultural framework of the profession.

Conversely, where a wrongdoer is unremorseful, disciplinary bodies have taken a much sterner line – in some cases, arguably more so than is objectively justifiable. Thus, in *Mitry v New South Wales Bar Association (LSD)*,[96] the lawyer had been convicted of an offence under company law legislation for assisting a company financing the purchase of its own shares (although in his capacity as a director of related companies and not in his capacity as a lawyer). The court fined Mitry $2,500. Such an offence is arguably regulatory in nature, and not one that would usually lead to an order striking the lawyer off. However, the approach of the lawyer was decidedly unrepentant. He attempted to minimize the significance of his role, arguing that the conviction was not sustainable and that he lacked intent (being an 'unwitting pawn'). This argument flew in the face of the evidence, including the proven fact that the lawyer had attempted to mislead an auditor.[97]

The court upheld the findings of the tribunal below in striking off the lawyer, and observed that:[98]

> there was no basis at all for Mr Mitry to claim that he was not guilty of the offence. It is also clear, in our opinion, that what was done by him was done deliberately and with an intention to help Mr Donlon perpetrate a dishonest scheme which involved deceiving an auditor, the Australian Stock Exchange and the investing public.

Once such a finding had been made, the inescapable conclusion was that the lawyer refused to acknowledge that what he had done was criminal (or arguably even inappropriate). Arguably, there would have been little risk to the public in allowing the lawyer – properly corrected – to have continued to practise. However, the lack of contrition was unable to be tolerated and the striking off order was upheld.

In contrast in *New South Wales Bar Association v Sahade*,[99] the lawyer engaged in a persistent and extensive fraud to be allocated shares in a public listing over his legal entitlement. He was acquitted of criminal charges for lack of *mens rea*. In an initial hearing, the professional tribunal found him guilty of serious professional misconduct. However, by the time the tribunal convened to impose a penalty, the lawyer had expressed considerable contrition, a significant change of tack from the earlier argument that in the absence of criminal law dishonesty (i.e. a subject-ive appreciation of wrongdoing) a finding of misconduct could not be made. In light of this turnaround, he was merely fined and reprimanded.[100]

These cases can be analysed simply on the basis of whether the person at the time the relevant tribunal makes its decision is a fit and proper person to remain a practitioner. Such an approach asks simply what the likelihood of wrongdoing in the course of practice might be, or (arguably) what risk exists of wider harm to the community or profession in allowing the practitioner to continue to practise. More insight is, however, to be gained if such remorse is seen in terms of submis-sion to and acceptance of professional values.

10.2.14 *Proportionality and deterrence*

It is well established that professional sanctions cannot be objected to on the basis of double jeopardy as the protective function of discipline is entirely different from the punitive function of the criminal courts.[101] Despite this, the courts are acutely aware of the effect that disciplinary orders (and especially striking off or suspension) can have. Thus it has been said that:

> I own I can conceive of no jurisdiction more serious than that by which a man may be deprived of his degree and status as a barrister, and which, in such a case – perhaps, after he has devoted the best years of his life to this arduous profession – deprives him of his position as a member of that profes-sion, and throws him back upon the world to commence a new career as best he may, stamped with dishonour and disgrace.[102]

However, it is clear that there is an element of deterrence in the approach of the courts. Apparent in some cases is the deterrent role of professional sanctions both against the wrongdoer and as a salutary warning to the profession at large. Thus, in one case, Mason P stated that 'protection of the public also includes deterring the legal practitioner in question from repeating the misconduct, and deterring others who might be tempted to fall short of the high standards required of them'.[103]

10.3 Conclusion

Law societies' regulatory authority to discipline lawyers for personal misconduct is generally accepted. In most cases, courts and tribunals justify the – sometimes significant – orders they impose by reference to the protection of the public. This chapter doubts that this is in fact the motivation for the orders imposed. Such claims do not withstand scrutiny, and an examination of the cases shows that, as currently applied, the regulation of personal misconduct is incoherent. It rests on doubtful assumptions about the existence of 'character' and the predictability of human conduct across highly variant circumstances.

It is suggested that an outdated approach of social acceptability to professional peers underlies the decisions of the courts and disciplinary tribunals that discipline lawyers. To an extent, the cases can be analysed in a way that on its surface shows a coherent legal approach. However, a close examination reveals that old values such as honour, tradition, reputation, transgression and repentance still underpin the way in which questions of professional discipline are addressed.

Notes

1 *Law Society of Alberta v Sychuk* [1999] LSDD 15. Maurice Sychuk was also a professor of law and a leading expert in oil and gas law.
2 Ibid., para. 60.
3 *Bolton v Law Society* [1994] 1 WLR 512; [1994] 2 All ER 486.
4 Although as discussed below, there are certainly reasonable arguments to be made against it, and indeed against the whole nature of 'character' as a meaningful concept. See, for example, J. M. Doris, 'Persons, situations, and virtue ethics', *Noûs*, 1998, vol. 32, 504–30.
5 It is recognized that in contemporary times disciplinary authorities and prosecuting bodies are no longer exclusively the courts or arms of the relevant law society. In Australia, Legal Services Commissioners have a role to play in the regulation of the legal profession as a first port of call in respect of complaints with the further function of prosecuting disciplinary matters before the relevant tribunal. In New Zealand, the Legal Complaints Review Officer acts as a quasi-appellate body from Standards Committees, and may discharge a summary disciplinary jurisdiction on review, or may act as a prosecutor before the relevant tribunal.
6 *New South Wales Bar Association v Cummins* [2001] NSWCA 284 at para. 20. See also *Re Prescott* (1971) 19 DLR 3d 446 per Branca JA at 452 for similar Canadian dicta. For a very different view, however, see *Re Cwinn and Law Society of Upper Canada* (1980) 108 DLR (3d) 381.
7 *Supreme Court of NSW v Ziems* (1957) 97 CLR 279 at 290.
8 *A Solicitor v The Council of the Law Society of New South Wales* [2004] HCA 1; (2004) 204 ALR 8. This case is discussed in L. Haller, 'Lawyers and the third dimension: *A Solicitor v The Council of the Law Society of New South Sales*', *University of Queensland Law Journal*, 2004, vol. 23, 211–17 and more generally in L. Haller, 'Smoke and mirrors: When professional discipline may cause harm', *Legal Ethics*, 2005, vol. 8, 70–86.
9 *A Solicitor v The Council of the Law Society of New South Wales* [2004] HCA 1; (2004) 204 ALR 8 at para. 34.
10 See generally H. Drinker, 'The origins and persistence of standards of professional conduct in the practice of law', *Proceedings of the American Philosophical Society*, 1953, vol. 97, 652. Also M. Ritter, 'The ethics of moral character determination: an indeterminate ethical reflection on Bar admissions', *California Western Law Review*, 2002, vol. 39, 4–9; D. Rhode 'Moral character as a professional credential', *Yale Law Journal*, 1985, vol. 94, 494–502.
11 3 Edw 1 ch 24.
12 12 Geo 1 c 29 (1725) (Frivolous Arrests Act).
13 *Ex Parte Brounsall* (1778) 2 Cowp 829, 98 RE 1385; *Ex parte Burr* 22 U.S. 529 (1824).
14 Ibid., applied in *Re AB* (Superior Court of Suffolk County Massachusetts, reported in full in 'Removal from the Bar, power of the courts') *Quarterly Law Journal*, 1857, vol. 2, 65–70.

15 *Ex parte Burr* 22 US 529 (1824).
16 Ibid., at 530.
17 See, for example, the statement in S. Howe, *The Practice in Civil Actions and Proceedings at Law in Massachusetts*, Boston: Billard Gray & Co, 1834. Also J. S. Bradway, 'Moral turpitude as the criterion of offenses that justify disbarment', *California Law Review*, 1935, vol. 24, 9–27; S. DeVitto, 'Justice and the felonious attorney', *Santa Clara Law Review*, 2008, vol. 48, 155–80.
18 *State v Chapman* 11 Ohio 430. See *Re Burr* (1823) 1 Wheeler's Crim Cases 503.
19 *Re Mills* (1847) Michigan Reports 392.
20 Ibid., at 394.
21 *King v Southerton*, 6 East. 127.
22 See, for example, Legal Profession Act 2006 (ACT), s 387; Legal Profession Act 2004 (NSW), s 497; Legal Profession Act (NT), s 465; Legal Profession Act 2007 (Qld), s 419; Legal Profession Act 2004 (Vic), s 4(4)(3); Lawyers and Conveyancers Act 2006 (NZ), s 7(1)(b)(ii). For a discussion of the Queensland position, see R. Mortensen and L. Haller, 'Legal profession reform in Queensland', *University of Queensland Law Journal*, 2004, vol. 23, 280–88.
23 Lawyers and Conveyancers Act 2006 (NZ), s 241(d).
24 Law Practitioners Act 1981 (SA), s 5(1). Discipline for conduct involving 'moral turpitude' has a long history in the United States. See, for an (somewhat dated) analysis, Bradway 'Moral turpitude'.
25 The position is even odder in Tasmania. Under section 56 of the Legal Profession Act 1995 (Tas), there appears to be no basis for discipline by the Law Society other than conduct undertaken in the course of practice.
26 See, for example, *Law Society of Tasmania v Schouten* [2003] TASSC 143.
27 Serious is then defined as broadly indictable. See, for example, Legal Profession Act 2006 (ACT), s 389; Legal Profession Act 2004 (NSW), s 498; Legal Profession Act (NT), s 466; Legal Profession Act 2007 (Qld), s 420; Legal Profession Act 2004 (Vic), s 4(4)(4). The Western Australian legislation gives no guidance, simply stating that a finding of unsatisfactory conduct may be premised on the conviction of an offence: Legal Practice Act 2003 (WA), s 190.
28 Legal Profession Act 2006 (ACT), s 389.
29 It appears that there is no statutory definition or guidance in respect of what amounts to professional misconduct or conduct unbecoming under the Legal Profession Act 2002 (Man), the Law Society Act 1990 (Ont), the Law Society Act 1996 or (NB), the Legal Profession Act 2004 (NS), Law Society Act 1999 (Nfl), s 41.
30 See, for example, Legal Profession Act 1998, s 1, which defines 'conduct unbecoming' as conduct which is contrary to the best interest of the public or of the legal profession, or harms the standing of the legal profession; Legal Profession Act 1990 (Sask), s 2; Legal Profession Act 1988 (PEI), s 37; Legal Profession Act 1988 (NWT), s 22. See also Legal Profession Act 2000 (Alb), s 49(1) and Legal Profession Act 2002 (Yuk), s 24, defining conduct deserving of sanction.
31 This is particularly true in the Canadian cases. See, for example, *Law Society of British Columbia v Hall* 2001 LSBC 34; *Law Society of British Columbia v Hart* 1999 LSBC 26; *Law Society of Saskatchewan v Durocher* [2000] LSDD No. 23; *Law Society of Saskatchewan v Zunti* [1999] LSDD No. 65; *Nova Scotia Barristers' Society v Block* [2003] LSDD No. 2; *Nova Scotia Barristers' Society v Block* [1998] LSDD No. 1.
32 *Prothonotary of the Supreme Court of NSW v Alcorn* [2007] NSWCA 288; *NSW Bar Association v Somosi* [2001] NSWCA 285; (2001) 48 ATR 562.
33 *In Re Blake* (1860) 3 E & E 34.
34 Per Cockburn CJ at 39.
35 *New South Wales Bar Association v Hamman* [1999] NSWCA 404. See also *New South Wales Bar Association v Cummins* [2001] NSWCA 284, where a Queen's Counsel was declared not a fit and proper person to be on the Roll of Legal Practitioners on the basis of not

filing tax returns for 38 years; also *Law Society of Manitoba v MacIver* [2003] LSDD 29 and *Law Society of Upper Canada v Coles* [1997] LSDD 175, where similar conclusions were reached.

36 See also *Mitry v New South Wales Bar Association (LSD)* [2000] NSWADTAP, where the conduct complained of was assisting a company in structuring a transaction to finance the purchase of its own shares in contravention of Australian company law and deceiving the stock exchange (and auditors) as to the real size of shareholdings. In that case, the lawyer was struck off.

37 See *Council of the Law Society of New South Wales v A Solicitor* [2002] NSWCA 62, where a solicitor was struck from the roll for sexual offending (not being of the most serious nature) against children who were in his care at para. 101 per Sheller JA.

38 See also *Re Cwinn and Law Society of Upper Canada* (1980) 108 DLR (3d) 381.

39 *A Solicitor v The Council of the Law Society of New South Wales* [2004] HCA 1; (2004) 204 ALR 8 at para. 34.

40 See also, for example, L. Corbin and J. Carter, 'Is plagiarism indicative of prospective legal practice', *Legal Education Review*, 2007, vol. 17, 53–66 for an example citing *Re Humzy-Hancock* [2007] QSC 34; *Law Society of Tasmania v Richardson* [2003] TASSC 9; *Re Liveri* [2006] QCA 152; *Re AJG* [2004] QCA 88 Compare *Pou v Waikato Bay of Plenty District Law Society* (High Court, Rotorua CIV 2004-463-0511, 9 May 2005, Baragwanath and Courtney JJ).

41 See, for example, Law Council of Australia Model Rules introduction to rule 30: 'A practitioner ought also to act in ways which uphold the system of administration of justice in relation to which those privileges are conferred'. Canadian Bar Association Code of Conduct Chapter XIII: 'The lawyer should encourage public respect for and try to improve the administration of justice'. See also para. 3 of the commentary: 'The obligation outlined in the Rule is not restricted to the lawyer's professional activities but is a general responsibility resulting from the lawyer's position in the community'. See also Chapter XIX at para. 10.

42 *Achtem v Law Society of Alberta* (1981) 16 Alta LR (2d) 24 (CA) per Stevenson JA at 29.

43 *Barristers' Board v Darveniza* [2000] QCA 253; (2000) 112 A Crim R 438 at para. 29. See also *Law Society of Upper Canada v Morgan* [1998] LSDD No. 98.

44 *Barristers' Board v Pratt* [2002] QCA 532.

45 *Barristers' Board v Young* [2001] QCA 556 at para. 15 per de Jersey CJ. See also *Coe v NSW Bar Association* [2000] NSWCA 13 (barrister knowingly swearing a false affidavit in his own family proceedings). *Young* was relied on in *Legal Practitioners Complaints Committee v Palumbo* [2005] WASCA 129, where a practitioner solicited his nephew to bear responsibility for a traffic offence of which the practitioner was guilty (the practitioner there was also involved in certain drug offences). See also *Re a Practitioner; Ex parte Legal Practitioners Disciplinary Tribunal* (2004) 145 A Crim R 557 (perjury to conceal lawyer's own professional negligence).

46 *Law Society of Upper Canada v Mills* (2005) ONLSHP 5.

47 *Law Society of British Columbia v MacAdam* [1999] LSDD 38; [1999] LSBC 24. See also *Law Society of British Columbia v Stevens* [2001] LSDD 19; [2001] LSBC 12, where a reprimand was imposed for negligently failing to ensure the health of dairy cows (owned by the defendant and her husband) in breach of the Prevention of Cruelty to Animals Act 1996.

48 (2001) 52 NSWLR 279. See also *New South Wales Bar Association v Somosi* [2001] NSWCA 285.

49 Compare, however, *Law Society of Manitoba v Ament* [1993] LSDD 150, where a similar failure to file tax returns for five years was thought deserving only of a reprimand.

50 *New South Wales Bar Association v Hamman* [1999] NSWCA 404. See also *Re Milte & Ors, Legal Practitioners* [1991] SASC 3101; (1991) 22 ATR 740.

51 At para. 87, approving the opinion of Sanford M. Stoddard and Carl A. Stutsman Jr in *Income Tax Offences by Lawyers: An Ethical Problem* (1972) ABAJ 842 at 845. See also *Law*

Society of Tasmania v Schouten [2003] TASSC 143, where the breaches were less extreme and the result of lassitude rather than intentional fraud. However, the Supreme Court of Tasmania was of the view that the failure of the barrister to file tax returns was reflective of a dismissive attitude to legal obligations and amounted to professional misconduct. Also *Re Prescott* (1971) 19 DLR 3d 446.

52 *Re B* [1981] 2 NSWLR 372 per Moffitt P at 382 (although that case concerned admission). See also *Coe v NSW Bar Association* [2000] NSWCA 13.

53 *Ziems v Prothonotary of the Supreme Court of NSW* [1957] HCA 46; (1957) 97 CLR 279, 298.

54 (1964) 80 WN (NSW) 968. See also *Law Society of British Columbia v Hart* [1999] LSDD 44, [1999] LSBC 26 where a lawyer failed to comply with family court orders in respect of the custody of his son (although only a reprimand was imposed).

55 *Chamberlain v The Law Society of the Australian Capital Territory* [1993] FCA 527; (1992) 43 FCR 148.

56 At para. 54. For the taxation saga, see *Chamberlain v Deputy Commissioner of Taxation* [1988] HCA 21; (1988) 164 CLR 502 and *Chamberlain v Commissioner of Taxation* (1981) 28 FCR 21.

57 *Re Law Society of the Australian Capital Territory and Chamberlain* (1993) 116 ACTR 1 at 17 per Miles CJ (Supreme Court).

58 See, for example, Legal Profession Act 1990 (Sask), s 2; Legal Profession Act 1988 (PEI), s 37; Legal Profession Act 1988 (NWT), s 22. See also Legal Profession Act 2000 (Alb), s 49(1) and Legal Profession Act 2002 (Yuk), s 24, defining conduct deserving of sanction.

59 *Bolton v The Law Society* [1994] 1 WLR 512; [1994] 2 All ER 486. See *Hands v Law Society of Upper Canada* (1899) 16 OR 625 per Boyd C at 635 for a Canadian articulation (affirmed at 17 OR 41). For a US analysis along traditional lines, see C. Selinger, 'The public's interest in preserving the dignity and unity of the legal profession', *Wake Forest Law Review*, 1997, vol. 32, 861–86.

60 *The Law Society of South Australia v Rodda* [2002] SASC 274; (2002) 83 SASR 541 at para. 25. See also *Law Society of South Australia v Liddy* [2003] SASC 379 at para. 11; *Re Cwinn* (1980) 108 DLR 3d 381.

61 *Law Society of British Columbia v Stevens* 2001 LSBC 12 at para. 10.

62 Ibid., at para. 12.

63 *The Law Society of South Australia v Rodda* [2002] SASC 274 at para. 27.

64 *Ziems v Prothonotary of the Supreme Court of NSW* [1957] HCA 46; (1957) 97 CLR 279 at 298.

65 *In Re Weare; re the Solicitors Act 1888* [1893] 2 QB 439.

66 Ibid., at 446. See also the words of Lindley LJ at p. 447: 'What respectable solicitor would without loss of self respect, knowing the facts, meet him in business?'

67 *Prothonotary of the Supreme Court of NSW v P* [2003] NSWCA 320 at para. 17.

68 For example, Law Practitioners Act 1981 (SA), s 5(1).

69 *In Re Weare; re the Solicitors Act 1888* [1893] 2 QB 439.

70 Ibid., at 446.

71 *Re Shortland* (1893) 12 NZLR 137 (CA).

72 At least that is what this writer infers from the statement that the marriage was due to 'delicate reasons best known to her'.

73 *Re Shortland* (1893) 12 NZLR 137, 141 per Williams J.

74 *In Re a Solicitor* [1956] 1 WLR 1312. 1314. The solicitor was also sentenced to three months' imprisonment on the criminal charge.

75 *In Re H (a Barrister)* [1981] 1 WLR 1257.

76 In a similar vein, in *Re Thom; Ex parte Prothonotary* (1962) 80 WN (NSW) 968 it was found that a solicitor was guilty of professional misconduct when he failed to disclose his adultery in a suit for the dissolution of his marriage (in breach of the applicable disclosure rules). For an analysis of similar US cases, see Rhode, 'Moral character', 553.

77 Thus, in *Re Cwinn* (1980) 108 DLR 3d 381, Craig J noted that, despite American law, 'we do not regard it as unbecoming simply for a solicitor to go to Buffalo for the purpose of fornication' – although in the circumstances the wider conduct (seducing young girls) was considered conduct unbecoming. Note, though, *Barry v Law Society of New Brunswick* (1989) 102 NBR (2d) 118, in which the court was unwilling to preclude law society investigation of a student-at-law charged with an offence arising from public nudity.

78 *Legal Practitioners Complaints Committee v Tomlinson* [2006] WASC 211. Compare *Law Society of Manitoba v Bjornson* [1996] LSDD 258, where the offending was not considered serious and a fine was imposed.

79 *Legal Practitioners Complaints Committee v McKerlie* [2006] WASC 211 at para. 22.

80 Law Practitioners Act 1981 (SA), s 5(1).

81 In Canada, *German v Law Society of Alberta* [1974] 5 WWR 217 had stated that moral turpitude was a necessary ingredient of any finding of conduct unbecoming. That was overruled in *Trace v Institute of Chartered Accountants* [1989] 2 WWR 86. See also *Law Society of the Northwest Territories v Ford* [1996] LSDD 109.

82 *Law Society of Upper Canada v Johnstone* [2001] LSDD 59.

83 Ibid., at para. 37.

84 *Southern Law Society v Westbrook* (1910) 10 CLR 609 at 612; *Re a Barrister and Solicitor* (1979) 40 FLR 1 at 24–25, per Blackburn CJ, Connor and Davies JJ; *Re Maraj (a Legal Practitioner)* (1995) 15 WAR 12 at 25, per Malcolm CJ; *Wentworth v New South Wales Bar Association* (1992) 176 CLR 239 at 250–51; *Ziems v The Prothonotary of the Supreme Court of NSW* (1957) 97 CLR 279; *The Law Society of South Australia v Murphy* (1999) 201 LSJS 456 at 460–61: *New South Wales Bar Association v Evatt* (1968) 117 CLR 177 at 183–84; *The Law Society of South Australia v Murphy* (1999) 201 LSJS 456 at 460–61.

85 *Law Society of Alberta v Sychuk* [1999] LSDD 15.

86 *R v CAM* (1996) 105 CCC (3d) (SCC). See also *R v Sargeant* (1974) 60 Cr App R 74 at 77.

87 *Legal Practitioners Complaints Committee v McKerlie* [2007] WASC 119.

88 Ibid., at para. 10.

89 See *Re a Practitioner* [2002] WASCA 93; *Re a Solicitor* [2004] WASCA 283; *Law Society of Upper Canada v Mills* (2005) ONLSHP 5 at para. 26; *Law Society of British Columbia v Watt* [2001] LSBC 16.

90 *Prothonotary of the Supreme Court of New South Wales v P* [2003] NSWCA 320. Compare *The Prothonotary of the Supreme Court of New South Wales v Sukkar* [2007] NSWCA 341, also concerning drug trafficking offences where the lawyer was struck off. This was also influenced by the lawyer's failure to acknowledge the full extent of his involvement and the fact that he gave false evidence at his trial. Note that in Western Australia a more stringent approach seems to have been taken in *Re a Practitioner* [2004] WASCA 283. See also *Re Maraj (a Legal Practitioner)* (1995) 15 WAR 12 at 24–25.

91 In contrast, many states in the United States appear to follow the Californian approach and start from the presumption that drug offences involve moral turpitude and under the relevant legislation warrant disbarment with the absence of compelling mitigating circumstances: *Re Nadrich* (1988) 747 P (2d) 1146, 1148; *Re Leardo* (1991) 805 P (2d) 948, 953–54.

92 For an analysis of rehabilitation from a US perspective, see M. Gibson, 'Proving rehabilitation', *Journal of the Legal Profession*, 1996, vol. 20, 239–50.

93 *Prothonotary of the Supreme Court of New South Wales v P* [2003] NSWCA 320. Compare *Re a Practitioner* [2002] WASCA 93 and *Re a Solicitor* [2004] WASCA 283.

94 For a more detailed argument that discipline in such cases is preserving the professional community, see Rhode, 'Moral character', 509–12.

95 *Haimes v Mississippi Bar* (1992) 601 So 2d 851. For further analysis of the US position, and an endorsement of the importance of remorse and rehabilitation, see M. Carr, 'The effect of prior criminal conduct on the admission to practice law: A move to more flexible admission standards', *Georgetown Journal Legal Ethics*, 1995, vol. 8, 367–400.

96 *Mitry v New South Wales Bar Association (LSD)* [2000] NSWADTAP 9. The fact that the lawyer also made an unsuccessful argument that one of the tribunal members should have recused herself for bias would not have enhanced the disposition of the tribunal to the lawyer. See also *New South Wales Bar Association v Cummins* (2001) 52 NSWLR 279 at para. 30.

97 An argument that the conviction was not sustainable is not one the court is able to entertain (although it may investigate fully the facts surrounding the conviction): *Ziems v Prothonotary of the Supreme Court of New South Wales* [1957] HCA 46; (1957) 97 CLR 279 at 288.

98 *Mitry v New South Wales Bar Association (LSD)* [2000] NSWADTAP 9 at para. 22.

99 *New South Wales Bar Association v Sahade* [2007] NSWCA 145, affirming *New South Wales Bar Association v Sahade (No. 3)* [2006] NSWADT 39. It was of considerable interest that the Court of Appeal seemed to accept that dishonesty outside of the practice of law does not always translate to unfitness to practise law when it said at para. [86]: 'The conduct revealed a defect in character, because of its deceptive or deceitful nature. Whilst that aspect of character is of high importance in relation to practice as a legal practitioner, it may be accepted that individuals behave differently in different circumstances. It would be wrong in the present case simply to assume that a reasonably brief period of deceptive conduct in relation to private investments, is of weighty significance in relation to the practice of law'. See also *Law Society of British Columbia v Johnson* [1992] LSDD 13, where a lawyer acted dishonestly (although not necessarily illegally) in lying to a trustee in bankruptcy in order to obtain an advantage in respect of purchasing the insolvent's assets.

100 For a further example of lack of contrition, see *New South Wales Bar Association v Bryson* [2003] NSWADT 19, where a barrister argued that taking Smith and Wesson (which was loaded) and Glock pistols to a bar in breach of relevant firearms licences was not misconduct. The court, in disagreeing with the submissions of the practitioner (which were described as novel and inconsistent both with the legislative scheme, authority and practice), imposed a fine and required supervision of the barrister. It became apparent that the lack of contrition of the barrister (including his attempts to minimize the significance of the offending) reinforced the conclusions of the court that disciplinary orders were necessary.

101 *Ex Parte Brounsall* (1778) 2 Cowp 829, 98 RE 1385. *In re Weare; In re The Solicitors Act 1888* (1893) 2 QB 439 at 442, 448; *Southern Law Society v Westbrook* [1910] HCA 31; (1910) 10 CLR 609; *Ziems v Prothonotary of the Supreme Court of NSW* [1957] HCA 46; (1957) 97 CLR 279 at 290.

102 *Hudson v Slade* (1862) 3 F & F 390 at 411; 176 ER 174 184.

103 *Law Society of New South Wales v Foreman* (1994) 34 NSWLR 408 at 470–71. Approved in *New South Wales Bar Association v Hamman* [1999] NSWCA 404; and *Mitry v New South Wales Bar Association (LSD)* [2000] NSWADTAP 9. See also *Law Society of Manitoba v Bjornson* [1996] LSDD 258; *Law Society of Manitoba v MacIver* [2003] LSDD No. 29.

11 Legal ethics and regulatory legitimacy: regulating lawyers for personal misconduct

Alice Woolley

11.1 Introduction

Regulation of the legal profession is pervasive. In every common law country, lawyers operate within a complex series of formal and informal norms that determine, *inter alia*, who is admitted to the Bar, the extent of competition permitted by non-lawyers, when lawyers' conduct is lawful and/or ethical and when it is not. Legislatures, courts and regulatory bodies such as law societies impose requirements and restrictions on the practice of law, and sanction lawyers who violate them.

In the aftermath of the 2008 collapse of the international credit markets, and the association of that collapse with limited and inadequate regulation of the financial sector in the United States,[1] the fact of pervasive regulation of an economic activity does not require defending the way it might once have. Nonetheless – and perhaps even more so, given the newly discovered enthusiasm for regulation as a 'good thing' – it is important to ask, persistently and rigorously, why we regulate (and why should we regulate) what lawyers do. More significantly, why do we have the particular regulations that we have? What is the point and purpose of having disciplinary rules or standards? Which rules are specifically justifiable and which are not? And on what basis can that assessment be made? What is the benchmark that distinguishes good and legitimate regulatory activity from that which is bad and/or illegitimate?

In Chapter 10 of this volume, Professor Duncan Webb reviews law society and judicial regulation of lawyers' personal misconduct[2] in Australia, Canada, England and New Zealand.[3] His chapter outlines the history, legislative framework and proffered regulatory justifications for sanctioning lawyers for morally or legally opprobrious conduct outside of legal practice in those jurisdictions. Professor Webb suggests that this regulatory action is misplaced. It relies on poorly articulated and defended empirical assumptions, represents undue concern with the reputation of the profession as opposed to the public interest, and as often as not 'amounts to little more than an emotive exclamation that lawyers whose conduct shows no allegiance to the legal system are bad'.[4]

This chapter builds on Professor Webb's analysis of the regulation of extra-professional misconduct. It does so to critique the regulation itself, as well as to make some general claims about the appropriate methodology for assessing regulatory action (or inaction). The next section argues that while regulation need not be based on demonstrable empirical facts, problems arise where its asserted empirical foundations are falsifiable or doubtful. In that event, some non-empirical justification for the regulation must be offered – some explanation as to why its faulty empirical foundations can be ignored. The current approach to regulation of extra-professional misconduct rests on just such dubious empirical foundations. Specifically, the research of behavioural psychology suggests that the regulation rests on empirically doubtful assertions about the existence of ascertainable 'moral character' predictive of individual conduct across situational contexts. For the regulation to be justified, some alternative foundation must be provided.

The following section assesses the legitimacy of regulation of lawyers' personal misconduct through theoretical frameworks traditionally employed to justify and/ or critique regulatory activity: economic and democratic theories of regulation. It argues that these frameworks are justifiably used to assess regulation of lawyers, and that in this instance they support Professor Webb's conclusions that the current regulation of personal misconduct is unjustified. In economic terms, regulation of lawyers' personal misconduct cannot be normatively justified as necessary to correct for the numerous imperfections in the market for legal services. In democratic terms, regulation of lawyers' personal misconduct fails to achieve the necessary standards of legitimacy.

Finally, the chapter considers what, if any, regulation of personal misconduct might be justified in empirical, economic or democratic terms.

11.2 The requirement of empirical validity: does personal misconduct accurately predict professional misconduct?

11.2.1 Do facts matter?

In justifying various regulations governing the legal profession, courts and regulators frequently make empirical claims of one sort or another. In defending solicitor–client privilege, for example, the Supreme Court of Canada claimed that, without the privilege, 'clients could never be candid and furnish all the relevant information that must be provided to lawyers if they are to properly advise their clients'.[5] In articulating the rules around conflicts of interest, the court suggested that: 'Unless a litigant is assured of the undivided loyalty of the lawyer, neither the public nor the litigant will have confidence that the legal system, which may appear to them to be a hostile and hideously complicated environment, is a reliable and trustworthy means of resolving their disputes and controversies'.[6] In justifying a decision to discipline a member for incivility, the Law Society of Alberta claimed that: 'Professionals are expected to act professionally and must do so or they compromise the interests of not only their clients but society at large'.[7] Similar claims are made in other areas and/or jurisdictions.[8]

Does it matter whether these assertions are false? It may be that they are true. It may even be that courts and regulators are entitled, without evidence to the contrary (or where they are susceptible neither to proof nor disproof), to assume them to be true. But what if they are demonstrably untrue, or at least demonstrably doubtful? What if, for example, it can be shown that 'more people would talk to a lawyer *sans* privilege, than they would to a marriage counselor . . . In fact . . . most people [surveyed] were either unaware of the attorney–client privilege or believed that it extended to other professional relationships'?[9] What if decisions on retaining a lawyer are wholly unrelated to systemic concerns or perceptions of the profession as a whole?[10] It would go too far to claim that a regulation may only be justified where it is based on demonstrable empirical facts. However, it seems prima facie reasonable to suggest that if the empirical foundations of a regulation prove falsifiable, or doubtful, then that should be addressed. If nothing else, regulators should cease to assert factual premises that have been demonstrated to be dubious or, at minimum, should acknowledge the premises' empirical uncertainty. They should also explain why, in the face of doubt as to the factual foundations usually offered for a rule, that rule is nonetheless desirable and appropriate.[11] A foundational value of common law legal systems is rationality.[12] Reliance on empirically doubtful or falsifiable conclusions in exercising legal power is not rational. And there is certainly precedent for the position that, where beliefs prove false over time, the law should respond with change.[13]

11.2.2 Does personal misconduct accurately predict professional misconduct?

Professor Webb outlines the justifications offered for disciplining lawyers for personal misconduct in the various jurisdictions whose decisions he considered: they cannot be trusted; they do not respect the law; they cannot command the confidence of the court; they undermine the public reputation of the profession; they are not esteemed by their peers; they are infamous; they must be denounced. These justifications can loosely be grouped into two broader categories: justifications based on a concern that the personal misconduct demonstrates a propensity for misconduct in legal practice; and justifications based on a concern that failing to discipline the lawyer for personal misconduct will bring the profession as a whole into disrepute. Disciplinary justifications concerned with a lawyer's trustworthiness, with respect for law and with the need for the confidence of the court all generally flow from the asserted relationship between personal and professional misconduct; disciplinary justifications concerned with the public reputation of the profession, esteem from the offending lawyer's peers, infamy and denunciation, all generally relate to protecting the profession's reputation. In this section, I will assess the empirical validity of the claimed relationship between personal and professional misconduct – that is, the validity of the assertion that, based on one or more instances of personal misconduct, it can be determined that a lawyer is, generally, untrustworthy, disrespectful of the law and/or unworthy of the confidence of the court.[14]

When regulators claim a relationship between personal misconduct and a lawyer's legal practice, they make two empirical assumptions: first, they assume that a single incident (or incidents) of personal misconduct is demonstrative of a lawyer's general moral character; and second, they view the moral character so demonstrated as indicative of the likelihood of immoral (unethical) conduct by the lawyer in their legal practice. Both of these empirical claims are highly doubtful.[15] They rest on what social psychologists call the 'fundamental attribution error' – that is, the error arising from the tendency for people to 'seriously and routinely under-estimate . . . both the number of observations and the distribution within them that is required to warrant the attribution of . . . character traits such as honesty'.[16] We commit the fundamental attribution error when, without anything more, we discover that a friend has told us a lie and attribute to him the vice of dishonesty, when we see someone at a party eating too much food and attribute to them the vice of greed, or when we see someone being kind to a disabled person and attribute to them the general virtue of compassion.

Limited instances of behaviour do not warrant this kind of generalized assumption about an individual's character. They do not do so because the overwhelming evidence of social psychology is that, in general, circumstances are far more predictive of behaviour than is a generalized notion of 'character'. While individuals behave with significant temporal stability – the person who eats too much at a party today is predictably likely to eat too much at a party tomorrow – they demonstrate little 'cross-situational consistency' in their behaviour. As a consequence, a particular behaviour that occurs in a particular context almost certainly says more about the influence of that context than about the character of the person who engaged in it. That is, it likely suggests that other people in that same context will behave in the same way, but it does not suggest that that person will behave in the same way if placed in a different context.[17]

The experiments supporting these conclusions have been summarized at some length in my chapter in the earlier companion volume to this book, *Reaffirming Legal Ethics*, which addressed the empirical problems with the regulation of the 'character' of applicants for Bar admission.[18] For the purposes of the argument here, it is sufficient to note that this evidence from social psychology undermines significantly 'protection of the public'-related justifications for disciplining lawyers for personal misconduct. The context of personal misconduct is – by definition – significantly variant from the context of legal practice. There is no reason to believe that reprehensible behaviour in one context says much at all about the likelihood of reprehensible behaviour in the other, particularly where there is no suggestion that there has been reprehensible behaviour in legal practice. And the more variant the circumstances, the less predictive the behaviour in one circumstance is to another. Thus assertions like the following, where a Canadian court rejected the argument that a lawyer's sexual misconduct did 'not impair or reflect upon the integrity or competence of the solicitor in any dealings that he may have with clients',[19] are, as currently articulated, empirically unsustainable:

[Cwinn] took advantage of these young girls in the relationship of dependence, trust and confidence that existed in all the circumstances outlined in the report of the Discipline Committee. I accept the guidelines of the Law Society (and also the submission of counsel for the solicitor) as to what must be shown before conduct is 'conduct unbecoming a barrister and solicitor'. Having done so *it is my view that his conduct was not only reprehensible, but that it does seriously reflect upon and shatter his professional integrity to the point where the protection of the public is involved.* In my opinion, therefore, Convocation was correct in finding the solicitor guilty of conduct unbecoming a barrister and solicitor.[20]

The court's statement about the relationship between the misconduct and Cwinn's professional integrity is simplistic and certainly not true simply because it was believed to be true by the court. However repellent Cwinn's behaviour might have been, it did not, prima facie, 'shatter his integrity' so as to place his clients at risk. Protection of young girls unfortunate enough to come under Cwinn's sphere of influence was at issue, but that protection occurs through the criminal justice system. Absent some other evidence, or some cogent explanation as to why there was some relationship between Cwinn's misconduct with these girls and protection of his future clients, the court gave insufficient justification for upholding the decision to disbar Cwinn.

This is not to say that ethical regulation must be dictated by the findings of behavioural psychology, or that behavioural psychology renders *any* regulation of a lawyer's personal misconduct unjustifiable. As noted, within behavioural psychology it is acknowledged that even if robust character traits – traits that dictate behaviour reliably across a variety of circumstances – do not exist, there may be 'local' character traits that create significant temporal stability in human behaviour.[21] The greater the similarity between the context of personal misconduct and the context of professional practice, the greater is the empirical justification for regulating that personal misconduct.

Moreover, observations about how, in general, situations affect human behaviour do not explain or predict how any given individual will behave, or eliminate the ability to make psychological judgments or assessments about individuals. As recently noted by David Luban, situational psychology does not explain why, as situations change, the behaviour of some remains the same.[22] In the end, situations may help explain human behaviour, but they do not determine it.[23] Finally, in many contexts – such as determination of custody cases or likelihood of reoffending – courts rely on psychological evidence, and on psychological assessments of individual character, to make legally required determinations of future conduct from past behaviour.[24]

Nonetheless, behavioural psychology does demonstrate the insufficiency of the bare assertion by a regulator that a lawyer who has evaded or avoided tax, or one who has sexually offended or has lied, is untrustworthy, generally disrespectful of the law or unworthy of the court's confidence. Absent some reason to relate the circumstances of the personal misconduct to the lawyer's professional practice, or some independent evidentiary basis for concern with the lawyer's conduct as a lawyer, the most empirically justified assumption is that the personal misconduct has little probative value for the lawyer's professional conduct. This suggests that it is only where personal misconduct by a lawyer is closely related to his or her professional practice (where, perhaps, it is only through a technicality that the misconduct can be said to be non-professional), or where the misconduct is coupled with issues related to the lawyer's conduct of his professional practice, that regulatory action against the misconduct is justified on the grounds of protection of the public. If, for example, a lawyer served as a volunteer on a not-for-profit board and misappropriated funds belonging to the not-for-profit, the lawyer should not be permitted to avoid discipline on the grounds that such volunteer service did not constitute 'legal practice' or 'professional misconduct'. By contrast, evading personal income taxes, or committing fraud to obtain a home mortgage, however reprehensible, must be coupled with some evidence of professional misconduct to warrant *professional* discipline. Other regulatory mechanisms such as the criminal justice system exist to discipline personal misbehaviour; professional discipline requires some relationship to professional practice. The evidence of behavioural psychology demonstrates that such a relationship does not exist through the mere fact of the personal misconduct; more is required.

11.3 Regulatory theory

Perhaps because so much of the thinking on the regulatory aspect of legal ethics has focused on the question of who should regulate lawyer conduct, it has sometimes got lost that decisions made by regulators of the legal profession – whether courts, legislatures or administrative bodies, and whether self-regulatory or including significant non-lawyer involvement – are properly understood and analysed as regulatory action. Regulation of the legal profession is obviously distinct in important ways from usually discussed spheres of regulatory activity like the determination of electricity rates, management of resource development or approval of pharmaceuticals as effective and safe. Nonetheless, as noted in the introduction, decisions about who is admitted to the Bar, about the extent of competition permitted by non-lawyers, and about what constitutes permissible (ethical) and impermissible (unethical) conduct constitute state regulation of individual (economic) activity. These decisions are empowered and authorized by legislation; a regulatory decision-maker with coercive power over individuals administers them; the regulatory decision-maker makes decisions on policy and adjudicates individual cases; and the decisions of the regulator are subject to judicial oversight. The fact that the regulator has historically been (and in some instances is currently) constituted of individuals subject to its authority does not change the fundamental nature of its decisions as constituting regulatory activity. Independence of the Bar has had, and likely continues to have, some relevance to the question of the manner in which lawyers are regulated, and as to the applicable norms to which lawyers should be subject, but it does not change the fundamental regulatory nature of the activity being undertaken.

While not widely applied to the regulation of the legal profession,[25] theoretical understandings of regulation as applied in other areas are sophisticated and can meaningfully be applied to critique the substance as well as the form of lawyer regulation. This part both assesses the regulation of personal misconduct by lawyers against the main forms of regulatory theory and justifies the use of each theory for such assessment. It considers the two main normative theories that can justify regulation – regulation to address market imperfections and failures, and regulation in pursuit of broader democratically legitimate norms – and the extent to which these theories succeed (or fail) in justifying the regulation of personal misconduct by lawyers.

11.3.1 *Economic regulation*

Economics dominates regulatory theory.[26] Some have gone so far as to suggest that, while regulation 'is quintessentially an interdisciplinary subject, those lawyers, political analysts, and sociologists who look at regulation seem often to have surrendered the value debate to welfare economists'.[27] This section considers the 'public interest'[28] economic justification for regulation, and looks at whether it provides normative support for regulation of lawyers' personal misconduct. Public-interest theories argue that regulation is justified in those circumstances where, because the normal operation of market forces fails, or the imperfections of the market are sufficiently great, the benefits of regulation outweigh its costs. The value orientation of public-interest theories is towards creation of economic efficiency, towards generation through regulation of the same efficiency gains that would exist if the market were perfect.

Before considering the application of public-interest economic theory, however, some analysis of why economics should inform lawyer regulation is required; the argument that the norms of economics, and economic efficiency, are relevant to the regulation of the legal profession is not self-evident. The most notable treatments of legal ethics consider the lawyer's duties from the perspective of the lawyer as a moral agent, or as an actor within the legal system. The idea of the lawyer as an actor within the economic system, and appropriately regulated as such, is less prevalent. Part of the reason for this may be, as noted by Julia Black, that once economic analysis enters the debate, it has – if taken seriously – a tendency to consume its competitors whole, leaving no room for the acknowledgement of the relevance of other considerations to the identification of appropriate legal or regulatory norms.[29] And to understand lawyers exclusively as economic actors, with no consideration of the claims of moral or political philosophy, is simplistic; in no sector of the regulation of legal practice should 'our primary concern . . . be the efficiency of legal markets and their capacity to promote the efficiency of other markets'.[30]

Nonetheless, the role of lawyers in the economy, and the identification of the effect of imperfections in the market for legal services on the interests of clients and others, is normatively significant for the assessment of lawyer regulation. Lawyers *are* economic actors. They sell their services for money. Further, the actions they take affect the functioning of the economy more generally, and can often be better understood if considered in economic terms. And, most importantly, it is generally accepted that the market for legal services is highly imperfect.[31] These imperfections make it difficult for clients effectively to monitor the services they are given. They can make it nearly impossible for them to ensure that they are not billed unfairly.[32] They additionally have the tendency to make lawyers less affordable and accessible.[33] And they create the risk that lawyers will improperly pursue client interests, imposing negative externalities on others in particular and on society in general.[34] Absent regulatory response, the market for legal services will allow these problems to persist; the costs of them doing so must therefore be assessed against the costs of regulation to address them. Regulation that responds to these imperfections can be justified if it is cost-effective in that sense. Other bases for regulation are legitimate, and regulation justified on economic grounds can nonetheless be criticized if it undermines other regulatory goals; however, the existence of other reasons does not change the fact that lawyers are economic actors and appropriately regulated as such.

The remainder of this section will thus apply public-interest economic analysis to the specific question of extra-professional misconduct: is regulation of lawyers' personal misconduct necessary to supplement imperfectly operating market forces?

With respect to such regulation in its current form, the answer to this question is 'no'. To understand why this is the case, it is first necessary to understand something about the nature of the relevant imperfections in the market for legal services – that is, the type of market imperfections likely to justify regulation of a lawyer's personal misconduct. The two most relevant issues with the market for legal services are product non-homogeneity and informational asymmetry.[35] In brief,[36] legal services are not homogenous. The needs of different clients, and the quality of services provided by different lawyers, can vary radically, and the 'winner-takes-all' nature of legal services makes these differences disproportionately important. This makes it very difficult for consumers to engage in the type of 'comparison' shopping that is possible in, for example, the economy car market, where the basic features of cars made by Honda, Toyota, General Motors and Ford are much the same, and consumption decisions can be made based on price. A consumer of legal services has no such luxury. In addition, the consumer who purchases an economy car will likely end up with something functional to his purposes and budget – an economy car is an economy car; by contrast, a consumer of legal services may quite easily end up with a lawyer inappropriate to his purposes, with too much or too little expertise and time. Further, that inappropriate lawyer may impair the client's pursuit of his legal interests, given that such pursuit may require not only that his lawyer be good, but also that his lawyer be better than the lawyer on the other side.

Second, the legal services market features significant informational asymmetry and even informational impossibility. Lawyers know more than clients about the law and about what is required to solve a legal problem; clients depend on the advice of the lawyer to determine what legal services they need. At the same time, even lawyers cannot always know what is necessary to solve a problem, and even *ex post* it may be difficult to know how much of a good or bad outcome is attributable to the quality of legal services provided, as opposed to other unrelated facts. This makes it difficult for consumers to decide which lawyer to employ. Again to contrast to the economy car market, a consumer looking for a car has significant information in the form of consumer ratings, manufacturer history and even personal experience with which to determine the appropriate car to purchase. This gives consumers economic power in the economy car market that they simply do not have in the legal services market, where they have very little basis on which to judge which lawyer is the right one for solving their legal problem.

The relevance of these imperfections to the question of whether regulation of lawyers' personal conduct is justified, is that if (a) personal misconduct by a lawyer affects the quality, cost or effectiveness of legal services, or may otherwise be important to a client in choosing a lawyer, and (b) market imperfections mean that there is no way for the client through the market to identify and make consumption choices based on that information, then arguably regulation of that misconduct is justified.

When stated in this way, however, the problems with a public-interest economic rationale for regulation of personal misconduct quickly become apparent. As noted earlier, it is by no means evident that a lawyer's misconduct outside of legal practice affects the legal services that will be provided. It is also not evident that a client would care about a lawyer's personal misconduct when choosing whether to retain them. For example, that Maurice Sychuk murdered his wife was notorious; the Alberta oil and gas community was aware of what he had done. Yet Mr Sychuk was able to obtain work providing legal services to clients as a 'Consulting Landman', who is responsible for oil and gas-related legal agreements. The market provided the necessary information about Mr Sychuk and clients made their decision with that information in hand. Further, if the market is not effective in providing this information – and in less notorious cases, or with the passage of time, clients may be ignorant of what the lawyer has done – then the obvious regulatory response is to require that the information be provided. There is no economic reason for the extreme response of denying clients the choice as to whether or not to retain the lawyer in question. Nor is there any justification for fining or imposing like sanctions on the lawyer; doing so punishes the lawyer but provides no additional information for the client to use to make a decision about which lawyer to retain.

Finally, and most importantly, much of the time the regulation of personal misconduct by lawyers is only indirectly related to protection of the public – through protection of the profession's reputation. As explained by Professor Webb (Chapter 10 in this volume), regulators argue that individuals will not go to lawyers when they need them unless the profession as a whole is held in good repute. Framed in economic terms, and trying to be charitable, the economic argument in support of this position might look something like this: due to the absence and asymmetry of information, and the problem of product non-homogeneity, consumers making a decision about whether to retain a lawyer and which lawyer to retain necessarily rely on status as a decision-making heuristic.[37] Not knowing whether or to what degree they need a lawyer, or which lawyers are better (or more appropriate for their particular legal problem), they look at lawyer status to decide whether to hire a lawyer and which one to hire. As part of this process, consumers rely on the reputation of the profession as a whole. If the reputation of the profession is inappropriately compromised, consumers will be impaired in their ability to rely on status; their assessment of status will be irrationally distorted. Therefore, regulation to protect the profession's reputation where it will be inappropriately compromised is warranted.[38]

There are a variety of problems with this argument. The most obvious is, of course, the doubtful validity of the underlying empirical claim that consumers decide to retain individual lawyers based on the broader reputation of the profession.[39] Also suspect is the related claim that the reputation of the profession is undermined if lawyers who have misbehaved personally are not sanctioned by the profession in some way, as is its corollary – the assertion that the reputation of the profession is protected simply through the sanctioning of the misbehaving lawyer.[40]

In addition, and more importantly, the use of status by consumers is essentially a method for consumers to compensate for existing market imperfections, and emphasis on the status of the profession as a whole is an irrational addition to that consumer heuristic. If economic regulation is justified in this area, it should be oriented at reducing the need for consumers to rely on status,[41] not at artificially bolstering the profession's status so as to heighten any existing irrationality that consumers are building into their consumption decisions. To analogize, if consumers are making irrational decisions because they misconceive the risk associated with a particular activity (for example, flying), the response would be to correct their misconception about the risk (by providing accurate safety information), not to hide information from them because there is a danger that it will heighten their misconception (e.g. concealing information about a plane crash). It is possible that the heightening irrationality approach will ultimately produce the appropriately economically efficient result (that perhaps consumers retain lawyers when they will benefit from doing so), but it will do so largely through coincidence not because it has appropriately identified and resolved the market imperfection problem.

An alternative public-interest economic argument in favour of regulation of personal misconduct to protect the profession's reputation might be based on the economic concept of externalities.[42] An externality is an economic cost (or benefit) associated with an activity which is borne (or received) by someone other than the economic actor, and which, as a consequence, can distort economic behaviours in undesirable ways. The externality argument here would be that if lawyer A engages in personal misconduct, and as a consequence lawyer B suffers reputational injury resulting in economic costs for lawyer B, that cost constitutes a negative externality. If subjecting lawyer A to discipline eliminates the harm to lawyer B – that is, if it effectively transfers the cost from B to A – then regulation is justified on this basis. A internalizes the cost of the externality, and he (and others like him) are thereby appropriately disincented from acting in a way that will impose the cost on B.

This argument is, however, also problematic. Without some empirical support for the claim that personal misconduct by lawyer A has a negative economic effect on lawyer B – that disciplining lawyer A effectively transfers the economic cost of the externality (requires that A internalize the cost); and that the effect of regulation is proportionate (that the cost transferred to A is proportionate to the cost avoided for B and others like B) – regulation on this basis reaches too far. And such empirical support seems unlikely to be forthcoming. While Maurice Sychuk's murder of his wife was reprehensible, it seems most unlikely that it had any measurable economic impact on other Alberta lawyers. In that light, the argument simply seems too theoretical to warrant regulatory action as potentially extreme as disbarment.

In sum, then, neither of the categories of justifications for regulating personal misconduct is supported by public interest economic analysis. Even if empirically sustainable, regulation to protect the public could be accomplished simply through providing greater information to consumers; there is no reason to prevent consumers from making an informed choice about which lawyer to retain. And regulation to protect the profession's reputation rests on doubtful empirical claims about the relationship between professional reputation and consumer choice – in fact, does little to foster such choice – and cannot be rationally justified in economic terms.

Before moving on to consideration of democratic legitimacy, the other significant economics-based theory of regulation – private-interest economics, or 'public choice' – merits some acknowledgement. Public-choice analysis of government regulation rests on two central observations about human behaviour and activity. First, public choice asserts that government actors are like all humans as understood from an economic perspective: they are utility maximizing and instrumentally rational – that is, they will act in ways most likely to further their personal utility.[43] Second, public-choice theory identifies the problem of collective action for the individual in the state,[44] and observes that groups with a special interest in political outcomes – who tend to have greater information, smaller numbers (lower organization costs) and higher economic stakes – will spend the most time and money lobbying the government, and will be the most effective in doing so. Large groups with broad and disparate interests will not be able to organize effectively to advocate for government policies in their favour.[45]

From these two observations, public choice draws its conclusion: special-interest groups have a disproportionate influence on government policy. They are able to mobilize and persuade government actors that a particular course of action will maximize those actors' utility. In its first clear articulation by Stigler, the focus of public choice-based analysis was on the power exerted by a particular special-interest group, regulated industry, and on the tendency of industry to 'capture' government regulation for its own benefit. The analysis almost immediately departed from this 'industry takes all' approach, however, moving to the more general observation that: 'Compact, well-organized groups will tend to benefit more from regulation than broad, diffuse groups'.[46]

The analytical significance of public-choice arguments is relatively limited – the observation that democracy tends to fall prey to 'special-interest' groups is close to being a truism. Further, public-choice analysis of regulation tends to be tautological: whichever group benefits most from regulation is presumed to have had the most influence over the regulation. Public choice does, however, provide some important colour and context to the normative analysis from other regulatory theories. Specifically, when a group has the features of a group likely disproportionately to influence regulation, and the regulation in question significantly benefits that group, there is reason to subject that regulation to additional scrutiny, to require better empirical support, more persuasive economic analysis and/or more rigorous democratic legitimacy before viewing that regulation as justified.

Such additional scrutiny is warranted in the case of extra-professional misconduct. As Professor Webb cogently argued in his paper 'Are lawyers regulatable?',[47] lawyers have the capacity to capture the process of regulation, whether that process has significant non-lawyer involvement or not:

> My suggestion is that lay persons who are involved in the regulation of legal professions face considerable pressure to co-operate in significant ways with the profession. Where the lay person is a member of a regulatory body, that pressure will, simply by virtue of group dynamics, be immense. Even where the layperson is a regulator who is independent of the regulated profession, there will be considerable motivation to ensure a workable relationship between regulator and regulated.
>
> The wider problem of regulatory capture has been recognized and documented. This is the phenomena whereby regulators over time increasingly advocate for the interests of the bodies they are tasked with regulating, rather than promoting the interests of the general public. Capture is a natural result of the development of a significant and ongoing relationship between the regulator and the regulated, in contrast to the sporadic contact that the regulator has with different members of the public. This can lead to the regulator having a detailed understanding of the problems facing the profession, without a counterbalanced understanding of the problems facing the public. Capture of this kind may also result from more concerted lobbying of an overt kind.[48]

Moreover, the substance of regulation of extra-professional conduct appears most obviously to benefit lawyers themselves; it sends a message that lawyers are a certain sort of person, concerned with moral probity and excluding those whose behaviour is dubious or reprehensible. It helps to maintain the sense of the legal profession as exclusive, as not including those on the societal margins, and as legitimately able to assert itself as worthy of respect (however little it may actually be respected).

When viewed through the lens of private-interest economics, therefore, the weaknesses in the empirical foundations and public interest economic justifications for regulation of extra-professional misconduct become more acute. The following section will consider the assessment of lawyer regulation in general – and of this regulation in particular – from the perspective of democratic legitimacy.

11.4 Democratic theories of regulation

11.4.1 Framework

As noted earlier, regulatory theory has been overwhelmingly dominated by economics-based explanations and justifications for regulatory action. Recently, however, some regulatory theorists have rejected this exclusive emphasis, suggesting that there is no *a priori* reason in a democratic state for economic values to dominate in this way. They assert instead that the core justifications for regulatory action must be based in democratic legitimacy, not economic efficiency.[49]

What does it mean to say that regulation must have democratic legitimacy? There are two ways to consider this problem. First, what is meant by legitimacy in a general sense? Second, how does one establish whether legitimacy can be claimed for regulatory action?

The answer to the first question is relatively straightforward.[50] Legitimacy is the claim of political actors to allegiance and conformity from the citizenry for reasons other than merely the coercive power of the state. It is the claim that there are reasons for citizens to accede to political power grounded in something other than the fact of brute political force.[51] To say that a political act is illegitimate, or has a weak claim to legitimacy, is not of course to say that a citizen should not adhere to it,[52] but is to say that the political actor has failed to provide a reason specific to that political action for the citizen to justify adherence, and is subject to criticism on that basis.

The answer to the second question – How do we know when the political claim to legitimacy is made out? – is more challenging, and can be answered at varying levels of complexity. The simplest (and weakest) form of this argument asserts that the actions of regulators must reflect their legislative jurisdiction – that an action must lie within the regulator's statutory mandate.[53] Given the breadth of the jurisdiction granted to legal regulators, it is clear that the regulation of personal misconduct satisfies this minimal standard of democratic legitimacy.

A slightly more complex and stronger articulation of democratic legitimacy asserts that regulatory action is legitimate only when it is within a regulator's statutory mandate and when that mandate itself can claim democratic legitimacy.[54] What is necessary for a statute to satisfy that standard goes beyond what can be explored here, and is likely irrelevant given that, on any mainstream consideration, the legislation pursuant to which regulators govern personal misconduct would be considered democratically legitimate, reflecting the necessary 'institutional accountability'.[55]

The problem with both these articulations of a democracy-based theory of regulation, however, is that their focus on legislative authority and legislative legitimacy does not recognize the self-defining nature of regulatory action.[56] As clearly articulated by Habermas, regulatory activity in the modern administrative state is not 'normatively neutral, technically competent implementation of statutes within the framework of normatively unambiguous responsibilities'.[57] Regulatory actors have normative power. Within highly generalized and/or normatively non-directive legislative authority, they have the power to determine our societal ends, the goods that we as society hope to achieve, and the extent to which state power may be exerted against individuals.[58] Limits on regulatory action are imposed by the process of judicial review but, given the breadth of statutory power under which regulators operate, those constraints do not remove regulatory actors' normative authority, nor do they remove the requirement that, one way or another, the norms relied on by regulators in the first instance, or courts on judicial review, must be democratically legitimate.

Given this observation, a robust theory of democratic legitimacy requires that regulators acting pursuant to statutory mandates that do not themselves legitimate the regulatory action (e.g. where they are general or non-directive), independently justify their actions on a democratic basis. They must establish that the norms that they assert to govern their decisions are democratically legitimate:

> Insofar as the administration cannot refrain from appealing to normative reasons when it implements open legal programs, it should be able to carry out these steps of administrative lawmaking in forms of communication and according to procedures that satisfy the conditions of constitutional legitimacy. This implies a 'democratization' of the administration that, going beyond special obligations to provide information, would supplement parliamentary and judicial controls from within . . . [P]articipatory administrative practices must not be considered simply as surrogates for legal protection but as procedures *ex ante* effective in legitimating decisions that, from a normative point of view, substitute for acts of legislation or adjudication.[59]

As suggested by this quotation from Habermas, these justifications can be procedural. Indeed, most who argue for the importance of democracy to regulation do so to assert and explain the necessity of appropriate procedure for both quasi-judicial and public policy decisions by regulatory actors.[60] These justifications can also be substantive, however. They can arise from the relationship between the norms justifying the regulatory action and other democratically recognized norms, such as constitutional requirements;[61] norms arising from the general and institutional operation of the law (e.g. principles of interpretation[62] and the rule of law); the common law; or norms embodied in other statutes. On this last point, while a regulator has no jurisdiction to implement statutes outside its jurisdiction simply because of legal norms contained in other legislation,[63] it can justify action generally authorized by its own statute through identification of its consistency with norms or directions contained in other legislation.[64]

To be democratically legitimate on this robust conception of democratic legitimacy, therefore, the regulation of a lawyer's personal conduct must incorporate three claims: (a) that there is legislative authorization of the regulation which sufficiently legitimizes the normative claim made by the regulator in regulating the conduct;[65] (b) that the regulation flows from a process which independently legitimizes the normative claim made by the regulator in regulating the conduct;[66] and (c) that the norms protected by the regulation are found and justified elsewhere in the legal system.

These claims do not have to exist simultaneously – the democratic argument is not that a regulatory act or policy must satisfy all the grounds in order to be legitimate. But nor is the argument that a bare ability to make one claim for legitimacy is sufficient. The claim to legitimacy rests on some operation of all three claims to a greater or lesser extent. For example, if a regulatory policy follows from a robust process with an appropriate degree of public input, then even if it is not specifically legislatively endorsed (although legislatively authorized), and even if it is inconsistent with some other recognizable democratic norms, it can claim legitimacy. Conversely – and this is the argument that will be made with respect to the regulation of lawyers' personal conduct – even if the policy has some claim to legislative authorization, and even if it follows from a recognizably valid process, if those claims are weak or marginal, and if the regulation is inconsistent with other fundamental democratic norms, then the policy has only a week to claim to legitimacy.[67] The regulator has failed to articulate a sufficient reason, other than its coercive power, for the regulatory action to be respected.

With respect to the regulation of lawyers, a further point about the relevance of democratic principles must be noted. Lawyers are not merely the subject of democracy; they are a constituent part of democracy in action.[68] The legal rules that represent the response to the problem of moral pluralism in a democratic society[69] are made effective in part through the actions of lawyers. As a consequence, democratic values have relevance for the regulation of the legal profession not only because lawyers, like any citizens, have the right to require justification before state action is brought to bear upon them, but also because the norms of a democratic society, of the legal system in which lawyers play a part, are particularly relevant to the question of what should be judged as proper conduct in a lawyer. How lawyers act, the choices lawyers make, the rules with which they must comply – these all help to determine the shape and effectiveness of our legal system, of democracy itself. In constraining and shaping those acts and choices, therefore, the needs and requirements for the functioning of a democratic legal system should be taken into account.

11.4.2 *Legislative legitimacy*

As set out by Professor Webb, the legislation pursuant to which regulators in Australia, New Zealand and Canada regulate personal misconduct by lawyers falls into roughly three categories: (a) legislation that permits regulators to determine that a lawyer is a 'fit and proper person', and permits consideration of conduct outside the practice of law;[70] (b) legislation that permits regulators to discipline lawyers for criminal convictions where the conviction 'reflects on his or her fitness to practice, or tends to bring his or her profession into disrepute';[71] and (c) legislation that permits discipline of lawyers for 'conduct unbecoming' where the conduct is 'contrary to the best interests of the public or of the legal profession, or harms the standing of the legal profession'.[72] The question is whether this legislation validates and legitimates the norms used by the profession to justify its discipline of lawyers for personal misconduct. Does it bridge the regulatory 'gap' so as to ground the profession's disciplinary norms?

There is a reasonable argument that the legislation bridges the gap. Where legislation expressly authorizes the regulator to consider the interests of the public, and a lawyer's fitness to practise, it arguably renders legitimate the regulatory assertion that discipline for personal misconduct is appropriate because that misconduct suggests a predilection to professional misconduct. If the personal misconduct has that effect, then surely it is contrary to the public interest and demonstrative of unfitness to practise. Similarly, where legislation expressly permits consideration of whether the conduct brings the profession into disrepute, or harms its standing, it arguably renders legitimate the regulatory assertion that discipline for personal misconduct is warranted in order to protect the profession's reputation. If the profession's reputation suffers from a failure to regulate personal misconduct, then regulation of personal misconduct is warranted to protect that reputation.

On further examination, however, this source of legitimacy is less obvious. This is clearly the case in the legislation, which simply authorizes regulation to ensure that a lawyer is a 'fit and proper person'. To take that legislation and to use it to discipline lawyers for personal misconduct requires the insertion of a further regulatory norm: that 'fit and proper' encompasses both intra- and extra-professional misconduct, and that regulation of such misconduct can take place to protect the profession's reputation. That further norm may be authorized by the legislation;[73] however, since the regulatory action does not by necessity follow from the legislative power provided, it must have some basis for claiming democratic legitimacy apart from that legislative grant. In other words, regulators are making a choice. They are not simply 'doing what they've been told to do'. As a consequence, they need to justify that choice as democratically legitimate; the legislation alone is insufficient to demonstrate that that norm is a norm reflecting the democratic will.

This may also be the case, albeit less obviously, in legislation such as that prevalent in some Canadian jurisdictions, where regulation is expressly permitted to be directed at protecting the profession's standing. This is because regulators have identified the standing of the profession as normatively important in a particular way. Specifically, they have seen the standing as of independent significance – as not needing to be tied to any other normative concerns. It is one thing to say that the reputation of the profession is important because that reputation serves some useful function for the public interest, or for the functioning of the legal system. It is quite another thing to say that high standing for the profession is, in and of itself, a good thing. There are, as noted, some attempts to see reputation as instrumentally important, as related to consumers' willingness to go to a law-yer;[74] however, the overarching concern does seem to be with lawyers' reputation *simpliciter*. Again, while the legislation authorizes concern with the profession's reputation in general terms, it does not do so specifically. It is regulators themselves who have chosen to see it in this way.

This argument may seem somewhat attenuated – how specific does legislation have to be to provide democratic legitimacy to a regulatory norm? On the other hand, in this case it is also difficult to see the legislation as embodying the democratic will in the same way, for example, as does a debated and contested piece of legislation that has been the subject of committee proceedings and public debate, particularly in light of the observations of private-interest economics noted above. While legislation empowering the regulation of the legal profession is legislation properly passed by an institutionally accountable body, it also looks a lot like legislation that demonstrates the occasional (if not consistent)[75] truth of public-choice explanations for legislative and regulatory action. If regulators of lawyers have been given this power legislatively, it may say more about the power of lawyers over the legislative process, and the 'stickiness' of historical models of professionalism, than about the consistency of the norms found in the legislation with broader democratic principles. As a consequence, the norms adopted by regulators under that legislation warrant greater scrutiny – require a closer relationship to the legislative authority – to claim democratic legitimacy.

In sum, when the norms against which they justify their conduct are assessed against their enabling legislation, regulators have only modest grounds for asserting legitimacy in their regulation of personal misconduct. The argument that the legislature has considered and endorsed the profession's approach appears more technical than substantial as a 'reason' for viewing the action as reflective of the democratic will.

11.4.3 Process legitimacy

Democratic legitimacy does not flow simply from legislative decision-making. Judicial and executive decision-making is also legitimating. It is so in significant part because of its independent procedural requirements and norms. As noted, democratic theories of regulation place particular emphasis on the relationship between procedurally sufficient regulatory decision-making and democratic legitimacy.[76] Decisions to discipline lawyers for personal misconduct are required to follow a fair, relatively rigorous, generally quasi-judicial process. That fact bolsters the legitimacy of those decisions, and may well be the best argument in their favour. It is a 'reason' to think that the regulatory action is justified.

11.4.4 Democratic norms

The final ground for assessing the democratic legitimacy of regulating lawyers' personal misconduct is the consistency of the norms underlying that regulation with other democratic norms. This section assesses this possibility.[77]

The objective of ensuring that prospective clients are protected from practitioners likely to be unethical is consistent with the norms embodied in the overall law of lawyering (which places primacy on protection of client interests); in the law of fiduciary obligations; in the general democratic commitment to access to justice; and in the recognition of the importance of legal representation to that access (in the criminal context, the right to counsel).[78] However, pursuing that objective irrationally by excluding lawyers who do not demonstrably pose a threat to treat their clients unethically, and in addition denying clients an ability to make an informed choice about whom to retain, does not further those or other democratically legitimate norms. In fact, it is arguably contrary to them.

Rationality – 'reason' – is a significant and recognized norm of the legal systems discussed here. For example, in a recent administrative law decision, the Supreme Court of Canada abandoned a distinction in substantive judicial review cases between a 'patent unreasonableness' standard and a 'reasonableness' standard, in part on the basis that it is unacceptable to suggest that an administrative decision which was unreasonable could stand so long as it was not 'patently' unreasonable. The court said that it was 'inconsistent with the rule of law to retain an irrational decision'.[79] To strike a lawyer from the rolls simply because of the regulator or court's naïve faith in the relationship between distasteful personal conduct and a predilection to unethical conduct in practice is irrational. While the prejudice upon which it rests may not be as intuitive and offensive as traditional exclusions based on religion or race, it is still a form of prejudice – a decision based on false intuitions not on reasoned analysis from the evidence.

The lack of rationality in this form of regulation means regulators treat too lightly the rights and interests of the lawyer being disbarred (and the clients who retain them). While in none of the jurisdictions examined by Professor Webb – unlike the United States – is a licence to practise law considered a property right, it is also fair to say that it is an interest with legal significance. This is reflected in, for example, the considerable procedural rights awarded to lawyers facing disciplinary sanctions, and by cases recognizing the legal significance and importance of an individual's right to a livelihood.[80] Given this, to take away that licence based on an empirically doubtful relationship between personal and professional misconduct, or because of the reputation-protecting instincts of other lawyers, is dubious.

It also ends up making the professional discipline appear duplicative of that which has already been applied to the lawyer elsewhere in the legal system, like a form of double jeopardy. While, as noted by Professor Webb, professional regulators are quick to assert that they are not duplicating sanctions already imposed[81] – that their concern is not with the personal misconduct per se – the lack of a compelling and forward-looking justification for sanctioning the misconduct makes this perspective uncredible. As made clear in Professor Webb's discussion of the cases, as often as not it appears that the distasteful conduct is driving the professional discipline. This is illustrated by *Sychuk*. While the Law Society of Alberta claimed that continued disbarment was necessary so as not to undermine the denunciatory effect of the life sentence, the reality of the disbarment was to add to the (backward-looking) denunciation – it was an additional prosecution and sanction imposed on Sychuk in large part because he murdered his wife. While murdering his wife was a wicked thing to do, and warranted sanction, it is inconsistent with the fundamental and long-standing reluctance to permit double jeopardy for the Law Society of Alberta to add its prosecution and punishment to that which has already taken place under the penal justice system. If the penal justice system, for all its denunciation in a life sentence, permits Sychuk to live in relative freedom and to hold employment, and the employment he is qualified for is that of a lawyer, then the law society needs some cogent reason to refuse him the licence for which he is otherwise qualified. Such a reason is not evident in the decision.

This is in part because regulatory action in order to protect the reputation of the profession is even more difficult to legitimate in light of other recognized democratic norms. In all of the jurisdictions we have examined, there is clear recognition of the importance of maintaining a competitive market, and in preventing anti-competitive behaviour such as price fixing and economic collusion. While professions have traditionally enjoyed exemptions from the application of competition legislation,[82] the norms embodied in such legislation nonetheless provide a legitimate measure against which to assess the profession's regulatory policy. When this regulatory policy is measured against those norms it fares poorly; it appears more than anything to represent an attempt by lawyers to maintain and protect their professional standing in furtherance of their own interests, and without regard to the interests either of the lawyer struck from the rolls or the general public. In a sense, the type of economic analysis considered under the economic theories of regulation can be incorporated as relevant in consideration of democratic norms as well: the numerous body of legislation and case law endorsing and valuing the operation of the competitive marketplace suggests that, absent some other important norm to justify it, regulation that impairs the operation of the marketplace is problematic.

Finally, although this dynamic is complicated, a fundamental and overarching norm of the law of lawyering is respect for client autonomy and decision making. Client consent is a standard requirement for many ethical decisions, and an exception to the application of many ethical rules. It also underpins the ethics of lawyers in a more fundamental way, through justifying the role that lawyers play. If lawyers have an obligation of partisanship, and have any moral distance from their clients, it is because it is partisanship, on the one hand, that allows a client to pursue her goals in the legal system and on the other hand, since they are not the lawyer's goals – goals with respect to which they are the moral agent – the lawyer is distanced from them. While ethics debates for decades now have contested the morality of the lawyer's role, focusing on the extent to which the lawyer's own moral agency is affected by it (if it should be), no one denies that the client's moral agency is relevant to understanding what lawyers do, and how they should do it. This means that to deny an individual their choice of counsel requires justification; it must be something important, a risk that the client cannot adequately appreciate or something of other social importance, such as a risk that the lawyer will harm others or undermine the administration of justice. In the cases on regulation of personal misconduct, the regulators and courts appeal to justifications such as these. As has been suggested, however, their attempt to do so largely rings hollow, except to the extent that regulation usefully could alert clients that their prospective lawyer has engaged in personal misconduct. A client who is informed, who knows who Maurice Sychuk is and what he did, should be given the choice of whether to retain him or not.

11.5 Summary

Disciplining lawyers because they have acted badly in their personal lives requires justification. No matter how wicked, distasteful, sleazy and unpleasant a lawyer's conduct of their personal affairs may be, professional discipline of that lawyer must be a legitimate exercise of regulatory authority. The previous section suggested that, when assessed against the traditional justification of regulatory action in market imperfections and attainment of economic efficiency, regulation of personal misconduct fails. This section has considered the regulatory action more broadly, against the procedural and substantive norms of the democratic state as embodied in the legislation pursuant to which this regulation takes place, the process through which it is done and other existing democratic norms. The best argument in favour of this regulation lies in the fact that it occurs pursuant to a quasi-judicial (and, when subject to review, a judicial) process. The worst – most troublesome – argument arises when the regulation is assessed against other democratic norms. Not only do those norms not support this type of regulation, they also suggest that this regulation is positively inconsistent with principles fundamental to a democratic legal system – rationality, fairness, double jeopardy, market functioning and client autonomy.

Given this assessment, can the current regulation of lawyers for personal misconduct claim democratic legitimacy? In my view, it cannot do so. While there are process grounds to support these regulatory norms, and some limited legislative legitimacy for them, the most significant point is their inconsistency with broader democratic norms. In the end, the impression arising from this analysis is that there is 'no good reason' for this regulation to persist. Without a good reason, there is no legitimacy.

11.6 Justifiable regulation of extra-professional misconduct

This chapter has argued against the current regulation of extra-professional misconduct, in which lawyers who act badly in their personal lives are subject to professional regulatory consequences ranging from a fine or reprimand to suspension and disbarment. This section takes a more constructive approach. Specifically, given the grounds of empirical justification, correction for market failure and democratic legitimacy, what type of regulation of extra-professional misconduct, generally speaking, might be justifiable?

First, as was noted in the discussion of empirical justifiability, misconduct that technically falls outside of the practice of law, but in which the lawyer could reasonably be understood to have in some way engaged her legal skills or expertise, can be justified for much the same reasons that ordinary regulation of professional misconduct is justified – it creates proper disincentives and sanctions for those violating their professional obligations. In this case, the expansion of the regulatory scope is simply to ensure proper implementation of those regulatory goals, not to shift to different regulatory goals. Regulation of extra-professional misconduct in its current form can best be understood as prophylactic, as directed at preventing some other as yet unknown harm. Regulation of extra-professional misconduct that is in substance professional misconduct is not prophylactic, but is rather directed at the specific misconduct in which the lawyer engaged.

Second, regulation that provides clients with additional information that might be relevant to their consumption choices, but which the market will not provide, could be justified. It may not be desirable – a lawyer with criminal convictions could conceivably use a requirement that she publish those convictions as an opportunity to attract clientele interested in a lawyer they perceive as likely to circumvent legal rules (even if such perceptions are empirically suspect) – but it could be justified on economic grounds.

Third, a democratic society that wishes to sanction particular types of conduct, could legitimately include as part of that sanction a restriction on the individual's ability to pursue particular livelihoods or types of work. As part of the criminal sentence for fraud or embezzlement, for example, a person could be prohibited from managing trust funds as part of the sentence. The important distinction here is that in that case the sanction is a sanction for the crime or misconduct in question, and does not need to be justified as connected to the legislative mandate given to a professional regulator.

Finally, and less directively, whatever form regulation of extra-professional misconduct takes, regulators need to embrace far greater rigour in their implementation. No regulation to protect the profession's reputation should be permitted, and those jurisdictions that have legislatively eliminated that possibility are to be commended. Regulators should not assert that personal misconduct shatters a lawyer's integrity such as to warrant disbarment of the lawyer; some other reason for the decision must be provided, and such statements tempered given their dubious empirical validity. And overall, all regulatory activities should be directed towards the regulator's most important mandate: ensuring that lawyers play their fundamental role in a pluralist democracy and that they do not abuse the power that they have been given. Regulation of extra-professional misconduct, to the extent it is done at all, must be directed at that end.

11.7 Conclusion: regulatory pluralism

The vexing question for legal ethicists has traditionally been: what constitutes right action in the practice of law? When is a lawyer's conduct properly described as ethical, and when is it properly described as unethical? The analysis in this chapter suggests that, as challenging the task of answering that question may be, answering its follow-up – how do we properly regulate what lawyers do to create the conditions for, and the outcome of, ethical legal practice so defined? – is even more difficult. It is one thing to provide a convincing explanation of what being an ethical lawyer would look like. It is quite another thing to ensure that, in fact, lawyers practise in that way.

This accomplishment may not be fully achievable. But if it is to be achieved, or even pursued, the most significant mechanism for doing so will be the regulatory norms governing the legal profession, both formal and informal. As a consequence, regulation of the legal profession needs to be the subject of serious engagement, critiquing the regulation that occurs and identifying regulation that should occur but has not.

Then, as posed at the outset of this chapter, the question becomes: On what basis should regulatory activity (or inactivity) be assessed? The answer given here is: on multiple bases. Regulation is at its heart pluralistic; there is no one norm or value that all regulations should or must adhere to at all times. Regulation needs to be empirically rigorous; it must not be based on empirical assertions that are in reality no more than beliefs stated with confidence, and that may be falsifiable as facts. Regulation needs to respond to the imperfections in the market for legal services to ensure the accomplishment of economic efficiency but also, and more importantly, to ensure that those market imperfections do not enable unethical activities. And, finally, regulation needs to be democratically legitimate; it needs legislative authorization, procedural rigour and consistency with democratic norms, particularly those related to fostering lawyers' role as actors within the democratic legal system.

What a critique of regulation on these bases looks like is illustrated by the analysis of the regulation of lawyers' personal misconduct. That regulation fails on each basis offered for assessment; if it could succeed on one, it would be defensible and perhaps even desirable. But when it is identified as based on dubious empirical presumptions, as bearing no relationship to addressing the imperfections in the market, as of doubtful democratic legitimacy and as explicable as an example of regulatory capture, the logical conclusion is that the regulation in its current form should be abandoned. Another approach to such regulation may be justifiable, but not this one.

Notes

1 See, for example, M. Lewis and D. Einhorn, 'The end of the financial world as we know it' and 'How to repair a broken financial world' *New York Times*, 4 January 2009.
2 Like Professor Webb's (Chapter 10), this chapter deals only with misconduct by lawyers outside of legal practice, which it refers to as 'extra-professional misconduct' and 'personal misconduct' interchangeably.
3 Professor Webb also gives some consideration to case law in the United States.
4 D. Webb, 'Screamin' Mo Sychuk: nefarious conduct and the fit and proper person test', MS p. 9.
5 *Smith v Jones* [1999] 1 SCR 455 at para. 46.

6 *R v Neil* [2002] 3 SCR 631 at para. 12.

7 *Law Society of Alberta v Pozniak* [2002] LSDD No. 55 (QuickLaw) at para. 17.

8 For an American example, see the discussion on the website Legal Ethics Forum regarding exceptions to confidentiality to prevent wrongful incarceration or execution. Available from: <www.legalethicsforum.com/blog/2009/06/sacrificing-the-client-to-save-the-innocent-man.html#comments> (accessed 30 October 2009).

9 A survey cited by D. Luban in *Lawyers and Justice: An Ethical Study*, Princeton: Princeton University Press, 1988, p. 218, n. 26. Although for a strongly contrary view see M. Freedman and A. Smith, *Understanding Lawyers' Ethics*, 3rd edn, Newark, NJ: LexisNexis, 2004, pp. 139–40.

10 See, for example, R. D. Rotunda, 'The legal profession and the public image of lawyers', *Journal of the Legal Profession*, 1999, vol. 23, 51; and W. B. Wendel, 'How I learned to stop worrying and love lawyer-bashing: Some post-conference reflections', *South Carolina Law Review*, 2003, vol. 54, 1033–41.

11 An excellent example of this is the case of *R v Lyons* [1987] 2 SCR 309, where the Supreme Court of Canada considered the validity of the dangerous offender rules in light of the overwhelming evidence that psychologists cannot predict future dangerousness with any degree of reliability. The Supreme Court acknowledged the validity of the evidence, but held that given the uncertainty of future danger, and the offender's past history of offending, it was appropriate that the risk arising from the uncertainty of identification be placed on the offender. That is, they offered a reasoned justification for the rule despite the empirical problems underlying it.

12 See note 79 below and accompanying text.

13 See, for example, *Reference Re Same-Sex Marriage* [2004] 3 SCR 698.

14 The relationship between personal misconduct by lawyers and the protection of the profession's reputation is also empirically uncertain. It does not, however, require consideration of a separate body of scholarship, and so is simply discussed in the context of my later assessment of regulation to protect the profession's reputation against the requirements of regulatory theory.

15 For a discussion of the empirical problems associated with the concept of 'character' in the context of the good character requirement for law society (Bar) admission, see D. Rhode, 'Good character as professional credential', *Yale Law Journal*, 1985, vol. 94, 491; A. Woolley, 'Tending the Bar: The "good character" requirement for law society admission', *Dalhousie Law Journal*, 2007, vol. 30, 27; A. Woolley and J. Stacey, 'The psychology of good character', in *Reaffirming Legal Ethics* (Routledge, 2010, pp. 165–87).

16 G. Sreenivassan, 'Errors about errors: virtue theory and trait attribution', *Mind*, 2001, vol. 111, 441. Sreenivassan himself is, however, a sceptic about the attempts of social psychologists to undermine the notion of character.

17 See J. M. Doris, 'Persons, situations, and virtue ethics', *Noûs*, 1998, vol. 32(4), 504; J. M. Doris, *Lack of Character: Personality and Moral Behavior*, New York: Cambridge University Press, 2002; L. Ross and R. E. Nisbett, *The Person and the Situation: Perspectives of Social Psychology*, New York: McGraw-Hill, 1991; P. Zimbardo, *The Lucifer Effect: How Good People Turn Evil*, New York: Random House, 2007; G. Harman, 'Moral philosophy meets social psychology: Virtue ethics and the fundamental attribution error', *Proceedings of the Aristotelian Society*, 1999, vol. 99, 315; G. Harman, 'The nonexistence of character traits', *Proceedings of the Aristotelian Society*, 2000, vol. 100, 223–26. David Luban provides an interesting discussion of the relationship between this social psychology evidence and legal ethics in Chapters 7 and 8 of *Ethics and Human Dignity*, New York: Cambridge University Press, 2007; as noted below, Luban is sceptical about pure situationist approaches. He has some reason to be. As many psychologists emphasize, while situations are highly significant in influencing human behaviour, they do not determine human behaviour. How people act involves a complex interaction of situation, personality, culture and other facts. See in general, D. Matsumoto, 'Culture, context, and behavior', *Journal of Personality*, 2007, vol. 75(6), 1285.

18 See Woolley and Stacey, 'The psychology of good character'; Woolley, 'Tending the Bar'.
19 *Re Cwinn and Law Society of Upper Canada* (1980) 108 DLR (3d) 381 at para. 8.
20 Ibid. at para. 10, emphasis added.
21 Doris, 'Persons', 507. It is a truism of psychology in general that the best predictor of future behaviour is past behaviour.
22 Luban, *Ethics and Human Dignity*, p. 283.
23 Ibid., p. 284. See also Matsumoto, 'Culture, context, and behavior' – although this does not show that 'character' does exist or is determinative.
24 Although such assessments are highly problematic: Woolley and Stacey, 'The psychology of good character'.
25 There have been some attempts to consider economic theory relative to regulation of the legal profession. See below notes 30 to 37.
26 See in general B. Barton, 'The theoretical context of regulation', in B. Barton et al. (eds), *Regulating Energy and Natural Resources*, Oxford: Oxford University Press, 2006; R. Baldwin, C. Scott and C. Hood (eds), *A Reader on Regulation*, Oxford: Oxford University Press, 1998; S. Breyer, *Regulation and its Reform*, Cambridge: Harvard University Press, 1982.
27 J. Black, 'Proceduralizing regulation part I', *Oxford Journal of Legal Studies*, 2000, vol. 20, 598.
28 The public-interest–private-interest terminology is used within the regulatory sphere. See, for example, R. Baldwin and M. Cave, *Understanding Regulation*, Oxford: Oxford University Press, 1999. Private interest refers to theories of regulatory capture, also known as public or social choice, or as political economy. The relevance of private interest economic analysis is considered briefly at the end of this section.
29 For example: 'Our central claim is that the welfare-based normative approach should be exclusively employed in evaluating legal rules.' L. Kaplow and S. Shavell, *Fairness Versus Welfare*, Cambridge, MA: Harvard University Press, 2002, p. 3.
30 G. K. Hadfield, 'Legal barriers to innovation: the growing economic cost of professional control over corporate legal markets', *Stanford Law Review*, 2008, vol. 60, 143. Hadfield argues that in some segments of the market for legal services democratic values dominate and in others economic values dominate. I am not sure that the market can be divided quite that neatly – in most circumstances, account must be taken of both economic and democratic values.
31 M. J. Trebilcock, C. J. Tuohy and A. D. Wolfson, *Professional Regulation: A Staff Study of Accountancy, Architecture, Engineering and Law in Ontario Prepared for the Professional Organizations Committee*, Toronto: Ontario Law Reform Commission, 1979; P. Slayton and M. Trebilcock (eds), *The Professions and Public Policy*, Toronto: University of Toronto Press, 1978; G. Hadfield, 'The price of law: how the market for lawyers distorts the justice system', *Michigan Law Review*, 2008, vol. 98, 953; M. Trebilcock and L. Csorgo, 'Multi-disciplinary professional practices: A consumer welfare perspective', *Dalhousie Law Journal*, 2001, vol. 24, 1; A. Woolley, 'Imperfect duty: Lawyers' obligation to foster access to justice', *Alberta Law Review*, 2008, vol. 45(5), 107; M. Trebilcock, 'The regulation of the market for legal services', *Alberta Law Review*, 2007, vol. 45(5), 215; B. H. Barton, 'Why do we regulate lawyers? An economic analysis of the justifications for entry and conduct regulation', *Arizona State Law Journal*, 2001, vol. 33, 430.
32 A. Woolley, 'Time for change: Unethical hourly billing in the Canadian legal profession and how to fix it', *Canadian Bar Review*, 2004, vol. 83(3), 859.
33 Woolley, 'Imperfect duty'.
34 Lawyers were relevant participants in the abuse associated with, for example, the Enron scandal – that is, the unlawful pursuit of client interests in that case imposed significant external costs on those relying on the accuracy and validity of the Enron financial statements.
35 It must be noted that, despite common assertions to the contrary, the market for legal services is *not* an economic monopoly. While lawyers as a whole have a monopoly,

within the legal profession itself there are numerous buyers and sellers of legal services such that no participant is likely to be able to extract market rents solely because of that monopoly effect. Because of the sheer numbers of lawyers in the market, it is also not obvious that, absent other market issues, the monopoly of lawyers themselves would lead to the extraction of economic rents.

36 My paper, 'Imperfect duty', provides a relatively detailed analysis and review of the literature on imperfections in the market for legal services.

37 See Woolley, 'Imperfect duty'; J. Podolny, 'A status-based model of market competition', *American Journal of Sociology*, 1993, vol. 98, 829.

38 Brad Wendel was helpful in formulating this 'best case' economic justification and the problems with it.

39 See Rotunda, 'The legal profession and the public image of lawyers'.

40 Ibid.

41 Although, given the information impossibility problem, reliance on status is probably inevitable to some degree.

42 Thanks to Frances Woolley for helping to formulate this argument.

43 E. Rubin, 'Symposium: getting beyond cynicism – New theories of the regulatory state public choice, phenomenology, and the meaning of the modern state: keep the bathwater, but throw out that baby', *Cornell Law Review*, 2002, vol. 87, 310.

44 M. Olson Jr, *The Logic of Collective Action*, Cambridge, MA: Harvard University Press, 1965.

45 S. Peltzman, 'The economic theory of regulation after a decade of deregulation', *Brookings Papers on Economic Activity: Microeconomics 1989*, 1989, 13.

46 See R. Posner, 'Taxation by regulation', *Bell Journal of Economics and Management Science*, 1971, vol. 3, 22; Peltzman, 'The economic theory of regulation', 13; S. Peltzman, 'Toward a more general theory of regulation', *Journal of Law and Economics*, 1976, vol. 19(2), 217; G. S. Becker, 'A theory of competition among pressure groups for political influence', *Quarterly Journal of Economics*, 1983, vol. 98(3), 371.

47 D. Webb, 'Are lawyers regulatable?' *Alberta Law Review*, 2008, vol. 45(5), 235.

48 Ibid., 251–52.

49 M. Feintuck, *'The Public Interest' in Regulation*, Oxford: Oxford University Press, 2004, p. 17. See also C. Sunstein, *After the Rights Revolution: Reconceiving the Regulatory State*, Cambridge: Harvard University Press, 1990.

50 For a general articulation of this perspective on democratic legitimacy, see: W. B. Wendel, 'Civil obedience', *Columbia Law Review*, 2004, vol. 104, 363.

51 B. Williams, 'Pluralism, community, and left Wittgensteinianism', in B. Williams, *In the Beginning was the Deed: Realism and Moralism in Political Argument*, Princeton, NJ: Princeton University Press, 2005, p. 29.

52 The arguments on this point are complex, and beyond the scope of this chapter. For a stringent (and somewhat odd) articulation of this view, see I. Kant, *The Metaphysics of Morals*, trans. M. Gregor, Cambridge: Cambridge University Press, 1991, pp. 129–33.

53 R. Baldwin and M. Cave, *Understanding Regulation: Theory, Strategy and Practice*, New York: Oxford University Press, 1999, pp. 76–78.

54 'Although such [political] power originates in autonomous public spheres, it must take shape in the decisions of democratic institutions of opinion- and will-formation, inasmuch as the responsibility for momentous decisions demands clear institutional accountability.' J. Habermas, 'Popular sovereignty as procedure', in J. Bohman and W. Rehb (eds), *Deliberative Democracy: Essays on Reason and Politics*, Cambridge, MA: MIT Press, 1997, p. 59.

55 Ibid.

56 Which is, of course, properly understood as executive decision-making, and therefore conceptually distinct from the legislature.

57 J. Habermas, *Between Facts and Norms: Contributions to a Discourse Theory of Law and Democracy*, trans. W. Rehg, Cambridge, MA: MIT Press, 1996, p. 440. It is questionable, of

course, whether administrative decision-making has ever been normatively neutral, although it certainly used to be less extensive.

58 T. Prosser, 'Theorising utility regulation', *Modern Law Review*, 1999, vol. 62, 216; P. P. Craig, *Public Law and Democracy in the United Kingdom and the United States of America*, Oxford: Clarendon Press, 1990, p. 136.

59 Habermas, *Facts and Norms*, pp. 440–41. For further articulation of Habermas's position in this respect, see J. Habermas, 'Paradigms of law', *Cardozo Law Review*, 1996, vol. 17, 771.

60 Ibid. See also J. Black, 'Proceduralizing regulation part I' *Oxford Journal of Legal Studies*, 2000, vol. 20, 597; J. Black, 'Proceduralizing regulation part II', *Oxford Journal of Legal Studies*, 2001, vol. 21, 33; A. Woolley 'Legitimating public policy', *University of Toronto Law Journal*, 2008, vol. 58, 153; M. Seidenfeld, 'A civic Republican justification for the administrative state', *Harvard Law Review*, 1992, vol. 105, 1512.

61 Prosser, 'Theorising utility regulation', 215: 'regulatory space should be seen as operating within a set of boundary constitutional principles'. Prosser goes on to argue that, given the absence of 'a relevant set of determinate constitutional principles' in the United Kingdom, it may be necessary to ground the search for such principles in a proceduralist model akin to that articulated by Habermas. In that sense, Prosser's work is consistent with that of Black and Woolley, 'Legitimating public policy', although Prosser places less emphasis on Habermas's deliberation theory and more on his articulation of how to institutionalize democratic processes.

62 Sunstein, *After the Rights Revolution*, although Sunstein clearly does not limit his identification of the relevant principles of interpretation to those currently employed in judicial decision-making.

63 See, for example, *Re Athabasca Tribal Council and Amoco Canada Petroleum Co Ltd* (1981) 124 DLR (3d) 1 (SCC).

64 Some argue that any democracy-based theory of regulatory action requires taking a position on the 'deeper controversies concerning different conceptions of the democratic society in which we live' (Craig, *Public Law and Democracy*, p. 4). For this chapter, the justificatory framework from the more robust democratic theories is proceduralist and positivist. It emphasizes democratic justification arising from a process linking the regulatory action to representative decision-making (whether legislative or internal to the administrative framework) and from compliance with substantive legal (including institutional) norms found and justified elsewhere in the democratic legal system within which this particular regulatory activity is taking place. It does not rest on, for example, broader substantive assertions that to be democratically legitimate regulation should ensure 'the democratic interests in equality of citizenship' (Feintuck, *'The Public Interest' in Regulation*, p. 250) or should comply with any other norms outside those articulated by the legal system within which the regulation is taking place.

65 This is not to say that the action is *ultra vires* – that is, the claim is not, as would be the claim in the first 'thin' conception of democratic legitimacy, that the action is illegitimate in the sense of being appropriately subject to reversal or nullification on judicial review. Regulators are given broad margins of manoeuvre by legislators, to the point where it is a unifying principle of common law judicial review that, within their jurisdiction, regulators are entitled to make incorrect decisions; as a consequence, a claim that regulatory action is illegal is a strong one. More robust democratic theories of regulation, like their economic counterparts, are theoretical frameworks for critiquing regulatory decision-making; they are not more stringent claims of regulatory illegality.

66 This form of legitimacy can be understood as flowing from the fact that regulatory decision-makers are fundamentally executive in nature, not legislative, and as a consequence can claim democratic legitimacy apart from legislative authority. This is most obvious in jurisdictions like the United States, where there is separation of powers, and rule-making and other agency processes are infused with democratic legitimacy through the office and authority of the President.

67 This approach is analogous to the approach adopted by William Simon to the exercise of ethical discretion in lawyering with respect to the measuring of the relative importance in a given case of the 'overlapping tensions between substance and procedure, purpose and form, and broad and narrow framing'. W. Simon, 'Ethical discretion in lawyering', *Harvard Law Review*, 1987–88, vol. 101, 1096. As in the exercise of ethical discretion, an element of judgment is inherent in assessing the grounds of legitimacy, and the three grounds need to be balanced against each other. So, similarly, here one 'can imagine a procedural context that is so reliable as to make superfluous' (1102) the need to assess the substance of the norm against other democratic norms. On the other hand, when the process (whether on the adjudication of a particular case, or at the level of policy) does not involve rigorous consideration of the norms, that process does not remove the need to assess the policy against them. It should be noted that the reliance on Simon here is by way of analogy, not a form of endorsement of the ethical discretion approach in general.

68 This argument is made by Brad Wendel, who uses it to develop his position that the fundamental ethical obligation of lawyers is one of fidelity to law. See, for example, B. Wendel, 'Professionalism as interpretation', *Northwestern University Law Review*, 2005, vol. 99, 1169. It is also developed by Tim Dare in his recent book: *Counsel of Rogues? A Defence of the Standard Conception of the Lawyer's Role*, Burlington: Ashgate, 2009.

69 See above, note 51 above and accompanying text.

70 See Webb, note 21.

71 See Webb, note 22.

72 See Webb, notes 28 and 29.

73 A number of Canadian jurisdictions, for example, expressly authorize regulation of conduct 'whether or not it occurs in the practice of law'. Having said that, even that authorization could be interpreted as simply ensuring that lawyers are not able to make technical arguments that they were not practising when they committed the misconduct in question. It does not, again, require by necessity that the law societies regulate in this way.

74 See text accompanying note 38, above.

75 See S. Croley, 'Theories of regulation: Incorporating the administrative process', *Columbia Law Review*, 1998, vol. 98, 1.

76 See Black, 'Proceduralizing regulation part I'; Woolley, 'Legitimating Public Policy'.

77 The assessment of these norms against other democratic norms creates significant interpretive issues. Norms within a legal system can conflict, and can within themselves reflect specific compromises of broader norms that are in tension. Those interpretive issues go well beyond the scope of this chapter, and are not resolved here. The claims made here are that interpretation is possible, and that while there can be more than one 'good' interpretation within law, there can also be demonstrably wrong interpretations: '[L]egal doctrine resembles a multi-generational compromise, with principles and counter-principles that roughly track the political fault lines of different stages of evolving society. The result is indeterminacy in legal doctrine. But it is indeterminacy of a special and limited sort – moderate, not global, indeterminacy . . . Brewster was wrong: *not* every proposition is arguable'. Luban, *Ethics and Human Dignity*, p. 197. In my view, the assertion that regulation to maintain the reputation of the legal profession, or regulation to prevent a risk to the public which is empirically undemonstrated (and likely untrue in general terms), is consistent with democratic norms is wrong, or 'not arguable'.

78 All of these norms can make independent claims to legitimacy – the law of lawyering in the process used in most jurisdictions prior to the enactment of codes of professional conduct (although such process is problematic in some jurisdictions given minimal participation by non-lawyers), the judicial process around the law of fiduciary obligations and the common law and legislative norms in favour of access to justice and the right to counsel (which also has constitutional significance).

79 *Dunsmuir v New Brunswick* 2008 SCC 9 at para. 42.
80 *Wilson v BC Medical Services Commission* (1988) 53 DLR (4th) 171, although it is noted that this case is of doubtful precedential authority.
81 Courts have expressly found that this regulation does not constitute double jeopardy, as discussed by Webb, MS p. 4, discussing *Ex Parte Brounsall* (1778) 2 Cowp 829, 98 RE 1385.
82 See in Canada, *Jabour v Law Society of British Columbia* (1980) 115 DLR (3d) 549 (BCCA) (aff'd [1982] 2 SCR 307).

12 The problem of mental ill-health in the profession and a suggested solution

Michelle Sharpe

In recent years, the mental health of legal professionals has attracted considerable attention in the media. After the death of a senior Victorian barrister in May 2007 from a drug overdose, much of this media attention in Australia was focused on the Victorian Bar. In the media scrum that followed the death of Peter Hayes, it was claimed that mental ill-health was rampant at the Bar and that the Victorian Bar had failed to provide support for its barrister members.

Drawing on the experience of the Victorian Bar and wider research, it will be shown that mental ill-health is a very real problem for the Bar – as it is in the profession at large – which urgently needs to be addressed. It is a problem that takes root in law school, in the way lawyers learn to think like lawyers, and is compounded by legal practice. It follows that the Victorian Bar (or any other legal organization) cannot fully meet this problem of mental ill-health on its own. It is too large and ingrained a problem for any one organization to deal with effectively. Instead, it will be proposed that the legal profession must work together with law schools and legal regulators to tackle the problem in an integrated and comprehensive way, both in legal education and practice and also in handling complaints. One way in which this might be achieved is through the vehicle of an independent organization charged with the task of educating and providing support to law students and lawyers on issues of mental ill-health. For the Victorian Bar, this approach can also be found locally. The Victorian Doctors Health Program (VDHP), modelled on the physician health program established in North America, has been successful in educating and supporting Victorian medical doctors for a number of years.

12.1 Is mental ill-health a problem for the legal profession?

To examine whether mental ill-health is a problem for the profession generally in Australia, it will first be explored within the microcosm of the Victorian Bar. It is the Victorian Bar, more than any other Bar in Australia, that to date has received the most media attention and the greatest criticism about the way it has handled issues of mental ill-health among its barristers. This examination of the Victorian Bar will also serve to provide a personal and human backdrop to the many studies conducted into mental ill-health in the profession. Indeed, the results of these studies are neatly reflected in this microcosm. In determining the extent of the problem of mental ill-health in the profession, studies undertaken both in Australia and in the United States will be examined. There is, as yet, very little empirical research into mental ill-health in the profession in Australia. The bulk of this research has been conducted in the United States. Despite the differences that exist between Australia and the United States, what little research that has been conducted in Australia reveals a striking similarity to the results of studies conducted in the United States. Thus US research over the past 50 years may well be helpful in illuminating the depths of mental ill-health in the profession that have yet to be plumbed in Australia.

12.2 The microcosm of the Victorian Bar

Anecdotes have long abounded at the Victorian Bar of barristers struggling to cope with anxiety and depression. Former Victorian County Court judge John Dee recounts in his autobiography his abuse of alcohol to manage feelings of anxiety during his legal career.[1] Dee notes that he only sought help for his alcoholism after it began to have a serious impact on his health.[2] On Father's Day, 2 September 2006, a Victorian barrister committed suicide.[3] He had battled with clinical depression.[4] In an article following his obituary, in the Victorian Bar's *Bar News*, Victorian barrister Geoffrey Gibson acknowledged that depression is rife in the legal profession.[5]

On 11 May 2007, a senior Victorian barrister was found unconscious in an Adelaide hotel room. He never regained consciousness and died 11 days later in an Adelaide hospital. Unlike the death of the barrister in 2006, this death was reported widely in the media.[6] The Victorian Bar was criticized for failing to recognize the existence of mental health issues at the Bar and failing to provide support to barristers. Among one of the Bar's most vocal critics was Peter Faris QC, who claimed that the Bar was 'awash with cocaine'.[7] This led to widespread calls by the public for random drug testing of lawyers.[8] In response to these calls, the Bar has vigorously denied that any such drug problem exists. In a television interview, Victorian barrister Robert Richter QC claimed never to have seen any evidence of a drug problem at the Bar, and condemned any move randomly to drug test lawyers.[9] However, during the interview Richter did confide that he had suffered from depression himself, and observed that mental ill-health was widespread among barristers and judges. The then chairman of the Bar, Peter Riordan SC, publicly denied that the use of drugs at the Bar was any more prevalent than it was in the general community.[10]

12.3 Empirical studies

The scant research that has been undertaken in Australia on the mental ill-health of lawyers has revealed alarming levels of depression and substance abuse in the profession. In 2007, a study conducted by Beaton Consulting and BeyondBlue reported that lawyers are significantly more likely than the general population to experience depression.[11] The study also reported that lawyers are more likely than any other profession to use alcohol or other drugs to manage depression or anxiety.[12] Another study examining the various trauma suffered by criminal lawyers in Australia compared with non-criminal lawyers also found that about two-thirds of the total sample reported using alcohol and one-third reported using medication to cope with stress at work.[13] The most recent and comprehensive study into lawyer mental ill-health was conducted by the Brain and Mind Research Institute at the University of Sydney in 2008.[14] The Institute found in its study that almost a third of solicitors and one in five barristers surveyed suffered from clinical depression.[15] These findings indicate that depression in the legal profession at large is about four times higher than that of the general population.[16] Just as troubling, the study also found that lawyers held certain perceptions and beliefs about mental ill-health that might create a barrier to seeking help. A number of the lawyers surveyed reported that they would prefer not to seek help if they were experiencing depression.[17] Even when help was sought from a professional, many lawyers surveyed thought that the most likely result would be that there would only be some improvement.[18] Most lawyers in the survey reported that they thought people suffering from depression would be discriminated against by others,[19] and just over half of those surveyed reported that they thought they would be discriminated against by an employer.[20]

Australian lawyers have much in common with their American counterparts. A study undertaken by Johns Hopkins University revealed that lawyers were 3.6 times more likely to suffer from a major depressive disorder than any of the 104 professions surveyed.[21] A study of lawyers in Washington found that 19 per cent of lawyers in that state suffered from 'statistically significant elevated levels of depression' compared with 3 to 9 per cent of people in Western industrialized countries.[22] A study of lawyers in Arizona found that Arizona lawyers suffered from depression at about twice the rate of the general population.[23] Another study revealed that 37 per cent of lawyers in North Carolina reported being depressed and 24 per cent reported suffering from the symptoms of depression, such as loss of appetite and insomnia, at least three times a month during the previous year.[24] In addition to the high rates of depression in the legal profession, studies have shown alarming levels of anxiety and other kinds of mental illnesses. One Arizona study found elevated rates of anxiety, hostility and paranoia among lawyers.[25] In the study of North Carolina lawyers, over 25 per cent reported having experienced the symptoms of extreme anxiety at least three times per month over the past year.[26] The study of Washington lawyers revealed indications 'significantly above [those in] the normal population' among lawyers for anxiety, social alienation and isolation, obsessive-compulsiveness, paranoia, phobic anxiety and hostility.[27]

Studies in the United States have found that lawyers reportedly contemplate and attempt suicide at a greater rate than the general population.[28] The study of North Carolina lawyers found that 11 per cent had thought about suicide at least once a month for the previous year. One study of Washington lawyers reported that lawyers were more likely than the general population to think about suicide and, on attempting suicide, more likely to succeed in killing themselves.[29] One researcher, on reviewing the death certificates of white male suicide victims by the National Institute for Occupational Safety and Health, has suggested that the suicide rate for white male lawyers in the United States may be twice that of other white males.[30]

Like the Beaton Consulting and BeyondBlue study, studies in the United States suggest that lawyers 'self-medicate' using alcohol or non-prescription drugs to manage feelings of depression or anxiety. The study of North Carolina lawyers reported that almost 17 per cent admitted to drinking three to five alcoholic beverages per day.[31] The study of Washington lawyers found that 18 per cent were alcoholics, almost double the rate found in the general population, which is estimated to be at 10 per cent.[32] One researcher has estimated that 15 per cent of lawyers in the United States are alcoholics.[33] Fewer studies have been done examining the rate of drug use by lawyers. The study of Washington lawyers found that 26 per cent reported to have used cocaine – more than double the rate of the general population at 12 per cent.[34]

Studies overseas and in Australia have yielded evidence that mental ill-health of lawyers begins at law school. In the Australian study conducted by the Brain and Mind Institute in 2008, law students were found to have significantly higher levels of distress than either solicitors or barristers.[35] Almost 40 per cent of law students were reported to be suffering distress severe enough to warrant clinical treatment, compared with 13 per cent in the general population.[36] The study also found that students had the same negative attitudes to depression as lawyers, which may well inhibit them from seeking help.[37] Studies in the United States have also revealed alarming levels of mental ill-health. In one study, conducted at the Yale School of Medicine and at the Yale School of Law in the early 1950s, law students were reported to have experienced more stress associated with academic demands and more stress 'related to personal reactions to the academic environment' than did medical students.[38] A study conducted at the Loyola University School of Law in New Orleans found law students were significantly more anxious and suffered from greater stress and anxiety than other non-law, undergraduate students.[39] Another study found Canadian law students were significantly less vocationally satisfied, worked against deadlines more often, and were more depressed and anxious than people in general.[40] A study conducted at the University of Arizona found that 12 per cent of law students were depressed enough to warrant clinical treatment compared with 3 to 9 per cent of adults in Western developed nations.[41] Further, and perhaps most revealing of all, the study found that law students reported normal levels of psychiatric distress shortly before commencing their law degree.[42] The study went on to find that these levels of distress significantly increased above average during students' first year of law school, rocketed to alarming levels during law school and never returned to pre-law school levels, even two years after graduation.[43] Finally, a disturbing national study of law schools in the United States revealed that, while the vast majority of law students begin consuming alcohol and/or using drugs before commencing law school, consumption or usage increased as students progressed through their law degree.[44]

12.4 Explanations of mental illness in the legal profession

It is easy to identify the existence of pressures both in law school and legal practice that could be blamed for the mental ill-health of law students and lawyers. It is also true, however, that similar pressures can be identified in just about any existing course, job or profession. Pressure or stress is an inescapable part of everyday life. It is not unique to the law. From the studies outlined above, what does appear to be unique to the law, however, is that lawyers seem to be significantly more vulnerable to mental ill-health than the general population. Several commentators have suggested that lawyers share a constellation of certain values or personality traits that are not conducive to good mental health. Patrick Schiltz, drawing from his own experiences in practice, suggests that law students and lawyers are materialistic and competitive.[45] Schiltz argues that it is these traits that draw lawyers into the 'game' of working harder for more money, thereby jeopardizing their happiness and their health.[46] Martin Seligman, Paul Verkuil and Paul Kang, in meeting with New York lawyers, suggest three principal causes of lawyer unhappiness: pessimism, high pressure and low decision latitude experienced by junior lawyers, and the zero-sum game of the adversarial system of justice.[47] The low decision latitude of junior lawyers does not provide an exhaustive answer to the mental ill-health of lawyers, not only for the reason outlined above but also because it does not describe the conditions in which all lawyers work. In particular, the work of barristers – who are self-employed – is characterized by a high degree of autonomy. The pessimism of lawyers and the zero-sum game in which they work, however, come closer to explaining the vulnerability of lawyers to mental ill-health. Seligman, Verkuil and Kang note that pessimism, 'the tendency to interpret the cause of negative events in stable, global and internal ways', makes lawyers more vulnerable to anxiety and depression.[48] The commentators also argue that the zero-sum game of the adversarial system prompts lawyers to become competitive and unsympathetic to the concerns of their clients. The commentators consider that this makes lawyers 'anxious, angry and sad'.[49]

Perhaps the most coherent description of the personality traits and values of lawyers is offered by Susan Daicoff, who points to various disparate studies conducted in the United States examining the personality traits of lawyers. She argues that it is possible to trace the outlines of a 'lawyer personality' from these studies.[50] It is interesting to note that to some extent this lawyer personality reflects the observations made by Schiltz and Seligman, Verkuil and Kang about lawyers outlined above. Daicoff identifies three main, general attributes of the lawyer personality.[51] The first attribute identified by Daicoff is competitiveness and aggression. Daicoff refers to two studies in support of this observation. A 1983 study found that female lawyers were more competitive and aggressive than female physicians.[52] A subsequent study in 1992 found that lawyers of both sexes were more competitive than nurses.[53] Daicoff also points to two further interesting studies in which lawyers' levels of testosterone, a hormone connected with aggression, were tested. A 1979 study found that female lawyers' levels of testosterone were higher than those of female nurses, teachers and athletes.[54] Perhaps an even more interesting study – particularly for what it might say about barristers – is one conducted in 1998 in which trial lawyers of both sexes were found to have higher testosterone levels than non-trial lawyers.[55]

The second general attribute identified by Daicoff is that lawyers are more likely to be achievement oriented. Daicoff refers to a study conducted in 1984 which found that lawyers were more often motivated by achievement and were only moderately motivated by power and less by any need for affiliation.[56] A subsequent survey conducted by the American Bar Association in 1995 of lawyers in the St Louis area, noted by Daicoff, lends support to this study. In this survey, lawyers reported that their most important goal was to 'do the highest quality work I can'. The goals that lawyers reported as being least important were to 'advance to a position of power' and to 'improve the public good'.[57]

The third general attribute identified by Daicoff is the overwhelming preference by lawyers for thinking over feeling. Daicoff points to four separate studies which all consistently found lawyers disproportionately to represent the 'thinking' type of personality in a Myers–Briggs Type Indicator personality assessment measure. A study conducted in 1967 of law students at four different universities found that 72 per cent were identified under a Myers–Briggs test to be 'thinking' types.[58] A 1981 study of law students found that 63 per cent were 'thinking' types,[59] as were 76.5 per cent of lawyers in a 1994 study.[60] A 1993 nationwide study of lawyers in the United States found that lawyers preferred thinking and judging more often than most people. The study also found that the majority of lawyers preferred introversion and intuition while the majority of non-lawyers preferred extraversion and sensing.[61]

Daicoff argues that these attributes directly contribute to 'lawyer distress'.[62] She points out that while these attributes might be useful, or even desirable, to lawyers professionally, they can be personally detrimental. Obviously, being a predominantly rational, achievement-oriented, competitive and aggressive person can be destructive of interpersonal relationships. Isolation is well known to increase vulnerability to mental ill-health. These attributes, Daicoff also notes, may lead to frustration, low self-esteem and depression if success and external rewards prove elusive.[63]

It might be argued that certain 'personality types' are attracted to a legal career, and that these personality types are inherently more vulnerable to mental ill-health. While studies in the United States have revealed certain attributes common to those undertaking legal studies,[64] this does not offer a complete answer. As outlined above, a study of law students from the University of Arizona revealed that law students were relatively 'normal' prior to the commencement of their legal studies.[65] Clearly, the answer is to be found within law schools and in legal practice.

The lawyer personality appears to take root in law school. The main – indeed, almost exclusive – aim of law schools is to inhere in students the process of legal reasoning or how to 'think like a lawyer' in preparation for legal practice. Law students are trained by the 'Socratic' method to identify and analyse legal rights in a given hypothetical problem or case. In this analysis, students are discouraged from considering the interpersonal, moral or psychological issues involved in the problem.[66] The justification for this approach to teaching law, as one commentator explains, is that: 'Just as the jousts of chivalry prepared the medieval knight for the carnage of battle, so the Socratic method may prepare the lawyer for the cool battle of wills required by the adversarial system'.[67]

Empirical evidence suggests, however, that far more than just getting students 'battle ready', law schools have a profound impact on the values and attributes of law students. In other words, law schools train students not only how to think like a lawyer but also how to '*feel* like a lawyer'.[68] Studies have shown that law school encourages and rewards the development of particular traits and conversely discourages others. The 1967 study of law students from four different universities in the United States found that those students who were identified as 'feeling' types under the Myers–Briggs test dropped out from law school at a rate four times greater than the 'thinking' types.[69] Another study of law students at the University of Virginia in 1987 tested students for optimism–pessimism with an attributional-style questionnaire (ASQ). The study then tracked these students throughout their degree and found that those identified under the ASQ as being pessimists out-performed those identified as optimists.[70] A study conducted of third-year students from six law schools in the United States in 1966 also found that higher-achieving students were more competitive in their interactions with their peers. Conversely, the study found lower-achieving students preferred more personally based relationships.[71]

Other studies have found that the attitudes of law students change over the course of their degree. A study conducted of law students in six different Australian universities found that law students at the conclusion of their degree had become more conservative and less idealistic.[72] The results of a subsequent study of law students at the Brigham Young University in the United States conducted in 1974 lend support to these findings. That study found that law students' interest in public service employment decreased and their interest in working for a private firm correspondingly increased during law school. This study also found that, during their first year of law school, law students became less sociable, less interested in people and less altruistic.[73] These studies on altruism have been criticized as being dated.[74] While this criticism has some validity, they and the other studies referred to above nonetheless show that that law schools do have some impact on law students' values during the course of their degree.

Another Australian study, however, reveals that law schools alone are not responsible for shaping the attitudes and values of lawyers. The national study conducted in 2001 to 2003 examined the responses of final-year law students and graduate lawyers to a set of hypothetical ethical dilemmas. The study found that graduate lawyers were influenced by their work environments to such an extent that they changed the value bases upon which they formed their answers to the dilemmas.[75] Clearly, legal practice plays an important role in shaping and reinforcing lawyers' values.

12.5 Gladiatorial culture in legal practice

Seligman, Verkuil and Kang, as outlined above, identified the adversarial system of justice as one of the root causes of lawyer unhappiness. As noted by these commentators, lawyers typically envision litigation as war and often use warlike terms in describing it.[76] Lawyers will, for example, talk of 'attacking' or 'shooting down' their 'opponent's' arguments.[77] This approach to legal practice is not limited to the courtroom but has been broadly adopted by lawyers working in areas of law other than litigation. A long-standing critic of the adversarial system, Carrie Menkel-Meadow, observes that:

> The adversarial model affects the way in which lawyers advise their clients ('get as much as you can'), negotiate disputes ('we can really get them on that') and plan transactions ('let's be sure to draft this to your advantage'). All of these activities in lawyering assume competition over the same limited and equally valued items (usually money) and assume that success is measured by maximizing individual gain.[78]

This approach to legal practice encourages and reinforces competitive, aggressive and even uncivil behaviour in lawyers.[79] Richter, in his television interview, notes that working in an adversarial system means he is required to adopt a façade of toughness and anything short of this might be seen as a weakness to be exploited.[80]

12.6 Policy reasons to address mental ill-health in the profession

Although numerous studies have shown that mental ill-health is an endemic problem in the legal profession, this in itself does not provide a reason for professional associations, law schools and regulators to address it.

In a world of limited resources, it could be argued that assistance should not be offered to lawyers for two reasons. First, lawyers are well-educated people who are also likely to be highly motivated and, compared with the rest of the population, well resourced. Such individuals are well placed to access assistance for themselves. Resources that could be used to assist lawyers could be better applied to those in greater need – for example, legal aid. Second, it could be argued that lawyers struggling with a mental illness may lack the requisite 'fibre' for legal practice.[81] It has been noted that 'legal practice is not "a sunny day" exercise' and that as such lawyers must be able to deal with stressful situations.[82] Those with a 'Darwinian' view of legal practice could well argue that assistance should not be given to struggling lawyers because this assistance provides a crutch enabling such lawyers to stay in a profession to which they are ill-suited.

Both arguments overlook the nature and extent of mental illness in the legal profession. As noted above, mental ill-health is endemic in the legal profession. Rates of mental ill-health are reported to be significantly higher than for the general population. Both legal training in law schools and the culture existing within the profession are argued to be at the root of this mental ill-health. It follows that, in such an unhealthy environment, all lawyers are vulnerable to mental ill-health. It also follows that leaving individual lawyers to access help for themselves does nothing to address the underlying cause of widespread mental ill-health in the profession.

More importantly, however, it can be argued that the mental ill-health of lawyers can have a direct and negative impact on professional standards. In the United States, it has been estimated that at least 60 per cent of malpractice cases involve lawyers who have been abusing substances.[83] Although to date no empirical data exist in Australia establishing a direct link between mental ill-health and poor ethical decision-making or lower professional standards, one can readily be inferred. The Legal Services Commissioner of Queensland, John Briton, has noted that 'emotional distress is the elephant in the room in a large proportion of the matters we deal with'.[84] Briton estimates that about 30 per cent of disciplinary matters handled by the Commission involve issues of lawyer mental ill-health.[85] A similar percentage of complaints received by the Victorian Legal Services Commissioner could also be seen to arise out of issues of lawyer mental ill-health. Very few complaints received by the Legal Services Commissioner of Victoria during the last year involved deliberate acts of dishonesty by lawyers.[86] The vast majority of complaints made by consumers of legal services (after costs)[87] concerned general negligence by lawyers, much of which is basic bad case handling.[88] This is followed by complaints about the failure of lawyers to communicate with their client, such as failing to return phone calls and provide progress reports.[89] A large number of complaints were also made about delays by lawyers.[90] These figures are, perhaps not unsurprisingly, largely reflected in the claims reported to have been made to the profession's insurer.[91] As already outlined, depression is rife in the profession and the symptoms of clinical depression provide a close fit with the kinds of complaints most frequently made about lawyers. Common symptoms of depression include working more slowly, making mistakes more often, inability to concentrate, absenteeism and an inability to delegate tasks.[92] Further, while a complete review of the case law is yet to be undertaken, there is no shortage of disciplinary cases in which the defendant lawyer has pointed to significant stress or mental ill-health as contributing to, or largely responsible for, the lawyer's misconduct.[93] It is plainly obvious that if law schools, professional associations and regulators aim to promote good ethical decision-making and high professional standards in lawyers, then they must also promote good mental health.

A related issue to poor ethical decision-making and lowered professional standards is the reputation of the profession. A poignant example can be found in the media scrum that followed the 2007 death. As it was widely reported that the barrister had died from a drug overdose, there was public debate as to whether a drug problem existed in the legal profession and whether or not lawyers should regularly be drug tested. In these circumstances, the public confidence in lawyers and the administration of justice may well be diminished.[94]

12.7 Strategies to address mental ill-health in the profession

The strategy proposed here is that an independent organization should be established to educate and support lawyers on issues of mental ill-health. Before outlining this strategy in any detail, however, it would first be useful to return to the microcosm of the Victorian Bar. Through an examination of the strategies adopted by the Victorian Bar, and their limitations, the usefulness of an independent organization in addressing mental health in the profession becomes more apparent.

12.7.1 The Victorian Bar microcosm revisited

In 2002, the Victorian Bar established the Bar Care scheme. Under the scheme, counselling was available to barristers at the Cairnmiller Institute, located in the Melbourne suburb of Camberwell. Initially, the scheme only provided one counselling session to barristers at the cost of the Victorian Bar. Any subsequent counselling sessions were at the barrister's own expense. In September 2006, the scheme was extended to six sessions.[95] The scheme worked entirely on a self-referral basis. The only barristers who were provided with counselling were those who sought it. It is perhaps not surprising then that the scheme was not widely used by barristers. The Victorian Bar had, as at June 2008, about 1726 practising members[96] but the scheme had only been used by 26 barristers since its creation.[97]

In September 2006, what was then known as the Bar Care Committee, and later the Health and Well-Being Committee, was established.[98] The stated purpose of the Committee is to promote cultural change at the Bar conducive to good mental health and to provide support systems for members of the Bar.[99] The Committee organized several seminars to raise awareness about mental health issues at the Victorian Bar.[100] The Committee also provided direct assistance to two barristers in distress who were said to have required immediate help.[101]

The Committee, however, is composed entirely of barristers who, while enthusiastic and well intentioned, do not have any formal training in psychology. Recognizing its own limitations, the Committee, in early May 2009, recommended the appointment of a psychologist to advise the Bar on issues of mental health and provide counselling services to members of the Bar and their immediate families.[102] Counselling is currently provided from premises in the city close to barristers' chambers, but not within the legal precinct in order to preserve the confidentiality of barristers. In addition to this, crisis counselling is available by telephone 24 hours a day, seven days a week. The Committee's objective of promoting cultural change at the Bar is further enhanced by having its resident psychologist become the human face of the Bar's health and well-being programme. It is the resident psychologist who runs seminars and other programmes on issues of well-being, and who attends meetings held by the various Bar committees to listen to and educate members about mental health.

While the Victorian Bar has clearly taken great steps to addressing the problem of mental ill-health at the Bar, its success in dealing with this problem will unavoidably be limited. A necessary prerequisite to signing the Bar roll is a formal legal education. The empirical evidence unarguably reveals that law school training plays a significant role in lawyer mental ill-health. In addition to this, many come to the Bar after years spent practising as a solicitor. During that time, any unhelpful behaviour or patterns of thought may be reinforced or even spawned by the prevailing culture of a law firm. As hard as the Victorian Bar works to improve the health and well-being of its members, each year it will receive an intake of new barristers who bring with them their own mental health problems.

12.7.2 *The Victorian doctors health programme*

Perhaps the template for a more comprehensive solution can be found in Victoria's medical profession. The medical profession is regulated by the Medical Doctors Board of Victoria, a statutory body established under the Health Professions Registration Act 2005 (Vic). Under section 6(2) of the Health Professions Registration Act, the Medical Doctors Board may refuse to grant registration of a doctor if the board considers the doctor unfit to practise by reason of mental ill-health. Under section 35, all medical doctors are required to notify the Medical Doctors Board of any medical student or doctor who they believe might be suffering from an illness which may seriously impair that person's ability to undertake clinical training or practise medicine. All notifications of a student or doctor's ill-health are dealt with by the Health Committee of the Medical Doctors Board.[103] The purpose of the committee is simply to determine whether a student or doctor is fit to undertake clinical training or to practise medicine. In determining fitness, the Health Committee is empowered under the Health Professions Registration Act to compel a student or doctor to undergo a health assessment.[104] If a health assessment reveals that the public would be at risk if the doctor were to continue to practise, the committee will seek to reach an agreement with the doctor to modify their practice to eliminate this risk. If agreement is reached, the Medical Doctors Board will impose conditions on the doctor's medical registration to reflect this agreement.[105] If, however, the health assessment indicates that the doctor cannot work safely, the committee will ask the doctor to give an undertaking to cease working until such time as the doctor recovers. If the doctor refuses to give such an undertaking, the Medical Doctors Board may suspend the doctor's medical registration.[106]

Although the Medical Doctors Board can suspend registration, the committee deals with notifications as a health issue, rather than a disciplinary one.[107] Accordingly, the committee's investigation into the health of a doctor is strictly confidential.[108]

In November 2000, the Medical Doctors Board, together with the Australian Medical Association Victoria, established the Victorian Doctors Health Program

(VDHP) further to address the issue of mental ill-health in the medical profession. The VDHP began full-time clinical service in May 2001.[109] It is modelled on physician health programmes established in most states in North America.[110] The VDHP is an independent organization that is fully funded by the Medical Doctors Board, which raises these funds by levying a fee on every medical registration. The VDHP runs offices close to the major public hospitals in Melbourne. The office is staffed by an administrative assistant, a psychologist case worker and three medical doctors on a rotating basis, who have expertise in dealing with mental ill-health.

The VDHP addresses the problem of mental ill-health in the medical profession at all three levels at which it can surface as an issue: in medical school training, medical practice and the regulation of the medical profession. In doing so, the VDHP plays three different roles: educator, counsellor and advocate. As an educator, the VDHP maintains a website,[111] produces a regular newsletter and runs seminars on mental well-being for all medical students and doctors in Victoria. Through these means, the VDHP seeks to promote behaviour that contributes to good mental health and otherwise to raise awareness of mental health issues in medical practice. As a counsellor, the VDHP provides a telephone crisis counselling service 24 hours a day, seven days a week. If a VDHP counsellor considers that a student or doctor might require clinical treatment, the VDHP will arrange for a medical assessment to be undertaken and will coordinate the services necessary for the appropriate treatment. Beyond clinical treatment, the VDHP provides ongoing assistance through a number of programmes such as support groups. The VDHP also provides counselling and support to the families of students and doctors. The counselling provided by the VDHP is entirely confidential; the VDHP is only subject to the obligation to notify under the Health Professions Registration Act when a student or doctor continues clinical training or the practice of medicine against its advice. This can be used as an effective 'carrot-and-stick' approach by the VDHP to prompt impaired doctors to take steps towards their recovery.[112] When a notification has been made, the VDHP can take on the role of advocate, and will seek to represent and safeguard the best interests of students and doctors in any investigation by the Health Committee. Where the Health Committee subsequently decides to place conditions on a doctor's registration, the VDHP will liaise with the Medical Doctors Board to ensure that such conditions are met. This may include, for example, ensuring that the doctor attends counselling or is routinely tested for drugs.

The VDHP has been highly successful. In 1998, the Health Committee received a total of 34 notifications.[113] Soon after the VDHP was established in 2001, the number of complaints spiked and then decreased rapidly.[114] In 2005, the Health Committee received 16 notifications[115] and in 2006 that number was 15.[116] The number of notifications received in 2007 was 27[117] and in 2008 it was 37,[118] figures that represent something of an aberration against the general sharp downward trend of notifications generally.

The success of the VDHP provides an exciting model on which to fashion a solution to the legal profession's own problem with mental ill-health. This is particularly so given the similarities between the regulation of lawyers and doctors. These similarities provide fertile ground for the creation of a lawyers' health programme that, like the VDHP, can work with and assist regulators of the legal profession.

12.8 A lawyers' health programme?

In order to practise, a lawyer, after first having been admitted to practice, must have a practising certificate, or 'ticket'. In order to obtain and retain a ticket to practise, lawyers must first prove their fitness to practise.[119] This requirement is intended to protect the public from, *inter alia*, lawyers who might be impaired by mental ill-health. Legal regulators in a number of jurisdictions have a statutory power to compel a lawyer to undergo a health assessment if the regulator has grounds to believe that the lawyer may be impaired by a mental illness.[120] Almost all regulators also have the ability to issue practising certificates subject to certain conditions. These conditions may include that a lawyer receive counselling or medical treatment.[121]

A lawyers' health programme, like the VDHP, could play an important role in working with a legal regulator in dealing with mental illness in the profession two main ways. First, a lawyers' health programme could assist a regulator by ensuring that a lawyer with a conditional practising certificate meets those conditions. A lawyers' health programme could do this perhaps more efficiently and successfully than a regulator. Such a programme will likely have greater access to, and an understanding of, the range of medical and counselling services available. Second, the lawyers' health programme, having as its main focus the well-being of the lawyer rather than the protection of the public, is likely to have a relationship with the lawyer that is more supportive and therapeutic than the lawyer's relationship with the regulator. Further, the lawyers' health programme, like the VDHP, could deal with mental ill-health in the profession before it even becomes a regulatory issue. Through education and counselling, the lawyers' health programme could teach law students and lawyers skills that might make them more resilient and less likely to suffer mental ill-health. This could be done in seminars at law schools, law firms and Bar Association meetings. The lawyers' health programme could disseminate information through a website and newsletters. Like the VDHP, a lawyers' health programme could set up offices not far from the legal precinct, from which it could provide face-to-face counselling services, and run support groups and a crisis telephone counselling service. Establishing and maintaining these services would be costly; however, legal regulators could raise the funds in much the same way as the Medical Board: by putting a levy on every practising certificate it issues.

12.9 Conclusion

Empirical studies, both in the Australia and in the United States, present a startling and deeply troubling picture of a profession in which mental ill-health is rampant. These studies strongly suggest that law schools and the legal profession contribute to the development and reinforcement of attributes, attitudes and values in lawyers that are not conducive to good mental health. In addition to the human cost, anecdotal evidence suggests that mental ill-health can have a negative impact on professional standards and ethical decision-making of lawyers. It is therefore imperative that the problem of mental ill-health in the legal profession be addressed. Some organizations, like the Victorian Bar, have become aware of this but the success of such organizations in dealing with mental ill-health will always be limited. The problem is so widespread – from law schools to law firms to the Bar – that it cannot meaningfully be addressed unless it is dealt with as a whole. In this regard, the VDHP provides a shining, tantalizing example of how the legal profession might unite to tackle mental ill-health.

Acknowledgements

The author is grateful for the assistance and comments of Associate Professor Christine Parker, Dr Linda Haller, Bernadette Healy and Phillip Priest QC. The author is also grateful for the comments of the anonymous referees.

Notes

1 J. Dee, *Bars and Benches: An Autobiography of John Dee*, Melbourne: John Dee, 2009, ch. 8.
2 Ibid., p. 63.
3 *Victorian Bar News*, 3 November 2006, obituary, 25.
4 Ibid.
5 G. Gibson, 'Surviving the law', *Victorian Bar News*, 3 November 2006, 26; J. Gibson, 'Does the Bar matter?' *Victorian Bar News*, 3 November 2006, 57.
6 C. Egan, 'Mystery surrounds collapse of top QC', *The Age*, 13 May 2007; C. Egan, 'Lawyer found naked, unconscious', *Brisbane Times*, 13 May 2007; 'Charges over QC's collapse', *The Age*, 15 May 2007; K. Kyriacou and R. Castello, 'Fears for Hayes visitor', *Herald Sun*, 20 May 2007; J. Roberts and M. Davis, 'Police check video for clues to barrister's collapse', *The Australian*, 17 May 2007; 'Prominent lawyer Peter Hayes QC, dies', *Sydney Morning Herald*, 22 May 2007; C. Crawford, 'Peter Hayes tributes flow', *Herald Sun*, 23 May 2007.
7 C. Buttner, 'Lawyer sniffs a cocaine problem in the profession', *Lawyers Weekly*, 25 May 2007; G. Fang, 'QC claims tops lawyers using illegal drugs', *World Today*, ABC Radio, 16 May 2007; K. Kissane, 'Cocaine and the law', *The Age*, 19 May 2007; L. Porter, 'Cocaine rife? Bar humbug, say lawyers', *The Age*, 20 May 2007; L. Houlihan and C. Tinkler, 'High society awash with drugs', *Herald Sun*, 20 May 2007; C. Merritt, 'Victorian Bar drops Peter Fairs misconduct probe', *The Australian*, 13 June 2008; D. Hoare, 'Barrister death sparks drug debate', *World Today*, ABC Radio, 22 May 2007; 'Lawyer Peter Faris facing disbarment over drugs comments', *Herald Sun*, 29 October 2007.
8 'Drug test lawyers, urges QC', *The Age*, 16 May 2007; One Nation, 'Legal profession should be drug tested like everyone else', media statement, 2 June 2007. Available from: <http://www.nswonenation.com.au> (accessed 20 September 2009); G. Hughes, 'Time for a dose of reality at the Bar', *The Australian*, 21 May 2007.
9 'Lawyers and the "Black Dog" ', *Sunday*, Channel 9, 17 June 2007.
10 C. Buttner, 'QC quits alleging gag attempt over comments about drugs at Bar', *Lawyers Weekly Online*, 9 November 2007.

11 BeyondBlue: The National Depression Initiative, *Annual Professions Survey: Research Summary*, April 2007. Available from: <http://www.beaton.com.au/pdfs/BC_Professions Survey.pdf> (accessed 28 October 2009). The study reported that respondents from legal professions were about 1.5 times more likely to report depressive symptoms than the total sample (15.2 per cent compared with 10.5 per cent).

12 Ibid. The study revealed that about 5 per cent of lawyers reported using alcohol or other drugs to manage depression and anxiety.

13 Study undertaken by Lila Vrkleski, Macquarie University. See J. Lewis, 'Risky business: a new study finds criminal solicitors' work can cause them psychological damage', *Law Society Journal*, 2007, vol. 45, 16.

14 The study surveyed a total of 2413 people, including 738 law students from 13 law schools, 924 solicitors and 751 barristers nationally.

15 The results of the study were presented at the Tristan Jepson Memorial Foundation Lecture on 19 September 2008. See University of New South Wales press release, 19 September 2008; N. Berkovic, 'Black dog gnaws at profession', *The Australian*, 19 September 2008; 'Call for early identification of lawyer depression', *Australian Lawyer 2B*, vol. 14, 11.

16 N. Kelk, G. Luscombe, S. Medlow and I. Hickie, *Courting the Blues: Attitudes Toward Depression in Australian Law Students and Legal Practitioners*, Sydney: Brain and Mind Research Institute at University of Sydney, 2009; 'Call for early identification', 11.

17 Kelk et al., *Courting the Blues*, p. 20. The survey found 37.6 per cent of students, 31.3 per cent of solicitors and 21.6 per cent of barristers would not seek help from anyone if they thought they were experiencing depression.

18 Ibid., p. 21. Of those surveyed, 35.5 per cent of law students, 46 per cent of solicitors and 46.8 per cent of barristers responded that they believed that the likely outcome of depression if treated by a professional (e.g. doctor, psychologist, psychiatrist or other counsellor) would be that there would be some improvement.

19 Ibid., p. 31. Out of those surveyed, 81.1 per cent of students, 83.3 per cent of solicitors and 75 per cent of barristers thought that a person suffering from depression would be discriminated against by other people who didn't know the person well.

20 Ibid. Out of those surveyed, 62.6 per cent of students, 56 per cent of employers and 47.3 per cent of barristers thought that a person suffering from depression would be discriminated against by an employer.

21 W.W. Eaton et al., 'Occupations and the prevalence of major depressive disorder', *Journal of Occupational Medicine*, 1990, vol. 32, 1079.

22 G. A. H. Benjamin et al., 'The prevalence of depression, alcohol abuse and cocaine abuse among United States lawyers', *International Journal of Law and Psychiatry*, 1990, vol. 13, 240. The researchers explain that 'statistically significant elevated levels of depression' is a significant elevation of a score given on a self-reporting instrument known as the Brief Symptom Inventory (BSI) 'is strongly correlated with clinical impairment, and suggests the need for clinical treatment'.

23 Ibid., 273.

24 North Carolina Bar Association, *Report of the Quality of Life Taskforce and Recommendations*, 1991, p. 4.

25 P. Schiltz, 'On being a happy, healthy, and ethical member of an unhappy, unhealthy, and unethical profession', *Vanderbilt Law Review*, 1991, vol. 52, 876.

26 North Carolina Bar Association, *Report*.

27 C. Beck, B. Sales and A. Benjamin, 'Lawyer distress: Alcohol-related problems and other psychological concerns among a sample of practicing lawyers', *Journal of Law and Health*, 1995–96, vol. 10, 1.

28 See generally D. Holmes, 'Learning from corporate America: Addressing dysfunction in the large law firm', *Gonzaga Law Review*, 1995–96, vol. 31, 377.

29 Benjamin et al., 'The prevalence', p. 234.

30 Schiltz, 'On being a happy, healthy, and ethical member', p. 880 citing C. Burnett,

'Suicide and occupation: Is there a relationship?', unpublished paper presented at the American Psychological Association – National Institute for Occupational Safety and Health Conference on Workplace Stress, location, 1992.

31   North Carolina Bar Association, *Report.*
32   Benjamin et al., 'The prevalence', 241.
33   E. Drogin, 'Alcoholism in the legal profession: Psychological and legal perspectives and interventions', *Law & Psychology Review*, 1991, vol. 15, 127.
34   Benjamin et al., 'The prevalence'.
35   University of New South Wales press release, 19 September 2008.
36   'Call for early identification', p. 11.
37   See above, notes 17–20.
38   See L. D. Eron and R. S. Redmont, 'The effect of legal education on attitudes', *Journal of Legal Education*, 1957, vol. 9, 520–21.
39   R. McCleary and E. L. Zucker, 'Higher trait- and state-anxiety in female law students than male law students', *Psychology Reports*, 1991, vol. 68, 1075.
40   K. F. Helmers, D. Danoff, Y. Steinart, M. Leyton and S. N. Young, 'Stress and depressed mood in medical students, law students and graduate students at McGill University', *Academic Medicine*, 1997, vol. 72, 708.
41   S. B. Shanfield and G. Andrew Benjamin, 'Psychiatric distress in law students', *Journal of Legal Education*, 1985, vol. 35, 65.
42   G. A. H. Benjamin, A. Kazniak, B. Sales and S. B. Shanfield, 'The role of legal education in producing psychological distress among law students', *Law and Social Inquiry*, 1986, vol. 11, 225.
43   Ibid.
44   American Association of Law Schools (AALS) Committee Report, 'Report of the AALS Special Committee on Problems of Substance Abuse in the Law Schools', *Journal of Legal Education*, 1994, vol. 44, 35.
45   Schiltz, 'On being a happy, healthy, and ethical member'.
46   Ibid.
47   M. Seligman, P. Verkuil and T. Kang, 'Why are lawyers unhappy?' *Deakin Law Review*, 2005, vol. 10, 49.
48   Ibid., 54.
49   Ibid., 61.
50   S. Swaim Daicoff, *Lawyer Know Thyself: A Psychological Analysis of Personality Strengths*, Washington, DC: American Psychological Association, 2004, p. 25.
51   S. Swaim Daicoff, 'Lawyer, know thyself: A review of empirical research on attorney attributes bearing on professionalism', *American University Law Review*, 1996–97, vol. 46, 1348, 1390–94.
52   Ibid., 1390. See S. W. Williams and J. C. McCullers, 'Personal factors related to typicalness of career and success in active professional women', *Psychology Women Quarterly*, 1983, vol. 7, 350.
53   Ibid. See J. M. Houston et al., 'Assessing competitiveness: a validation study of the Competitive Index', *Personality and Individual Differences*, 1992, vol. 13, 1155.
54   Daicoff, *Lawyer*, p. 26. See J. M. Dabs, E. C. Alford and J. A. Fielden, 'Trial lawyers and testosterone: Blue-collar talent in a white-collar world', *Journal of Applied Social Psychology*, 1998, vol. 28, 87–88.
55   Ibid.
56   Daicoff, 'Lawyer, know thyself', 1391. See L. H. Chusmir, 'Law and jurisprudence occupations: A look at motivational need patterns', *Commercial Law Journal*, 1984, vol. 89, 231.
57   Ibid. See J. Dionese, 'Striving for happiness', *American Bar Association Journal*, 1995, 41.
58   Ibid. See P. Miller, 'Personality differences and student survival in law school', *Journal of Legal Education*, 1967, vol. 19, 460. The four universities surveyed were: Northwestern University, University of California (Berkeley), University of Pennsylvania and University of Virginia.

59 Ibid. See F. Natter, 'The human factor: psychological type in legal education'. *Research into Psychological Type*, 1981, vol. 3, 55.
60 Ibid.
61 Ibid. See L. Richard, 'How your personality affects your practice – The lawyer types', *American Bar Association Journal*, 1993, vol. 79, 74.
62 Daicoff, *Lawyer*, p. 149.
63 Ibid.
64 See generally ibid., pp. 51–56.
65 Andrew, Benjamin et al., 'The role'; see Daicoff, 'Lawyer, know thyself'.
66 D. P. Stolle, D. B. Wexler and B. J. Winick, *Practicing Therapeutic Jurisprudence: Law as a Helping Profession*, Durham, NC: Carolina Academic Press, 2000, pp. 26–27; S. Keeva, *Transforming Practices: Finding Joy and Satisfaction in the Legal Life*, Chicago, IL: Contemporary Books, 1990, pp. 99–109.
67 J. Taylor, 'Law school stress and the "deformation professionelle"', *Journal of Legal Education*, 1975–76, vol. 27, 266.
68 M. Meltsner, 'Feeling like a lawyer', *Journal of Legal Education*, 1983, vol. 33, 624.
69 Miller, 'Personality differences', p. 466. The drop-out rate of 'thinking' types was only 6.7 per cent but the drop-out rate of the 'feeling' types was 28.1 per cent.
70 J. Satterfield et al., 'Law school performance predicted by explanatory style', *Behavioral Sciences and the Law*, 1997, vol. 15, 95.
71 M. Patton, 'The student, the situation, and the performance during the first year of law school', *Journal of Legal Education*, 1968–69, vol. 21, 10.
72 D. Anderson, J. Western and P. Boreham, 'Conservatism in recruits to the professions', *Australian and New Zealand Journal of Sociology*, 1973, vol. 9, 42.
73 J. M. Hedegard, 'The impact of legal education: an in-depth examination of career-relevant interests, attitudes and personality traits among first year law students', *American Bar Foundation Research Journal*, 1979, vol. 4, 836.
74 K. Tranter, 'The different side of society: *Street Practice* and Australian clinical legal education', *Griffith Law Review*, 2006, vol. 15, 1.
75 A. Evans and J. Palermo, 'Preparing Australia's future lawyers: An exposition of changing values over time in the context of teaching about ethical dilemmas', *Deakin Law Review*, 2006, vol. 11, 127.
76 Seligman et al., 'Why', 62. See also S. D. O'Connor, 'Professionalism', *Oregon Law Review*, 1999, vol. 78, 388, referred to by the commentators.
77 Ibid.
78 C. Menkel-Meadow, 'Portia in a different voice: Speculations on a women's lawyering process', *Berkeley Women's Law Journal*, 1985, vol. 1, 49.
79 Daicoff, *Lawyer*, pp. 12–13, 146. See also C. Menkel-Meadow, 'The trouble with the adversary system in a post-modern, multi-cultural world', *Journal for the Institute of Legal Ethics*, 1996, 49; M. E. Aspen, 'The search for renewed civility in litigation', *Valparasio University Law Review*, 1993–94, vol. 28, 513.
80 Lawyers and the 'Black Dog', Channel 9.
81 *Gregory v Queensland Law Society Inc* [2001] QCA 499 at 27.
82 Ibid.
83 Daicoff, *Lawyer*, p. 13, citing C. Greene, 'Half of lawyer malpractice and discipline stems from substance abuse', Annual Meeting of the National Conference of Bar Presidents, 6 August 1988.
84 J. Briton, Legal Services Commissioner, 'Lawyers, emotional distress and regulation', paper presented at the Bar Association of Queensland 2009 annual conference, Gold Coast, 7 March 2009.
85 Ibid.
86 Legal Services Commissioner, *Annual Report 2007–2008*, pp. 40–41. The total number of complaints received by the LSC in 2007–08 was 2903. Of this number, the LSC received 138 complaints about dishonest or misleading conduct by lawyers,

92 complaints about duress, pressure or intimidation and five complaints of sexual impropriety.

87 Ibid. The LSC received 845 complaints about costs.

88 Ibid. The LSC received 465 complaints about general negligence of lawyers.

89 Ibid. The LSC received 250 complaints about the failure to communicate by lawyers to clients.

90 Ibid. The LSC received 116 complaints about delays.

91 Legal Doctors' Liability Committee, *2007 Annual Review*, pp. 7, 13.

92 M. Naylor, 'Depression in lawyers', *Brief*, 2004, 12.

93 See, for example, *Gregory v Queensland Law Society Inc* [2001] QCA 499; *A Solicitor v Law Society of NSW* (2004) 216 CLR 253; and *Quinn v Law Institute of Victoria* [2007] VSCA 122.

94 It is also important to note that the ranks of the judiciary are almost entirely composed of lawyers, and in particular barristers. Issues of mental ill-health, if not dealt with in law schools or in the profession, inevitably become issues for the judiciary – for example, see Justice M. Kirby, 'Judicial stress', *Australian Bar Review*, 1995, vol. 13, 101. Arguably, at this level these issues can have an even greater impact on public confidence and the administration of justice.

95 The Victorian Bar Inc, *Annual Report for the Year Ending 30 June 2006*.

96 The Victorian Bar Inc, *Annual Report for the Year Ending 30 June 2008*.

97 The Victorian Bar Inc, *Annual Report for the Year Ending 30 June 2004*, reported that three barristers had used the scheme; the Victorian Bar Inc, *Annual Report for the Year Ending 30 June 2005* reported that one barrister had used the scheme; the Victorian Bar Inc, *Annual Report for the Year Ending 30 June 2006* also reported that only one barrister had used the scheme; the Victorian Bar Inc, *Annual Report for the Year ending 30 June 2007* reported that five barristers used the scheme; and the Victorian Bar Inc, *Annual Report for the Year Ending 30 June 2008* reported that 16 barristers had used the scheme.

98 The Victorian Bar Inc, *Annual Report for the Year Ending 30 June 2006*.

99 The Victorian Bar Inc, *Annual Report for the Year Ending 30 June 2008*, p. 22.

100 Ibid.

101 Ibid.

102 Bernadette Healy of the Re-Vision Group. The New South Wales Bar has also appointed a psychologist to provide support to its barristers. In March 2008, Penny Johnston was appointed to the position of Director, Care & Assistance, in the New South Wales Bar's BarCare scheme.

103 Health Professions Registration Act 1958 (Vic), Div. 7.

104 Ibid., s. 68.

105 Ibid., s. 38.

106 Ibid., s. 40.

107 The approach of the Health Committee is outlined on the Medical Board's website. Available from: <http://medicalboardvic.org.au/content.php?sec=27> (accessed 28 October 2009).

108 To this end, all hearings are conducted in private: Health Professions Registration Act 1958 (Vic), s. 69.

109 Medical Doctors Board of Victoria, *Annual Report 2001*, p. 14; see also N. Warhaft, 'The Victorian Doctors Health Program: the first three years', *Medical Journal of Australia*, 2004, vol. 181, 376.

110 Ibid. A list of the state physician health programmes in North America is provided by the Federation of State Physician Health Programs (FSPHP) on its website. Available from: <http://www.fsphp.org> (accessed 28 October 2009).

111 Victorian Doctors Health Program website. Available from: <http://www.vdhp.org .au> (accessed 28 October 2009).

112 Ibid. Warhaft, 'The Victorian Doctors Health Program'.

113 Medical Doctors Board of Victoria, *Annual Report 1998*, p. 18.

114 Information taken from Medical Doctors Board of Victoria, *Annual Reports* for the years 1998 to 2007.
115 Medical Doctors Board of Victoria, *Annual Report 2005*, p. 13.
116 Medical Doctors Board of Victoria, *Annual Report 2006*, p. 12.
117 Medical Doctors Board of Victoria, *Annual Report 2007*, p. 11.
118 Medical Doctors Board of Victoria, *Annual Report 2008*, p. 17.
119 In the Antipodes, this requirement can be found in the following legislation: Legal Profession Act 2006 (ACT), s. 11; Legal Profession Act 2004 (NSW), s. 9; Legal Profession Act 2006 (NT), s. 11, Legal Profession Act 2007 (Qld), s. 9; Legal Practitioners Act 1981 (SA), s. 15; Legal Profession Act 2007 (Tas), s. 9; Legal Profession Act 2008 (Vic), s 8; Legal Profession Act 2008 (WA), s. 8; Lawyers and Conveyancers Act 2006 (NZ), s. 55.
120 See Legal Profession Act 2006 (NT), Div. 3; Legal Profession Act 2007 (Qld), Div. 3; Legal Profession Act 2008 (Vic), s. 2.5.4.
121 Legal Profession Act 2006 (ACT), s. 47; Legal Profession Act 2004 (NSW), s. 50(3)(e); Legal Profession Act 2006 (NT), s. 70(3)(e); Legal Profession Act 2007 (Qld), s. 53; Legal Practitioners Act 1981 (SA), s. 20AA; Legal Profession Act 2007 (Tas), s. 55; Legal Profession Act 2008 (Vic), s. 2.4.14; Legal Profession Act 2008 (WA), s. 47(3)(f); Lawyers and Conveyancers Act 2006 (NZ), s. 55.

Index